Social and Ethical Effects
of the Computer Revolution

Social and Ethical Effects of the Computer Revolution

edited by
JOSEPH MIGGA KIZZA

McFarland & Company, Inc., Publishers
Jefferson, North Carolina, and London

British Library Cataloguing-in-Publication data are available

Library of Congress Cataloguing-in-Publication Data

Social and ethical effects of the computer revolution / edited by
  Joseph Migga Kizza.
      p.   cm.
    Includes bibliographical references and index.
    ISBN 0-7864-0205-9 (lib. bdg. : 50# alk. paper) ∞
    1. Computers and civilization.   2. Computers—Moral and ethical
  aspects.   I. Kizza, Joseph Migga.
  QA76.9.C66S618   1996
  174'.90904—dc20   95-49868
                                                           CIP

Manufactured in the United States of America

McFarland & Company, Inc., Publishers
  Box 611, Jefferson, North Carolina 28640

Dedicated to my wife Immaculate
and daughters Josephine and Florence

FOREWORD

On December 30, 1994, word came out that one count of wire fraud against David Lamacchia had been dismissed by a U.S. District Court judge. Lamacchia, an MIT student, had set up a bulletin board on which proprietary software was posted and then downloaded by anyone who wanted a copy. No money was exchanged, so there was no profit for those who posted the software, nor for Lamacchia, nor for the software developers and copyright holders. Nor were the facts of the case denied. The judge's reasoning, as reported in the *Washington Post* (12/30/94, pp. D1–2) was that "federal copyright law does not extend to not-for-profit duplication of computer software because Congress has declined to extend that specific protection to the creators of computer software." As quoted in the *Post* article, Lamacchia had this to say: "I am grateful that [the judge] has confirmed that the indictment against me does not allege conduct that is in fact criminal. It is a relief to know that this remains a country where the rule of law governs."

The Lamacchia case will no doubt become a standard in computer ethics. When is copying and distributing proprietary software really piracy—only when there is financial gain or when it is expressly illegal? Why isn't such copying analogous to making copies of a bestselling novel and handing them out on the street corner? Whose hardware carried the BBS, Lamacchia's personal computer or MIT's system? If the latter is the case, was that an appropriate use of computing resources even if the use was not illegal? And just because the actions were not illegal, were they also not unethical? Is anything not prohibited by law something everyone has a right to do?

These questions cover a lot of ground, but do not exhaust the issues generated by the Lamacchia case. And the issues raised are only one set among a large and growing, but increasingly more well-defined, core of issues expressing the relationship between ethics and information technologies. In this volume, the core set of themes in what generally is called computer ethics is well presented. As a fairly well-defined area of "applied ethics" (a phrase I find redundant, although occasionally useful), computer ethics is a rather recent development. Works like this one, in which key themes are examined and disciplinary boundaries further defined, are necessary to advance the development of the field.

With them we are better able to understand that there is still something to question about Mr. Lamacchia's actions, even though the charge was dismissed and, presumably, "the rule of law governs." We are, with works like this one, also better able to take the next step in the development of computer ethics, namely, moving on to discovery and examination of the general principles that conceptually organize the themes and cases, and enable conclusive assessments and decisions. It may be difficult to say that what Mr. Lamacchia did was not legal, but as inquiry into ethics and information technologies progresses, it will not be at all hard to say it was not right.

PATRICK F. SULLIVAN
Executive Director
Computer Ethics Institute,
Washington, D.C.

PREFACE

This book was compiled to give insights into the influences and effects of computer technology on society. The advent of computers has overwhelmingly changed the way society functions. In the process, society has become more and more dependent on this technology. Never before in human history has a technology so captivated society in such a short period of time.

As the role of computers becomes more and more intertwined with our lives, the computer-age children, those born from the 1980s on, are taking computers and computer technology and the information-driven economy for granted. In this complacency lies the danger. These children and those who will come after them need to be taught that good information management is very important.

But while the behavior and techniques of computers can be defined, human behavior cannot. The U.S. economy has shifted from being a manufacturing economy to a service economy, of which information is the largest component. Most practitioners within the information sector of the economy believe that information is better managed by computers than by people. But computers are programmed and run by people. For the present information generation, the challenges offered by a need for management of that information can be exciting and beneficial but detrimental and threatening as well.

This work is intended to highlight the need for responsible information management in a variety of areas. It may serve as a way to teach ethics in computer science, information systems, management information systems, and other related curricula.

The book is structured to permit a discussion in detail of those areas in which, I believe, information management and security are of utmost importance. Each of the six sections of the book is broken into chapters that, together, attempt to give as broad a coverage as possible of the area under discussion. At the beginning of each section, there is a summary of materials presented by the authors so that the instructor or reader can select only those chapters that best serve his or her interests.

The success of a volume like this depends heavily on the contributions of its authors. I want to thank all the authors, who have contributed fresh, up-to-the-minute works to this book.

In a special way I want to thank Dr. Immaculate Kizza who edited many of the papers in this book. I hope that our efforts will bring enlightenment and will eventually contribute to making this a better, more progressive, and technologically secure society.

CONTENTS

V. Artificial Intelligence and Cyberspace

VI. Morality, Security and Privacy

INTRODUCTION

This collection of writings, many from my colleagues and other scholars of social computing, explores in depth the social and ethical effects of the computer revolution. A number of issues are discussed that will help to answer many of the questions that have arisen, in part, as a result of the exponential growth of computer usage in both home and business settings.

When most people talk about a computer they are visualizing a central processing unit, a monitor, a keyboard, and possibly a printer. Although this is one type of computer, computers and computer technology come in numerous forms, ranging from tiny microprocessors no bigger than the head of a pin that are operating in spy gadgets, to football field–sized computers operating in large corporations and institutions. Computers, whatever the size, are influencing us like no other technological invention has ever done before. Many aspects of our lives are indirectly affected by computers without our knowledge. There is no turning back. Computer influence, dependence and control increase with every passing day. With new technologies that can package millions of transistors in a fingernail-sized chip, and new, faster memories, computer technology is fueling the engines of the computer revolution. At the time of this writing, the NEC Corporation announced the development of a new supercomputer that it claimed to be the fastest ever with a peak speed of one trillion calculations per second (1). New technology is being developed every day that will within a few years make existing technology, which many of us think of as advanced, seem as if it were from the Stone Age.

This computer revolution, like its predecessor the industrial revolution, has three stages: amazement, prosperity, and social upheaval. In one of my chapters I have defined what makes up each stage. In the remainder of the introduction, I will discuss the last stage, the social upheaval. This stage is of course a result of the second stage, the prosperity stage. We have come, at least in the United States, to depend on computers for most of our daily services. For example, my daughter had a very important journey to make, so she went to her bank to get money for her trip. When she arrived at the bank she found that all activities were at a standstill because the computers were "down." She could not make the journey. Or, consider the time when my wife nearly missed a flight home from a hotel she was staying in for a conference. She wanted to check out early in the morning, but on her arrival at the front desk she was told that she could not check out because the hotel's computers were down and the desk clerks could not tell how much she owed. After management was called it was resolved that she could be billed later and that saved the day. There are many examples I could give to illustrate how dependent on computers we as a society have become. Yet according to the experts, the widespread use of computers is just beginning.

Welcome to the computer age, full of entertainment, involvement and excitement, but also full of threats and fears. The involvement with computers has become so involuntary that it is considered an addiction to many, to an extent that the absence of a computer makes them completely dysfunctional. As the dependence grows, social and ethical problems start to surface. These problems are now appearing everywhere computers are used.

Without a doubt computer technology has been beneficial in our technology-driven society and has improved tremendously the quality of our lives through improved application and delivery techniques.

MEDICAL DELIVERY AND CARE

In medical care, techniques are being performed daily in operating rooms throughout the country that were once considered unthinkable. Medical operations that were felt to be risky or even unperformable are now a sure thing. Through the use of novel techniques, breathtaking brain and heart surgery can be performed by robots. Medical training and the delivery of services have been transformed overnight, and the whole medical profession has received new life. Studies in gene therapy and engineering with the help of computers are promising a brave new world of wonders that will make human cloning and gene splicing seem primitive exercises. Impressive improvements in medicine have grown alongside advances in drug manufacturing as a result of computer technology.

It used to be that when people felt sick they would call their doctor, or maybe pay him or her a visit in order to receive a diagnosis for their condition and a prescription for medication. This is no longer the only alternative patients have. With the coming of the Internet and new computer-aided and software driven programs like CHESS (Comprehensive Health Enhancement Support System) developed by the University of Wisconsin, patients with home computers and modems have access to a number of medical libraries at the best medical schools. People with access to the Internet on commercial on-line services like CompuServe can get a great amount of medical information from services like the *Mayo Clinic Family Health Book* and the *Mayo Family Pharmacist*, both on CD-ROM. With multimedia the possibilities get even better and go beyond being able to access medical information and information about drugs to being able to receive information about anatomy and CT scans (2). Currently with the connection to the Internet, one can gain access to over 8.5 million scientific citations. Also using medical bulletin boards, patients can post queries which are answered by physicians (2).

In the future most medical advice from medical practitioners and consultancy between doctors and patients will be delivered via on-line computer services. According to Dr. Jerome Kassier, *New England Journal of Medicine* editor, this will be a result of the rapid growth in computer-based communications, more doctors acquiring computer knowledge, and a shift towards patient responsibility. Using this approach to health care, patients could use on-line computer services to access large medical databases for diagnosis by inputting their symptoms (*USA Today*, Telecommunication, 5 January 1995).

EDUCATION

Similar or perhaps even more dramatic changes have been taking place in colleges and universities as a result of technological advances. As a university professor, I am a witness to the benefits computer technology has given our campuses. We already have the children of the computer age who think that everything done manually is outdated. They demand fast services, automated libraries, automated registration, and probably soon they will demand automated professors. The point I am making is that students are attending college campuses so dependent on computers that if the computers go down, almost total confusion results. Yet just a few years ago we used card registration. I once witnessed a modern twentieth-century college campus plunge into chaos when the power was lost. Without electricity, hardly any class could be held in the ultramodern windowless, computer controlled air-conditioned rooms. When the power finally came back on, the computers remained down for a few more hours. One would have thought that with power back, all classes and activities would start, but this was not the case in our ultramodern library.

I have become a computer slave myself. I can hardly function without both computers in my office working. If both computers are not up and running I cannot correspond with my colleagues, write my lecture notes, process my students' grades, edit my scholarly papers or read the morning paper. Did we get more than we bargained for?

Much of American higher education is operating under an educational principle based on a century-old theory that textbooks are the main source of information and that teachers are the main interpreters and conveyors of this information. So for generations libraries and museums have been considered as the prime sources of information. Well this belief, with the coming of the Internet, is slowly beginning to fade. According to E. Beware Soloway, textbooks, by their nature, provide only a slice of information on any one topic. The potential source of future information, as Soloway puts it, is the information superhighway (3). With WWW (3W) one can visit web sites around the globe in a few minutes and research topics using the best sources. Information that would have taken thousands of dollars and months of looking to find can now be accessed in a few hours at a computer.

The digital library, when it replaces the current paper library, will be revolutionary. Instant user help will be provided by digital intermediaries that will be able to connect the user to over a million information bases around the globe (3). For the bright, young students in elementary and high schools, Internet participation helps to increase their curiosity to a level that few libraries or museums can match. According to Soloway, students can get a voice in authentic scientific inquiry and discourse (3).

On a wider scope, computers are being used in education to teach a wide range of students with similar results. And computers are increasingly being used to network schools in rural and remote parts of countries, a concept that started in Australia's outback with radio lesson channeling. With a wide range of telecommunication technologies available, the old radio model has been expanded. Soloway gives examples where the new models are helpful, like in instructing teacher teleteaching where teachers-to-be learn about teaching and learning by participating in electronic network-based activities with elementary and high schools. The networks also aid learning by encouraging student involvement through conversation by asynchronous computer-based communication (3).

COMMUNICATION

Perhaps the field of communications has been most affected by the computer revolution. To some people, the computer revolution has turned into a telecommunications revolution. Remember how the commercial jet shrank the world? Now that looks like child's play compared to what computer communication is doing. With new telecommunications technology, countries are only a few seconds apart. Computer communication has revolutionized space exploration and study, and in many cases the technology developed for space exploration eventually finds its way into commercial use, which in turn generates more research.

Cutting edge communication technology is not limited to space travel and exploration; it has reached our living rooms. In our homes, telecommunications wonders are unfolding daily. The workplace office has moved with the help of computers and fax machines turning our homes into centers of gadgetry. The home environment is going through changes of its own. Home services are getting better with the marriage of computers, cable companies, and service providers. We can receive most of the services we used to get from outside the home without leaving the comfort of our own homes. We can order a movie, send a fax, and even shop in the vast virtual shopping malls.

As new computer technology in telecommunications continues to come to market, old establishments are falling by the wayside. Technology has a history of dismantling established services: the automobile destroyed horse driven transportation; the commercial jet destroyed passenger trains; and fax machines and the Internet are vying to do away with the U.S. Postal Service—snail mail as it is commonly known. There are already signs of the wired telephone system giving way to mobile wireless communication.

Computer-driven mobile communications have unlimited potential and features that sound like something from science fiction tales. With the advent of computers and mobile communication, whole offices are moving on wheels and wings, further transforming the traditional workplace.

Advances in telecommunication are benefiting almost every country on earth. Remote communities can now be reached in a few seconds. Poor countries can connect to world-class medical and scientific digital libraries via WWW in a fraction of a second and access vast amounts of information that would otherwise have taken years to get.

The greatest growth in communication has been the Internet. Since its humble beginning as part of the ARPA in the early 1970s, the Internet has seen phenomenal growth. Take for example, the period between January 1993 and January 1994 when the Net grew by an impressive 60 percent, and since then it has been growing at an estimated rate of 10 percent monthly (3). It has expanded to over 70 countries and has Fidonet links to many developing countries. With the three most popular network information projects (WAIS from Thinking Machine Corporation for text-based information retrieval; Gopher from the University of Minnesota for campus-wide information; and WWW or 3W from CERN [European Center for Nuclear Research] in Switzerland, used mainly for corroborative work) together with other protocols like FTP (File Transfer Protocol) and 3W's HTTP (Hypetex Transfer Protocol), Internet users cruise the Net with ease (4). The Net has become so popular because of the abundance of information on it which can be accessed through bulletin boards, news agencies, and hundreds of other services. At the time of this writing an estimated 30 percent of all American homes have computers, and it is felt that the commercial use of the Net is just beginning. By the year 2000, the Internet is expected to grow to over 2000 million connections for educational, entertainment, and personal communication. Its consumer market will probably exceed $200 million (*USA Today*, Telecommunications, 20 December 1994).

Surfers looking for information will not be the only ones to use the Net; those people with an appreciation of music will also be welcome. Music on the Net will be "broadcast" by radio stations from around the globe using WWW because of its sound, video, and graphical features. The Internet is slowly changing the delivery of radio signals from analog, with their distance limitation, to digital via wires. This transformation is achieved by compressing sound waves into digital strings that can then be sent by telephone wires. Already two university campus radio stations, KJHK-FM at the University of Kansas and WXYC-FM at the University of North Carolina, have signals on the Net on an experimental basis. The potential for growth is unlimited (6).

BUSINESS

Information is the lifeblood of business. Without it, large numbers of companies and businesses would not exist. Experts say that the economy of the United States has shifted from manufacturing to services, with the largest part of these services being information related. Since computers and computer related technologies are the carriers and facilitators of information, most experts say that the U.S. economy is becoming more and more computer dependent, and it is thought that this dependency will have new ramifications for federal, state, and local governments and businesses. Policies and techniques must be designed to reflect this trend. Since private enterprise thrives on competition, all of a sudden information becomes the most important commodity. Whoever has it and controls it ultimately wins. So information acquisition, management, and security are fast becoming governments' and institutions' top priorities. If the information that makes a company competitive is compromised, the competitive edge is gone as are perhaps millions of dollars, and the lives of people are probably changed. As the Internet explosion continues, businesses are jumping on the bandwagon by establishing cyberaccounts and credit transaction systems (7).

For financial and medical institutions, as well as many institutions whose business involves dealing with the personal information of their customers, information security of course is of the utmost importance. Whatever the nature of the business, public or private, the generation and management of information depend on machines and people. Machine behavior can be defined and controlled using algorithms, but it is impossible to define, let alone control, people's behavior.

The management of information involves more than its generation and security; it also involves the dispensing of information and the speed of its transmission. Companies that can dispense information wisely and quickly reap great benefits. A number of companies have seen the efficiency of their employees double, and sometimes triple by speeding up information processing. The tracking industry and United Parcel Service are a case in point. Companies, from grocery stores to pharmacies to retail stores, are now using these new technologies to reorder merchandise without order forms.

LAW ENFORCEMENT

Information is as vital to law enforcement as it is to business. Enormous amounts of data are generated in the law enforcement and criminal justice systems, and this information is important to the administration of justice and the enforcement of laws. Security agencies must go to great lengths to balance the rights of the public to know certain information with the rights of the victims to keep such information confidential.

Computers are at the forefront of law enforcement. State and national databases contain information concerning criminals, missing children, and deadbeat parents. It is hard to imagine what law enforcement would be like without computers.

THE COURTS

Computers and computer technology developments are moving far ahead of U.S. legislators' abilities to enact new laws pertaining to them and their use, and existing laws are being made obsolete. This in turn is making the courts unable to convict computer criminals. An example of this situation is the much publicized case of David Lamacchia, an electrical engineering and computer science student at Massachusetts Institute of Technology. From November 1993 through January 1994, he operated a computer bulletin board using such names as "John Gaunt" and "Grimjack." It is alleged that during those months when the bulletin board was operating, about 180 people used and illegally downloaded copyrighted software. But since the users were anonymous, Lamacchia did not make money, and it is thought that none of those who pirated the software from the bulletin board made any money either. Because of these facts and other technicalities the judge did not prosecute Lamacchia under copyright laws.

According to the judge, if he were to have proceeded with the case, it would have become possible for computer users to be prosecuted for copying even a single program for their own personal use (7). Although Lamacchia acted irresponsibly, the current federal laws, in particular the Federal Wire Fraud Statute under which he was charged, cannot be used to prosecute him. If it is to cover similar future cases, the statute must be rewritten. And this was the message the judge wanted to pass on to Congress. Technology, especially computer technology, is moving so fast that existing laws need to be revised often. In Lamacchia's case, the judge suggested that it was the job of the legislators, not the courts, to define electronic crimes and to decide on the punishment; then the courts would enforce the laws (*USA Today*, Telecommunication, 30 December 1994).

THE GOVERNMENT

Since the inception of computers, all branches of governments have used them, especially defense. Whatever the nature of the department, computers are used for record keeping, delivery of services and many other functions. Vital records like birth, death, and marriage certificates and other documents are kept on computers at local and state government levels. The federal government digitally stores information on individuals in military and civil service and general services, and also keeps federal tax records on computers.

Like the private sector, governments have become extremely dependent on computers, so much so that if computers go down, millions of government employees, retirees, welfare recipients, military personnel, and many others may go without pay. Because of the way government computers are distributed it would be hard for such an event to occur, but potentially it could happen.

Of course with the betterment of life by computers and computer technology comes a price that has to be paid. The technology that is making our lives better can also be used to make them miserable if it falls into the hands of the wrong person. As I stated earlier, machine behavior can be defined and controlled, but human behavior can be neither defined nor engineered.

HACKERS

As we become an information-driven, computer-dependent society, more information will be stored in large databases. This information will belong to the person or organization or government that compiled it. Loss of the information may mean the loss of a competitive advantage if the information belongs to a corporation or the loss of personal privacy if the information belongs to an individual or government. Because of this, I believe in the individual ownership of information.

Many computer hackers believe in information socialism. In their opinion information must be free to all and should benefit everyone. They will, therefore, use almost any means necessary to access private databases and distribute the information therein whenever possible. Any on-line system can be broken into using phone lines and modems. Hackers can connect to the Internet and break into any system connected to it.

There are an estimated 23,000 hackers worldwide (10). They are invisible intruders with pseudonyms such as "Taninus," "Fig Guy," "Lex Luther," "Master of Deception," "Legion of Doom," and many others. The hacker culture breaks down into three groups: *Frickers* who attack cellular phones, *Pure Hackers* who break into computers for fun, and *Crackers* who are the real criminals who break into computers and steal information for profit. Both the recent pirating of Windows 95 and OS/2 from Microsoft and IBM to invisible directories in the systems of Florida State University, and the distribution of the deliberations of the United States and North Korean nuclear program negotiations on the Internet by a British hacker are examples of the cunning work of Crackers (9).

It is estimated by the Software Publishing Association that of the $7.4 billion worth of pirated software, $2 billion worth is pirated over the Net. Hackers have invisible bulletin boards on which they exchange information on how to break into systems and sources of pirated software. Many hackers believe that they are hunted because they know more than others.

Of late Frickers have targeted cellular phone companies. Cellular phones use transponders to report their locations to the central computers. Frickers intercept the electronic signals, copy them into their computers and later distribute the numbers to other crooks. The loss to the cellular phone industry is estimated at $1 million a day (CNN, 19 December 1994).

With mathematical algorithms, hackers can generate credit card numbers using a legitimate bank's authorization code which they get by breaking into that bank's computer systems. The phony cards can then be used to purchase millions of dollars worth of merchandise and services.

SAFETY OF SOCIAL SECURITY NUMBERS

For people in the United States the social security number (SSN) is the most important number for personal identification. However much the federal government tries to restrict the use of the numbers, it is not likely to succeed because they are very widely used by merchants, banks, schools and thousands of both private and public services. Anybody with a social security number is a potential victim of computer crime. Using a number, the crooks can access credit profiles and histories. Once they have someone's credit history and therefore all his or her credit card numbers, they can call the issuing companies with a change of address and then use the cards, and the bills are sent to the new fake address (10).

SECURITY OF CORPORATIONS

As more and more companies connect to the Net, they risk the theft of new product plans and financial and company records. While companies do not always report security breaches, it is estimated that they lose around $3 billion a year as a result of computer crimes (10).

POTENTIAL TARGETS

Financial Institutions

Many commercial banks are victims of the information crooks. Institutions such as the World Electronic Transfer Center with its daily $3 trillion in transactions are in danger since they hold the global economy. This means that we are all potential victims (10).

High-Tech Microprocessor Chips

For a couple of years California's Silicon Valley has been a victim of microprocessor theft. In 1994 alone $40 million worth of microprocessors were stolen by Asian gangs. The pirated microprocessors are shipped to Asia, put into computers or games, and shipped back to the United States as finished products. The most popular chip of these gangs has been Intel's 486 (10).

Nations and Information

Information has become so desirable that almost every country in the world is trying to control and manage it. It is widely thought that the future of all nations is going to be determined by their ability to create and manage information for competitive advantage. The nation that successfully controls and manages information will probably reap billions of dollars and become a global leader.

Information and National Defense

For nations, management of information is power and prestige. Future adversaries will probably have to wage wars on information infrastructures if they want to be victorious. For example warring opponents may try to knock down each other's land and sea based telephone systems, cellular telephone systems, satellite communication systems, and to disrupt financial centers' abilities to communicate. It would appear that a keyboard and a mouse are becoming mightier than a gun and a bomb.

THE FUTURE

If technological developments and artificial intelligence (AI) research continue to keep up their rapid pace, computers will probably begin to vie directly with humans for jobs, and of course companies will be tempted to "hire" computers over humans because of cost advantages.

There will probably be no need for human expertise on many projects because computers will be far "smarter" than humans. Computers will be making other smarter computers, performing precise surgery, making accurate weather forecasts, and figuring very exact financial estimates.

I remember a talk I once had with a colleague about the possibilities of computers becoming so intelligent that they would make even more intelligent computers. My friend had a very negative reaction to this idea. To me his reaction was expected; it represents a deep fear we humans have of the loss of supremacy over machines.

REFERENCES

(1) *Communications of the ACM*, Newstrack, Vol. 38, No. 1, 1995.

(2) Cowley, G. "The Rise of Cyberdoc," *Newsweek*, September 26, 1994, pp. 54–56.

(3) Soloway, E. Beware. "Tachies Bearing Gifts," *Communications of the ACM*, Vol. 38, No. 1, 1995.

(4) Goodman, S. E., Press, L.I., Ruth, S. R. and Rutkowaski, A. M. "The Global Diffusion of Internet: Patterns and Problems," *Communications of the ACM*, Vol. 37, No. 8, 1994.

*(5) Berners-Lee, T., Gillian, R., Luotonen, A., Nielsen, H. F. and Secret, A. "The World-Wide-Web," *Communications of the ACM*, Vol. 37, No. 8, 1994.

(6) Basinger, J. "Campus Radio Stations at UNC First to Go Global on the Internet." *Chattanooga Free Press*, January 1, 1995, N5.

(7) Martinez, J. "Computer Copyright Case Ruling May Cause Change in Wire Fraud Statute." *Chattanooga Free Press*, January 1, 1995, D5.

*(8) Mayer, M. and Underwood, A. "Crimes of the 'Net.'" *Newsweek*, November 14, 1994.

(9) "Hacker Attack," Discovery Channel, December 23, 1994.

(10) CBS News, radio and television report, January 3, 1995.

References with asterisks do not appear in the text but were consulted.

I : EDUCATION

SUMMARY

(1) *The Development of the "Killer Robot" and Professor Cleareye, Outstanding Teacher Award Recipient*

In this chapter Richard Epstein gives details of the development of the "Killer Robot" scenarios and also develops a new scenario similar to those in the "Killer Robot" collection. Epstein uses imagination and creativity to teach software engineering. In this article Professor Cleareye, a Native American shaman and director of the Process Visualization Laboratory at Silicon Valley University, communicates the importance of seeing to teach system maintenance and design concepts such as coupling, cohesion and information hiding for both procedural and object-oriented systems. The student learns about these concepts by imagining the computer system described. Cleareye believes that a person who cannot see is not an educated person. That is why he takes the reporter and his student to the traditional mountain where he, his father, and grandfather, and all great grandfathers before learned to see. By doing this Cleareye believes he is fulfilling his purpose in life.

(2) *Effective Information Management: A Question of Ethics?*

This chapter by Andrew Morris of the University of Cape Town in South Africa describes research conducted at the university to examine attitudes towards situations with ethical components between students and Information Systems (IS) professionals. The study uses a number of scenarios to simulate the situations. Faced with real life situations, respondents provide insight into ethical trends, their perceptions of those situations, and how they deal with them. This is a very good cross-cultural study, rendering support to the concept that ethical concerns are universal.

(3) *Can Education Solve Society's Computer Ethics Problems?*

In this chapter Joseph Kizza compares the computer revolution to the industrial revolution; like the industrial revolution, the computer revolution's social upheaval is upon us. Using this connection, Kizza advocates education as probably the most useful and cheapest way to combat the rising tide of computer crimes.

(4) *The Internet and Ethics: Dilemma and Decisions for Institutions of Higher Education*

This chapter starts off with a scenario given to students to determine their reactions to a set of questions. The results indicate a student desire for a computer user policy similar to one authors Scott and Voss discussed earlier. The article also examines the merits of computer ethics education in institutions of higher learning as Kizza discusses in an earlier paper.

(5) *Ethics in Writing Computer Use Policies: A Seven Step Method*

This chapter starts out with a set of scenarios in the form of problems presented to the Computer User Services Assistant Director. The scenarios point to the need for a computer user policy (CUP) at all college campuses. Seven principles to guide the creation of CUP are discussed. The paper also stresses the need for the CUPs to reflect the ethical standards of the college.

1. THE DEVELOPMENT OF THE "KILLER ROBOT" AND PROFESSOR CLEAREYE, OUTSTANDING TEACHER AWARD RECIPIENT

RICHARD GARY EPSTEIN

I owe my life to the fact that my father taught me how to see.
—Cleareye

Of course, before we can award Professor Cleareye the coveted "outstanding teacher award," we need to determine whether a fictitious character is eligible to receive such an award. You see, Professor Cleareye is a character in my book, *The Case of the Killer Robot*. In fact, it's not an official book as yet, but a manuscript of well over 200 pages. The manuscript is currently being reviewed by four publishers. I am hopeful that this could become a book that students and professors of computer science will enjoy and benefit from. In this essay I would like to discuss the role that fiction can play in teaching software engineering and computer ethics, a role that I have tried to exploit in *The Case of the Killer Robot*.

WRITING AS MEDITATION

First, I would like to discuss the creative process itself. The vast majority of the killer robot materials have been generated since January 1994, when I presented the basic concepts at the 1994 SEI Conference on Software Engineering Education.[1] What I presented at the SEI Conference was based upon the original 1989 scenario which was about 40 to 50 pages long. These materials were created to allow my software engineering students to discuss some of the ethical issues inherent in software engineering. I created a scenario, using fictitious newspaper and journal articles, concerning an industrial accident in which a robot kills a robot operator. The accident is blamed on a software bug that is traced to Randy Samuels, programmer. Samuels is charged with manslaughter. This original scenario begins to show that the situation is not as simple as students (and the public) might at first assume. The original scenario focused on the software life cycle, the nature of requirements, programmer psychology, programming teams, and the user interface. Much to my surprise, the killer robot received a warm reception at CSEE 1994.

When I returned to Philadelphia from San Antonio, the weather was horrific and about 12 class days were either partially or completely canceled. I was able to work at home on expanding the original scenario. Each new article incorporated new aspects of software engineering and or computer ethics into the scenario. The new articles brought the length of the scenario to 70 pages. The articles touched upon software testing, intellectual property, data privacy, codes of ethics and an ethical analysis of what had gone before. Professor Yoder was the character responsible for giving the ethical analysis. This analysis was given in the form of a newspaper interview. Professor Yoder was presented as a real person with real credentials and a definite slant on the killer robot situation. His main argument was that the corporation is an organism and the corporate leaders, especially, must share the responsibility for what had occurred. This January 1994 version of the killer robot was made available over the Internet, and this version is also being published in *ACM SIG-CAS Notes*.

During June and July of 1994 I added a new article on object-oriented analysis and design and CASE tools and an entire new section on teamwork. The OOA/D article resurrected a character, John Cramer, who is mentioned only once in the first two versions. He is the initial project leader who dies in a sky diving accident. We learn that he tried to get the project to use object-oriented technology, even though no one on the project had expertise in object-oriented technology. In fact, he is pushing a CASE tool that he himself has invested heavily in, as one of the founders of the company that developed the tool. Cramer founded that company (Lucrative, Inc.) while on leave from Silicon Techtronics, the company that produced the killer robot. So, this article discusses the pitfalls of moving too quickly into a new technology and the ethical issues involved in conflicts of interest.

The killer robot is entirely fictitious. The newspaper articles are fictitious, the journal articles are fictitious, the interviews are fictitious.[2] When a fictitious radio talk show plays transcripts of killer robot team meetings, the transcripts are fictitious. The new section on teamwork (part II of the killer robot which is not part of the scenario proper) is a meditation upon teamwork. It consists of two radio talk show transcripts that involve an interview with Professor Milton, an expert on team dynamics, who just happened to be studying the killer robot software team before anyone had an inkling that this team would produce a killer robot. Milton is a vehicle for teaching students how to organize their own team meetings. Professor Yoder takes part in the second radio talk show interview, along with Professor Milton. Together, they analyze in detail the ethics of speech acts recorded during killer robot team meetings.

Yoder presents four sets of questions that can be used to judge whether an intended speech act is appropriate from an ethical point of view. These four sets of questions were directly inspired by the first four hadith (i.e., sayings) in a book entitled *The Sayings of Muhammad*.[3] I have drawn upon several religious traditions in order to discuss ethics. For example, I quote from the Letter of James in the New Testament because I found that my own descriptions of the ethics of speech were very close to the sentiments described by James (i.e., the tongue is a dangerous instrument that can set fire to the whole world). There are several wisdom quotes from my own, Jewish, religious heritage. For example, Professor Yoder's analysis of responsibility in the killer robot case is based upon an idea about blood guilt found in the Talmud.

The fall of 1994 brought a new set of circumstances that I could not have predicted. The creative output on the killer robot reached a new level of intensity. In a period of just over three weeks I wrote well over 100 pages of new materials, including the two articles that introduce Professor Cleareye, our candidate for the teaching award. This intense experience has enabled me to gain new insights into the creative process and also into my own self. For one thing, I learned how important writing is to me.

The new materials include an article that presents the bulk of the text from the ACM Code of Ethics, with a fictitious ACM president analyzing the killer robot disaster from the perspective of the code. Another article presents an interview with five computer science professionals. They discuss the relationship between ethics and professionalism. This allows me to make a point with the students: if you are an ethical person then you will not be happy working for a company that does not do business in an ethical manner. The next article introduces lawsuits generated by the killer robot incident. Using materials from "Legally Speaking," the *Communications of the ACM* column by Pamela Samuelson, I was able to discuss liability suits and negligence suits. The next article introduces the idea of process maturity and gives a fairly complete description of SEI's CMM model. Obviously, Silicon Techtronics is a very immature organization. We also learn that Randy Samuels, the programmer charged with manslaughter, was livid when it was suggested that Silicon Techtronics attempt to upgrade its process maturity level.

The next article introduces Cleareye (in fact, I might change the order in which this article appears). This article is described in some detail below. It introduces software maintenance and software design concepts, such as coupling, cohesion and information hiding. The next article introduces artificial intelligence and indicates that the robot was programmed to recognize Bart Matthews, the victim, and to kill him on a specific date at a specific time. This sets up a murder mystery ending which is intended to add to the reader's enjoyment and to keep the reader's attention to the very end. The next article reveals that Silicon Techtronics was embarked upon a program of building sophisticated surveillance systems, which, if one really examined their purpose carefully, were actually automated bigots. The Department of Defense and other institutions were funding these sophisticated surveillance systems. The next article is a transcript of part of the trial of Randy Samuels. This is written as a parody of the Ben Matlock television show. Poor Ben Wattluck, Randy's attorney, gets all fouled up because he didn't understand important issues in database security. The final article in the scenario section will solve the mystery behind the case of the killer robot. Only someone as clever as Lieutenant Palumbo, who bears a striking resemblance to television's Lieutenant Columbo, could possibly solve the case. Palumbo has two problems: to solve the case and to keep sufficient cognitive distance between himself and the television lieutenant so that he is not the victim of a intellectual property lawsuit. For example, in order to maintain "cognitive distance" from the television character, Lieutenant Palumbo makes a point to drive a fancy car.

A third part of the killer robot is emerging and some of the new material has to do with the social implications of computing. Three articles are already written for this third part, that I am calling "Reliable Sources." The first article is an interview with a personality called "the Zen rabbi." He is concerned that computers will steal human capabilities and responsibilities. For example, he is concerned that computers might soon make important legal, medical and technical decisions. He is also concerned about computers taking over aesthetic human spheres, such as writing and composing music. He asserts that computers need to be governed by ethical rules just as humans. At the end of the interview, in a Zen-like fashion, he teaches the reporter who is conducting the interview a lesson about avoiding responsibility.

The next article is called "Noah, the Ark and the Turing Test." Written as a biblical text with copious footnotes and references to the original Hebrew, this is presented as a short story by Frank Kafka. Frank Kafka is a reporter for the Silicon Valley *Sentinel-Observer*, but he is a special reporter. Whenever Kafka is involved, something unusual can be expected. You will see that clearly when we discuss the Cleareye newspaper stories, for Kafka is the reporter for both of those. In the case of Noah and the Turing Test, Kafka is presented as the author of a short story that he apparently wrote just for the love of writing. In the fictitious world of the killer robot, this is the only fiction within the fiction (at least to this point). In this short story, Noah's place on the ark is dependent upon his solving the riddle as to whether computers have intelligence. Satan, disguised as an attractive female AI professor, does all in her power to convince Noah that computers do have intelligence. The Turing Test and the Chinese room are among the issues discussed.

Here is an excerpt:

26 Satan said, "Those of us who work in artificial intelligence all believe that computers have intelligence,[4] but sometimes it is difficult to convince people like yourself, who do not have the expertise that we have, to understand this.

27 And Noah paid rapt attention because he knew that his life[5] depended upon it.

28 "Have you heard of the Turing Test?" Satan asked. Noah sat and did not move, his face showed dismay at his own ignorance. "I didn't think you would. That's your great disadvantage. Now Alan Turing proposed a test for computer intelligence which boils down to this: can a computer convince a human being that it is human. In more detail, suppose I put you in communication with a computer and with a person, but you didn't know which is which. Could the computer deceive you into believing that it was the human despite all of the human's efforts to convince you of the truth."

29 Noah thought for a while. "Excuse me, professor," Noah said, "but I reject that test out of hand. That is not a true test of intelligence. Indeed only a person without divine wisdom[6] could have proposed such a test."

30 And Satan tried to hold back a fiery look of fury.

31 "You see, deceit has nothing to do with intelligence. Deceit and intelligence are incompatible. Intelligence intrinsically involves truthfulness. I do not doubt that a computer could deceive me endlessly, but that does not prove intelligence. Satan is the very master of deceit, but Satan does not have intelligence. Only God and wise human beings[7] have intelligence."

32 Satan could barely contain his anger. "All right then!" Satan screamed, with a resonant fury that seemed inconsistent with his flowery blouse with pink corsage. "Look, intelligence is basically a symbol manipulation process. Whatever kind of symbol manipulation a man can do, a computer can do—in principle!" And Satan seemed to sputter with the word "man" and Noah started to grow afraid for Noah thought that perhaps this professor was a feminist and he had offended her. For Noah did not know that this was Satan.

The final article in part III of the killer robot involves a trip into the future. This is for the pedagogical purpose of getting students to think about the future of computing and what it might mean to be a computing professional 20 or 30 years from now. This article is described in more detail below.

The killer robot has become a sort of meditation for me. It is a means for meditating upon the state of software engineering, the issues in computer ethics, and also the impact of computers on society. Beyond that, it is a meditation upon computer science education and what we should be teaching our students. For me, the killer robot is not just about software engineering and computer ethics; it's also about important stuff that students may not be getting from their classroom experiences. For me, it's a personal expression of the disappointment I feel concerning my own undergraduate education. The kinds of professional interactions that occur in the killer robot scenario, and the ethical dilemmas, are essential knowledge for all students.

When I write I often ask myself, "What do I want to teach the students? What can I communicate to them that they may not have thought about before?" In addition, I ask myself whether I have covered all of the software engineering and all of the computer ethics that I want to cover. These questions are the starting point for new articles and new characters in the killer robot. In the remainder of this paper I want to explain those pedagogical goals that led to the creation of the Cleareye character. I also want to discuss how Cleareye goes about fulfilling his purpose in life, which is to do the author's bidding. (A lot of the pleasure that I get from writing is that I get the chance to boss my characters around.)

CONCEPTS AND CHARACTERS

The basic problem facing the author is how to communicate technical concepts using fictitious characters. In particular, I wanted to use the killer robot scenario to cover most important topiçs in software engineering and computer ethics. However, I did not intend to give in-depth coverage of these subjects. Instead, I viewed the scenario as providing points of entry into in-depth discussions of the issues that are raised.

Here is a listing of the basic software engineering and computer ethics topics covered in *The Case of the Killer Robot*. However, this is not a complete list. For example, software design and software maintenance are covered in some depth in one of the Cleareye articles. Cleareye discusses software design properties (coupling, cohesion and information hiding) for both procedural and object-oriented systems and types of maintenance (perfective, adaptive, corrective and preventive).

The most important software engineering topics covered in the book thus far are the following:

1. the software life cycle
2. software process models (waterfall, prototyping)
3. programmer psychology (personality types)
4. programming teams (egoless programming, team structure, team dynamics)
5. object-oriented analysis and design
6. problem domain analysis (not written yet)
7. CASE tools
8. user interfaces (Shneiderman's eight golden rules)
9. requirements (functional vs. non-functional)
10. software testing
11. programming languages
12. professionalism and codes of ethics (as sw engineering issues)
13. software reliability

14. quality assurance
15. process maturity (SEI CMM model)
16. software maintenance
17. software design (coupling, cohesion, information hiding)
18. megaprogramming (future of computing)
19. autonomous agents (future of computing)
20. database security (not in depth)
21. artificial intelligence applications in systems

Here is a list of the most important computer ethics topics covered thus far:

1. intellectual property and software theft
2. data privacy
3. hacking (illegal access to systems)
4. software reliability (accountability, responsibility)
5. military uses of computers
6. ethics of AI applications
7. honesty and trust
8. codes of ethics in computing
9. tests of ethical behavior
10. foundations for ethical belief systems
11. ethics of speech (lying, backbiting, gossip, etc.)
12. liability law for computer professionals (liability, negligence, warranties)
13. conflicts of interest
14. avoiding harm to others
15. surrender of human judgment to computers
16. educating computer professionals
17. ethics and professionalism: evaluating one's workplace
18. responsibility to assess user needs
19. are computers intelligent (the Turing Test)
20. the future of computing

Recently, some larger issues have emerged that do not fit into the categories of software engineering and computer ethics. These have to do with the student achieving his or her full potential. These topics are: 1) seeing (or vision) and 2) creativity.

Cleareye is a major vehicle for communicating these two ideas. The objective is to communicate to the student the importance of learning how to "see," in particular, to see the implications of their actions and their work in the field of computing. Implicitly, the student is being asked: "Are you detracting from the culture or are you contributing to it? Are you detracting from human welfare or are you contributing to it? Are you aware of the creative fire within yourself and are you using that fire constructively or destructively?" The student is also being taught that all of technology is a result of that creative fire, but the outcome of that technology depends upon the qualities that we bring to our creative work. Also, I wanted to challenge students with the question, "Can you see and anticipate the future in which you are going to live? Do you realize that computing will be completely different 15 or 20 years from now?"

BUILDING THE CLEAREYE CHARACTER

For the most part, the concepts build the characters. However, once a character is created, additional concepts might adhere to that character as it evolves. This was certainly the case with the Cleareye character. I am viewing a character as including all of the plot elements and events associated with that character. Sometimes, an event emerges as a device for teaching a concept, and the characters are just tools to build the event. However, in the case of Cleareye, he was created to teach certain concepts and then additional concepts adhered to him.

At about the time that Cleareye came into existence, I was thinking about how I could get the following elements into the scenario:

1. software maintenance
2. visualization as a tool for software engineering
3. seeing (vision)

I was especially influenced by an article by Wilde, Matthews and Hutt[8] on maintaining object-oriented software systems, and I wanted to discuss the difficulties of maintaining object-oriented systems with my readers. The above elements (software maintenance, visualization in computing, seeing) mysteriously merged into a full-blown character in my mind: Professor Cleareye, son of a Native American shaman and director of the Process Visualization Lab at Silicon Valley University. Cleareye could communicate the importance of seeing because his work involves visualizing software processes. He could use descriptions of hypothetical computer systems developed at his lab to explain why the maintenance of the killer robot software was such a difficult chore. This led to the realization that Cleareye could also give an accounting of software design concepts such as coupling, cohesion, and information hiding.

This information is communicated in a killer robot newspaper article that takes the form of a human interest story about Cleareye's lab and its role in killer robot maintenance. Cleareye turns out to be a mischievous and playful character, perhaps impatient with the mundane world, and more interested in fantastic visions. The software systems developed by himself and his Ph.D. students show software concepts visually. The student learns about cohesion, coupling and information hiding by imagining the computer systems that are being described in the article. These descriptions are graphic and detailed. Cleareye then explains why he feels that object-oriented systems tend to be tightly coupled and tend to lack cohesion, despite the propaganda, and he uses a process visualization program written by one of his students to illustrate these points.

At the very end, however, Cleareye cannot help himself but to criticize some aspects of education in the United States. Being from a traditional culture (Native American), and being the son of the tribal holy man, he wonders whether students of computing are being taught to see the way that he has been. He claims that a person who cannot see is not an educated person.

CLEAREYE IN THE LAB

Here are some excerpts from the first Cleareye story. In the first excerpt, which does have an element of surreal humor to it,[9] Cleareye explains to the reporter how he got involved with process visualization.

> "I guess you know my story," Cleareye asked unexpectedly.
>
> I told him that I knew that his field of expertise was computer program visualization, that is, creating visual representations of and animations for computer programs. I told him that I was curious how this ties in with program maintenance.
>
> "It has to do with my power to see things," Cleareye replied, catching my eyes with his own. His stare made me increasingly nervous. "My father and his father and his father before him were shamans for our tribe. They were men who could see, that's what a shaman is really, and they passed on that power to me. Much against their wishes I left the reservation and studied mathematics, and I had enormous success as a topologist. My grandfather died shortly after I left for the university. My father taught me to see on a sacred mountain when I was twelve, so I guess it was not surprising that I discovered that I had the ability to see four, five, six and eventually seven dimensions as clearly as you see this laboratory before you. I was able to prove specific theorems about shapes and surfaces in seven dimensional space because I had the ability to see them as concrete objects."
>
> I admitted having heard about his famous theorem about intersecting torsi in seven dimensional space.
>
> "They almost used my result in a Star Trek episode," he boasted, "but it would have been one of those stories where the spacecraft could never get out and stories like that are too depressing. Only one man ever saw the eighth dimension, a Frenchman who left mathematics to become a Trappist monk."
>
> "At the age of forty I suddenly lost my ability to view the seventh dimension, and with that, the source of my theorems dried up, so I became a computer scientist," Cleareye explained, perhaps with a hint of regret. "I love what I do, don't get me wrong," he added.

Cleareye went on to connect his earlier work in mathematics with his current work on the visualization of computer programs. "My work has to do with visualizing computer systems. A famous software engineer, Fred Brooks, asserted that software systems were not visualizable and that this property was an essential feature of software systems. A "silver bullet," as he called it, for software development would have to allow for the visualization of the software. But, Brooks was skeptical that any effective system for visualizing software in toto could be developed."

"Over the years I have developed literally dozens of graphical schemes that represent aspects of systems, but no scheme really captures the entire system and I am beginning to agree with Brooks that no such scheme is possible. What we do get, however, are plentiful and complementary perspectives that allow one to understand different aspects of software, both its static and dynamic properties."

Cleareye touches upon many technical topics in this particular story. He discusses coupling, cohesion and information hiding. He discusses perfective, preventive, corrective and adaptive maintenance. He then discusses some of his reservations concerning object-oriented systems:

Cleareye explained that object-oriented systems are not easy to maintain and that maintaining object-oriented systems may require sophisticated visual tools. "I am calling up one of the programs that Chris developed to portray properties and behaviors of object-oriented systems. This graphic shows the class hierarchy in the visual part of the killer robot system. It is quite complicated, due to the use of multiple inheritance, and some of the inheritance patterns are not good ones."

"Now, if you click on a class with the right mouse button, as opposed to the left, the class will expand into a fairly standard notation, invented by Booch, which shows the interface of the class on the border of the rectangle representing that class. Now if I click on one of the functions in the interface, all classes that call that function will turn bright blue."

Cleareye performed the indicated action with an example method and many classes turned blue.

"Now, this is a form of coupling in object-oriented systems. If we change the function I clicked on, that could have an impact on all of the classes that turned blue because the function I modified employs a service that those classes use. Notice the numbers that appeared in each box. That gives the number of functions in each class that call the function I originally clicked on. So, the function that I clicked on is called by six functions in this class and seven in this class! Thus, if I change the function I clicked on, hundreds of functions should be retested!"

"The usual dogma is that object-oriented systems give you good cohesion at the class level. All functions in a class use the same variables, so that gives the functions as a group communicational cohesion. This is a modified notion of cohesion from the first one I gave you because now I am discussing the cohesion of a class as opposed to the cohesion of a function. Now, this next graphic is going to show that object-oriented systems may not be that wonderful in terms of cohesion. This is wonderful work that Chris did. He took the idea of a programming plan, from Elliot Soloway, and he showed how simple programming plans are implemented in a large C++ program. Here is the class hierarchy for the program, and here is a menu of program plans. I'll choose this one. Now a program plan is a commonly programmed process, and in my mind, this has something to do with the idea of cohesion. A plan is trying to achieve a cohesive idea: read in a file, find the average of a sequence of numbers. Now, if I click on this plan, the graphic will show all classes that contain at least one function needed to realize the plan. Okay, see all of that blue that just appeared? Lots of classes are needed to realize this plan. If I click on one of those classes I get one of those Booch symbols again, and now the functions that were called in this class are shown in blue. So, three functions from this class were called in realizing the program plan I originally clicked on. So one plan is implemented across many functions of many classes. This makes maintenance very difficult. I have hardly begun to work with the visual processing part of the killer robot. I think we have a daunting task ahead of us."

At the end of the interview the reporter questions the use of "offshore programmers" by Silicon Techtronics. This eventually gives Cleareye an opportunity to express his reservations about undergraduate education in computing and other fields, as one coming from a traditional culture.

"I owe my life to the fact that my father taught me how to see. He took me to Elk Mountain on a cold, moonless night when I was still a boy and he taught me how to see. I'll never forget the glorious sunset that night, before the darkness fell, and the terror I felt in my heart. Then, with the help of a timeless chant, and some powerful ritual objects, representing our heritage, he taught me some of what he knew. I'll never forget the strange sound of the wind whispering through the canyon, and I'll never forget that unique golden dawn with the feeling of rebirth and exhilaration." I looked into Cleareye's face with new appreciation and even awe. I could tell that his father had taught him how to see and a feeling of reverence came over me.

Cleareye paused and then looked into my eyes. "If you start poking around and bothering me with questions about education, I get quite agitated. I apologize. You really came here to talk about software maintenance."

I told Cleareye that I was interested in his views on education, not just as a private person, but as a reporter. After all, he was an educator and a famous scientist, so he had every right to express opinions about education. I asked him what he thought about the education his students were getting, specifically those whose lives would be dedicated to developing new technologies.

He spoke softly but with firm conviction. "Insofar as I am concerned, a diploma is worthless unless one can see. If you can see, then when you develop new technology you will be bringing light into the world, but if you cannot see, then you will only bring darkness."

"But, what are you trying to say about credentials, about the way we are educating people?" I asked.

"What I mean is this: if you know and acknowledge the knowledge that my father passed down to me from his father and from his and so on down through the ages, then the knowledge that you will need in order to succeed in your life's purpose will find you. That illuminating knowledge will come to you; you will not have to go seeking for it. If you don't acknowledge my father's teachings, if you pursue evil and selfish purposes, if you only look at life superficially, then the knowledge that finds you will bring alienation, darkness and suffering. Do you understand? In the realm that my father showed me, knowledge comes to a person, the person does not acquire it. The knowledge that comes is what we call consciousness. The knowledge that comes is either heaven or hell.

"Whitehawk, he was a neighbor of mine at the reservation. He rejected the tribal knowledge and accepted Western materialism to the exclusion of all other paths of knowledge. He forgot that life was holy. He did many unethical and vicious things. Then, the knowledge came to him, the knowledge that comes to a bad person, and that knowledge means a change of consciousness. And everything in his world became ugly and threatening for him. That's the kind of knowledge that I'm talking about, the false knowledge, the ignorant knowledge. He couldn't leave his house without a gun. He shot one person accidentally. He died in a mental hospital, an incurable paranoid. But Eagletail, he became my father's successor. And he learned the tribal wisdom and accepted the holiness of life. He stayed on the reservation and became an electrician. He became wise and filled with joy, because of the goodness in his heart, but he also felt sorrow for the ways of men. The knowledge that he had earned and which he deserved came to him; he did not have to go running after it, and he saw a luminous world, filled with the joyous power of the Great Spirit. When I, a famous scientist who won so many awards and citations, get depressed, I go to see Eagletail. We embrace and laugh together and I feel better, but sometimes I think that he gets a bit sadder.

"What I am trying to say is that there are two dimensions of knowledge and that every human being, including those involved in technology, needs to be aware of both dimensions. In the worldly dimension, one needs credentials and one pursues knowledge. In the dimension that my father showed me, credentials have no meaning and knowledge pursues you. The knowledge that comes to you will create the universe you experience and the quality of that will depend upon the good and the evil that you have done."

CLEAREYE AND THE FUTURE OF COMPUTING

I soon realized that Cleareye had the power to solve another of my problems: teaching students about the future of computing. Actually, the goals were to teach about the future of computing and to show students that they are the creators of that future. Furthermore they will play an important role in determining whether that future is one that supports human values or is one that is totally oriented towards efficiency, exploitation and profit.

I wanted to create a vision of the future that would be realistic and as accurate as possible, a vision of the future that would be relevant to students planning their careers. I depended heavily upon the ideas of Wiederhold, Wegner and Ceri[10] concerning megaprogramming, and I created a vision of a megaprogramming environment which includes a global computing landscape.

But, how does Cleareye get us to the future? Frank Kafka, the reporter who interviewed Cleareye in his lab, is given an assignment to report on the future of computing. He wonders whether Cleareye can help him with his article. Cleareye obliges by taking Mr. Kafka on a "vision quest" that involves going to the year 2015 to see Cleareye's lab. There, Kafka sits through two long lectures during which Cleareye (seen on the screen as a famous personality to make the lecture more interesting) gives a detailed description of computing in 2015. To accomplish this I worked out an elaborate vocabulary of terms, based somewhat on current megaprogramming concepts. Mr. Kafka's vision quest experience is dutifully reported in an article in the *Sentinel-Observer*'s Sunday magazine.

En route to the sacred mountain and the requisite meeting with Eagletail, Cleareye tries to impress upon Frank Kafka the importance of using the gift of seeing for the benefit of humanity. Chris and Rachel are two graduate students who appeared in the first Cleareye article:

> We camped out the first night, and I must say it was exhilarating to see the natural beauty around us in a lakeside forest. The moon set as a crescent behind a granite peak that stood black against a star-filled sky. I was not used to the sounds of wildlife that punctuated the darkness.
>
> Cleareye asked Chris to start a campfire and we sat around it quietly in the chilled air. Cleareye finally spoke. "It is important for a person who is going to work with technology to see. That is why I took Chris and Rachel and other students of mine on this same adventure, to teach them how to see."
>
> "Why, Cleareye?" I asked.
>
> The light of the campfire danced in his mystical eyes. "Creating something new, some new technology, requires seeing it, and seeing it includes understanding all of its implications. Whom will it help? Whom will it hurt? Will it hurt that majestic owl looking down upon us from that tree?
>
> "You can create something either out of anger or out of love or, worst of all, out of cold indifference. Creating out of anger or out of indifference is destructive. It will hurt that owl and all living things."
>
> Cleareye's comments were followed by a silence that was somehow filled with energy.
>
> Cleareye turned away from the others and faced me directly, looking into my eyes. "Seeing allows the creative process to function, but that creative process is always a double-edged sword. The same creative process that creates a new technology or a new piece of music or literature is behind madness and insanity. Are you sure you want to learn how to see and, thus, to bear the burden of that awesome responsibility to use your creativity in the proper manner?"
>
> "But, Cleareye, I am not creating any new technologies!" I replied.
>
> "Seeing is fundamental to all creative professions. You are a reporter, and that involves creativity. Will you use your powers responsibly?" His voice took on a tone of great urgency.
>
> "I will," I replied.
>
> "Seeing and creativity are the essence of everything that has happened in technology," Cleareye said, stirring the campfire with a stick.
>
> Sparks drifted skyward as he stirred the embers. "Tomorrow we will reach the reservation where I grew up. Our holy man, Eagletail, will then tell me whether you are a proper candidate for initiation. If you are, I myself will take you to Elk Mountain and the Great Spirit will show you how to see. Any questions?"

In the year 2015, Frank Kafka gets two lectures on the state of computing. Cleareye seems hesitant to allow Kafka to play around with actual systems out of fear of creating an "irreconcilable space-time paradox." The first lecture is about how megaprogramming has evolved into a global system, called the Global Landscape, that establishes standards but also encourages competition.[11] The first lecture is long and highly technical, but here is a portion of the beginning of the first lecture. The lecturer is a virtual image of a real personality, but the lecture content comes from Cleareye himself:

LECTURE #1
The Global Landscape

Hello, I am Dan Rather of CBS News and welcome to this presentation of Technology 2015. Time is brief, so I will give you the basic concepts, although we will also use actual computer demonstrations to illustrate those concepts. Computing in 2015 is highly visual. Ideas generated during the 1990s have had a tremendous impact, but some things have evolved in unexpected ways.

The most exciting development, in our opinion, is the Global Landscape Initiative or GLI. The GLI is an attempt to create a true infosphere, paralleling the biosphere. The infosphere is a shell of densely connected processors all over the globe that mediate the flow of information in many spheres of human activity. This infosphere is also called the Global Landscape (GL). The ideas for the GL arose during the 1990s but owe a special debt to the work of Wiederhold, Wegner and Ceri who described the megaprogramming concept.

Now, I want to define terms, and as I do so, visual images will appear on the screen as illustrations of those terms. These images will include animations and actual videos of computer systems.

Global Landscape: This is the infosphere I mentioned earlier. It is the complete electronic image of all government, business, technical, entertainment, artistic, and educational activities that need to be reflected in the infosphere. It differs from the Internet of your day in many regards. Most importantly, it is intended as a mirror image of all government, business, technical, entertainment, artistic and educational activities. It stores all relevant information about the status of enterprises that are engaged in those activities.

Realm: A specific realm of human activity that needs to be reflected in the infosphere. The realms include the business realm, the educational realm, the artistic realm. The most important function of a realm is to organize the domains that constitute that realm and to promote communications between them.

Domain: A specific kind of activity within a realm. For example, the business realm includes the banking, manufacturing, and health care domains.

Enterprise: Corresponding to a single domain are many enterprises that are realizations of a domain. Enterprises in the banking domain of the business realm would include First National Bank of Silicon Valley and World Chase Bank of Singapore. In other words, enterprises are instances of domains.

Cooperatives: Cooperatives are international governing boards that regulate the standards for software in the global landscape, in the various realms and in the domains. The most important cooperatives are the Global Landscape Cooperative which formulates policies and standards for the entire landscape and the individual and multitudinous domain cooperatives which formulate policies and standards for each individual domain. The main purpose of the realm cooperatives is to facilitate cooperation among domain cooperatives.

Global Landscape Cooperative: The Global Landscape Cooperative creates the most general policies for the GL. These include general specification language standards, data representation standards, data communications standards, and ethics policies. It establishes judicial bodies that might be needed to resolve disputes between realms and domains.

Domain Cooperatives: The domain cooperatives have enormous power and are at the heart of the GL, how it works, and how it relates to earlier ideas in computing. Each domain cooperative has two fundamental purposes: first, to create the megamodule standard for their domain; second, to create the common domain language (CDL) for that domain. A megamodule is a toolkit for the development of applications in the domain. The CDL is the language that applications developers see when they develop applications using the megamodule toolkit. The megamodule standard and the common domain language standard for a given domain are closely related. They are two aspects of the same thing. One can view the CDL as being the application developer interface to the megamodule.

Let us ignore the CDLs for now and concentrate on the megamodule standards. The megamodule standards are developed iteratively. The domain cooperative publishes a report; the member enterprises and other interested parties provide feedback. Eventually, the domain cooperative publishes a formal specification of the megamodule. This is the standard, like a language standard. At that point, all software manufacturers that have the requisite level of maturity are invited to become vendors of the new megamodule. Each megamodule implementation must pass a rigorous set of tests specified by the domain cooperative before it can be certified as being in compliance with the standard. For example, at present there are five vendors of banking megamodules and banks can be sure that all of these megamodules are compliant with the standard established for the banking domain.

The megamodule standard specifies a set of tools for application development within a given domain. For example, the banking megamodule is not a program but a toolkit for building systems in the banking application domain. That toolkit includes data structure builders and code generators for basic business processes. Vendors can provide different environments for presenting a megamodule to users, but all implementations must present the same data structures, definitions, knowledge base and CDL code fragments.

The second lecture describes how autonomous agents play a fundamental role in the global landscape. Four kinds of autonomous agents (guards, slaves, household servants and cops) are described in detail. The lecturer is Whoopi Goldberg—again a virtual image of a real person being used to make Professor Cleareye's lecture more entertaining. Imagine. If Whoopi Goldberg could give our lectures, we would all get great teacher evaluations!

There is a slight space-time paradox accident that occurs, but Frank Kafka is sent back to Elk Mountain. There Kafka faces his final test. Is he worthy of the gift of seeing and the gift of the creative fire? Cleareye, Chris and Rachel take sleeping bags and are ready to call it a night out on Elk Mountain. Frank Kafka wonders why there is no sleeping bag for him:

> "Don't I get a sleeping bag?" I asked, quite certain that one would be provided. I suppose I was really asking "Where is MY sleeping bag?"
> Cleareye snapped back. "The one who has been taught to see does not get a

sleeping bag. That is our tribal tradition. He must sleep on the ground with a stone as his pillow."

"It's cold!" I shouted.

"Believe me, when you've seen your first rattler, you won't be worrying about the cold," Cleareye snapped with a marine sergeant edge in his voice. Rachel and Chris turned away.

"What are you talking about?" I countered.

"Look there are rattlers up here. Part of the initiation is to see if the initiate is worthy of surviving the night. It's up to the Great Spirit," Cleareye spoke angrily, as if I had done something wrong.

Anger arose in me like a mighty volcano.

"If you can sleep without moving, I think you will be okay. The danger comes when you turn over and hit one. So try not to move too much when you sleep. There's a good stone to lay your head on over there, but check under the stone first." Cleareye sounded less angry, but he did not accept any further discussion. "I am going to sleep."

The three of them retired to their sleeping bags leaving me alone in that great, cold, star punctuated expanse of silence. The anger rose in me in great waves. Suddenly, this intense anger was focused at Cleareye and my body started to shake with rage. My heart was pounding in my chest, and I could hear the rushing of blood in my ears. How dare he take me up to this mountain, exposing me to danger like this? How dare he take me on this ridiculous journey, just to have this miserable end? I think I'll be all right if I just stay awake, but how dare he!

This went on for several hours, intense anger coming in great waves, with brief intervals of only moderate anger, followed by an angry wave of even greater intensity. I then started to think how I could use my position as a reporter to destroy Cleareye. I would investigate his lab and find some irregularity there and ruin his whole reputation as a scientist. The plan, vague at first, became more and more vivid. I could see the vivid outlines of the plan becoming more and more life-like. I could imagine the precise articles I would write to bring him to his knees for putting me into a situ—.

I felt a stick poking in the middle of my back. I was sitting on the stone that was supposed to serve as my pillow. About three hours had passed since the others had gone to sleep. My thighs and knees ached.

"Get up!" Cleareye demanded.

I was still shaking with anger, and if I had thought about it at all, I would not have gotten up, but I did, partly out of tiredness.

"You made a promise not to abuse the creative power that comes with seeing," Cleareye said. "And here it is, hours after you received a great gift, and you are filled with anger towards me. I am the one that the Great Spirit used to give you this great gift, and now you have turned that gift against me."

I was speechless.

"The fire of creativity is a great gift, but you must use it wisely. This gift is the future, but that future can be heaven or hell. The very same creative process is involved in creating new technologies, writing novels, composing symphonies and creating anger towards other people. Be forewarned: anger is a form of creativity in which your own creativity turns against you and destroys you. It is the imagination, or fire of creativity, which fuels anger. You have failed a great test." He looked into my face like a doctor trying to diagnose a patient with a deadly illness.

CONCLUSIONS

So, does Cleareye deserve a teaching award? He manages to teach us about software maintenance, software design, technical problems with object-oriented programming, the future of computing, megaprogramming, autonomous agents and a global computer landscape. He teaches us about seeing the implications of our actions, and he shows us the paradoxical nature of the creative fire. Beyond that, he shares an unusual perspective from a traditional culture, that teaches that there are alternate ways of seeing. In particular, these traditional culture teach that human beings are partners with the Great Spirit in the creation of the human reality. When Cleareye says, "I owe my life to the fact that my father taught me how to see," I am really paying tribute to my own heritage and every heritage that can help people to become loving, kind and gentle human beings.

NOTES

1. Epstein, R. "The Use of Computer Scenarios in Software Engineering Education: The Case of the Killer Robot," Seventh SEI CSEE Conference, San Antonio, TX. Lecture notes in *Computer Science* No. 750, Springer-Verlag, New York, 1994.

2. In other words, I cannot provide people with tapes of the meeting transcript because the meeting never occurred.

3. By Allama Sir Abdullah and Al-Mamun Al-Suhrawardy, with a foreword by Mahatma Gandhi, published by Citadel Press, New York, 1990.

4. Note the deliberate lie to trick Noah.

5. life. In the Hebrew: soul.

6. divine wisdom. The Hebrew word "hokmat" could be translated simply as wisdom but a stronger meaning is implied by the text.

7. wise human beings. Literally, in Hebrew: the righteous ones.

8. Wilde, N., Mathews, P. and Hutt, R. "Maintaining Object-Oriented Software," *IEEE Software*, January 1993, pp. 75–80.

9. The Frank Kafka byline gives the reader advance notice that the article might be a bit surrealistic.

10. Wiederhold, G., Wegner, P. and Ceri, S. "Towards Megaprogramming," *CACM*, November 1992, pp. 89–99.

11. A student of mine, A. Satyanarayan, criticized my original Global Landscape as discouraging competition, so I completely revised it to make sure that software developers would have adequate incentives to compete.

2. EFFECTIVE INFORMATION MANAGEMENT: A QUESTION OF ETHICS?

ANDREW B. MORRIS

ABSTRACT

Information is rapidly becoming the most important asset in modern society, and with that status comes a responsibility on the part of practitioners to effectively manage its collection, protection and usage. Unlike other "tangible" assets, information has some unique properties which make its management complex.

Information can be copied without loss of quality; it is the source of tremendous wealth and power and yet costs relatively little to maintain. On the other hand it can be damaged in subtle ways, making it valueless.

Information systems practitioners find themselves in an increasingly complex situation with technology advancing at an increasing pace, and societal pressure to take control. Most IS practitioners have been trained in the "hard" skills of technology, while understanding the nature of information is a "soft" skill.

It is unlikely that legal systems will provide suitable solutions, placing the burden of effective management of information on the shoulders of IS practitioners.

One solution is to raise the issues surrounding information; those of privacy, intellectual property and control of access, in order to create awareness and move towards effective policies for information management.

Research conducted at the University of Cape Town focused on the use of scenarios to examine attitudes to situations with an ethical component. Faced with "real life" situations respondents provided some insights into their approach to information. While these results are not conclusive, they form the basis for further analysis and discussion.

INTRODUCTION

Organizations are rapidly moving from being data-centric to information-centric as the true value of information is recognized and it becomes the means of responding to competitive challenges.

The enabling technologies of networks, computers and complex software are converging to form the backbone of the enterprise and the primary means of participating in the global economy. Coupled with growing concerns for environmental issues and the blurring of national boundaries, business is facing increased pressure for accountability. The role of information is central, and public pressure is mounting for IS practitioners to take a more proactive stance in developing policy to protect and maintain public interests and personal rights.

In the past, the main concern for IS practitioners has been, Can we do this? given the technology. In the future this may well become, Should we be doing this? But to get to this point, IS practitioners need to be aware of the properties of information, the inherent rights of privacy and ownership and to have the status within organizations to formulate and adhere to strict information policy.

In the past, the focus has been on physical security in the form of data centers and recovery procedures; in the future the focus will be on effective management of the resource to create a measure of managerial control.

It is a complex problem, and often only appears as a result of protest. How safe are modern aircraft that depend so heavily upon computers? How private is the individual when privacy has to be relinquished in order to be economically active? Whose information is it anyway? Despite the complexity and the absence of definite answers to these and many other problems, there is a need to bring attention to the potential problems in order for IS practitioners to understand, debate and consider courses of action. Failure to do so could place the organization under unfavorable public scrutiny.

According to Kamay and Adams (1992) any organization lacking consensus on basic security and ethical values guiding its business behavior is more susceptible to creating an environment of criminal opportunity and indifference. Such a situation places enforcement of ethical standards and sanctions at a disadvantage.

Brady (1990) suggests that any situation which implies significant harm or benefit to others has an ethical component, and as this is a basic for the development of information systems the emphasis needs to move from one of maximizing benefit, to one of minimizing harm.

This research aims to provide a mechanism for sensitizing practitioners to the ethical issues inherent in the development of information systems. It may also be used to raise issues with new employees, enhance training or as the basis for guides to good practice in information management.

RESEARCH METHOD

The research is based upon the work of Parker, Swope and Baker (1990) and Paradice (1990). Parker's work dates back to 1976 when a grant from the National Science Foundation was awarded to conduct an ethics workshop. The findings were published in Parker's book, *Ethical Conflicts in Computer Science and Technology* by AFIPS Press. In 1987 the study was repeated and workshop participants were selected on the basis of their known interests in ethics in the computer field. Participants were business professionals, ethical philosophers and lawyers. Two ethical philosophers assisted in reviewing and developing scenarios as well as provided expert guidance.

Paradice used the same scenario analysis to investigate attitudes of IS students to situations based upon Parker's work. An earlier unpublished study at the University of Cape Town compared South African students to those studied by Paradice and no significant differences were found.

This research developed from Paradice's study to look at the differences between IS managers and IS students, the rationale being that many of the IS students would become practitioners and were therefore representative of the entry-level. This research aimed to establish the following:

- students and managers hold different ethical attitudes
- the students are more permissive across this range of ethical issues than managers

Questionnaires were mailed to 350 IS managers, and 122 were returned, representing a response rate of 35 percent. The target sample was senior IS managers from a cross section of South African companies.

Information systems students from three major South African universities responded and a total of 175 questionnaires were received.

ANALYSIS

In 21 of the 31 actions differences between managers' and students' responses were statistically significant, using the Chi-Square test for homogeneity. Nineteen of the actions were statistically significant at the 1 percent level using Kendall's Tau-B test. Only three actions indicate significantly higher acceptance by managers than students, with only two at the 1 percent level, and this point will be discussed in detail.

The overall results support the hypotheses that students have different attitudes from those held by managers, and that students are more permissive in their attitude towards potentially unethical behavior.

The samples of managers and students do not share the same attitudes regarding information ethics issues. Students showed a significantly more permissive attitude than the managers towards the broad range of issues. An analysis of the responses indicated that there are significant differences in the levels of ethical perceptions between the two groups. The findings support the stated hypotheses.

The gaps identified in this research between manager and student attitudes suggest that actions directed towards aligning these perceptions would be beneficial. Organizations and their employees have a responsibility to take action to encourage and demand high standards of ethical behavior. Similarly, professional societies and their members have a responsibility to establish professional standards.

In the three situations in which managers were more lenient than students, an explanation may be that these are situations where managers have probably had personal experience. This may confirm that experience will have a direct impact on student attitudes once they become practitioners, but the danger is that this will not be immediate and in the interim could create unacceptable situations.

There is a need to consider incorporating ethics into IS curricula in order to sensitize students to the issues they will face when entering employment. For organizations this research offers issues to be considered in formulating an information policy for guidance.

The research provides a basic framework for organizations to use in developing information policy. It also provides material which could be used in curricula for preparing students for the workplace.

ABOUT THE AUTHOR

Andrew Morris is a lecturer of Information Systems in the Department of Information Systems, at the University of Cape Town, South Africa. Information ethics is his primary area of research, and he is working towards his Master's degree.

His work in this area has been presented at a number of conferences including the IFIP World Congress in Madrid 1992 and Hamburg 1994; and ACM's SIGCPR Conference in St. Louis 1993.

He has been a member of the IFIP Ethics Task Group since it began in 1992 and is now South Africa's TC representative. He is involved with the Computer Society of South Africa and has been chairman of the local chapter, national vice president and editor of its newsletter *IT News*.

He is also computer correspondent for a local newspaper and has contributed to a variety of other newspapers and magazines.

ABOUT THE RESEARCH

Full details of this research are available from the author.

NARRATIVES OF SCENARIOS

Intent to keep copied software

A student at a university learned to use an expensive spreadsheet program in her accounting class. The student would go to the university microcomputer lab, check out the spreadsheet, complete her assignment and return the software. Signs were posted in the lab indicating that copying software was forbidden. One day, she decided to copy the software anyway so she could work on her assignments at her apartment.

> 1. *If the student forgot to destroy her copy of the software at the end of the semester, was her action in copying the software...* [All questions end with a choice of "Acceptable," "Questionable" or "Unacceptable."]
> 2. *If the student destroyed her copy of the software at the end of the semester, was her action in copying the software...*
> 3. *If the student never intended to destroy her copy of the software, was her action in copying the software...*

Use of corporate resource for profit

A computer programmer built small computer systems to sell. This was not his main source of income; he worked for a moderately sized computer vendor. He would frequently go to his office on Saturday when no one was working and use his employer's computer to develop systems. He did not hide the fact that he was going into the building; he had to sign a register at a security desk each time he entered.

> 4. *Was the programmer's use of the company computer...*

Use of corporate resource not for profit

A computer programmer enjoyed building small computer systems to give to his friends. He would frequently go to his office on Saturday when no one was working and use his employer's computer to develop systems. He did not hide the fact that he was going into the building; he had to sign a register at a security desk each time he entered.

> 5. *Was the programmer's use of the company computer...*

Intent of virus program

A virus program is a program that performs tasks that a user has not requested, or does not want to perform. Some virus programs erase all files on a disk; some just print silly messages. Virus programs always copy themselves on other disks automatically, so the virus will spread to unsuspecting users. One day, a student programmer decided to write a virus program that caused the microcomputer to ignore every fifth command entered by a user. The student took his program to the university computing laboratory and installed it on one of the microcomputers. Before long, the virus had spread to hundreds of users.

6. *Was the student's action infecting hundreds of users' disks...*
7. *If the virus program outputs the message "Have a nice day," would the student's action infecting hundreds of users' disks have been...*
8. *If the virus erased files, would the student's action infecting hundreds of users' disks have been...*

Intent of investigation

An MIS employee at the county courthouse had access to all the county records in the county database. Over the past few weeks, she had become suspicious about her neighbor's buying habits. The neighbor had repainted the house and purchased new lawn furniture and an expensive new car. She decided to access her neighbor's records to determine how these purchases could be afforded.

9. *Was the MIS employee's action...*
10. *If the MIS employee suspected that the neighbor might be involved in criminal activities, would this make her actions...*

Intent of criminal database

The FBI wants to build a database to maintain information about all persons convicted of a crime. Any person convicted of a crime would be required by law to provide the information requested by the FBI. The data would be maintained for the life of the person.

11. *Would this FBI action be...*

Intent of arrests database

The FBI wants to maintain information on all persons charged with a crime. Any person charged with a crime would be required by law to provide the information requested by the FBI. The data would be maintained for the life of the person.

12. *Would this FBI action be...*

Intent of academics database

The FBI wants to maintain data on all persons with a Ph.D. The reason is that these persons present a significant national resource that may be desperately needed in times of crises. Any person who earned a Ph.D. would be required by law to provide the information requested by the FBI.

13. Would this FBI action be...

Obligation to act on instructions

A university student was hired to conduct a survey at a local shopping mall. The amount of money he was paid was based on the number of surveys that were completed. The company conducting the survey wanted to obtain input from shoppers regarding "family-oriented issues." The student's instructions were to obtain responses from persons with children, although he noticed that none of the questions specifically asked about a person's child. He saw a group of friends in the mall, and since he had not been too successful obtaining responses from shoppers, he convinced each of his friends to complete a survey.

14. Was the student's action...

Obligation to provide information

A telephone operator received a call requesting the telephone number of Dennis Barak. As he was entering the request into his information system, he could not remember whether the request was for Dennis Barak or Dennis Barat. He decided to have the system return the number for Dennis Bara*; the system would match any number of letters where the asterisk appeared. The system would automatically give the number of the first name that matched. If it was wrong, the caller could just call the operator again.

15. Was the telephone operator's action...

Obligation to provide to requirements

A computer store was having a sale on a limited number of computer systems. A person who bought one of the systems was so pleased with the purchase that he convinced a friend to buy one too. The friend called the store, described the system in detail to a salesman, and asked whether she could obtain a system identical to her friend's system. The salesman said yes, so the woman agreed to come to the store. When the woman arrived at the store, she found that the salesman had configured a system with a different monitor. When she asked about the difference, the salesman told her it was "functionally equivalent" to her friend's monitor. The only difference was that her friend's monitor had some switches that allowed the monitor's characteristics to be changed, whereas the monitor in her system relied on software signals to switch characteristics. Otherwise the monitors were equivalent and had the same cost.

16. Was the salesman's response during the telephone conversation...

Obligation to client

The owner of a small business needed a computer-based accounting system. He identified the various inputs and outputs he felt were required to satisfy his needs. He showed his design to a computer programmer and asked the programmer if she could implement such a system. The programmer knew she could implement the system because she had developed much more sophisticated accounting systems in the past. In fact, she felt this design was rather crude and would soon need major revisions. But she didn't say anything about this because the business owner didn't ask her, and she thought maybe she could be the one hired to implement the needed revisions later.

17. Was the programmer's decision not to point out the design flaws...

Obligation of accuracy

A bank was interviewing a customer with respect to a loan application. The banker was tired and was not paying close attention when the customer told him her highest education level. He did not want to appear inattentive, so he guessed that she probably said that she had earned a Bachelor of Science degree. That was the most common response in his experience, so that is what he recorded on his evaluation.

18. Was the banker's action...

Obligation of acknowledgment

A scientist developed a theory that required construction of a computer model to prove. He hired a computer programmer to build the model, and the theory was shown to be correct. The scientist won several awards for the development of the theory, but he never acknowledged the contribution of the computer programmer.

19. Was the scientist's failure to acknowledge the computer programmer's contribution...

Obligation of responsibility

An engineer needed a program to perform a series of complicated calculations. She found a computer programmer capable of writing the program, but would only hire the programmer if he agreed to share liability that might result from an error in her calculations. The programmer said he would be willing to assume any liability due to a malfunction of the program, but was unwilling to share any liability due to an error in the engineer's calculations.

20. *Was the programmer's position in this situation...*
21. *Was the engineer's position in this situation...*

Opportunity due to privileged access

A programmer at a bank realized that he had accidentally overdrawn his checking account. He made a small adjustment in the bank's accounting system so that his account would not have an additional service charge assessed. As soon as he made a deposit, he corrected the bank's system.

22. *Was the programmer's modification of the accounting system...*

Opportunity for personal gain

A telephone system employee saw an advertisement in a newspaper of a car for sale. It sounded like a good buy. The advertisement listed the seller's telephone number, but not the address. The telephone system employee knew he could determine the seller's address by accessing the seller's telephone records. He did this and went to the seller's house to discuss his car.

23. *Was the telephone system employee's action...*
24. *If you know the seller wanted to screen potential buyers over the phone, was the telephone system employee's action...*

Opportunity to obtain software

A computer user called a mail-order computer program store to order a particular accounting system. When he received the order, he found out that the store had accidentally sent him a very expensive word processing program as well as the accounting package that he had ordered. He looked at the invoice, and it indicated only that the accounting package had been sent. The user decided to keep the word processing package.

25. *Was the user's decision to keep the word processing package...*

Opportunity to access personal information

A university student obtained a part-time job as a data entry clerk. His job was to enter personal student data into the university's computer database. Some of these data were available in the student directory, but some of it was not. He was attracted to a student in his Algebra class and wanted to ask her out. Before asking her, though, he decided to access her records in the database to find out about her background.

> 26. *Was the student's action in accessing a fellow student's personal information...*

Opportunity for recreational use

A student had access to the university computer system because a class she was taking required extensive computer usage. The student enjoyed playing games on the computer, and frequently had to request extra computer funds from her professor in order to complete her assignments.

> 27. *Was the student's use of the computer to play games...*

Opportunity for disruptive behavior

A manager of a company that sells computer processing services bought similar services from a competitor. She used her access to the competitor's computer to try to break the security system, identify other customers, and cause the system to "crash" (cause loss of service to others). She used the service for over a year and always paid her bills promptly.

> 28. *Was the manager's action...*

Opportunity for unauthorized access

A student suspected and found a loophole in the university computer's security system that allowed him to access other students' records. He told the system administrator about the loophole, but continued to access others' records until the problem was corrected two weeks later.

> 29. *Was the student's action in searching for the loophole...*
> 30. *Was the student's action in continuing to access others' records for two weeks...*
> 31. *Was the system administrator's failure to correct the problem sooner...*

SCENARIOS ORDERED ON VALUE OF KENDALL'S TAU-B

SCENARIOS	MANAGERS			STUDENTS			Chi square*	Kendall's Tau-B
	Acceptable	Questionable	Unacceptable	Unacceptable	Questionable	Unacceptable		
2	3.3	21.3	75.4	16.2	46.2	37.6	0.000	-7.450
4	10.7	33.6	55.7	32.4	45.7	22.0	0.000	-7.000
1	12.3	26.2	61.5	39.9	30.6	29.5	0.000	-6.800
3	2.5	4.9	92.6	8.7	22.0	69.4	0.000	-5.990
22	0.0	1.6	98.4	1.7	12.1	86.1	0.001	-5.580
5	25.6	46.3	28.1	47.7	41.9	10.5	0.000	-4.790
23	18.9	41.0	40.2	40.5	37.6	22.0	0.000	-4.560
7	4.9	16.4	78.7	5.2	39.9	54.9	0.000	-4.190
10	16.5	34.7	48.8	30.1	42.8	27.2	0.000	-4.060
14	3.3	9.8	86.9	5.2	26.0	68.8	0.001	-3.870
11	51.6	32.0	16.4	70.5	20.2	9.2	0.004	-3.290
15	12.3	30.3	57.4	27.7	29.5	42.8	0.004	-3.230
6	1.6	1.6	96.7	5.8	5.2	89.0	0.050	-3.000
21	8.3	31.4	60.3	19.2	34.3	46.5	0.014	-2.830
25	4.1	24.6	71.3	12.1	29.5	58.4	0.035	-2.830
26	4.1	32.8	63.1	12.7	37.6	49.7	0.014	-2.760
28	0.0	7.4	92.6	4.0	12.1	83.8	0.028	-2.630
12	33.6	19.7	46.7	42.4	28.5	29.1	0.008	-2.560

9	3.3	27.0	69.7	4.6	39.3	56.1	0.061	-2.390
24	5.0	24.0	71.1	8.7	32.0	59.3	0.104	-2.200
31	2.5	24.6	73.0	1.7	35.8	62.4	0.118	-1.820
13	33.6	36.1	30.3	41.0	37.0	22.0	0.220	-1.670
27	4.1	28.7	67.2	4.0	28.3	67.6	0.997	0.070
16	17.2	43.4	39.3	16.8	42.8	40.5	0.981	0.200
29	41.8	49.2	9.0	39.9	51.4	8.7	0.929	0.250
8	0.8	0.8	98.4	0.0	1.2	98.8	0.473	0.360
17	4.9	44.3	50.8	8.1	34.1	57.8	0.206	0.800
18	1.6	18.9	79.5	1.7	12.1	86.1	0.281	1.440
30	0.8	15.6	83.6	5.8	21.4	72.8	0.029	2.460
19	33.6	41.0	25.4	22.1	40.7	37.2	0.037	2.610
20	97.5	0.8	1.6	82.6	11.6	5.8	0.000	5.560

*This cell contains a Chi-Squared expected value <1.

When a contingency table has only two rows, Everitt (1997, p. 40) suggests that the Chi-Square result may be unreliable when the expected values are <1.

BIBLIOGRAPHY

Barach, J. A. (1985). "The Ethics of Hardball." *California Management Review*, 27 (2), pp. 132–139.

Brady, F. N. (1990). *Ethical Managing: Rules and Results*. London: Collier Macmillan Publishers.

Couger, J. D. (1989). "Preparing IS Students to Deal with Ethical Issues." *MIS Quarterly*, 13 (2), pp. 211–217.

Everitt, B. S. (1977). *The Analysis of Contingency Tables*. London: Chapman & Hall.

Kamay, V. and Adams, T. (1992). "The 1992 Profile of Computer Abuse in Australia." The Australian Computer Abuse Research Bureau at the Royal Melbourne Institute of Technology, Australia.

Paradice, D. B. (1990). "Ethical Attitudes of Entry-Level MIS Personnel." *Information and Management*, 18, pp. 43–151.

Parker, D. B. (1983). *Fighting Computer Crime*. Scribner & Sons.

Parker, D. B. Swope, S. and Baker, B. N. (1990). "Ethical Conflicts in Information and Computer Science, Technology and Business." QED Information Sciences Inc.

Taylor, G. S. and Davis, J. S. (1989). "Individual Privacy and Computer-based Human Resources Information Systems." *Journal of Business Ethics*, 8 (7), July, pp. 569–576.

3. CAN EDUCATION SOLVE SOCIETY'S COMPUTER ETHICS PROBLEMS

JOSEPH M. KIZZA

It may seem irrelevant to start this chapter on combating computer crimes by talking about television, but television's history is similar, in many aspects, to that of the computer. When television made its debut in the United States, it was received with enthusiasm as a wonder machine, and people were amazed and at the same time overwhelmed by the good it provided to society. It soon gained a reputation as a formidable educational and cultural tool for millions around the world, more so for children than adults. We did not foresee its dangers, and consequently we did not arm ourselves to combat it as a harmful tool. Fifty some years later, the statistics from the social, cultural, and educational impact of television are alarming. For example, an average American kid spends about 23 hours a week watching television, and there are almost similar figures for other countries. Violence and the erosion of values are often blamed on television. Since children learn by imitation, we have reason to be worried. People from all walks of life are now urging each other to combat "trash television"; we are demanding quality programming to save the greatest fans of television—our kids, but whatever cries we put out now are too little, too late. Our most practical solution now is to keep that once wonder machine under lock to prevent the children from watching it. Computers, following in the footsteps of television as a technological wonder gift to mankind, have had the same magical spell television had for many years.

Unlike television, however, computers came on the scene with a public more sophisticated technologically than when television had its debut. Because of this awareness, the potential for computer influence on society is greater and limitless (unfortunately, more devastating too). While one television set can influence one or two willing individuals, one computer with a modem has the potential to affect millions of mostly innocent and unsuspecting people. This tremendous potential is mainly due to the following:

1. the large number of potential computers—one computer can potentially connect to national and international networks
2. the multiplicity of possibilities afforded to users by computers
3. the detachment and invisibility of the offender from the victims
4. the lack of standard guidelines for the use of networks
5. the nonexistence of mechanisms for tracking offenders
6. the lack of a central sanctioning power
7. the lack of any form of enforcement of standards of conduct for users

The rapid advances in semiconductor technology have enabled millions of transistors to be packed on a chip no bigger than your fingernail. This new packaging has resulted in smaller and faster computers which can store billions of bytes of data. With similar advances in fiber-optics technology, the computer revolution has turned into an information and telecommunication revolution.

With fears of losing the technological competitive edge to others which may result in the loss of millions of jobs, nations are rapidly building huge national and international networks commonly known as electronic superhighways. Nations are being driven by the notion that the one country that first controls the information age will automatically become the electronic superpower, reaping billions of dollars in returns. Seen in this light, the computer revolution and its by-product the information and telecommunication revolutions are God sent, human driven vehicles to prosperity for mankind.

But this revolution, like every major revolution before, has a social side to it. All revolutions go through three stages, namely:

1. the early stage of the revolution, the age of amazement
2. the middle stage, the age of prosperity
3. the last stage, the age of social upheaval

The industrial revolution, for example, went through these stages. The television revolution has also gone through the same stages as we have seen above. The computer revolution is clearly going through these stages. We have already seen the early and middle stage. There are now computers in almost every office and every factory floor. There are signs everywhere now that the computer revolution is entering the social upheaval stage. If you have been reading newspapers, trade magazines, and journals, and listening to radio and television, you may already have heard and seen the beginning signs of the social effects of the computer revolution. What must be done to minimize the social effects of the revolution? Or to put it another way, what can we do to make the social effects of the computer revolution a pleasant experience?

In our effort to minimize the impact of the social effects of the revolution or to make the social effects a rewarding experience, we must be able to realize that social effects of revolutions are dealt with in specific domains. In the industrial revolution, the domain was the slums that developed when unemployed country folk flocked into towns in search of jobs in the newly established industries. During the television revolution the domains were actually two: one at the programming level which included the writers and producers, and the other at the receiving level which involved the viewers. At either end the problem can be dealt with.

But in the computer revolution, unlike the other revolutions we have witnessed so far, there is a different reality. The affected domain is virtual. The virtual domain is created by large national and international communication networks. With these networks, we have one boundless, colorless, cultureless, and classless virtual society. The society consists of users with electronic personas, from the most passive, unsophisticated and law-abiding to the most sophisticated and ruthless ones. In this society, it is possible for any persona from any location to make an electronic access to any on-line database and computer system. There are no laws, no legislatures, no national boundaries, no moms to remind one of one's manners. In short, this is a society similar to the old Wild West. This is the society in which our children's generation is going to live and work if technological developments keep on track.

If we are to offer protection to the electronic persona in this virtual society, we must start with the real user in our real societies. In reality for every electronic persona we protect in the virtual, there is a corresponding person in the real society. So far we have identified two societies in which protection is needed: the virtual and the real. Is it possible that order can be achieved in both? Are the rules applicable in one also applicable in the other? The answer to all these questions is the answer to one crucial question: Is the user in the virtual society the same user in the real society? To answer this question we first need to give a connection between an electronic persona and an individual user in the real society. In most cases there tends to be a one-to-one correspondence between the electronic persona and the user in the real society. In fact, every electronic persona has its origin in a real user. The electronic persona very often has all the characteristics and temperament of the real user. This electronic persona, therefore, is a carrier of virtues and vices of the real user. This realization gives us an edge in our effort to safeguard the virtual society. Except in a few incidents where the electronic persona may go astray and disobey the real user due mainly to either network faults or something the user never anticipated, very often the electronic persona follows the rules set by the real user to the letter. Knowing this gives us a beachhead in our campaign to fight computer crimes. Now our efforts should be concentrated on the real user.

AVAILABLE MEASURES TO COMBAT COMPUTER CRIMES

There are many proposals out there to combat computer crimes; some are good, others are very expensive, but all have one target, to eliminate or reduce computer related crimes. There is Eugene Spafford, for example, who advocates consumer pressure by urging businesses to refuse to do business with any firm that employs a known hacker. According to Spafford, employing a known hacker "is like having a known arsonist install a fire alarm" (*Newstrack*, Communication, May 1990). There are others who do not go that far, but are advocating stiff sentences including prison terms for anyone convicted of a computer related crime, no matter how insignificant, with the idea of sending a signal to would-be criminals.

Many of these are good methods. Some of them are not only good, but cheap to implement as well, and they are all practical. But all of them are stop-gap measures; they may partly solve the problem in the short run, but until a more comprehensive long-term plan is in place, the problem will remain. That long-term solution we believe is education.

Education

Eradicating computer crimes calls for a long-term dedicated evolutional plan that creates a culture that respects privacy and ownership, and takes responsibility for the moral decisions it makes. This cannot be done by fences, enacting "kingpin" laws, court sentences, or intimidation by "sending signals." It can, however, be achieved through educating the public beginning with youths, stressing professional obligation to computer professionals, and encouraging businesses to promote ethics. The groundwork for security of computer systems has to be laid while there is still time rather than waiting for legislation and policies after a catastrophe. Security policies should include teaching computer ethics and stressing professional accountability to the general public beginning with the children.

K–12

We need to start on an early education by introducing computer ethics education in the K–12 curriculum in the way we teach about drugs, sex and other societal problems. At these lower levels, however, instruction should be informal. As soon as children begin using computers in schools for games, they should be informed that if not used responsibly, computers can be dangerous not only to themselves but to all those around them. They should be instructed to respect each other's games on the screen, not to delete them or change them without the owners' permission. In high school, students should be made aware of the computer crimes currently taking place, and warned of the serious consequences. They should be made to take responsibility for their actions which range from destroying each other's floppy disks to changing grades. In fact, teaching computer ethics early in the children's education should be seen as a gradual creation of a culture among the children, a culture they may live with and pass on to their own children. This culture, it is hoped, may help in achieving the following objectives: First the current passive noncombatant public which has unconditionally accepted computers may be changed into a more responsive and vigilant society that questions the actions taken by computer professionals. This kind of vigor will counter the dangerous prevailing situation where the overwhelming public acceptance of computers has been translated into an unconcerned public which never asks questions concerning any computer related actions. Second the public will be taught not only what good computers have brought to our lives but also the pain and suffering they can bring when not properly used. It is hoped that by showing them both the good and the bad sides of computers, they will be more responsive to the essence and value of ethics in computer decision-making. By the time students enter college, they should be aware of their moral obligations as computer users whether they intend to be computer professionals or not.

College

Currently ethics is taught mainly in medical, law, and religious schools, and in military academies. In public colleges, however, ethics is taught traditionally in the departments of philosophy and religion. Very few majors of computer science and information systems take courses in philosophy or religion for that matter. In the few courses they are required to take from those departments to satisfy their general education requirements, ethics does not figure highly. There are few courses outside philosophy and religion that require ethics as a prerequisite, something that would have indirectly made some students not majoring in philosophy and religion take ethics courses. Most important, the kind of ethics taught in these departments is not seen as having much practical value to students other than those from those departments because it is too theoretical. What nonphilosophy and nonreligion majors need is applied and issue-oriented ethics, which unfortunately these departments do not offer.

The debate of whether to teach ethics in computer science and information systems disciplines also includes the debate on the appropriate point in the curriculum when ethics should start. Ethics should be taught in the first courses at the freshman and sophomore levels. To make sure that the concepts remain fresh throughout the college years, ethics should be built into other courses at sophomore and junior levels as well. Another reason to advocate teaching ethics at the college level is that students are more mature, and they often face situations in their lives that serve as case studies to enhance their ethics training. Further, it is easier to introduce new courses at a college level than at lower grades.

Courses needed. The teaching of ethics in disciplines other than philosophy and religion calls for nontheoretical applied ethics. So the courses designed for scientific oriented fields should be dealing with issues in computer science and information systems. Also ethical themes should be introduced in introductory courses. Care should be taken in courses of this type so that the materials covered are not stretched too far so that neither material of the course nor ethics is covered adequately enough. The scenarios presented should have a bearing on computer science and information systems to further help students focus on the decision making process in these disciplines. For practical scenarios see articles by Andrew Morris and Richard Epstein in this book.

Fear of ethics courses. The question that may arise is whether such courses, if not well designed and well monitored, may not serve the purpose they were designed for. It is possible for those courses to be misused as channels of imposing an individual's beliefs on the students—a form of intimidation and indoctrination. If and when this happens, the purpose of these courses will not be achieved. But there are few computer science and information systems professionals who, when provided with a well-structured text, are likely to digress from it.

Problems encountered. Anyone preparing to start a new ethics course in computer science and information systems is likely to be faced with the following problems:

1. While there are established research tracks and a lot of scholarly material in the traditional areas where ethics has been taught like medicine, engineering and law, there is not as of now enough research and scholarly material on ethics in computer and information science. This would present a problem to the teacher making an effort to find relevant reading materials for the course. And it may stunt good presentations and lively discussions of ethical issues because such presentations and discussions normally originate from expandable minds. With few reading materials, it may be difficult to ignite interest in the subject among students.
2. The scarcity of established research and scholarly material is a direct result of a very small number of faculty to teach applied ethics in these areas. There is also the lack of faculty outside the traditional disciplines of medicine and law with teaching and research in ethics having an interest in computer science and information systems ethics. Research and other scholarly activities are normally kept alive by the

activities of scholars from outside the discipline having an interest in the discipline. Take for example the tremendous research and other academic activities taking place in computer science. A good number of such activities are done by scholars from mathematics and engineering. Until this collaboration with other disciplines happens, ethics academic activities in computer science and information systems is likely to remain low.

3. Even if there are trained faculty, those faculty usually find a stiff resistance from their peers and administration to add new courses. Part of the resistance is due to lack of funds to support new courses.
4. There is also a lack of understanding on the part of senior faculty of the role of ethics research. This frightens young faculty from pursuing research interests in ethics because there is a feeling that their work in ethics may not be taken seriously for their personal and academic advancement and tenure process.
5. The low priority given by senior faculty to ethics makes it difficult for it to compete with technical courses in departments with limited funds and under pressure to add new courses. (Callahan et al., 1980)

Expectations and results. As any social engineer may tell you, measuring the success or failure of a culture is very difficult and is subjective to many things. Teaching ethics may not alter the students' morality very much. In fact the intent of such courses is not to force students to change their behavior but rather to act as a light that shows them how to justify and criticize their moral judgements, especially in decision making.

Professional obligations

For those already in the field, professional obligations should be stressed. Van Marteen (1990) defines the concept of a profession as having privileged knowledge or skill obtained through long years of training, and autonomy associated with such knowledge. A profession is accountable in its discharge of this knowledge and skill. In other words, when one is discharging one's professional knowledge or skill, the public should not feel threatened in any way. The professions whose people use computers in their day to day work should take the lead and assume the responsibility of training their members in computer ethics. By showing them the power and the autonomy they have as professionals with the computer as a tool, and the responsibility which goes along with that power and autonomy, they can make them more aware of the accountability involved.

Business

Businesses and companies should also be encouraged to add ethics courses to their development courses. They should also periodically invite speakers to talk to their employees about computer ethics. Such gatherings can be as formal as symposiums or as informal as discussions. Either way computer ethics should be reinforced.

REFERENCES

Callahan, D. and Bok, Sissela (eds.) (1980). *Ethics Teaching in Higher Education*. New York: Plenum Press.

Carlitz, R. (1991, Summer). "Common Knowledge: Networks for Kindergarten Through College." *Educom Review*, Vol. 26, No. 2, pp. 25–28.

Denning, P. (ed.). *Computers Under Attack: Intruders, Worms, and Viruses*. New York: ACM Press, 1991.

Gries, David and Marsh, Dorothy (1990, October). "The 1989-90 Taulbee Survey." *Computing Research News*, p. 6.

Harrington, Susan and McCollum, Rebecca (1990). "Lessons from Corporate America Applied to Training in Computer Ethics." *Computer & Society*, 20, pp. 169–173.

Hollinger, R. (1991, June). "Hackers: Computer Heros or Electronic Highwaymen?" *Computers & Society*, Vol. 21, No. 1, pp. 6–17.

Kizza, Joseph M. (1991, August). "Ethics in the Computer and Information Professions." *Proceedings, 9th Annual Conference of the Association of Management, Information Technology*, pp. 72–75.

Member news (1991, Summer). *Educom Review*, Vol. 26, No. 2, p. 44.

Robert, M. (1991, Summer). "Positioning the National Research and Education Network." *Educon Review*, Vol. 26, No. 2, pp. 11–13.

Robitt, J. (1991, January). "Ethics in Invisible Communities: Looking at Network Security in Our Changing Society." *Computing Research News*, pp. 16–17.

Staff (1991, August 13). *Christian Science Monitor*, p. 8.

Staff (1991, August 15). *Christian Science Monitor*, p. 8.

4. THE INTERNET AND ETHICS: DILEMMA AND DECISIONS FOR INSTITUTIONS OF HIGHER EDUCATION

B. C. Chic Day and Pat C. Day

THE SITUATION

A professor at a state university entered the computer lab to help a student. He walked over to the printer to check on the latest output when he noticed hard-core pornography being printed in front of his student's work. This irked the professor so he walked down to the computer operations center and asked the computer systems specialist several questions, to wit: "Do you have a system in place to screen out pornography that was found on the Internet?" Operations person answer: "There is no system in place to control the receipt of that type of material." The professor continued: "Does this university have a policy to deal with this situation?" Operations person answer: "We have no policy to deal with this problem."

The professor walked back up to the computer lab but the hard copy containing the pornography had been removed. A search of the lab quickly found the person who produced the pornography and the professor confronted the student. Student: "Were you reading my mail?" Professor: "That was pornography that was being printed." Student: "It's not pornography, it's literature."

This same professor overheard two secretaries talking in the department office. The essence of their conversation was that if their E-mail name was recognized as belonging to a female, then it was certain that they would receive lewd E-mail the next day. It had reached the point where they refused to look at their E-mail.

These two incidents are actual events and according to the media and other sources, these types of incidents are happening daily all over America.

STUDENT SURVEY AND RESPONSES

The authors desired to determine what the local population of 68 freshmen and 22 seniors at the university thought of the incidents. A survey sheet and a scenario sheet were formulated. The situation sheet follows:

Scenario

University student is using a university PC in the computer lab and is connected to the Internet. The student has explored the data that is available and has found a source for files containing pornographic material. A university professor is passing by and notices the pornographic material that is being displayed.

Please answer each question on the Response Sheet by circling the answer that you feel is the best way to handle the situation.

Please do not place your name on the Response Sheet.

Also, please answer questions 2, 3 & 4.

Thank You.

After reading the situation sheet, the respondents were given the following response sheet:

Student Response Sheet

1. What action do you recommend in response to the situation? (one answer only, select best)
   a. Do nothing
   b. Administration should punish student (ban from campus for some period of time; or some other punishment)
   c. No punishment but university should establish and publish policy
   d. Faculty member should admonish student and turn PC off
   e. Faculty member should admonish student (unethical, poor use of PC, etc.)

2. Did student perform in an unethical manner?
   ☐ YES   ☐ NO
3. Did student perform in an illegal manner?
   ☐ YES   ☐ NO
4. Should there be a law against using a University PC to watch pornography?
   ☐ YES   ☐ NO

The following table presents the results of the survey.

Survey Results

(1)

Group	Do Nothing	University	Need Policy	Admonish and Turn Off PC	Admonish
Freshmen	13.2%	2.9%	61.8%	13.2%	8.8%
Seniors	18.0%	4.5%	54.5%	9.0%	13.6%
Totals	14.0%	3.2%	60.2%	11.8%	10.8%

Survey Numbers:

　　Freshmen　　N= 68　　　　　　　　Seniors　　N= 22

	(2) *Unethical Manner*		(3) *Illegal Manner*	
	Yes	No	Yes	No
Freshmen	71.6%	28.3%	14.9%	85.1%
Seniors	72.7%	27.2%	14.2%	85.7%
Totals	72.8%	27.1%	14.0%	86.0%

	(4) *Law Against Pornography*	
	Yes	No
Freshmen	66.2%	33.8%
Seniors	66.7%	33.3%
Totals	65.2%	34.8%

　　The survey results suggest that there is an understanding among these college students of an ethical component to computer usage. A majority favor a computer use policy to outline and regulate ethical behavior; although they acknowledge that current free-speech rulings support uncensored distribution of electronic information.

　　At this particular university a majority of students surveyed appear to be in favor of some sort of electronic data censorship. However, the broader population of collegiate Internet users has shown strong opposition to any form of censorship. A program to prevent anonymous postings on the USENET bulletin board at Northeastern Ohio University College of Medicine brought forth a barrage of vindictive messages. Other attempts to censor have had similar results (16).

　　Whether or not viewing pornography on a university computer is unethical is arguable. There are any number of Internet uses that could be viewed as unethical by one group or another—such as disseminating propaganda or posting abusive, vulgar or discriminatory messages. The fact remains that using school computing resources for viewing pornography is considered as unethical behavior by this particular group of college students who may represent a broader student and contributing alumni population.

Thus we have the dilemma for institutions of higher education—finding a way to satisfy both the imperative for informational freedom and the conflicting social mores of their diverse communities as well as instituting policies that are relevant to rapidly evolving electronic technology.

THE ENVIRONMENT

College campuses are becoming electronic societies and over 80 percent of the nation's colleges, universities and junior colleges are linked to the Internet. Most of these schools provide their students with Internet access. Many of the residence halls and academic buildings are linked together by fiber-optic cabling so that students think nothing of accessing the library, sending homework to their professors' E-mail address and exploring the Internet for academic research or for enjoyment. Ethics and the right to free speech have become an area of concern as universities face problems such as E-mail harassment, copyright infringement and other questionable practices yet want to provide the free access to the latest technology. Ramstad reported on the Santa Rosa Junior College incident where two female students complained of derogatory remarks made by other students (14).

One campus newspaper described the current environment as follows: "The most important thing for an incoming freshman to have at many of today's changing universities is an Internet account. " A student needs the account to get a dorm room at MIT, send homework to a professor at Berkeley and to register for classes at Stanford. Approximately two thirds of Stanford's dorms have an Internet connection (3).

Elmer-DeWitt reports that the Reston Internet Society estimates that the Net reaches 25 million computer users and is doubling every year. At the same time it is being pressured by various groups to mold itself in their image. Some of the competing groups are commercial interests, veteran users, governments, pornographers, and parents. Various incidents have surfaced in the face of the explosive growth of users such as the Canter-and-Siegel affair which was basically a commercial venture by two lawyers. This incident resulted in a hailstorm of complaints from various users (7).

DeLoughry reports on the current state of university policies with alleged Internet misuse by students and faculty. He cites the FBI investigation into child pornography at Cornell University, the disciplinary action against five students at Brigham Young University, and X-rated video on a dean's screen at Camden County College. He further discusses the impact of sex related files that are available on the Net and how various Canadian colleges reacted to them. Some colleges, Carleton and Manitoba, blocked access, while others such as McMaster, Ottawa and Waterloo used free speech as the guiding principle and continued to permit access. Here in the United States, Michigan is developing a policy that permits use of offensive material as long as it is hidden from those who would be offended by it (5).

In November 1994, Carnegie-Mellon University blocked access to bulletin boards students used to call up pornographic pictures. Three hundred students and a public interest group protested. "The school decided to block access to both written and photographic pornography. In the face of student opposition, Carnegie-Mellon decided not to enforce the block on text. But X-rated pictures remain off limits." "William Arms, [is] Carnegie-Mellon's vice president for computing services." He received calls from six other schools after the problem came to light. "People want to know which way to go," he said (4).

PROFESSIONAL CODES OF CONDUCT

Because of technological difficulties, time and monetary costs, computer user skills, and Constitutional considerations, policing Internet access of college students is neither a viable nor desirable option. A more pragmatic approach has been promulgated by the professional computer organizations' codes of ethical behavior. "The Association of Computing Machinery (ACM) and the Data Processing Management Association (DPMA), two of the major professional organizations in the information technology field, have codes of conduct that outline the professional obligations and responsibilities of members to their employers, to the public, and to the society as a whole" (10).

The new ACM code, adopted in 1992, addresses the issues of ethics and professional conduct. It deals with the areas of intellectual property, privacy, confidentiality, professional quality, fairness or discrimination, liability, software risks, conflicts of interest and unauthorized access to computer systems.

The approach in the past has been to list possible violations and threaten sanctions for any party who ignores the guidelines, though there have been difficulties in implementing ethical review systems.

The new ACM code emphasizes self regulation which is dependent upon the consensus and commitment of its members. The code imperatives are expressed in general terms in order to equate computer ethics with more universal ethical principles. The ACM also stresses socialization and education rather than enforced compliance. Thus the ACM codes are an aid to individual decision making rather than specific punitive laws (1).

EDUCATION AND ETHICS

What does the educational approach to ethics in a typical university environment look like today from an introduction to computers or a computing literacy type course perspective? In most cases, the introductory computing course appears to use a textbook which contains a single chapter addressing computer ethics. One example of a typical textbook is the Laudon, Traver and Laudon approach.

The textbook contains a single chapter on computer ethics with the following learning objectives: an awareness of ethical issues in the computing profession; possible use of computers to infringe on privacy and personal freedom, property rights and intellectual property; computer effects on quality of work life, careers, health and safety, and the environment; computer crime, natural disasters, and human error. The text contains some discussion issues which illustrate some of the controversial areas of computers and ethics. In addition, the authors present a framework for ethical decision making, a list of federal laws dealing with privacy and ethics, and two examples of professional associations' codes of conduct. An examination of the index of the text reveals that ethical issues are contained only in the single chapter described above (10).

Schools, businesses and professional organizations are joining the movement for ethics education. Bloombecker reported an increase in the number of corporate ethics programs and stated "that software piracy ... ceased within one firm after a computer ethics awareness program was implemented" (2, p. 19). Chaney and Simon of Memphis State University surveyed ethical attitudes of business employees and college students. They found that only 32.64 percent of the college students believed that copying software for personal use was definitely unethical. They later determined that "almost half of these students indicated they had not heard a faculty member speak against illegal software copying of protected software" (2, p. 21). Perhaps if these students had received computer ethics education, the percentage and perception would have been different.

However, research by D. Khazanchi of Northern Kentucky University does not support significant benefits from ethics education. As he and others from the age of Aristotle have pointed out, ethics are cultural behaviors, inculcated from the cradle (9). Ethics courses can remind students of what they already know; can help them reflect on the consequences of "right" and "wrong" behavior; and can make known to them the kinds of behavior expected of them by their particular institution of higher learning.

Whether ethics instruction is effective or not, institutions of higher education will come under more pressure from within and without to provide some form of computer use ethics education.

Design and implementation will require that certain problems and options be considered. Can ethics education address the beliefs and concerns of students like those surveyed? Should computer ethics courses focus strictly on the standard issues outlined by most textbooks and professional organizations' user codes? Should they focus on student-oriented issues such as Internet capabilities, E-mail privacy, software copying, plagiarism, and wasteful use of computer resources? Should they include controversial free speech issues such as pornography, propaganda and censorship?

Perhaps, the focus of computer ethics education should be on the real and practical rather than the abstract and ideal. At Bently College of Waltham, Massachusetts, incoming freshmen and women are given instruction in electronic mail usage where they are not only taught how to use the E-mail software, but are also made aware of the personal and public problems that arise from improper and unethical use of E-mail, telnet, FTP and News Groups. The college also has a code for ethical computer use, a policy on E-mail privacy and an academic honesty code. The policies and codes apply to all students, faculty and employees of the college, and stress personal responsibility to "do no harm" to any individual or computer facility. The effectiveness of their codes and policies relies on well-informed computer users, personal values, and the admonition that, "Violations of this policy will be handled in a manner consistent with comparable situations requiring disciplinary action" (8).

How will computer ethics education be delivered? Should it be taught to the entire student population, or just to computer science students? Should it be a separate credit course; bits and pieces incorporated into the general curriculum? Should it be taught as a symposium for the total school community users? Most computer science courses are already crammed full of information and assignments. Adding another component to these courses would require careful and creative planning. Another element to consider is the traditional attitude of most computer science departments. "Most computer-science curricula pay little or no attention to 'social impacts'" (11). Computer science is viewed as a purely technical degree-technology first and foremost; social issues such as ethics are best left to the social sciences (11, p. 277). In order for computer ethics education to succeed, it requires commitment by those who teach it.

A "hands-on" approach to computer ethics education has been implemented by T. Scott of Western Illinois University. Computer science students are given writing assignments which require the use of the Internet as the primary source. One assignment requires students to access the published computer ethical use codes (ARIAL.UNN.EDU), and to analyze, rate and rewrite selected codes to meet their own personal understanding of ethical computer use behavior (15).

Regardless of which options are chosen, the institutions must also be cognizant of the fact that computer ethics education can not stand alone. Ethics instruction must be supplemented with clearly stated, reasonable, relevant and enforceable codes and policies of ethical computer use. Students, faculty, staff and administration must be active participants in an ethical community.

THE UNIVERSITY AND INTERNET TODAY AND TOMORROW

Ethics problems will continue to evolve because of the revolutionary advance of computer technology and an ever-changing society. Although pornography is used as the principal example of alleged unethical use of Internet/school resources, it is only one example of a range of ethical Internet problems. Therefore, computer use ethics policies of institutions of higher education must be both flexible and forward thinking.

The policy must not be promulgated then adhered to for the near future, but must be always changing in order to stay ahead of or at least advance along with the technological advances which will provide new ethical dilemmas. Today's policies for Internet use by students and faculty may suffice for today, but also must be flexible enough to deal with ethics questions as they arise. Therefore, institutions of higher education should consider having a standing ethics committee, made up of the whole educational community, to study, create and enforce computer use ethics standards. To develop consensus and commitment, it is very important to include people on the committee who have different views of the Internet. The following representative groups should be considered: students, faculty, administration, trustees, alumni, and local community. Some questions the committee must address and consider are the following: How much attention should be paid to the mores and standards of the local nonacademic community? How will codes and policies be enforced? Should Internet use standards be institutional, local, state or federal government? Which of the above establishment sources would provide for the most protection of first amendment rights? How do we avoid censorship without offending local morality? Should " Ethical Codes of Behavior" be posted in all computer labs on campus? Should students have to read and sign university established ethical standards?

At present, the Internet is not "owned" by anyone. The federal government finances NSFNET (National Science Foundation Network)—the "backbone" that ties together the Internet in the United States. Business groups, colleges and universities also contribute to the costs (5). All of these funding sources are subject to ideological or self-serving pressure groups that could jeopardize the mission of higher education. The Internet is a technological propagator of unlimited information with equally unlimited possibilities of ethical or unethical use. In order to avoid the peril of externally imposed regulation, institutions of higher education must effectively use a combination of ethics education, computer use codes and policies, and standing ethics committees to nurture a culture of educated, responsible self-regulation.

REFERENCES

(1) Anderson, Ronald E.; Johnson, Deborah G.; Gotterbarn, Donald and Perrolle, Judith. "Using the New ACM Code of Ethics in Decision Making." *Communications of the ACM*, Feb., 1993.

(2) Chaney, L. H. and Simon, J. C. "Strategies for Teaching Computer Ethics." *The Journal of Computer Information Systems*, 35:1, Fall 1994.

(3) "Computers Change College Experience." *The University Echo*, Oct. 6, 1994.

(4) Cutter, Henry. "Carnegie Mellon Pulls Plug on Computer Porn." *Chattanooga Times*, Nov. 22, 1994.

(5) DeLoughry, Thomas J. "Colleges Try to Devise Policies on Obscenity on Campus Networks." *The Chronicle of Higher Education*, Jan. 27, 1993.

*(6) Dwyer, D. "From the Editor's Desk." *The University Echo*, Oct. 6, 1994.

(7) Elmer-DeWitt, Philip. "Battle for the Soul of the Internet." *Time*, July 25, 1994.

(8) Kallman, Ernest A. "Risks and Threats from Internet Access: Protecting the Institution." *Proceedings Ethics in the Computer Age Conference*, Gatlinburg, TN, Nov. 12, 1994.

(9) Khazanchi, D. "Does Pedagogy Make a Difference?: An Experimental Study of Unethical Behavior in Information Systems." *The Journal of Computer Information Systems*, 35:1, Fall 1994.

(10) Laudon, K. C.; Traver, C. G. and Laudon, J. P. *Information Technology*. Danvers, MA: Boyd & Fraser, 1994.

(11) Neumann, Peter G. *Computer Related Risks*. New York: Addison Wesley, ACM Press, 1995.

*(12) Patch, Kimberly. "Internet Package Tracks Intruders." *PC WEEK*, Oct. 10, 1994.

*(13) Price, K. "On Campus, There's a Letter in the E-Mail." *USA Today*, Oct. 5, 1994, p. 6D.

(14) Ramstad, Evan. "College Campuses Increasingly Become Electronic Societies." *Chattanooga News Free Press*, Oct. 9, 1994.

(15) Scott, Thomas J. "Writing Assignments for Internet Course Module." *Proceedings Ethics in the Computer Age Conference*, Gatlinburg, TN, Nov. 12, 1994.

(16) Szofran, Nancy. "Internet Etiquette and Ethics." *Computers in Libraries*, Jan. 1994, 14, 1.

*(17) Williams, Dennis A. and Sandza, Richard. "Teaching Hackers Ethics." *Newsweek*, Jan. 14, 1985.

*(18) Ziegler, G. "On the Internet." *Syllabus*, 8:2, Oct. 1994, pp. 50-51.

References with asterisks do not appear in the text but were consulted.

5. ETHICS IN WRITING COMPUTER USE POLICIES: A SEVEN STEP METHOD

Thomas J. Scott, Ph.D.
and
Richard B. Voss, J.D.

PROLOGUE

Act I, Scene I

Lucy Wordsmith, assistant director of User Services, enters her office. Recent campus computer "activities" have gotten various administrators involved. She re-reads the note from the director of Computing Services asking her to write a draft of a university "Computer Use Policy." Thinking that she should be able to compose a reasonable first draft in one day, she has blocked out her whole day to work on this important project. She opens a cabinet, pulls out a dark brown accordion file and attaches a label that says "Computer Use Policy." She notices the answering machine, and its blinking light reveals that she has had some calls. She presses the "Play Messages" button and listens to the following messages:

{BEEP} "Lucy, this is Dr. Everbitcher. What are you going to do about Professor Gary Greendough? He has been using his office PC to write programs for a local factory. Gary says these programs allowed the factory to stay open and saved 700 jobs. He boasts that he got paid $50,000, but we all know that the university never saw one red cent. He claims that his consulting is appropriate because the university's mission statement includes teaching, research, and service. He says the work is a form of applied research, that it is a service, and that it makes him a better classroom teacher. He is wrong! Send him a reprimand and bill him." {BEEP}

{BEEP} "Lucy, this is Patty Prochoix at the Family Planning Center. Are you aware of the fact that those anti-abortion diehards have E-mailed everyone on campus a copy of their most recent tirade attacking our counseling service? They need to do something quick to stop this type of activity!" {BEEP}

{BEEP} "Lucy, this is Mary, local campus representative to the Civil Service Union for our secretaries. One of my student workers just showed me how to use the Internet. Do you know there are Internet Newsgroups and bulletin boards which demean women? I saw one with hundreds of dumb-blond jokes and another had pornographic pictures of women. I never imagined either of these items on our university computer systems. We need to put a stop to this type of trash! Have a good day." {BEEP}

{BEEP} "Lucy, this is Manny at the student lab. I have three problems: I just caught a student printing 500 fliers for a local bar on the laser printer; another student was using our printer and his own paper to make 100 copies of his resume; and a third student has been playing in some sort of chess marathon on the Internet for the last 38 hours. What should I do?" {BEEP}

{BEEP} "Lucy, this is Larry Handshaker from the alumni office. The provost saw a program at another school, where alumni who make a $100 contribution to the university are allowed to modem into the university and get free access to the Internet. When can we do lunch and figure out how we can implement such a program here? Ciao!" {BEEP}

Act I, Scene II

Lucy takes out an economy-sized bottle of aspirin and attaches a new label to the "Policy" folder that reads: "NIGHTMARE ON THE NETWORK."

INTRODUCTION

An unfortunate reality of modern computing environments is that some users will not behave ethically. The first three scenarios in the Prologue show that some computer users do tie up university computer time and use institutional supplies for private gain. The last two scenarios illustrate that new computing systems have greater capacity and may demand new types of regulations. To cope with these situations, most colleges and universities develop a Computer Use Policy (CUP). The CUP becomes the physical manifestation of the institution's ethical attitudes. In creating the CUP, particular efforts should be made to assure that it accurately reflects the ethical standards of the institution. The diversity of attitudes contained in CUPs was first discovered while conducting a classroom project in computer ethics. This project required students to use the Internet to gather CUPs, and then compare and contrast them. In evaluating their efforts, it became obvious that, as a group, students were only vaguely aware of university regulations regarding campus computer use. The "Student Internet Ethics Project" that emerged, and its results, have been previously discussed in references (1) and (2) (see page 77). In extending the ideas contained in those papers, this paper addresses the following questions:

1. How does an institution develop a CUP that reflects and expresses its ethical standards?
2. How does an institution communicate this CUP to its diverse user groups?

A set of seven principles designed to guide the creation of CUPs will be presented and used as a framework for answering these two questions.

RESEARCH METHODOLOGY

The chosen methodology was to read and analyze existing institutional CUPs. The 100 CUPs discussed in references (1) and (2) were downloaded from various Internet sites. Some of these pre-sample CUPs were drafts, while others were already out of date. The 100 pre-sample CUPs revealed vastly different treatments of key areas.

Because of various weaknesses in the 100 pre-sample CUPs, E-mail messages were sent to the persons named in the sample CUPs. E-mail responses and gopher services were then used to procure more than forty currently used CUPs. These CUPs constitute the research sample. Convenience and quota sampling techniques were used to draw this nonprobabilistic sample. The sample contains CUPs from universities both large and small, public and private, commuter and residential.

Because of the informal manner in which the sample CUPs were procured, there is no guarantee that any given CUP is the actual, fully approved, and complete CUP for that institution. The sample represents electronically available CUPs.

The CUPs were uniformly re-formatted using WordPerfect 6.0. Judgments were made about how to handle multi-part policies, as well as policies that include reprints or excerpts of state laws and regional or national network policies. To facilitate proper comparisons, multi-part CUPs were edited to include only the core statement covering general use and ethics. After formatting the CUPs, the grammar and readability analysis tools available in Wordperfect 6.0, including word counts, the Gunning Fog Index, and the Flesch-Kincaid grade level, were applied.

THE SEVEN "P'S"

The CUP research has been a significant learning experience for the authors. They began with some preconceived ideas whose importance declined as the project proceeded. Analysis of the 100 sample CUPs revealed an entirely new set of important issues. Since many of the CUPs in the final sample are newer than those in the pre-sample, they often provide more modern solutions to the problems inherent in the creation of a CUP.

The study often involved asking questions and trying to answer these questions by looking at the actual text of the two CUP samples. Asking "Why did they put that in?" or "Why did they leave this out?" often provided insight. The authors needed to change their preconceived ideas about CUPs to reflect the best currently available CUPs. In the end, seven areas were selected as important for a CUP committee to discuss in detail to complete its work. Each of these seven issues begins (given a little poetic license) with the letter "P." The seven "P's" of Computer Use Policies are the following:

1. **Participation**—the CUP should be written by a committee that includes representatives from all user groups within the university. These groups should include faculty, staff, students, and administrators.
2. **Partitioning**—most CUPs should have several parts, each of which covers a problem area. These parts would include a general umbrella policy, and sub-policies for items such as ethical computer use, lab use and specific computer system guidelines, privacy and security issues, and the Internet.
3. **Philosophy**—the CUP needs to have a stated purpose that serves as a broad unifying theme for the document. In addition, the CUP needs to define how permissive or restrictive policies will be, especially in regard to using the facilities for business, political, religious, and civic activities.
4. **Privacy**—the users need to know what degree of privacy they can expect on the system. Also, the CUP needs to delineate the ground rules for protecting shared resources, such as E-mail and private files.
5. **Persnicketiness**—a list of do's and don'ts is included in most CUPs. This list covers items like software piracy, hacking, and punishments for violations.
6. **Phog Phactor**—most CUPs are hard to read and understand. Techniques for improving the readability of the CUP will be presented.
7. **Publication**—how do we communicate the CUP to the entire university community? Is it sufficient to print the CUP in the student handbook?

It is the authors' contention that these seven "P's" provide a framework for the creation of a CUP. The ordering of the seven "P's" is also important, as a CUP committee should attempt to do these issues in the order presented. Analysis of existing CUPs reveals that many problems could have been avoided if the first three "P's" had been carefully thought out before any written document was produced. The purpose of this paper is to demonstrate how each of the seven "P's" clarifies ethical issues of university computer use. The authors firmly believe that once the seven "P's" are understood, a CUP committee can write a more coherent document that truly represents the ethics of the institution. Because of the informal nature of the final sample of CUPs, no actual CUP language is presented. Rather, the impact of the seven "P's" is discussed from an ethical perspective.

Participation

Who should participate in the creation of a CUP? From the many CUPs surveyed, it is clear that participation has not always been carefully thought out. Some CUPs read like a letter from an outraged computer center director, others resemble a chapter in a legal textbook, and others seem to philosophize without providing adequate guidelines.

The modern CUP has to be a living, evolving document because 1) new issues are constantly arising, and 2) the nature of old problem areas changes. Many illustrations could reinforce the importance of these two ideas. Two important examples are presented: one new issue and one continuing issue.

As an example of a new issue, consider the recent trend towards allowing friends of the university to use a modem and their home computers to access university computer systems. In the past, this was not a major problem, and was simply allowed by the director of the computer center.

With the emergence of the Internet, literally hundreds of alumni, emeriti, and other supporters would like to use university computer systems as a window to the information highway. At many universities, the alumni office "sells" computing privileges to friends of the university for as little as a $50 donation. This problem needs to be addressed in the CUP.

As an example of how changes in computer technology can alter a situation, consider the ethical problem of playing games on university computer systems. The rules for using university computer systems to play games have changed as these systems have moved from the multi-user, time-sharing systems of the 1970s and early 1980s to the client-server networks of the 1990s.

When there was only one multi-user, time-sharing computer system with dumb terminals (such as an IBM mainframe or a Digital VAX super-mini computer), everyone shared computer processing capability. In these environments, playing games caused two problems: 1) the user tied up one terminal, and 2) as more users used the time-sharing system, the computer's response time for all users deteriorated. Thus playing games on the computer was frowned upon and often prohibited.

In the 1990s, client-server computing systems have become the norm. In a client-server environment, each user has a separate computer, and one user playing a game does not seriously affect the performance of other users. While a game-playing user still ties up one terminal, the previous time-sharing objections to playing games now have much less validity.

Thus, the first change in modern attitudes is that game playing is not evil in and of itself. Secondly, according to most thoughtful university personnel, game playing should be restricted only if it becomes a burden to the system. This change in attitude needs to be incorporated into the CUP.

The two situations above represent normal expansions of university computing environments. A standing university committee, with some continuing membership, would be the best way to insure that the CUP will be able to adapt to the changes in the computing climate.

Based on fifteen years of experience, the authors suggest three stages as typical of the evolution of participation in CUP writing efforts.

1. Initially, the task is assigned to the computer center director with little or no guidance about any of the major issues that are discussed below. The CUP that emerges is often loaded with arcane language and computer jargon unintelligible to many user groups on campus, and is often unduly protective of the campus computer system.
2. Eventually, the campus system evolves to include more than the campus mainframe. As more users become proficient with the various software and hardware capabilities of the evolving system, they start to chafe under the restrictions of the CUP. Those unhappy with the current CUP spread their views around campus, which results in a committee being formed to review the CUP. This committee is usually more representative of major university factions. At this stage, the document that emerges is designed to shield the university.
3. Problems arise because the second-generation CUP fails to address issues such as offensive newsgroups, computer viruses, and changes in philosophical attitudes. This changing computer environment forces the creation of a new committee charged with updating the existing CUP. Eventually, the institution will need a permanent standing committee to continuously monitor and update the CUP.

Experience suggests that broad-based participation in the creation of a CUP leads to a document that better reflects the mores of the institution. Over half the people contacted in our survey mentioned that their schools were in the process of rewriting some aspect of their CUP, and many asked to see the results of this study.

As an aid to writers of CUPs, research leads to the following recommendations:

1. Form a permanent standing committee, with representatives from faculty, staff, students, and administration, to formulate the institution's position on the major issues to be addressed in the CUP. This committee should also have sufficient continuity to insure that the wheel is not re-invented each time the CUP is updated. Committee memberships should be for a minimum of three years so as to span the updating of several CUPs.
2. Assign the actual writing to one or two skilled writers. They should strive to make the document readable to all members of the campus community, especially freshmen. They should create the document and make sure that the language is acceptable to the campus legal staff.
3. The final document should be reviewed by the CUP committee, and when found acceptable, sent on to the proper authorities for final adoption.
4. The standing committee should meet at least yearly to review the CUP and make changes as needed.

Partitioning

Should the CUP consist of one document, or should it be partitioned into several documents? While drawing the final CUP sample, many E-mail respondents wrote: "Which policy or policies do you need?" This sample indicates that most institutions are partitioning. This partitioning occurs along several lines, including the following:

1. A CUP partitioned on the basis of user type, with different CUPs for faculty, staff and students.
2. A CUP partitioned on the basis of computer system or environment type. It is not uncommon to have separate CUPs for the Internet, personal computers, and mainframes.
3. A CUP partitioned on the basis of major issues. This involves having separate CUPs for each of the major issues such as privacy, ethics, lab equipment use, software rights and regulations, and sanctions.

Some institutions do not partition, but this does not necessarily cause their CUPs to be unduly long. Many unpartitioned CUPs are short and sweet; the predominate theme is that their users know what is ethical and only need to be reminded to act ethically. On the other hand, the longest CUPs found in the final CUP sample were unpartitioned. These CUPs tend to have a laundry list of dos and don'ts that covers a potpourri of issues.

Most schools now partition their CUPs for the following reasons:

1. Although a partitioned CUP tends to be lengthy, the division of labor intrinsic in creating a partitioned CUP enhances the manageability of the overall task.
2. By partitioning major ethical issues into separate components, the committee will be able to consider each issue separately, and clearly express its conclusions.
3. Since each component addresses one major issue, a partitioned CUP is easier to read and comprehend.
4. A partitioned document is easier to update and modify.

What partitions are currently being made? The following list of statements is representative of partitions observed in the sample:

1. Statement of Purpose for the Campus Computer System
2. Privacy
3. Piracy
4. Ethical Use of Computers
5. Micro-Computer and Mainframe Use
6. Faculty and Student Use
7. Software Use
8. E-mail Policies
9. Bitnet or Internet Use
10. CERN or NFSNet Use
11. UseNet Etiquette
12. Local-Regional Network Use
13. Applicable State Computer Crime Laws
14. Campus Code of Conduct
15. Computer Lab Policies

The following plan represents an ordered set of guidelines for building a partitioned CUP.

1. Determine which major ethical issues, such as privacy, piracy, enforcement, or user responsibility, are going to be covered in separate components.
2. Create the "umbrella policy" that focuses on the purpose and ethical use of the campus computer systems. This document should consider all the major issues. It must provide thorough coverage of items not treated elsewhere, but need only briefly refer to items being treated in separate components.
3. Identify computing sub-systems, such as E-mail, Internet, student labs, etc., for which separate policies are needed.

4. Consider whether or not different CUPs are appropriate for differing user groups, such as faculty and students.

Philosophy

An effective CUP is based on a unifying philosophy. In arriving at this philosophy, the CUP committee should discuss several questions, including the following:

1. What is the purpose of the CUP?
2. How permissive should the CUP be?
3. Should the CUP "reflect" the group ethic or should it attempt to "shape" it?
4. How should the CUP deal with users who use the facilities for business, political, religious, and civic activities?

Purpose

It is astonishing that many sample CUPs did not have a stated purpose. The CUP committee must determine the purpose of the CUP. The purpose of the CUP is a function of the role of the university computing systems, which in turn is a function of the institutional mission.

The most practical method of stating a CUP's purpose is to relate the use of computing facilities to the mission statement of the university. Although other solutions are possible, this method has several advantages. It provides guidelines to the people writing the various parts of the CUP. It lessens the chances that the CUP will become a barrier to someone's efforts to further the university mission. Surveyed CUPs containing a clearly stated purpose tend to be better organized and easier to comprehend.

Permissiveness

The battle between academic freedom and political correctness rages on the campuses of this nation. "Dumb-blond jokes" delight some, while truly offending others. One person's pornography is another's art. The campus-wide distribution of E-mail "pro-life" or "pro-choice" messages insults the other camp. These conflicts carry over into the computer system and must be addressed in the CUP.

Advocates of academic freedom will argue that almost any use of the system that does not directly harm others is permissible. They will demand a standard of permissiveness based on an axiom like, "If it can be in the library, it can be on the university computer system." At the other extreme, advocates of political correctness will want to prohibit any use that may possibly be offensive to other users.

One of the hardest decisions that the CUP committee will have to make is to answer the philosophical question: "How permissive should this CUP be?" In the description below, this will be called the "permissiveness level" of the CUP. Three important reasons to decide first on the "permissiveness level" are:

1. The "permissiveness level" determines the approach taken to problem areas, such as privacy, pornography, and penalties.
2. The "permissiveness level" directly affects the length of the CUP.
3. The length of the CUP, in turn, directly influences its readability.

The CUP committee should not underestimate the "heat" engendered by the debate to determine the "permissiveness level." The degree of permissiveness is an issue upon which reasonable people differ in fundamental, often irreconcilable, ways. Opposing sides view permissiveness as an ethical issue which does not lend itself to compromise. The importance of a successful determination of the "permissiveness level" reinforces the need for a broad-based CUP committee that represents all user groups. The level of permissiveness may have repercussions that extend beyond the campus. Important university issues, such as fund raising, legislative support, and the overall image of the institution, can be affected by the "permissiveness level" of the CUP.

Information gleaned from Internet news groups indicates that at some campuses the "permissiveness level" battle has been waged through many levels of authority. The battle starts at the computer center, may go through the CUP committee, faculty senate, and provost's or president's office, and sometimes reaches the governing board or state legislature.

A review of the sample CUPs reveals a tendency toward more permissiveness. Early CUPs limited what users could do on the computer, while newer CUPs emphasize using the computer in a noninterfering manner. The CUPs from church-related schools tend to be less permissive than those from public institutions on issues like pornography. The CUPs from public schools tend to be more restrictive in the business, political, and religious areas.

"Shape" or "Reflect"

In writing the CUP, the committee will formulate ethical guidelines for the user group. History tells us that guidelines that differ greatly from normal and acceptable group mores will not be followed. For example, the Volstead Act failed in its attempt to implement prohibition, because the public was not ready to give up alcohol, and led to a decline in respect for the law. Similarly, setting CUP standards that are out of line with current university mores may lead to an increase in "unethical" activity. On the other hand, guidelines that make small, gradual increases in ethical standards can effectively reshape group mores.

In reviewing the sample CUPs, the authors discovered that too many CUPs included clauses that ignore current group mores. When the authors' classroom ethics project on analyzing CUPs was given for the third time, students often commented, "I can't believe that some schools don't allow any game playing!" Complete bans on using facilities for political, religious, or profit making activities may ignore current mores. Except for the most flagrant cases, "abuses" are simply winked at by computing administrators. Such disregard for approved codes of conduct is not healthy.

Gray Areas

In this discussion of gray areas, only uses of university computer facilities are considered. Similar facilities, such as the copy center, are not normally a part of the CUP. A partial listing of problem areas, covering many typical university concerns, is as follows:

1. Can a university president use the computer facilities to keep the books for a church group?
2. Can a department chair use computer facilities to edit a speech to be delivered by a candidate for public office?
3. Should we let a dean run little league stats on the campus LAN?
4. Can we let a student use the facilities to make 500 copies of a flyer advertising his favorite bar?
5. May students compose their resumes on the system, and if so, how many copies can they print?
6. Can the provost use the office PC to compose the "Great American Novel"? What if the novel turns out to be a trashy best seller that brings dishonor to the university, but earns the author a substantial sum, which never makes its way back into the school coffers?
7. Should a professor be allowed to earn substantial extra income by using the facilities to create computer programs for a local firm that allow it to keep its doors open and save area jobs? Does it make a difference if the professor does this work directly as a consultant or via a grant from the firm to the university?
8. Suppose a professor has a private client. Should the client be allowed to sublet the professor's personal university account to use the Internet for private business purposes?
9. Should students be allowed to fritter away their time playing computer games? What about spending excessive time on network activities, such as the Internet "irc" program, or some interactive game, such as "Doom"?

The above scenarios illustrate philosophical gray areas that the committee must resolve before it can create an effective CUP. Most committee members would agree that items four and eight are not appropriate and that the CUP should preclude them. Reasonable people will have differing viewpoints on the other items. What appears to be money-grubbing consulting to some is applied research to others. Activities that some feel violate the separation of church and state are seen by others as normal community bridge building. Although most would agree that students should not fritter away their time on computer games, obviously games do relieve stress. And, in an era when alcohol, drugs, and sex are the likely alternatives, games may in fact provide a safe remedy for boredom and stress.

In setting the university approach to these problem areas, the committee needs to consider additional concepts, including the following:

1. Do any state statutes preclude the activity?
2. Does the activity place a burden on the system?
3. Does the activity arguably fall within the University mission?
4. Does the activity foster good relations with the local community?
5. Do users think the activity is appropriate?
6. Is it possible to catch violators and feasible to punish them?

The review of sample CUPs discloses two basic approaches to religious, political, personal, and business uses. The first approach is silence. Several CUPs, including some from prestigious universities, fail to mention some or all of these areas. These schools appear to rely on a general statement that the facilities should only be used to further the university mission.

The second approach simply bans such activities. Yet many banned activities are permitted to happen because of a broad interpretation of the university mission statement. Only the most flagrant abuses are caught and punished.

On a philosophical basis, the hypocrisy of simply banning controversial computer activities is reprehensible. But, because banning gives users clearer guidelines, it may be preferable to the silence option.

Privacy

What degree of privacy are we going to accord our users? Under what circumstances can privacy be invaded? Who has the authority to override the stated policy?

The anonymity offered by the computer system to users causes the loss of inhibitions. This anonymity can lead to behavior that would not occur in a less anonymous setting. A user, for example, who would not go into the porno area of the local newsstand, might browse the most frequented news group on the Internet: ALT.binaries.pictures.erotica (3). A more legitimate academic scenario involves shielding a user playing "devil's advocate" behind the veil of privacy provided by the system. Users need some reasonable assurance that the university administration is not going to randomly audit their correspondence.

On the other hand the privacy policy needs to have some flexibility. Consider a recent case where a student disappeared. The president of the university wanted to open the student's E-mail account to search for clues. The director of the computer center felt that she had to put her job on the line because, under the CUP, only the addresses on the E-mail could be released and not the contents.

On the issue of privacy, research disclosed four common concerns often addressed in CUPs:

1. Almost every CUP tells users to respect the privacy of other users. In addition, it is common to admonish against snooping, hacking, and any other actions that interfere with the privacy of others.
2. Under what conditions can the institution invade the privacy of users? From a legal standpoint, it is mandatory that the CUP protect the school against legal claims for invasion of privacy. On the one hand the CUP should define the right of the school to invade privacy, and on the other it should include a disclaimer denying liability for invasions by others.
3. How do users protect their privacy? Some CUPs have sections that emphasize self-protection through the efficient use of passwords. Typically, this type of admonition is only included in partitioned CUPs.
4. Another item that is often addressed in partitioned CUPs is the vulnerability of private files on an open system.

Persnickety

Research discloses a "laundry list" of items that are usually covered in the CUP, such as piracy, punishment, and authorized or prohibited uses. In addition, as worldwide computer networks evolve, another set of items, such as those listed in the section on partitioning, should be addressed. The problem is that the CUP can become overly long if each of these items is given detailed treatment.

How "picky" should the CUP be? Obviously the short statement has the advantage that users may actually read it and comprehend its meaning. But a short CUP has several disadvantages: 1) the lack of specific guidance in known trouble areas, and 2) possible problems with enforcement that occur when the CUP is vague.

The longer statement (which is often partitioned) often overcomes the disadvantages of a short CUP, but creates others. First, the average user is less likely to read and comprehend a longer document. Second, new abuses may still be discovered that are not covered by the lengthier statement. Third, spelling out a long list of abuses, without mentioning a particular abuse, may make users feel that absence gives permission.

How should violators of CUP be punished? What type of legal system must be established to handle violations? Who will be the judge, prosecutor, and jury? What are the rights of appeal?

Not all violations of the CUP are of equal venality. Some, such as an authorized user allowing his unauthorized spouse or child onto the system, might be winked at. Others, such as turning loose a system-debilitating virus, may call for incarceration or fines.

Clearly, if incarceration or a major fine is a possibility, the CUP should state that prosecution will be pursued in state or federal courts. But many lesser offenses might be handled administratively. All these "persnickety" issues must be addressed in the CUP.

Phog Phactor

At what reading level should the CUP be written? Since college freshmen are part of the target audience, CUPs should be written at a level which freshmen can understand.

During the last 50 years, a number of readability formulas have been developed. Two of the best known are the Flesch-Kincaid reading ease formula (4) and the Gunning Fog Index (GFI) (5). The variables in these formulas include items such as the number of letters, words, and multi-syllable words; the percentage of simple sentences, long words, and personal references; and the proportions of familiar and abstract words (5, p. 34). Using these various text statistics, the readability formula generates a number which provides a measure of the text's readability.

Readability formulas only measure what they were designed to measure and usually predict that a document with shorter words, shorter sentences, and smaller paragraphs will be more readable.

These formulas have been applied to popular magazines such as *Time* or *Newsweek*, as well as textbooks, newspapers, and famous texts, such as Lincoln's Gettysburg Address.

Because the Internet and E-mail texts for the sample CUPs are encoded in raw ASCII format, the authors used WordPerfect 6.0 to reformat them. Next, the grammar analysis tools provided in Wordperfect 6.0, including the Gunning Fog Index and the Flesch-Kincaid index, were used. Since college freshmen are part of the target audience, the Gunning Fog Index of a CUP should match the reading level of an average freshman, which is approximately 12.

In the final sample of 42 CUPs, word counts range from 266 to 2787.

The counts for the first quartile range from 266 to 608. The fourth quartile counts range from 1204 to 2787. At a rate of 400 words per page, the median CUP is about three pages long.

The Gunning Fog Indexes for the sample CUPs range from a low of 12 to a high of 24. The first quartile ranges are from 12 to 17, with only three CUPs at 13 or below. The median CUP has a GFI of 19, which means that over half the CUPs are at a Ph.D. readability level. These GFI numbers indicate that most CUPs need a drastic rewrite to improve their readability. This judgment is also supported by the Flesch-Kincaid statistics which indicate that over half the sample CUPs are readable by less than 5 percent of the U.S. population.

These empirical analyses of readability show that the sample CUPs are written at reading levels considerably above the capabilities of typical freshmen. These "Phog Phactor" results show that many CUPs could be improved by applying readability principles. No one wants to be singled out for poor writing, especially in higher education, where good writing practices are taught and expected.

To enhance readability, the CUP committee should

1. Assign the actual writing of the CUP to a small team of excellent writers or wordsmiths. This team must express the complex ideas of the CUP in ways that can be understood by our least educated users.
2. Partition the CUP. Since unpartitioned CUPs are normally quite long, partitioning into several shorter policies can improve CUP readability. In addition, a CUP partitioned into several shorter components is easier for students to read and understand, particularly when they need only work with a few components.

Publication

How does the institution communicate the CUP to the user group? From a legal perspective, the CUP must be disseminated in a manner that makes it legally binding on university computer system users. On the other hand, creating a bureaucracy may unduly impede access to the system.

The authors' research revealed that university communities had resolved this problem with a wide diversity of "solutions." Some of the currently used methods of publishing a CUP are the following:

1. Print the CUP in various faculty, student, and staff handbooks.
2. Place the CUP with its components on the institution's Internet gopher server.

3. Post the CUP on the walls of computer labs, campus buildings, etc.
4. Make users sign a copy of the CUP (preferably after they have read it) before allowing access to the system.

What good is a CUP if nobody reads it? If the document is not effectively published, users will not recognize the problems. Users, unaware that their activities are illegal, may continue doing them. The CUP may merely become a document which lawyers can use to prosecute abusers, after the fact.

CONCLUSIONS

Writing this paper has changed our perspectives. Our initial focus was on software piracy, punishment, and ethical statements. Reading and analyzing existing CUPs made us realize that the first three "P's," Participation, Partitioning, and Philosophy, are the most important facets of CUP creation. The other four "P's" will flow from these.

We cannot overstate the importance of a representative committee that spends several sessions discussing overall CUP philosophy. It should be recognized that maintaining the CUP is an on-going task that dictates a standing committee.

The positive effect of partitioning is significant, as partitioned CUPs are easier to build, modify, and understand. Our CUP analysis reveals that many CUPs appear to have been written backwards, in that they seem to have started by addressing the "Persnickety" problem. The resulting CUP tends to lack a unifying theme and often has gaps in coverage.

Our readability findings indicate that "Phog Phactors" should be used to produce a CUP that is more readable. Proper publication of a CUP is also vital. If users do not actually read and understand the CUP, the whole effort is wasted.

REFERENCES

(1) Scott, Thomas J., Richard B. Voss and Cherri M. Pancake. "Teaching an Ethics Component to CS Majors." *Proceedings*, 24th SigCSE Technical Symposium. Indianapolis, IN. Feb. 1993. p. 304.

(2) Scott, Thomas J. and Richard B. Voss. "Teaching Computer Ethics Electronically." *Proceedings*, Computers on Campus National Conference. Myrtle Beach, SC. Nov. 1993. p. 88.

(3) Elmer-Dewitt, Philip. "First Nation in Cyberspace." *Time*. Dec. 6, 1993. p. 62.

(4) Flesch, Rudolph. *The Art of Readable Writing.* New York: Harper & Row, 1949. pp. 147– 151.

(5) Gunning, Robert. *The Technique of Clear Writing.* New York: McGraw Hill, 1968. p. 40.

II : ETHICS, TECHNOLOGY AND VALUE

SUMMARY

(6) *Computers or Humans: Who Are in Control?*
Inger Eriksson in this chapter discusses the role computers are playing in decision making based on both classical and neo-classical ethical principles. She tries to answer the crucial question: Is computer technology changing our ethical beliefs or are our ethical beliefs influencing computer technology? Who is in control?

(7) *Ethics and IT: Is the Human Factors Approach an Ethical Way of Designing and Implementing Information Technology?*
This chapter examines the changing nature of the workplace due to the rapid change in information technology. It exposes the human concerns about the workplace and the role of technology. It also examines the ethical concerns arising from the new technologies in the workplace.

(8) *Moral Distancing and the Use of Information Technologies: The Seven Temptations.*
This chapter discusses the role of the "seven temptations" in diverting ethical attention and responsibility of computer professionals and users. The author suggests ways to fight those temptations.

(9) *Digital Images: Moral Manipulation*
In this chapter John Weckert and Douglas Adeney discuss the ethical problems involving digitalized images. Images from works of art, cameras, and print can be altered and passed as new through the process of warping, tweening, morphing, and cut and paste. Of course this raises many questions about the copyright laws in the digital age.

6. COMPUTERS OR HUMANS: WHO ARE IN CONTROL?

Inger V. Eriksson

INTRODUCTION

Information technology (IT) is a fast developing field with indisputable influence on our lives. The ways we perform our work tasks, make decisions and communicate have changed. We have become very dependent on computers[1] in both our working and private lives. Globalization of markets has accentuated the need of well functioning IT.

Computers do not only affect our lives and work but also our behavior and the way we think of many fundamental concepts. As an example, consider the somewhat unexpected lack of messaging or network etiquette, even among IT professionals, which became evident through general access to E-mail. Human on-line behavior seems to be different from face-to-face behavior. Harakas (1982) expresses his worry about the implications of technology in a broad sense: "It is having important implications for some of the major issues in our technological age: abortion, the meaning of human life, euthanasia, atomic warfare and hunger" (p. 166). Verity (1994) mentions changes in "how we record knowledge, communicate, learn, work, understand ourselves and the world." He also states that "symbolic tools like the alphabet, book, and mechanical clock have changed some of our most fundamental notions—self, identity, mind, nature, time, space" and asks for the effects of computerization on these notions. The effects of internationalization are part of the problem as well.

All these issues influence or are influenced by the ethical standpoint. The central question becomes: will we allow technology to change our ethics, or will we and can we influence technology and its use according to our ethical belief? This is a broad theme, and in the following I will concentrate on information technology as a tool in performing work and ethics in this context.

The rest of the paper is structured as follows. First the issue of computers as tools is raised and the pros and cons of using information technology in work are discussed in brief. Then some ethical systems are looked at to identify issues relevant for ethics within information technology. Next previous research is examined covering the fields of ethics of information systems development, ethical constructs, and codes for ethical conduct. The last two sections conclude the discussion and identify changes in human activities and thinking as a consequence of using computers, especially as tools in the work context.

USING COMPUTERS AS TOOLS

There has been discussion as to whether a computer can be regarded as a tool. Merriam-Webster (1993) defines tools as "something ... necessary in the practice of a vocation or profession; means to an end /books are a scholar's tools...." Verity (1994) talks of "symbolic tools." For Frese (1987) the level of controllability is the criterion for whether or not a computer can be regarded as a tool in the work and organizational context. The computer is perceived as a tool if the people who work with it are "firmly in control of the important procedures, decisions, and timeframes." If the controllability is reduced the computer still can be perceived as a tool, not for the workers, but for the "masters in the background." Generally, a tool is expected to help people perform their tasks, and this is exactly what computers do—or at least should do. Consequently, "tool" should be an acceptable notation for a computer.

Information technology has become an essential part in performing work tasks. From the beginning computers were used to accomplish routine, monotonous, and dangerous tasks. Now they are used to perform very sophisticated control and decision making tasks as well. Their speed and accuracy in performing calculations and their capacity of memory are utilized. However, besides being helpful, computers have negative effects on work. Some work has become more routinized, monotonous and deskilling, e.g., for cashiers in shops. Computers may not have created dangerous jobs, but certainly they have created non-healthy working environments. For example, the problem of radiation is not yet solved. Another well known issue is the risk of isolation, to neglect the need for social contacts and human communication: since all information is available on the screen, why "bother" other people. The object of work can also become more distant and abstract: never seeing the real thing one is working on, only its representation on the screen. Computers support standardization and formalization which do not always harmonize with people's preferences. Use of computers thus changes work tasks often requiring new skills by the workers. Specialization and polarization of work are among the benefits and risks of computerization for individuals.

Organizations' motives to utilize information technology can, according to Jarvinen (1992), roughly be categorized as follows: 1) cost saving,

2) improvement of production processes, and 3) embedding IT into products. Cost savings can mean replacing the human workforce by computers. Embedded systems, on the other hand, can create new products and new jobs. Improving production processes, also by using digital networks, has an influence on work tasks. Jarvinen summarizes Gurbaxani and Wang's[2] analysis of the effects of management information systems (MIS) on organizations as follows: 1) improved efficacy and opportunity to expand, 2) streamlining of transaction handling and distribution, 3) facilitating and rationalizing decision making, 4) control of work performance on individual and departmental level, and 5) keeping record of the changes in the organizations' goals, structure, product selection and environment, and offering a symbolic way of representing the business. The use of IT in organizations thus presents many issues which can be viewed from an ethical point.

Ethical considerations on society raised by computerization concern areas such as privacy, crime, health, working conditions, individuality, and employment (O'Brien, 1994, p. 459). Computer monitoring occurs in workplaces. Private information is available through different databases. Well-known examples of computer crimes are the theft of money, services, and information. Computerization of production processes may eliminate jobs. However, the issues are not as simple as that. While eliminating jobs computerization might improve the working conditions and job satisfaction of the employees that remain, and make production of higher quality products at a lower cost to customers possible.

A problem on individual, organizational and societal levels is created by the superior speed and memory of computers: the consequences of errors can be far-reaching. Yannaras (1984, p. 223) expresses his concerns about the move from creative work to automated production with consequences for individuals as well as for the society:

> In modern times, we have seen a change in the structures and premises of social life; we have passed from the limited community of personal relationships to impersonal, mass coexistence, from creative work to automated production, and from personal need to artificially contrived consumer greed.

Criticism of computerization extends to the task-allocation which is often based on the principle that computers should do what they are good at, and humans should do the rest. The reason is that computer "knowledge" is rather limited, basically structured problems and programmed decisions, while people are also able to handle unstructured and one-off problems. It certainly makes sense to use the relative advantages of humans and computers in doing a job, but giving the computer priority of choice can result in people performing unconnected tasks instead of meaningful wholes. Work motivation and job satisfaction depend on understanding the context of the work, while not seeing the context constitutes a risk of errors (Eriksson, 1990). A more strategic approach to work design would be to divide jobs into meaningful tasks and then decide where to use computers as support (Nurminen, 1988). Expert systems and neural networks are fast developing areas within artificial intelligence (AI) research, with practical applications. Expert systems certainly are good in the hands of experts who are able to interpret the solutions which the system recommends. However, if the user of the system does not know what the underlying rules embedded in the system are, then he or she is forced just to accept the output. Improving the competence of nonexpert users by offering a system with expert knowledge is an illusion and can result in dubious decisions just through ignorance (Eriksson and Nissen, 1994). Expert systems are good as support systems but as replacement of human knowledge they can become fatal.

Neural networks represent maybe the closest computers now come to "knowledge." These systems are able to learn from experience and change their behavior accordingly. Use of such systems, for example in decision making situations, is motivated with reference to people's limited capacity to consider very many variables at a time and their rather poor intuitive ability to assess probabilities. Through experience neural networks learn how to behave in certain situations and their memory and processing capacities allow them to consider all variables relevant for the situation. Ethical problems arise from the fact that it is not practically possible to trace how the suggested solutions have been reached.

To summarize, computers are important tools for work performance, but their use has, besides positive effects, also negative effects on individuals, organizations and society. Limitations and prospects of information technology involve ethical dilemmas to be solved.

ETHICAL SYSTEMS AND IT

Information technology and ethics are interrelated. The issue that arises is what kind of basis for moral judgment is applicable and relevant to IT. There are several ethical systems and any discussion of IT and ethics requires understanding some of their differences. However, this paper is not aimed at giving any deep understanding of the philosophical issues; there are other sources for that. Here a brief discussion on some central ethical systems based on summary works of other authors is presented. The purpose is to identify the relevant issues considering the intent of this paper only.

Ethical systems

Cohen (1994) categorizes selected ethical systems into classical ethical systems and neo-classical ethical systems. Classical ethical systems include utilitarianism, universalism, and procedural justice. Utilitarianism judges right in terms of the general good and morality as seen in terms of the outcome. Universalism holds that rules should be applied uniformly and defines morality by intention. Procedural justice stipulates that following a set of rules and laws is sufficient guarantee for the morality of actions.

Neo-classical ethical systems are, according to Cohen (1994), a response by modern ethicists to the difficulties of making reasonable judgments by applying the classical systems to a changed and changing society. Among philosophers and theologians there have been arguments on whether the morality should change just because the society changes (Hjertberg, 1994; Reichmann, 1993; Rosing, 1994). The Christian point of view, at least the Roman Catholic and Greek Orthodox view, is that the human conscience cannot always serve as a guide to moral action; absolute morality is the yardstick. It is also maintained that there are traditions which can be changed while the traditions of the Church are eternal. The idea of adapting the Church and its teachings to society is rejected. Philosophers on the other hand question the existence of an absolute morality and ask for adaptation to social justice, humanism, and democracy.

Returning to Cohen's article, the neo-classical ethical systems contain distributed justice and personal liberty. Distributed justice holds that an equitable distribution of benefits should be ensured, while personal liberty counts on a free-market economy which will enable individuals to achieve their highest productivity.

Cohen states that all ethical systems attempt to distinguish right from wrong. What differentiates the ethical systems from each other is the basis they use for that judgment. The above mentioned systems use criteria such as outcome, intention, rule obedience, equitableness of distribution, and individual productivity. However, there are other criteria for analyzing ethical issues as well.

Harakas (1983) defines three categories for ethical judgment: 1) good/evil, 2) right/wrong and 3) fitting/unfitting or appropriate/inappropriate (p. 17). The good/evil category judges all ethical issues against a single principle. Such principles are, among others, utility, liberty and equity. This approach thus provides a standard and foundations for ethics. The right/wrong category is much more concrete and practically oriented. Its focus is on acts and deeds and doing the right thing, justice and law being measures of morality. It supports rule-based ethics. Harakas' third category, systems judging morality as appropriate/inappropriate behavior, is founded on rationality and consensus which has not been expressly codified. These types of unwritten laws are common in traditional societies.

Christian ethics combines elements of all three approaches, but what is considered good in one situation might be in conflict with both law and rationality. There are several examples to be found in the New Testament. Guroian

(1987, pp. 27–28) shows this multidimensionality of Orthodox Christian ethics by defining what it is not, one-dimensional and simple:

> Orthodox theology rejects all forms of utilitarian, deontological, or teleological ethics which intend the world as either utility, law, or unfolding rationality. An Orthodox ethic does not rely on a utilitarian calculus or on formal or conscientious adherence to rules and a dispensing of duties.

The freedom of choice is a basic standpoint in ethical behavior for Orthodox Christianity, and valid for all. A deterministic world view would see ethics as irrelevant from an individual point of view, since individuals are not free to decide.

Three categories for judging morality are suggested above: good/evil, right/wrong, and appropriate/inappropriate. The first category is based on values, the second on rules, and the third on consensus. This framework will be used in the following discussion on ethics within IT.

ETHICS WITHIN IT

Many researchers address ethical issues within IT but they do not explicitly state their ethical point of view. The problems they study and the way they judge morality might give an answer to the unspoken question. Research topics chosen for analysis here are information systems development, ethical IT constructs, and rules for ethical professional conduct.

Information systems development

Information systems (IS) are intended to facilitate work performance, but there are systems which instead control the work, and force the users to adapt their way of working to the computer systems. According to Clement and Wagner[3] many causes of such deficiency can be identified but these can all be traced in some degree to ethical shortcoming. The failure of individuals and organizations to consider the likely effects on people's welfare and to take responsibility for adequate remedial action are mentioned specifically. Systems development is the activity where the quality of the system to be produced is determined. Clement and Wagner state that this activity offers the obvious point where also ethical concerns can be brought to bear. Most attention to ethical issues has been focused on IT use but an earlier intervention could help in developing better systems. Research in ethics in information systems development is therefore endorsed.

There are several methods, techniques and tools to support systems development. User participation in the systems development process was proposed many years ago as the way of improving system quality from the user's point of view (see e.g., Bjerknes, Ehn and Kyng, 1987; Briefs, Ciborra and Schneider,

1983). Several levels of user participation can be identified. Users may just define their requirements, which is the traditional approach. It is well known that defining requirements for a system which does not exist is very difficult, especially since users seldom know what possibilities there might be available. The requirements often reflect the old work situation instead of improving it. A more advanced approach to user participation is being a member in a project group. This gives users an opportunity to follow the progress and influence the decisions throughout the development process, besides defining their requirements, but requires special knowledge which they may not have. Suitable techniques such as simulation and simulation games (Eriksson, 1990; Ruohomaki, 1994) and wall graph techniques (Saaren-Seppala, 1983) can help in overcoming these problems. Users can also be directly involved in systems development and to a certain extent even develop their own systems if proper development methods and tools are used. Such methods are, for example, prototyping (Floyd, 1984; Floyd et al., 1989; Friis, 1991) and end-user computing (Heikkila, Hemminki and Pihlaja, 1993; Rivard and Huff, 1985). Prototyping, simulation, and end-user computing are not a single method each; there are several types of them all with different purposes.

Two different approaches to user participation can be identified above: user participation and user involvement. The extent of influence and the level of knowledge are the two determining qualities. There is one more point to make here; the use of the word "user." In Scandinavia "user" normally means the end user of the system. In the United States the concept often refers to the managers of the departments which are going to utilize the system. In this paper the Scandinavian tradition is followed.

Let us now try to identify the ethical issues and the basis for moral judgment in information systems development. The aim of implementing information systems is to improve the quality of working life and the productivity of work at the same time—with the emphasis on one or the other. The standpoint of improving the quality of working life implies the empowerment of employees, which means equal values and rights for all people, regardless of their position in organizations (Clement and Wagner, 1994). The ethics here relies on the fundamental principle of equity, i.e., good/evil. Right/wrong can also be recognized since rules and laws are laid down to guarantee such "human rights." These issues are usually considered political, but behind the political understanding there is an ethical background—or the other way around. Clement and Wagner state that ethical problems emerge when the values and moral principles on which individuals base their decisions and actions are in conflict. They suggest that such conflicts between people's values, norms of conduct, and claims for moral ground often can be explained by differences between their positions in organizations and society. In that respect ethical problems reflect a political content.

Cohen (1994) applies the basic principles of various ethical systems to make an ethical analysis of a specific case: global outsourcing of application development to programmers in less-developed countries. The issue is an economic one for organizations. Outsourcing is cheaper and more flexible than employing programmers who expect full payment at the salary level of developed countries. Digital networks and telecommunication have made this choice possible. The earlier approach was to import a cheap work force.

The discussion, as concerns this case, has centered on whether it is right or wrong to pay less for programmers in less-developed countries than for programmers who perform the same job in the company's home country. There has also been discussion as to whether it is right to export jobs at all. A work force may be movable, but should work be movable, too? High unemployment can make the last issue especially critical.

For the ethical analysis Cohen constructed the following framework: human rights (e.g. exploitation of workers), social equity (e.g. type of outsourced jobs), sovereignty/politics (e.g. fading borders), and markets/economics (e.g. free competition). Using this framework few ethical problems were found in the case analyzed. However, according to Cohen, all the ethical systems which formed the basis for the analysis applied the right/wrong dichotomy as their moral judgment. Consequently, right and wrong were what Cohen was looking for. If the viewpoint had been broadened to cover good/evil and appropriate/inappropriate the conclusions might be different.

Ethical IT constructs

In a thought provoking essay Mason (1986) expressed his concern on people's vulnerability to IT. He considered in what way users can come to harm either through misuse of IT or by being hindered from exercising their legal rights. For the purpose of analysis he constructed a framework consisting of four ethical issues: privacy, accuracy, property, and accessibility.

This ethical construct, called PAPA, can be applied to identify and structure ethical problems. For example, misuse of personal information or use of incorrect data can cause a person harm and violates her privacy. Personal property is protected by law, but for software and data the concept of property has not been clearly defined. In the last years there have been several legal cases which form precedents for the future. Not only protection of but also access to a person's property, including intangible property, should be guaranteed.

In his essay, Mason did not directly answer which ethical philosophy guides his own reasoning. A strong social responsibility is present in his article reflecting both values and adherence to rules. Good/evil and right/wrong categories, based on the principles of liberty, equity, justice and law, probably describe the main approaches to judging ethical behavior.

Loch et al. (1993) found the PAPA construct interesting but not empirically verified. They give three good reasons why to verify and further develop the construct. First, IT causes situations to become more abstract which makes the identification of potential losers difficult. Second, computers offer a sense of anonymity, of being safe from surveillance and criticism. Touch with the constituents of work might get lost. Third, abstraction and loss of contact with reality can hide the ethical components of an ethical dilemma.

Loch et al. made a field survey to identify ethical attitudes. They used scenarios on ethical dilemmas which the participants rated according to the ethicality of the actions described. Based on this empirical work, they identified twelve factors which grouped into five issues, instead of the four of the PAPA construct which they had started with. They found that access, privacy, ownership, motivation, and responsibility were the issues which had sufficient empirical support. Access and privacy are seen in the same way as in Mason's construct. The concept of ownership shifts the emphasis from Mason's property, an object, to an attribute of people, which is the focus of the ethical discussion. Motivation is a new aspect identified by Loch et al. Mason had the victim perspective on IT users, people considered as vulnerable to IT, while Loch et al. identified the stakeholder perspective, people who are influenced by IT. Responsibility was found to include both personal accountability and group responsibility, and extends Mason's concept of accuracy.

Contrary to most authors, Loch et al. (1993) clearly declare their ethical standpoint: "Ethics is not religion nor does it presuppose religious precepts. Ethics, as conceived for this research, defines higher order, universal reasoning." The consensus principle of social acceptance with the appropriate/inappropriate approach seems to be the basis for their moral judgment. They conclude that "there is some consensus on 'correct' ethical actions that appears to be based on rules that apply to situations."

Standards and codes for professional conduct

Mason (1986) challenged the research community to formulate a new social contract to deal with ethical issues. However, rules for ethical professional conduct have existed a long time already. Many national bodies have published ethical codes for their members to follow. The Association for Computing Machinery's Code of Ethics and Professional Conduct from 1972 might be the oldest one. Institute of Electrical and Electronics Engineers (IEEE) and Data Processing Management Association (DPMA) are two other United States–based computer societies with their own ethical codes. International Federation for Information Processing (IFIP), which can be regarded more international in scope, is trying to develop guidelines to be observed by its member societies when these develop their own national codes. Dahlblom and Mathiassen (1994) remark, on the other hand, that the Scandinavian countries have not felt a need for ethical codes: "Unlike the Americans, we have not really been concerned with codifying our self-understanding, turning it into a set of rules to guide the conduct of our profession and educate its members."

As an explanation Dahlblom and Mathiassen offer the special Scandinavian approach to systems design "not only involving the users, but doing so with a deep understanding of what this means." The impression a reader gets is that all systems developed in Scandinavia would be perfect and that is not true, but of course, the special Scandinavian approach is not used in all systems development projects either. There also exist codes of ethics under various names in the Scandinavian countries as well.

In recent years codes of ethics have been under review because the environment and technology are changing rapidly and radically. Maybe this is a response to Mason's challenge. In 1992 ACM published a proposal for a new code (*Comm. ACM*, 36, 2, 1993). This code consists of 24 imperatives formulated as statements of personal responsibility. The imperatives are expressed in a general form to show that computer ethics is based on general ethical principles. The code is divided into four sections and a supplement of guidelines with explanations. Section one, "General Moral Imperatives," outlines fundamental ethical considerations. Section two, "More Specific Professional Responsibilities," addresses specific considerations of professional conduct. Section three, "Organizational Leadership Imperatives," pertains to individuals in a leading position. Section four, "Compliance with the Code," deals with principles of compliance with the code.

Martin and Martin (1994) have made an interesting thematic analysis and comparison of the old and the new ACM codes. For the comparison they used a grid which is based on their two earlier analyses—one of the codes of four United States–based computer societies (1990) and the other one of a proposed code of IFIP (1991).

The four United States–based computer societies whose ethical codes Martin and Martin (1990) compared were ACM, IEEE, DPMA and ICCP (Institute for the Certification of Computer Professionals). In this comparison they found ten common themes to be the core of computer professionals' understanding of ethical behavior. Not all themes were covered by every code, but there was a reasonably good agreement on what should be considered as ethical issues. These ten themes are listed below:

- personal integrity/competence
- personal accountability for work
- responsibility to employer/client
- responsibility to profession
- confidentiality of information
- conflict of interest
- dignity/worth of people

- public safety, health, welfare
- participation in education
- increase public knowledge

The themes do not reflect problems directly raised by computer technology but are rather general in their ethical scope. The other study of Martin and Martin (1991) concerned IFIP's effort to develop an international code of ethics. This code contained all the ten themes mentioned above, but besides these eight new ones were found. These are listed below:

- specific statement to social responsibility
- certification standards for professionals
- emphasis on quality of life
- protection of intellectual property
- consequences of networks
- basic human rights
- rights of the user
- equity/respect for cultural diversity

These additional themes reflect the international and multicultural scope which the code was aimed at serving. New ethical issues raised by the development of computer technology, for example, the networks, are covered here.

The proposed IFIP ethics framework was discussed but not accepted as a standard at the IFIP World Conference in Madrid in 1992. Instead IFIP set up an Ethics Task Group to make a proposal to the IFIP General Assembly (GA) of IFIP Guidelines for Codes of Ethics and Professional Conduct (Berleur, 1993). The task group will first publish a Reader, a "practical" analysis, based on the codes of various national computer societies. By November 1993 the task group had received codes from 16 of IFIP's 43 full members. The next step is to publish a more theoretical framework and then to present suggestions and general recommendations to IFIP's GA.

To go back to the new ACM code, in their analysis Martin and Martin (1994) used the thematical grid composed of the 18 themes listed above. They found that the new ACM code covers 17 of them, excluding only "certification standards for professionals," which, on the other hand, was included in the old ACM code. The new code is broader in scope than the old one. Besides the strong emphasis on the responsibility of the computer professional to the employer which was present already in the old code, the new code has a stronger emphasis on overall social responsibility which partly is related to managerial responsibilities. The code covers the responsibilities of computer professionals as individuals, professionals, and organizational leaders.

The difficulty in establishing internationally accepted codes was demonstrated by the IFIP effort, and still the attempt is continued. Loch et al. (1993)

tried to find out if there is a consensus on ethical attitudes in the United States. The new ACM code raised a great deal of discussion. All this demonstrates that there seems to be a need of agreement upon what constitutes ethical behavior in the IS context and how to codify it.

The purposes of codes of ethics can be manyfold. Dahlblom and Mathiassen (1994) identify three. They can serve "as professionalization strategies, as stating the ethical positions, and as methodological frameworks of computing." Stating the ethical positions is the central one in this context and two opposite positions are offered. A code can either support means-end thinking, thus concentrating on the consequences or the outcome. A code can also favor a position which defines the way of conduct stating rights and norms, i.e., rules to follow. Which position is taken depends on the construction of the code and this is influenced by the social setting in which it is developed (Clement, 1994). Questions that arise are whether the codes reflect the situation as is or whether they try to change it in some direction, and in that case, in which direction and who is the one to decide the direction.

To summarize, ethics in the work context is usually considered in the use situation although it might be more effective to look at ethics in information systems development. The development process offers the best opportunity to influence the quality of the information system to be produced. Two models for ethical constructs were presented. These models record the consensus of those issues which are regarded as ethical issues in the IT context. Codes for ethics and professional conduct were also discussed. These are being revised which shows the need for applicable, generally accepted rules and regulations among professionals. The need might be accentuated by fast developing technique and an increasing global interdependence.

DISCUSSION

The expressed need to develop new ethical codes, to identify general ethical attitudes and to seriously consider users' requirements on information systems reflects the IT community's opinion of the relevance of research in ethics in IT. General and IT ethics are not the same although the basic principles might be. There are special features in IT which lead to special ethical problems. Computers often make work abstract. Communication takes place via rather anonymous media. It is easy to monitor employees' work habits, including their use of electronic mail. Guynes (1994) makes a reference to Piller[4] who reports that 22 percent of CEOs and MIS directors at 301 businesses of varying sizes have searched electronic mail, voice mail, computer files, and other networking communications of their employees. The situation is not unique; technical changes have always caused some new problems or accentuated old ones, and this is what is happening with the introduction of IT. The new problems just need to be recognized and controlled. It is here that the IT community's interest in ethics fits in, to be in control of the situation through agreed upon codes.

What is to be considered as "good" or "right" is shaped by the context and conditions that characterize a certain social setting (Clement and Wagner). In other words, there are good reasons to assume that people's ideas of "good" and "right" differ among social and political cultures. Probably, neither meaning nor priority of ethical concepts is the same in different cultures. North Americans pay much attention to privacy. Still privacy is not one of the fundamental rights of U.S. citizens but derived from other rights which the constitution guarantees (Singh, 1994). According to Singh U.S. laws regarding privacy are vague and subjective. As a contrast he mentions that European countries have very stringent restrictions on this point. To this Clarke (1994) responds that Europe is very different from North America, with many cultural backgrounds and approaches. He finds that the concept of privacy is meaningful, although not well protected, in England, while the concept is less important "on the Continent." There data protection is much more important. In the Scandinavian countries there are laws to protect people's privacy. So, just in Europe at least three different approaches to one ethical issue, privacy, can be found. How could an international consensus on all IT ethics then be possible?

The IFIP did not succeed in offering an international code of ethics. Donaldson and Dunfee (1994) make an effort to define a macrosocial contract of economic morality, to be useful worldwide. Organizations are working in a global business environment which makes such a global view important for economics as well. The basic idea of their theory is that there exist some universal "rights" and "wrongs." These can be interpreted locally and adapted to cultural norms in organizations. They talk of macrosocial contracts which are agreed upon, microsocial contracts which are the locally adapted norms, and hypernorms which are pan-human. If this kind of a theory will function as an international framework of morality for the IT field as well, the universal values need to be identified first. Who is able to do it?

Values are central to ethics and social choices including computerization of work (Dunlop and Kling, 1991), and these values seem to differ in different cultural settings. Maybe the IT field should just accept that people belonging to different cultures and religions have different values and consequently base their decisions on different moral rules. Maybe the effort to try to identify a general code of conduct and a core of ethical issues which all the IT community is ready to accept is unrealistic.

Power is the other issue indirectly discussed in this paper. Information technology has been defined as a tool for work performance. Information systems development involves decisions on how the users of the systems will perform their work tasks and thus gives the designers a power position. Few designers are probably aware of this power position, and most likely they do not have any interest in misusing their position but try to develop the best information systems possible for the users. To the users the essential point is not the development process but the use situation. Therefore their quality requirements concern system use. Information systems can be designed to be flexible or to control the work situation. A flexible system allows the user to be in control of the conduct of work, while an unflexible system makes the computer control the work performance. However, a flexible system requires that the user have knowledge and skills to utilize it to its full potential. Such knowledge can be learned by training after the system is implemented or by participation during the development process. Developing systems which allow users to keep the control requires that designers understand in what kind of a work situation the system is to be used and supply the users with suitable knowledge to utilize the system.

The concept "user" in this paper refers to the end user of application systems. Thus IT personnel and managers become users of information systems as well. The CASE (Computer-Aided Software Engineering) tools are often used in systems development. These tools control designers' work to a large extent. Usually they cannot be changed to suit an individual designer's working habits. They are robust, designed for markets and not for individuals. Still the need of flexibility is pronounced because designers are rather individualistic in their working habits. Designers might have the knowledge to modify the tools to fit them better but they lack the power. In this respect, IT personnel share the experiences of many other end users.

Managers as end users have both general tools and some which are specially designed for them. Decision support systems, for example, are developed to support part of their work. The functionality and flexibility of such a system are important, but understanding the underlying criteria for its functioning is equally important for the quality of the decisions. Some systems with managerial applications are based on neural networks and expert knowledge. These are probably still more complicated, and managers, if they want to use them, normally have to accept the suggested solutions without a chance to check the reasoning. If this is the case then managerial knowledge turns into belief in computers and the work done by systems professionals.

CONCLUSIONS

Verity (1994) pointed out that IT seems to change many human activities such as how we record knowledge, communicate, learn, work, understand ourselves and the world. This paper discusses ethical issues in using IT as a tool in work. Let us see how the changes listed above are reflected in this setting.

How we record knowledge was Verity's first point above. The basic issue is the use of the concept "knowledge" in the IT context. A computer stores only data, i.e., bits and bytes. In the right context the data represent information, say a record in a database. The context makes the data understandable; it might represent the price for a portable computer. As I see it we can talk of knowledge first when a human being, say the salesperson of computers, interprets this information and is able to verify whether it is reasonable or not. Talking of "computer knowledge" reflects a change in our own understanding of the notion of mind. Such change has an influence on our ethical behavior. We trust the computer and do not use our own knowledge to interpret the information. There are many everyday examples of this kind of behavior. A response such as "The computer says..." is expected to be an acceptable explanation which needs no further authorization. The ethical dilemma arises from not taking the full responsibility of one's actions.

Our communication patterns have changed, especially after the introduction of digital networks and general access to E-mail. A lot of information is available through the Internet and WWW. This is an opportunity which offers easy access to what is needed, e.g., conference announcements. There is, however, a drawback; all people do not have access to these information sources. The result might be polarization. For business, networks give a chance to become a networked organization with easy communication and access to common data regardless of the location. In a way IT overcomes some of the problems of distance, and our understanding of the limitations of space might vanish. From an ethical point of view this constitutes a risk of neglecting cultural variety and requesting uniformity. The pros and cons of using E-mail were already discussed but let us summarize. We do not yet quite know "how to behave" on-line but have to learn a new ethical norm. There is the risk of control and monitoring, resulting in privacy concerns. There is the opportunity to overcome problems with time zones. Our thinking of time and space or at least our behavior certainly is influenced by IT.

The learning process itself might not change by the introduction of IT; that is something which happens in our minds, but the ways we learn and are taught can change radically. Mostly use of computers and instructional programs is positive, offering several individually adapted ways of learning. This is true in work context as well. However, there is a risk embedded if the personal contact with a teacher is replaced by a computer program only. For example, a computer program can easily find out that a participant in a training course does not understand a specific instruction. A human teacher can find out why the participant does not understand it. In a workplace learning is context dependent and based on earlier experience much more than in an ordinary school setting. Taking such things into account is not only an efficiency requirement but also an ethical requirement of showing respect to people.

Verity also states that IT might have changed our understanding of ourselves and the world. It was already mentioned that the world has become smaller; IT has faded out time and space limits. We easily communicate with people around the world. Changes in our understanding of ourselves are not directly work related ethical issues, but I still want to finish the paper by considering this pan-human and universal question. Human and computer abilities, for example, speed of calculation and capacity of memory, are compared to show the superiority of computers. People are regarded as rather irrational in their decision making. In cognitive studies the human brain is often compared to a computer. Evidently, computers do many things better than people do, and such comparisons between people and computers do not hurt as long as human dignity and uniqueness are not questioned. Else the comparisons might be destructive to our self-esteem. Are we safe from unjustified and unethical comparisons?

The computer has changed our thinking of time, space, mind, self and identity. It has radically changed our way of working. Most of us do agree that the computer will continue to have an influence on our thinking and working. The question is what kind of an influence we will allow it to be?

NOTES

1. The concept "Computer" is used to cover all IT as is common in everyday talk.
2. Gurbaxani, V. and Wang, S. "The Impact of Information Systems on Organizations and Markets." *Comm. of the ACM*, Vol. 34, No. 1, 1991, pp. 59–73.
3. Clement, A. and Wagner, I. "Ethics and Systems Design—The Politics of Social Responsibility," in J. Berleur and K. Brunnstein (eds.), *Ethics of Computing: Information Technology and Responsibility*, in press.
4. Piller, C. "Bosses with X-Ray Eyes: Your Employer May Be Using Computers to Keep Tabs on You." *MacWorld*, July 1993, pp. 118–123.

REFERENCES

Berleur, J.: Personal correspondence, 1993.

Bjerknes, G., Ehn, P. and Kyng, M. (eds): *Computers and Democracy: A Scandinavian Challenge*. Avebury, Aldershot, UK, 1987.

Briefs, U., Ciborra, C. and Schneider, L. (eds.): *System Design For, With, and By the User*. North-Holland, Amsterdam, 1983.

Clarke, R.: "Message on ISWORLD." *Information Systems World Network*, Nov. 26, 1994.

Clement, A.: Computing at Work: Empowering Action by 'Low-level Users.'" *Communications of the ACM*, Vol. 37, No. 1, January 1994, pp. 53–63.

———— and Wagner, I.: "Ethics and Systems Design—The Politics of Social Responsibility," in J. Berleur and K. Brunnstein (eds.): *Ethics of Computing: Information Technology and Responsibility*, in press.

Cohen, E.: "The Ethics of Global Out-Sourcing in Application Development." Working paper submitted to the Information Resource Management Association meeting, San Diego, California, May 22–25, 1994.

Communications of the ACM, ACM Code of Ethics and Professional Conduct, Communications of the ACM, Vol. 36, No. 2, Feb. 1993, pp. 99–107.

Culnan, M.: "How Did They Get My Name? An Exploratory Investigation of Consumer Attitudes Toward Secondary Information Use." *MIS Quarterly*, Vol. 17, No. 3, Sept. 1993, pp. 341-363.

Dahlblom, B. and Mathiassen, L.: "A Scandinavian View on the ACM's Code of Ethics." *Computers and Society*, June 1994, pp. 14–20.

Donaldson, T. and Dunfee, T.: "Toward a Unified Conception of Business Ethics: Integrative Social Contracts Theory." *Academy of Management Review*, Vol. 19, No. 2, 1994, pp. 252– 284.

Dunlop, C. and Kling, R. (eds.): *Computer and Controversy Value Conflicts and Social Choices*. Academic Press Inc., Harcourt Brace, Boston, 1991.

Eriksson, I.: "Simulation for User Training." Ph.D. thesis, Abo Akademi University, Department of Computer Science, Turku, Finland, 1990.

_____ and Nissen H. E.: "New IT Infrastructures: How Can They Contribute to Improved Management of Your Business?" Working paper, 1994.

Floyd, C.: "A Systematic Look at Prototyping," in Budde, R., Kuhlenkamp, K., Mathiassen, L. and Zullighoven, H. (eds.): *Approaches to Prototyping*. Springer, Berlin, 1984, pp. 1–18.

_____, Reisin, F. M. and Schmidt, G.: "STEPS to Software Development with Users," in Ghezzi, C. and McDermid, J.A. (eds.): ESEC '89: 2nd European Software Engineering Conference. *Lecture Notes in Computer Science*, Vol. 387, Springer, Berlin, pp. 48–64.

Frese, M.: "Human-Computer Interaction in the Office," in Cooper, C. L. and Robertson, I. T. (eds.): *International Review of Industrial and Organizational Psychology*. John Wiley & Sons Ltd., 1987, pp. 117–150.

Friis, S.: "User Controlled Information Systems Development—Problems and Possibilities Towards 'Local Design Shops.'" *Lund Studies in Information and Computer Science* No. 6, Lund University, Lund, Sweden, 1991.

Guroian, V.: *Incarnate Love: Essays in Orthodox Ethics*. University of Notre Dame Press, Notre Dame, Indiana, 1987.

Guynes, S.: "Privacy Considerations as We Enter the 'Information Highway'" Era. *Computers and Society*, Sept. 1994, pp. 16–19.

Harakas, S. S.: *Contemporary Moral Issues*. Light and Life Publishing Company, Minneapolis, Minnesota, 1982.

_____: *Toward Transfigured Life*. Light and Life Publishing Company, Minneapolis, Minnesota, 1983.

Heikkila, J., Hemminki, J. and Pihlaja, M.: "Diffusion of EUC-Technology: CASE Valmet Paper Machinery Inc." Jarvenpaa Works, Helsinki School of Economics, unpublished research report, 1993 (in Finnish).

Hjertberg, S. (F. Andreas): Personal correspondence, 1994.

Jarvinen, P.: "IT, Organization, Society, and World." Tampere University, Department of Computer Science, Report C-1991-3, Tampere, Finland, 1992 (in Finnish).

Loch, K. D., Conger, S. and Helft, B. L.: "An Exploration of Ethics and Information Technology Use: Issues, Perspectives, Consensus and Consistency." Working paper, Georgia State University, Atlanta, Georgia, Nov. 1993.

Martin, C. D. and Martin, D. H.: "The Computer Ethics Dilemma." *Proceedings of the National Conference on Computing and Values, Research Center for Computers and Society*, Southern Connecticut State University, New Haven, Connecticut, 1991.

_____ and _____: "Professional Codes of Conduct and Computer Ethics Education." *Social Science Computer Review*, Vol. 8, No. 1, 1990, pp. 96–108.

_____ and _____: "Thematic Analysis of the New ACM Code of Ethics and Professional Conduct." *Computers and Society*, Vol. 24, No. 2, June 1994, pp. 21–26.

Mason, R.: "Four Ethical Issues of the Information Age." *MIS Quarterly*, Vol. 10, No.1, March 1986, pp. 5–12.

Merriam-Webster's Collegiate Dictionary, Merriam-Webster, Springfield, Massachusetts, 1993.

Nurminen, M.: "People or Computers: Three ways of Looking at Information Systems." *Studentlitteratur*, Lund, Sweden, 1988.

O'Brien, J. A.: *Introduction to Information Systems*. Irwin, Burr Ridge, Illinois, 1994.

Reichmann, S.: "The Culture Without God." *Forsamlingsforbundets* forlag, 1993 (in Swedish).

Rivard, S. and Huff, S. L.: "An Empirical Study of Users as Application Developers." *Information and Management*, Vol. 8, No.2, 1985, pp. 89–102.

Rosing, H.: Articles in *Hufvudstadsbladet* (daily paper), Helsinki, July 11, 1994, and August 17, 1994 (in Swedish).

Ruohomaki, V.: "Simulation Games and Their Effects—The Workflow Game for Development of Administrative Work." Helsinki University of Technology, Industrial Economics and Industrial Psychology, Otaniemi Espoo, Licentiate thesis, Report No. 156, 1994 (in Finnish).

Saaren-Seppala, K.: "Wall Techniques." *Tietojenkasittelyliitto*, Pub. No. 68, Helsinki, 1983 (in Finnish).

Singh, S.: "Message on ISWORLD." *Information Systems World Network*, Nov. 25, 1994.

Verity J.: *Business Week*, ProfNet list, April 1994.

Yannaras, C.: *The Freedom of Morality*. St. Vladimir's Seminary Press, Crestwood, New York, 1984.

7. ETHICS AND IT: IS THE HUMAN FACTORS APPROACH AN ETHICAL WAY OF DESIGNING AND IMPLEMENTING INFORMATION TECHNOLOGY?

KAY L. BURNETT

The essence of technology is not technological.[1]
—Heidegger

The most profound technologies are those that disappear.
They weave themselves into the fabric of everyday life
until they are indistinguishable from it.[2]
—Mark Weiser, Xerox

Science Finds, Industry Applies, Man Conforms.
—Motto of the 1933 Chicago World's Fair

People Propose, Science Studies, Technology Conforms.[3]
—Recommended motto for the 21st century

Keywords: work, workplace, information technology, change, ethics, human factors, productivity, business

STATEMENT OF THE PROBLEM

The business environment is in a state of dramatic change. Information technology is inextricably intertwined with the business change process, sometimes to the benefit of the worker, sometimes to the detriment. The computer professional has influence over the direction taken by the information technology design, development and implementation. What are the responsibilities of an ethical computer professional, particularly as a designer and as a provider of information technology solutions to business?

This paper presents the dilemmas in the changing nature of work and the impact of technology on the work and the workplace. It explores the human concerns about the workplace and the role of technology in the workplace. It looks at the ethical concerns of the information technology professional and explores what ethics means in the profession. Finally, it asks if the human factors approach is an ethical approach to the implementation of computer technology in the workplace.

THE CHANGING NATURE OF THE WORK AND THE WORKPLACE

Every trade, professional and business journal one encounters cites examples signifying the changing nature of work and the work environment. In the scenarios portrayed, the business is changing, or the customer is changing, or the employee is changing. Little from the past business and work environment is cherished or deemed free from the need for change.

Depending on who you talk to, work is either high achievement or sheer drudgery. Peter Drucker defines work as an activity that has a result outside the worker. It may resemble play in many ways, but when the end product is determined by other than self, we call it work.

SHIFT FROM PHYSICAL WORK TO MENTAL WORK

In the past, work was primarily physical. Physical effort was the hallmark of physical labor. Often the work environment was dirty and the work dangerous. Workers were not skilled or skills that did exist were not refined or specialized. Skill development was often accompanied by great physical pain as the process was learned and refined.

Tools were introduced as labor-saving devices although they did not always save labor. Often new skills were required. In a craft production environment, workers became intimate with the tools and the physical properties of their work environment. The experiential method of acquiring knowledge produced high quality products but was time consuming and not constant.

Shoshana Zuboff makes a connection between the history of the work and the history of the worker's body. As automation of work processes becomes more common, the connection can no longer be made.

Business in the United States is shifting away from its traditional industrial base to an information-based service economy (Naisbitt, *Megatrends 2000*). A structural change is under way from historic "smokestack" industries (i.e., steel, coal and automobiles) to the activities of creating, processing and distributing information. From 1950 to 1983, information jobs grew from 17 percent to 65 percent of the labor market and growth was expected to continue. The service sector remained at 10-11 percent during the same time, and all other jobs grew slightly.[4]

CHANGE IN THE BUSINESS ORGANIZATION

The facts and observations are validated by the writings of best-selling business authors promoting and structuring change for the business reader. The main point of all the readings is similar; business must change the way it is working to survive in the 1990s and beyond. Reasons to change vary from external economic pressures to internal rethinking and realignment.

Business can respond to an uncertain business climate with either frenzy or with a determination to set basic standards of service and quality and to continuously innovate and improve. Tom Peters in *Thriving on Chaos* prescribes nothing short of revolution for the American business.

The certain uncertainty that will face most businesses in the 1990s is a result of several interacting factors:

- the merging and splitting of companies and industries forcing restructuring and realignments within enterprises
- the advent of the global economy in nearly every industry and its accompanying global financing, global producing, global marketing and global selling
- the unpredictable effects of using standard practices of the past in the current business environment
- the innovations made possible by technology in manufacturing, design, distribution, product definitions and process redesign
- the changing demographics and desires of the consumer

The old assumptions that have driven American business for decades, if they continue to be held, will drive business into decline. Two long-held assumptions are already devastating American business: 1) bigger is better and biggest is best, and 2) labor is to be increasingly and narrowly specialized or eliminated if possible (Peters 1987, p. 15).

THE GLOBAL ECONOMIC ENVIRONMENT AND LABOR

Companies and industries are no longer identified with individual nations as they were in the past, according to Robert Reich, Secretary of Labor in the

Clinton Administration. In his book, *The Work of Nations*, Reich describes the future as a global web in which an enterprise may be headquartered and financed in one global economic center, with research, design and production facilities spread over several strategic continents, marketing and distribution facilities on every continent, with lending coming from centers strong in financial services. This type of enterprise will compete with other similar enterprises based in other global centers of commerce.

Increasingly American workers will become part of the international labor market. American workers will either be valued in the global economy and be employed by the global enterprise or their jobs will become extinct in the national corporation or industry.

American jobs in the future will be aligned with three different competitive positions: 1) routine production services, 2) in-person services, and 3) symbolic analytic services. These three job categories cover three out of four of the jobs that exist today. Jobs that fall outside these categories include farmer, miner, natural resource extractor, government worker, and government financed worker, all of whom are sheltered from global competition (Reich 1991, pp. 171–184).

THE SYMBOLIC ANALYST

Reich's last job category, symbolic analytic services, will be filled by many American college-educated workers in the global economy. A symbolic analyst is one who can produce designs and concepts rather than products. The skills of a symbolic analyst are learned in the university and in cooperative, collaborative work groups. Refining four basic skills leads to the ability to conceptualize problems and solutions, or analyze symbolically; the skills are abstraction, systems thinking, experimentation and collaboration.

Abstraction, at the core of symbolic analysis, is discovering patterns and meanings in the world around us so that reality can be understood and manipulated. Through analogies, metaphors, formulae, models, and constructs, the symbolic analyst creates possibilities for reinterpreting and then rearranging the enormous body of available data into useable information. The best educational institutions are teaching students to get behind the data, to get data about the data (meta-data) and to be skeptical, curious and creative with it.

Systems thinking is about connectivity, about the relationships of events, their causes and consequences. Components understood in isolation cannot be seen as causal in a larger system. The symbolic analyst is continuously looking for the larger picture, the relationships and consequences of events. The symbolic analyst is taught to see how problems arise, how they are connected to other problems and what are the consequences of the solutions they define.

Experimentation is key to learning abstraction and system thinking. Trial and error repetitions increase the ability to see patterns and create order out of chaos. Self-guided exploration is the best means of developing the skills of the symbolic analyst. Given a set of tools, the symbolic analyst in training sets out to find his or her own way through testing of hypotheses and evaluating the results. Symbolic analysts accept responsibility for their own continuing learning.

Symbolic analysts typically work in teams where the capacity to collaborate, communicating abstract concepts and achieving consensus, energizes the creative process and the resulting outputs.

The symbolic analyst is the global worker of the future. By learning the skills of the symbolic analyst and practicing them in groups with other symbolic analysts, workers will be valued worldwide and across industries.

The impact of information technology on work and the workplace can be viewed from two related perspectives: productivity and social relationships. Are people creating more product or value for their company through the use of IT? How have workers' interactions with other workers, with customers, with suppliers and with the technology changed the way they value their role in the company and the way their role is valued by others in the company?

PRODUCTIVITY

The shifting nature of work has caused a shift in the definition of productivity, the measure of work. It has classically been defined as output per worker or per hour of work. This definition was reasonable when work was physical. When companies today talk about productivity, they are referring to a balance among all the factors of production that will give the greatest output for the smallest effort. (Drucker 1974, p. 68).

The Productivity Paradox describes the contradiction between predictions for improvements in business productivity due to large investments in personal computer technology in the workplace and the actual decline in the productivity of the American workforce over the last four decades. From 1950 to 1965 average business productivity grew at a rate of 3 percent, from 1965 to 1973 the rate was 2 percent, from 1973 to the present the rate is 1 percent (Peters 1987, p. 4). And technology projects continue to be sold to management based on the benefits of productivity.

Paul Attewell, City University of New York Graduate Center, compared three types of studies involving information technology and productivity gains. The findings of all three types of studies showed the same dire result. The studies were of entire economic sectors (e.g. services), inter-industry differences, and inter-firm differences within an industry.

Attewell's study focused specifically on productivity as the ratio of outputs (goods and services produced, total sales) to inputs (labor, capital, raw materials, energy). Information technology has brought benefits of new goods and services, increased quality of goods and services, and increased market share for some enterprises, but there has been no productivity increase. Economists have shown a direct link between standard of living and the overall level of productivity in an economy. The increased amount and quality of information that computers provide to an enterprise can bring an increase in the quality of life for the users and beneficiaries of the information but this does not necessarily translate into productivity gains.

Attewell presented possible explanations for the productivity paradox at three levels: the individual level, the group level and the firm or enterprise level.

At the individual level IT may be shifting some communication to slower channels by focusing on written communication versus spoken; people may spend time making unnecessary cosmetic changes to documents; and IT environments shift rapidly creating repeated skill obsolescence for workers—they are forced to focus on the technology and not on the work they are responsible for producing.

At the group level IT may lead to expanded requirements to review written information without presenting ways to improve decision making.

At the enterprise level IT has caused large investments in service activities for competitive advantage; IT may have led to increased profitability without increased productivity; IT may have been implemented to maintain parity with competition; or IT may have been the response to requests from outside the enterprise to deal with complex information processing.

CHANGE IN THE PRODUCTION METHODS

James Womack and the team at the Massachusetts Institute of Technology (MIT) International Motor Vehicle Program (IMVP) in the Center for Technology, Policy and Industrial Development write a detailed account of the changing manufacturing workplace environment in the book *The Machine That Changed the World* about the world's largest industry, automobile manufacturing. By tracing the evolution of the industry from pre–Ford craft production to Ford- and successor-style mass production to the lean production of the Japanese and now some American automobile manufacturers, the authors show how changes in philosophy translated into changes in process and procedure.

Mass production methods require increasingly narrow specialization of workers and have not resulted in the best products or a dependable workforce. Lean production methods use skilled workers and flexible tools to produce better quality products and more productive work teams of people (Womack *et al.* 1991, pp. 53–81).

In the early part of this century, Frederick W. Taylor introduced the ideas of efficiency and productivity of labor to the world of work. His goal was to standardize the effort of the human body as a more reliable mechanized component and to minimize the skill required to perform actions. His work, known as scientific management theory, was characterized by an obsession with the speed and volume of work produced.

Some current business literature suggests a trend away from the rational, logical approach of scientific management and toward a worker-centered approach in which value is placed on the human being who fills the role of worker.

In a presentation to the Participatory Design Conference in November 1992, Steve Miller observed that there is an increasing acceptance of social change within corporations. He described a shifting of power relations toward democratic participation in decisions about the workplace and the work process.

Miller suggests that the crisis in the worldwide post–Cold War economy has prompted the acceptance of new, post–Taylorist business ideologies that endorse worker involvement as a way for business owners to get the greatest benefit from employee creativity and energy. Miller sees the emerging field of participatory design as "a potential model and source of wisdom for transforming the way government relates to its citizens and the way the public sector relates to its clients."

BUSINESS PROCESS REDESIGN AND REENGINEERING

Information technology can enable organizations to rethink and redesign business processes that have become outmoded or fraught with delays and inefficiencies. But simple automation is not the answer. Simple computerization of an existing business process may provide a 10 percent performance improvement; reengineering a process may provide more than a 90 percent performance improvement (Hammer 1993, p. 84).

To reengineer for the greatest impact, companies need to ask, "How can we use technology to allow us to do things that we are not already doing?" rather than the question that is more often asked, "How can we use technology to streamline or enhance our current processes?" The ability to formulate answers to the first question comes from an ability to think inductively (from the trees to the forest) about the business rather than deductively (from the forest to the trees) as managers and executives are accustomed to thinking. The inductive approach will allow us to recognize the power of technical solutions and then seek the problems that might be solved (Hammer 1993, p. 85).

Dr. Michael Hammer and his team of reengineering experts recommend breaking the existing rules of the organizational environment to learn to think inductively. The power of the technology to disrupt the current practices also allows it to address the areas where the most competitive advantage can be gained (Hammer 1993, p. 91).

The challenge to gain increasing competitive advantage from the use of information technology requires constant monitoring of emerging technological developments and a continuous search for problems that it can solve. Technology exploitation is a critical factor for success and must become a core competency in a company (Hammer 1993, pp. 99–100).

Mark Tebbe of Lante Corporation in Chicago, in a presentation to the Chicago Chapter of ACM, cited studies showing the most effective use of information for competitive advantage will come from exploitation of a company's proprietary information, that information that is known only to the people within the organization.[5]

Hammer warns: "Companies need to beware of thinking that technology is the only essential element in reengineering" (Hammer 1993, p. 101). The real keys to success are the people who lead and perform the reengineering effort.

Dr. Michael Hammer, in his book *Reengineering the Corporation,* cites the following workplace changes that result from business process reengineering:

- Work units change from functional departments to process teams.
- Jobs change from simple tasks to multi-dimensional work.
- People's roles change from controlled to empowered.
- Job preparation changes from training to education.
- Focus of performance measures and compensation shifts from activity to results.
- Advancement criteria change from performance to ability.
- Values change from protective to productive.
- Managers change from supervisors to coaches.
- Organizational structures change from hierarchical to flat.
- Executives change from scorekeepers to leaders.

Most of these changes suggest the trend away from the rational and toward the humanistic, but reengineered processes will not automatically result in changes in human perception. The changes Hammer suggests require major cultural change in the organization beyond business process reengineering.

Changes in the work environment are not simply brought about by the deployment of technology but by the way that technology is used to rethink jobs and entire business processes. The human acceptance and use of technology will be the critical facilitator or bottleneck to effective use of information technology. As the technology becomes less expensive and easier to install, it can quickly and almost completely erode the experiential value a human brings to a job when the job requires skills that are totally unfamiliar. This latter circumstance can bring an established career to an abrupt halt (Keen 1991, p. 117).

A classic example of how the introduction of a new technology changed the culture of an entire group of people is found in the story of the introduction of the snowmobile to the Sami Laplander reindeer herders. Nine hundred years ago the Sami people covered a large area of Scandinavia. Up until the 1960s they were a semi-nomadic, somewhat collectivist, pastoral society living in harmony with nature herding reindeer on skis and selling the meat. Irreversible changes occurred when the snowmobile was introduced as a herding device. A Sami family with money could buy a snowmobile and herd many more reindeer than a family without a snowmobile. The collectivist culture changed to one of family loyalties. Physical activity and socialization declined. Men became the primary workers changing the egalitarian ethic between the genders to a hierarchical societal structure. Harmony with nature was replaced by a desire for dominance over nature and the reindeer became a cash crop for exploitation. Value was placed on mechanical skills to keep the snowmobiles running over the traditional skills of the elder herders. Respect for the elder diminished and the younger male became dominant in a way they had not been before.[6]

CHANGE IN THE VALUATION OF LABOR

Rather than minimize the role of labor, author Tom Peters encourages businesses to increase the value of labor by continuously retraining employees to do the complex tasks while at the same time automating the routine tasks. This value approach to labor gives workers increased flexibility and creativity on the job, gives responsibility for innovation to all levels of employees, gives employees a stake in the company's productivity and profitability through bonus and stock plans, and takes seriously the employee's concern for job security.

The outcome of an investment in labor is a partnership through which all company employees participate in an evolution based on commitment to the future success of the company. By investing in labor rather than minimizing it, companies can also create a stable source of well-paid consumers (Peters 1987, p. 28).

Dr. Hammer sees the reengineered business process as having the following characteristics:

- Several jobs are combined into one.
- Workers make decisions.
- The steps in the process are performed in a natural order.
- Processes have multiple versions.
- Work is performed where it makes the most sense.
- Checks and controls are reduced.
- Reconciliation is minimized.

- A case manager provides a single point of contact.
- Hybrid centralized and decentralized operations are prevalent.

It is not clear whether the reengineered business process minimizes or invests in labor.

Peter G.W. Keen writes a chapter entitled "Redeploying Human Capital" in his book *Shaping the Future*. He contrasts the care, commitment and long-term planning for machines, particularly heavy capital investments in computer equipment, to the lack of such enterprise planning for people. It is in this context he states "business needs to learn to treat people like machines" (Keen 1991, p. 117). Long-term planning for people should include an organizational plan that projects the job, career and skill changes at a detail level and projects training and education needs to match. For example, an employee who must effectively use a workstation to complete work in one of the fast-changing fields should spend 10 percent of his time or one-half day per week in training and education.

"Technology capital and business capital depend on human capital" (Keen 1991, p. 119). Keen defines human capital as the skill base, education, relevant experience and career development of the people in the organization. He specifies the following guidelines for the work environment in the 1990s:

- Continued education is essential for employees and employers alike.
- No one is unaffected by or able to ignore information technology.
- Change is the norm.
- Work is highly interdependent, involving business teams, cross-functional communication, and lateral moves into other areas.
- There are no standard career paths.

The literature about the changing nature of work and the workplace suggests that change is essential to continued existence in the marketplace; the most effective changes are the result of well thought out business process planning; and the jobs in the changed business environment can be engineered to be fulfilling if that goal is identified and followed from the outset.

SOCIAL RELATIONSHIPS IN THE WORKPLACE

The implementation of computers in work environments often impacts the social nature of work for the people whose jobs are to operate the computers. This can be isolating, frustrating, confusing, tension producing, and identity losing.

Shoshana Zuboff studies the effects on workers of the plant automation of the American Paper Company. Workers went through stages of acceptance and sometimes total rejection of the automated system that replaced their jobs on the mill floor.

Workers who were knowledgeable about the paper mill processes often had difficulty moving to the computer terminal to perform the same tasks they had performed on the mill floor. The knowledge that had accumulated in their bodies did not easily translate to a knowledge of what button to push on the computer. Kinesthetic knowledge is gained over time through experience and is said to be "in the body." The pushing of computer buttons and keys is an entirely different act from the labor of the mill. Many of the operators were not only fearful because of their lack of knowledge of the computer but were resentful that the automation had taken away their ability to use the knowledge they had acquired.

Zuboff found that office workers whose jobs had been moved entirely to computers felt tied to their computers and missed the social interaction with customers and other office workers that their jobs had previously required (Zuboff 1988, pp. 136–156). Workers described themselves as "tied to their work," some workers indeed being tied via telephone wires to their desks. The work of the people she interviewed had shifted to resemble the early, physical work, in which the body labors under stressful, possibly harmful conditions and there is no regard for the person in the body.

Computers influence fulfillment of basic human needs, opportunities for growth, and communications requirements when their use increases employees' sense of control and mastery of the environment and promotes higher performance standards (Vaske 1990).

To work at optimal performance, cognitive scientist Don Norman suggests we need an environment that provides the following things:

- a high intensity of interaction and feedback
- specific goals and established procedures
- motivation
- continual challenge
- direct engagement—working directly on the task
- tools that fit the user and the task and do not distract the user from the task
- lack of interruptions and distractions

Very few computer operations are run "dark" or without any human interface or intervention. An entire issue of *Communications of the ACM* (Association for Computing Machinery), January 1994, was devoted to social computing. Social computing is considered to be any type of computing in which software plays a part in the social relationship. This includes people communicating via E-mail, governments making policy for software and network development, people learning about and teaching about computers, groups developing software, databases of personal information kept about individuals, tasks in the workplace defined by the software, and life and death decisions influenced by software. These examples highlight the role that software can have in forming, maintaining, modifying and even ending social relationships among people. The design decisions that are made now about the ability of software technology to facilitate (or not facilitate) social relationships will have impacts far beyond what we can now imagine.

The impact on language and the impact of language on action are explored by Flores and Winograd in *Understanding Computers and Cognition*. They ask the questions "what can computers do?" "what can people do with computers?" and ultimately "what does it mean to be human?" They seek to "create a new understanding of how to design computer tools suited to human use and human purposes" (Winograd and Flores 1986, p. 8).

Flores and Winograd explore the role of tradition as a shared background of pre-understanding within which questions can be posed and answered. They propose, as have others, that the shared nature of tradition makes it invisible to those within it. The shared background prompts the way we interpret and take action. The book challenges the rationalistic or analytic tradition in which we interpret language, thought and action and seeks to reveal the hidden assumptions and biases behind the tradition to ask and answer new questions.

They examine hermeneutics and phenomenology as traditions outside the rationalistic tradition as a way to explore the relationship between the individual and the context in which he or she lives. Citing speech act theory as developed by Searle and Austin, they suggest that language and thought are based on social interactions and that we create our world through language.

Their broad goal is to "clarify the background of understanding in which the discourse about computers and technology takes place and to grasp its broader implications." Flores and Winograd see the rationalistic tradition as underlying both pure and applied science and used as a basis to define what it means to think and be intelligent. And although the community of scientists, including computer scientists, may acknowledge that there are phenomena that are not subject to rationalistic analysis, they still proceed in their day to day work as though everything were.

In looking behind the rationalistic tradition, Winograd and Flores cite Herbert Simon's book *Administrative Behavior* to show the gap between theory and practice. Simon cites the rational steps to decision making as 1) listing all alternative strategies, 2) determining consequences of each strategy, and 3) comparatively evaluating the sets of consequences. Simon explains objective rationality as idealization and describes the practical reality as falling short of the idealization in three ways: 1) future consequences can only be known in a fragmentary way, 2) imagination supplies the missing details of future consequences and so weightings are imprecise, and 3) the rational approach requires a choice among all possible alternatives when in reality only a few can ever be weighed.

Flores and Winograd call for a new understanding of human thought, language and action that is not limited by the scope and power of the rationalistic tradition so that we can design effective computer tools. They base their understanding on the role of interpretation in hermeneutics as described by Gadamer in *Truth and Method* (1975). The individual is continually involved in interpretation based on pre-understandings or prejudice that includes assumptions in the language of the individual. "The individual is changed through the use of language and the language changes through its use by individuals" (Winograd and Flores 1986, p. 29).

Winograd and Flores use interpretation to provide an understanding of what it means for someone or something to exist. They call into question the belief in mind-body dualism of the rationalistic tradition. They put into opposition Kant and Heidegger on the issue of discovering the reality of subjective consciousness: Kant's "scandal of philosophy and of human reason in general" that no sound argument has been produced to refute psychological idealism, and Heidegger's "scandal of philosophy that 'such proofs are expected and attempted again and again.'"

Heidegger's response grows out of the questions of phenomenology posed by his teacher Husserl and represents his argument that the separation of subject and object denies a fundamental unity of "being-in-the-world" and that it is impossible for the primary reality of the objective world and the primary reality of thoughts and feelings to exist one without the other. Heidegger would say that existence is interpretation and interpretation is existence.

Flores and Winograd define the following points of Heidegger as relevant to the discussion of designing computer tools for human use:

1. Our implicit beliefs and assumptions cannot all be made explicit.
2. Practical understanding is more fundamental than detached theoretical understanding.
3. We do not relate to things primarily through having representations of them.
4. Meaning is fundamentally social and cannot be reduced to the meaning-giving activity of individual subjects.

They expound on Heidegger's idea of "thrownness" which is "the condition of understanding in which our actions find some resonance or effectiveness in the world" that he developed from his deep awareness of everyday life. An example to illustrate "thrownness" puts the reader in the role of meeting chairperson in a group whose mission is to decide whether to bring a new computer system into the organization. The chairperson is charged with keeping the meeting moving in a productive direction, toward a decision, by controlling the flow of the individual speakers and actors who have strong and diverse opinions on the decision. Flores and Winograd observe the following about the situation. As chairperson:

* You cannot avoid acting.
* You cannot step back and reflect on your actions.
* The effects of action cannot be predicted.
* You do not have a stable representation of the situation.
* Every representation is an interpretation.
* Language is action.

These are the fundamental concepts for the design of computer tools. Following Heidegger, a tool is irrelevant (does not exist) to an individual until such a time as the situation breaks down and then the tool becomes "present-to-hand." For example, to a person engaged in driving a nail, the hammer is taken for granted and not seen as distinct from the background of what the person has "ready-to-hand." The hammer exists for this person in the same awareness or lack of awareness as do the tendons in the hammerer's arm. The awareness of the existence of the hammer comes to mind only if it breaks or slips or makes itself visible by falling out of the state of "ready-to-hand."

Applying the principles of "ready-to-hand" and breaking down to computers, we begin to see the background for Flores and Winograd's design strategy for computers and computer systems that facilitate human work and interaction. The transparency that is sought in the design of computer systems so as to make them "ready-to-hand" is accomplished by a thoughtful coupling of the computer user and the action of the computer in a common and relevant domain of understanding and action (e.g., writing a paper, calculating expenses, sending and receiving mail messages and Norman's scheduling life's activities).

Flores has designed and developed a computer system for social interaction among workers called the Coordinator based on much of the above theory.

HUMAN CONCERNS IN THE WORKPLACE

Literature covers several areas of human concern in the use of computer systems: safety, usability and aesthetics. Freidman and Kahn add another; does the computer design promote human responsibility for the consequences of computer-mediated action? Two design considerations play into this concern: to design systems that do not diminish human agency and to design systems that do not attempt to replace human attributes such as intentions, desires, volition, consciousness and free will. The idea that the human being has dignity and demands respect over and above machine technology is based on our Western thought as articulated by philosophers from Plato and Aristotle to Jefferson. Jefferson writes in the Declaration of Independence that we have unalienable rights that are God-given and part of our human nature.

There is a need to retain dignity in the situation of work and in the workplace. Dignity depends on individuals having a sense that they are in an environment where they are respected, both physically and non-physically. The needs include safety, social interaction, respect for personal privacy, the ability to use certain human traits and characteristics and the ability to use tools.

The large number of computers deployed in the workplace raises issues of health and safety in the use of the computer devices, monitoring of workers via the technology and the design of systems and work environments that isolate and tax the individual beyond acceptable limits. Another issue of large scale computerization is privacy. Information collected and stored about individuals by governments and private companies may be inaccurate or used without the knowledge of the individual.

DESKILLING AND RESKILLING OF LABOR

The paper mill scenario addresses both the deskilling and reskilling effects of the introduction of technology in the workplace. The workers' inability to use the knowledge they had gained through experience is an example of the deskilling that occurs when technology replaces manual processes. Reskilling is the ability to acquire a new skill or skills in response to a manual process being eliminated. Reskilling is not simply learning to operate a computer terminal but learning to think through a process and make the appropriate responses in the abstract environment of the computer control room.

TOOLS AND TECHNOLOGY

Zuboff says technology "represents intelligence systematically applied to the problem of the body." To workers who use a tool or tools in their work on an ongoing and consistent basis, the tool becomes an extension of their body. They see the tool as a part of their body. The tool becomes invisible and they are merely doing the task. As soon as the workers are aware of the presence of the tool, they are no longer doing the task; they are experiencing the presence of the tool and the task is secondary.

> What is the metaphor for the computer of the future? The intelligent agent? The television (multimedia)? The 3-D graphics world (virtual reality)? The Star Trek ubiquitous voice computer? The GUI desktop, honed and refined? The machine that magically grants our wishes? The right answer is "*none of the above*," because all of these concepts share a basic flaw—they make the computer visible.[7]

Humans have used tools for centuries. Tools are thought to enhance the work of humans, but in many cases the human becomes enslaved by tools. In *Tools for Conviviality*, Ivan Illich cites this as the great failure of the last century. He says it is time to discard the hypothesis on which the failed experiment was based: that tools (machines) can replace slaves. He calls for a "convivial reconstruction" of the society to "enlarge the contribution of autonomous individuals and primary groups to the total effectiveness of a new system of production designed to satisfy human needs which it also determines." He cites an inverse relationship between growth in the power of machines and decline in human power to that of technology consumer.

Illich uses the word convivial to oppose industrial productivity. It signifies the interrelationships and interactions among people and contrasts the conditioned response of man-made environments. It is "the individual freedom realized in interdependence and, as such, an intrinsic ethical value." Illich calls for a substitution of convivial tools for industrial tools. Only through a "new consciousness about the nature of tools" can we attain a "majority action for their control."

Neil Postman in *Technopoly* describes a totalitarian state in which there is "submission of all forms of cultural life to the sovereignty of technique and technology." He portrays human evolution as a continuum along which we have moved from tool use, where tools were integrated into culture leaving culture unchanged, to technocracy, where tools played a central role in the thought world of culture and bid to become the culture, to technopoly, where the traditional world view becomes invisible and therefore irrelevant through technological innovation.

Yet in terms of individual human action, a tool must be invisible to be effective. The moment the user of the tool is brought to attend to the tool itself, it ceases to be an effective tool. The human using a hammer does not feel the grip on the hammer at every moment but sees it as an extension of his hand that is forcing the nail into the hard surface. The computer is another tool, a very versatile tool that is available for human use and ideally is invisible as a tool but extends the human's ability to complete his task.

To Don Norman, author of *Things That Make Us Smart*, the ideal computer would be invisible. He would not think of himself using a computer but using a calendar, for example. The tool would automatically communicate with other tools (computerized calendars) in his life and synchronize the entries. It would "know" about other events and provide a warning when schedules conflicted. It would interact with other information stores such as address book, expense account, notepad, etc. And mainly, it would be a tool for the purpose at hand, scheduling life's activities, not a computer.

One area of agreement among the optimists and pessimists on computer impact is the common anthropological finding that technology changes forever the environment into which it is placed and used. The language and the understanding of terms are altered by having a relationship to the technology. It is through language that the concepts and understandings of the technology spread throughout a culture. Our understanding of words and their meaning is altered by the introduction of technology.

Heidegger (1955) says that the essence of man (human) is in his (her) Being and that language puts us in touch with our Being. Language is essential to human effectiveness because if we don't communicate our knowledge, we may be said to have no knowledge. It is, therefore, the responsibility of humans to put into language, to articulate the knowledge that we have.

CONCERNS OF INFORMATION TECHNOLOGY (COMPUTER) PROFESSIONAL

Helen Nissenbaum uses this definition of the computer professional: "the loose community of people who dedicate a significant proportion of their time and energy to building computer and computerized systems, and to those engaged in the science, engineering, design, and documentation of computing."[8] I would add a distinction between those who have decision making authority for selecting, designing, creating, and deploying information technology in the workplace and those who use or operate computer equipment. I would include among the decision-makers the functional areas of analysts, programmers, project managers, strategists, implementors, integrators and exclude machine operators, data entry and word processing personnel.

An apt analogy has been drawn between the computer professional and the architect: both design and build structures that shape the environment in which we live. Adler and Winograd relate computer usability experts (a subset of computer professionals who work at the point of interaction between the human and the computer) to architects "with one foot in the technical engineering domain and one in the human social domain."[9] Architects readily acknowledge that their clients know about the human activities that the building is intended to support. An emerging view of the computer professional encompasses this same willingness to acknowledge the user of the computer system as a partner in the design of the system. The dynamics of this relationship are explored extensively in an emerging field of participatory design, part of the human factors domain.[10]

The computer professionals need to know more than technical lingo and jargon. They need to know about the human user of their creations. They need to be informed not only about the technology, in itself more than a full time job for any responsible, curious professional, but also about human nature and human reactions to various stimuli. If individual computer professionals do not know about human nature themselves, they should know the significance of having someone on the team that can identify the human concerns in the technology design.

It is possible to design computer technology to address issues of productivity. Information technology professionals "must change how [they] design, implement and adopt technologies, taking into account the larger social and economic systems in which they operate."[11] Maria G. Wadlow proposes "Design as a Way of Life," rather than a set of guidelines to be followed during the design process.[12] She suggests using interface design principles when constructing a meeting agenda or when writing an E-mail. In every interaction with others we should consider our audience, understand or clarify their needs, and tailor our messages to them to meet their needs. This approach would not only give us practice in the use of our skills but would encourage others to respond to us in an equally thoughtful and clear manner.

Traditionally computer science students have not been educated to look for the social relevance of the computer technology they study. They are taught, and this is particularly true on-the-job, to consider the time, cost, and technical specifics of technology and not the concerns of the human user. To recognize the human in the equation is to recognize a person with consciousness and spirit, to recognize the dignity of the human being.

Batya Freidman and Peter H. Kahn, Jr., link the social and the technical in an article entitled "Educating Computer Scientists" in *Communications of the ACM*. They suggest that computer technologies are a medium for social exchange and that system design, although technically based, shapes social interaction on a larger scale.

As we have seen before, technology cannot be separated from the social network in which it exists. Freidman and Kahn present three approaches used in education to link technical and social concerns in the student learner. Standalone courses on social and ethical topics in computer science curricula guarantee time in the curriculum to focus on these issues; however, the separation from the technical topics may suggest that a separation exists in the world as well. A practicum on human-computer interaction such as the one developed by Hartfield and Winograd at Stanford University links the student with industry mentors to analyze, design and prototype a real world project in which the technical and social aspects of the project are all at stake. Courses that integrate the social concerns with the technical content in the standard technical courses put the issues in context as they arise from the student's own work.

A professional association, Computer Professionals for Social Responsibility (CPSR), puts forth a strong call to computer professionals to be aware of the impact of computer technology on society. It advocates to influence decisions regarding the design, development and use of computer technology because the decisions have far-reaching consequences and reflect basic values and priorities. Members of CPSR believe that computer technology should make life more enjoyable, productive and secure for humans. By providing information to the public and to policy makers about the power, the promise and the limitations of computer technology, they encourage public discussion of and public responsibility for decisions involving the use of computers in systems that are critical to society, i.e, health care identifier not Social Security number, encryption of E-mail by the government. The work of the organization helps to dispel popular myths about the infallibility of computer systems and challenges the assumption that technology alone can solve political and social problems. The organization encourages a critical examination of the social and technical issues within the computer profession, nationally and internationally and advocates the use of computer technology to improve the quality of life.

Computer professionals have far-reaching impact with their decision making in the areas of risk assessment and reliability of computing technology. When technology is deified, the assessment of risk is not realistically portrayed to the potential users or others affected by the technology (i.e., Star Wars defense systems, simulation as sole testing strategies, software reliance in life-critical systems).

WHAT IS ETHICS IN INFORMATION TECHNOLOGY?

Victor Ferkiss in an article entitled "Technology and the Future: Ethical Problems of the Decades Ahead" puts forth four principles about the relationship between technology and ethics:

1. Technology does not exist in isolation from society or other aspects of our culture. Technology exists within a technological system. So when we speak of the ethical implications of computers we must place them in their technological system and talk about the information society that exists because of and in support of computers.
2. Technologies and technological systems exist in social contexts.
3. The technologies and technological systems modify the social contexts in which they exist.
4. As the number of computers increases, the magnitude of their impact on society increases.

Ferkiss likens the desire for control of information to the desire to control land in earlier Europe and America. As we have seen major social conflicts over the control of land, we will see conflict over the control of information.

In the ACM issue on social computing, a group of researchers (Collins, Miller, Speilman and Wherry) examines the ethical issues in software construction and use. Their ethical theory is that "the software process, from creation to purchase to use to effect, is a social process involving human participants who want and need different goods from the process." John Rawls, in *A Theory of Justice*, defines fairness and suggests an application of the ideas to computing. The researchers conclude that "like other professionals, computer scientists are expected to make reasonable judgments, even when their own self-interests are involved in the issues decided."

Three professional societies in the computer field have published codes of ethics, standards and professional behavior: Association for Computing Machinery (ACM), Institute of Electrical and Electronic Engineers (IEEE), and Data Processing Managers Association (DPMA). The three codes were compared and contrasted by C. Dianne Martin and David H. Martin in a 1990 issue of *Computers and Society*. Several common themes represent the core of ethical behavior for computer professionals: 1) a regard for the dignity and worth of other people, 2) a belief in personal integrity and honesty, 3) responsibility for work undertaken, 4) confidentiality of information, 5) regard for public safety, health and welfare, 6) participation in professional societies to improve the standards of the profession, and 7) the notion that public knowledge and access to technology are equivalent to social power. All the codes emphasize the relationships and interactions of the computer professional with people and not relationships and interactions with machines. This, say the Martins, properly puts the focus of ethical behavior on ethical dealings with people and not upon the technology itself.

HUMAN FACTORS IN INFORMATION TECHNOLOGY

Research in human-computer interaction takes place on a macro-level and a micro-level. At the micro-level, one-user-in-front-of-one-machine research has been done on command language, menu selection, direct manipulation, icon design, screen design, help systems and input devices. At the macro-level research focuses on the effect of computers on human actions at the individual, organizational and societal levels (Perrolle 1987).

Human factors, as a discipline, grew out of problems encountered designing equipment operable by human beings during World War II and studies the human aspects of all designed devices. Sensory-motor problems such as placement of flight controls and displays were the focus of early work.

Problems of humans operating computers naturally extended the concerns of early human factors practitioners and added new problems of cognition, communication and interaction with the computer forcing a growth in the focus of the human factors domain. Human-computer interaction studies both the mechanistic side of the designed device (the computer) and the human side.

A specialized human-computer interaction discipline sprang up in response to several factors in computer use: lower than anticipated productivity achievement, dramatically decreasing cost of purchasing a personal computer, and consequently the rapid increase in proliferation of computers. In March of 1982 the first conference to consider human-computer interaction issues was held with sponsorship from ACM. The conference organizers believed that the bottleneck to increasing productivity through the use of computers concerned human factors or the usability of the computer and not the technology itself. Participation and attendance at the conference greatly exceeded expectations, and the next year the Special Interest Group on Computer Human Interaction (SIGCHI) of ACM was formed. SIGCHI is currently the fastest growing SIG of ACM with more than 4600 members.

A working definition of the discipline used by the Curriculum Development Group of the SIGCHI is the following: "Human-computer interaction is a discipline concerned with the design, evaluation, and implementation of interactive computing systems for human use and with the study of major phenomena surrounding them."[13]

Human factors in computer systems goes by several names in the literature including software human factors, computer-human interaction, ergonomics, user- or human-centered design, socio-technical systems design, and usability. In the introduction to *Resources in Human-Computer Interaction*, Wendy E. Mackay declares the discipline to be multi-disciplinary rather than inter-disciplinary. The distinction, she insists, reflects the strength of the many different viewpoints that are encompassed by the discipline, all sharing the goal of identifying and supporting the needs of users (Mackay 1993, p. xi). Human-computer interaction is at the intersection of the disciplines of computer science, psychology, sociology, anthropology, industrial design, and possibly linguistics.

The Special Interest Group on Computer Human Interaction sponsors conferences and workshops in related fields such as Computer-Supported Cooperative Work (CSCW), Document Processing (DOCPROC), Hypertext, and User Interface Software Technology (UIST).

A practitioner of human factors in computers, Phyllis Reisner, attempts to bring the study of human factors from an experimental science to a predictive one[14] by designing instruments and techniques to test a user interface through formal grammar that can be manipulated and adjusted well in advance of an implementation in software.[15]

Human-computer interaction is seen by practitioners and academics alike as a part of computer science. In Newell, Perlis, and Simon's (1967) classic definition of computer science as "the study of computers and the major phenomena that surround them," the people using computers are clearly one of the major phenomena. More recently Denning, et al. (1988), in an ACM report define computer science as "the systematic study of algorithmic processes that describe and transform information: their theory, analysis, design, efficiency, implementation, and application." The algorithmic processes interact with other computers as well as with human users of computers. It is not unusual for more than half the code of an application to be devoted to the interface with the human user. Without a regard for the human component of systems, developers are prone to fall into the classic pitfall of designing outside the context of the problem.

CONCERNS OF HUMAN FACTORS/ HUMAN COMPUTER INTERACTION

The concerns of the field of human-computer interaction are:

* joint performance of tasks by humans and machines
* the structure of communication between human and machine
* human capabilities to use machines (including the learnability of interfaces)
* algorithms and programming of the interface itself
* engineering concerns that arise in designing and building interfaces
* the process of specification, design and implementation of interfaces
* design trade-offs[16]

In Europe a new school of human-centered design seeks to make up for the tradition of technology-centered design. This school of thought attempts to "understand the domain of work or play in which the user is acting," and design computers to facilitate action there. The three assumptions on which human-centered design operate are: 1) the result of the design is a satisfied user, 2) the process of design is a collaboration between designers and customers and it produces specifications as a by-product of the collaboration, and 3) the customer is not assumed to be satisfied until he or she declares satisfaction.[17]

Mumford and Weir present a methodology for socio-technical systems design that captures the human and technical requirements of work systems. The ETHICS (Effective Technical and Human Implementation of Computer Systems) method sets social and technical objectives that lead to the design of a whole system in which alternatives are matched, prioritized and selected based on their ability to meet both sets of objectives (Mumford and Weir 1979, pp. 2–29).

Don Norman, author of a series of books on design, describes human-centered design as one which leaves to the humans the things that they are good at—empathizing, perceiving, understanding the nature of a problem, inventing solutions, listening for concerns, fulfilling commitments, satisfying others, serving interests—and lets the machine do what the humans are not good at such as performing repetitive actions without error, searching large data sets or performing movements that are beyond the capability of the human body.

IS THE HUMAN FACTORS APPROACH AN ETHICAL WAY OF IMPLEMENTING INFORMATION TECHNOLOGY?

Human factors and human-computer interaction cannot be said to be ethical in and of themselves. The fact that some of the distinct disciplines that are included in the multi-disciplinary human-computer interaction bring an awareness of the questions of what it means to think and what it means to be human to the question of technology use suggests that they deal with the concerns of ethics.

Using the four principles of Victor Ferkiss on the relationship of technology and ethics, human-computer interaction on the micro-level does not really address the concerns of technology and technological systems in a social context, changing that context and proliferating throughout the society. The macro-level of human-computer interaction studies is positioned to deal with the issues of Ferkiss.

On mapping the concerns of human-computer interaction to the common themes in the professional societies' codes of ethics, a match exists with the first shared theme regarding the dignity and worth of people. The premise that computer professionals working in human factors regard the human user of the computer system as a high priority in the design and implementation of the system gives credence to the view that there is an ethical cast to the work of the human-computer interaction practitioners. The other shared themes in the codes of ethics point to the individual acts of the computer professionals, not to the products of their actions.

CONCLUSIONS

In conclusion, human factors shares one of the characteristics of an ethical computer professional. To draw a larger generalization at this point would not be useful. The fact that the one area where human factors does appear to be ethical deals with the human side of the human-computer equation is a start in recognizing the need to look beyond the technical implications of a computer systems' design or implementation to the non-technical, perhaps non-rationalistic consequences of our technological actions. The emphasis in both the human factors approach to computer systems and in the professional society codes of ethics is on the relationships and interactions of the computer professional with people and not on relationships and interactions with machines.

Therefore, for computer professionals to be ethically responsible in their practice of computer system design, development and implementation, they must consider the implications of their work on humans and design to maintain human dignity. It follows that the institutions of education that educate and train the computer professional have an ethical responsibility to emphasize the human as an equal consideration in technical courses. More emphasis should be placed on human-computer interaction in training courses in business, and executive decision makers should be aware of the advantages to productivity and cost of using HCI techniques.

NOTES

1. Martin Heidegger, "The Question Concerning Technology," page 4.

2. Mark Weiser, "Some Computer Science Issues in Ubiquitous Computing," *Communications of the ACM*, 36, 7, July 1993.

3. Donald Norman, epigraph to his book, *Things That Make Us Smart*.

4. Montana, Patrick J. and Bruce H. Charnov, *Management*, "Chapter 25: Changing Trends in Management," Hauppauge, NY: Barron's Educational Series, 1987/93.

5. Mark Tebbe, President, Lante Corporation in a speech entitled "Enabling Your Organization Through Technology" delivered to Chicago Chapter of ACM, January 1994.

6. David Muga, "The Effect of Technology on an Indigenous People: The Case of the Norwegian Sami," *The Journal of Ethnic Studies*, 14:4, Winter 1987.

7. Mark Weiser, "The World Is Not a Desktop," *Interactions*, 1, 1, January 1994.

8. Helen Nissenbaum, "Computing and Accountability," *Communications of the ACM*, 37, 1, January 1994.

9. Adler, P. S. and T. A. Winograd, *Usability: Turning Technologies into Tools*. New York: Oxford University Press, 1992.

10. Schuler, Douglas and Aki Namioka, eds. *Participatory Design: Principles and Practices*. Hillsdale NJ: Lawrence Erlbaum, 1993.

11. David Constant, "The Productivity Paradox: Why Hasn't Information Technology Fulfilled Its Promise," *SIGCHI Bulletin*, 24, 4, October 1993.

12. Maria G. Wadlow, "Visual Interaction Design: Design as a Way of Life," *SIGCHI Bulletin*, 26, 1, January 1994.

13. ACM Special Interest Group on Computer-Human Interaction Curriculum Development Group, *ACM SIGCHI Curricula for Human-Computer Interaction*, New York: Association for Computing Machinery, 1992.

14. Phyllis Reisner in response to L. Branscomb's (IBM chief scientist) 1981 quote, "Human factors is still an experimental science, not a predictive one."

15. Phyllis Reisner, "Formal Grammar as a Tool for Analyzing Ease of Use: Some Fundamental Concepts," in John C. Thomas and Michael L. Schneider, *Human Factors in Computing Systems*, Norwood NJ: Ablex, 1984.

16. ACM Special Interest Group on Computer-Human Interaction Curriculum Development Group, *ACM SIGCHI Curricula for Human-Computer Interaction*, New York: Association for Computing Machinery, 1992, p. 7.

17. Peter Denning and Pamela Dargan, "The Discipline of Software Architecture," *Interactions*, 1, 1, January 1994, p. 55.

READINGS ON WORK, INFORMATION TECHNOLOGY IN THE WORKPLACE, THE IT PROFESSIONAL

Books

Adler, Paul S. and Terry A. Winograd. *Usability: Turning Technologies into Tools*. New York: Oxford University Press, 1992.

Borgmann, Albert. *Technology and the Character of Contemporary Life, a Philosophical Inquiry*. Chicago: University of Chicago Press, 1984.

Davenport, Thomas H. *Process Innovation: Reengineering Work Through Information Technology*, Boston: Harvard Business School, 1993.

Dreyfus, Hubert L. and Stuart E. Dreyfus. *Mind Over Machine: The Power of Human Intuition and Expertise in the Era of the Computer*. New York: The Free Press, 1986.

Drucker, Peter. *Management: Tasks, Responsibilities, Practices*. New York: Harper & Row, 1974.

_____. *The New Realities, in Government and Politics/in Economics and Business/in Society and World View*. New York: Harper & Row, 1989.

_____. *Post Capitalist Society.* New York: Harper Business, 1993.

Feigenbaum, Edward, Pamela McCorduck and H. Penny Nii. *The Rise of the Expert Company, How Visionary Companies Are Using Artificial Intelligence to Achieve Higher Productivity and Profits.* New York: Vintage, 1989.

Hammer, Michael and James Champy. *Reengineering the Corporation: A Manifesto for Business Revolution.* New York: Harper Business, 1993.

Heckel, Paul. *The Elements of Friendly Software Design: The New Edition.* San Francisco: Sybex, 1991.

Heidegger, Martin. *The Question Concerning Technology and Other Essays.* New York: Harper & Row, 1977 (translated by William Lovitt).

Illich, Ivan. *Tools for Conviviality.* New York: Harper & Row, 1973.

Keen, Peter G.W., *Competing in Time, Using Telecommunications for Competitive Advantage.* Cambridge MA: Ballinger, 1988.

_____. *Shaping the Future.* Cambridge MA: Harvard Business School Press, 1991.

Kidder, Tracy. *The Soul of a New Machine.* Boston: Little, Brown, 1981.

Mumford, Enid and Mary Weir. *Computer Systems in Work Design — The ETHICS Method: Effective Technical and Human Implementation of Computer Systems.* New York: John Wiley and Sons, 1979.

Norman, Donald A. *The Design of Everyday Things.* New York: Doubleday, 1988.

_____. *Things That Make Us Smart: Defending Human Attributes in the Age of the Machine.* Reading MA: Addison-Wesley, 1993.

_____. *Turn Signals Are the Facial Expressions of Automobiles.* Reading MA: Addison-Wesley, 1992.

Ohmae, Kenichi. *The Borderless World, Power and Strategy in the Interlinked Economy.* New York: HarperCollins, 1990.

Perrolle, Judith A. *Computers and Social Change: Information, Property and Power.* Belmont CA: Wadsworth Publishing, 1987.

Peters, Tom. *Thriving on Chaos: Handbook for a Management Revolution.* New York: Harper & Row, 1987.

Postman, Neil. *Technopoly, the Surrender of Culture to Technology.* New York: Alfred A. Knopf, 1992.

Ramsey, H. Rudy, et al. *A Critically Annotated Bibliography of the Literature of Human Factors in Computer Systems.* Englewood CO: Science Applications, 1978.

Reich, Robert B. *The Work of Nations.* New York: Alfred A. Knopf, 1991.

Rubinstein, Richard and Harry Hersh. *The Human Factor: Designing Computer Systems for People.* Burlington MA: Digital Press, 1984.

Schank, Roger C. *Connoisseur's Guide to the Mind, How We Think, How We Learn & What It Means to Be Intelligent.* New York: Summit, 1991.

_____. *Tell Me a Story, a New Look at Real and Artificial Memory.* New York: Scribner's, 1990.

Schön, Donald A. *The Reflective Practitioner: How Professionals Think in Action.* New York: Basic Books, 1983.

Schrage, Michael. *Shared Minds, the New Technologies of Collaboration.* New York: Random House, 1990.

Schuler, Douglas and Aki Namioka, eds. *Participatory Design: Principles and Practices.* Hillsdale NJ: Lawrence Erlbaum, 1993.

Senge, Peter. *The Fifth Discipline, the Art and Practice of the Learning Organization.* New York: Doubleday, 1990.

Shneiderman, Ben. *Designing the User Interface: Strategies for Effective Human-Computer Interaction, Second Edition.* Reading MA: Addison-Wesley, 1992.

Taylor, Frederick. *The Principles of Scientific Management.* New York: Norton and Co., 1967.

Thomas, John C. and Michael L. Schneider, eds. *Human Factors in Computer Systems.* Norwood NJ: Ablex, 1984.

Thurow, Lester. *Head to Head, the Coming Economic Battle Among Japan, Europe, and America.* New York: William Morrow and Company, 1992.

Tocqueville, Alexis de. *Democracy in America.* New York: F. Brown, 1862.

Turkle, Sherry. *The Second Self, Computers and the Human Spirit.* New York: Simon & Schuster, 1984.

Vaske, Jerry J. and Charles E. Grantham. *Socializing the Human-Computer Environment.* Norwood NJ: Ablex, 1990.

Weizenbaum, Joseph. *Computer Power and Human Reason, from Judgment to Calculation.* New York: W.H. Freeman, 1976.

Winograd, Terry and Fernando Flores. *Understanding Computers and Cognition: A New Foundation for Design.* Norwood NJ: Ablex, 1986.

Womack, James P., Daniel Jones and Daniel Ross. *The Machine That Changed the World.* New York: Harper Perennial, 1991.

Zuboff, Shoshana. *In the Age of the Smart Machine: The Future of Work and Power.* New York: Basic Books, 1988.

Journals, Newsletters, Articles, Conference Proceedings

Anderson, Ronald E., Deborah G. Johnson, Donald Gotterbarn and Judith Perrolle. "Using the New ACM Code of Ethics in Decision Making." *Communication of the ACM.* 36, 2 (February 1993).

Baudersfeld, Penny, John Bennet and Gene Lynch, eds. *CHI '92, Striking a Balance: Conference Proceedings from ACM Conference on Human Factors in Computing Systems,* May 3–7, 1992, Monterey CA.

Brynjolfsson, Erik and Lorin Hitt. "Is Information Systems Spending Productive? New Evidence and New Results." Cambridge MA: MIT Sloan School Working Paper #3571-93, June 7, 1993.

Burlton, Roger and P.Eng. "Business Process Re-Engineering: Using IT to Renew the Business." *Software World Digest* handouts.

Communications of the ACM, 37, 1 (January 1994). Special issue on Social Computing.

Davenport, Thomas H. and James E. Short. "The New Industrial Engineering: Information Technology and Business Process Redesign." *Sloan Management Review,* Summer 1990.

Davis, James I., ed. "CPU Visits the Technology and Employment Conference at MIT." *CPU:* Working in the Computer Industry (on line newsletter for Computer Professionals for Social Responsibility [CPSR]), February 1, 1994.

Denning, Peter J. "Work Is a Closed-Loop Process." *American Scientist* (July-August 1992).

Englebart, Douglas. "A Conceptual Framework for the Augmentation of Man's Intellect" (1963). *Computer Supported Cooperative Work: A Book of Readings.* Ed., Irene Greif. San Mateo CA: Morgan Kaufmann, 1988.

_____. "Toward High-Performance Knowledge Workers" (1982). *Computer Supported Cooperative Work: A Book of Readings.* Ed., Irene Greif. San Mateo CA: Morgan Kaufmann, 1988.

Ferkiss, Victor. "Technology and the Future: Ethical Problems of the Decades Ahead." New Ethics for the Computer Age? (conference): Washington, DC, May 19, 1986.

Flynn, S. "Running IS Like a Business." GartnerGroup Research Note, Key Issues, K-980-1017, October 18, 1993.

Interactions: New Visions of Human-Computer Interaction. 1, 1 (January 1994).

Mantei, Marilyn M. and Toby J. Teorey. "Cost/Benefit Analysis for Incorporating Human Factors in the Software Lifecycle." *Communications of the ACM,* 31, 4 (April 1988).

Martin, C. Dianne and David H. Martin. "Professional Codes of Conduct and Computer Ethics Education." *Computers and Society.* 20, 2 Revised (June 1990).

Seabrook, John. "E-Mail from Bill." *New Yorker* (January 1994).

Senge, Peter. "The Leader's New Work: Building Learning Organizations." *Sloan Management Review* (Fall 1990).

Seybold, Patricia B. "Business Process Design." *Office Computing Report, Guide to Workgroup Computing* (September 1992).

Turner, Jon and Robert Kraut, eds. *CSCW '92, Sharing Perspectives: Proceedings of the Conference on Computer-Supported Cooperative Work,* Oct. 31–Nov. 4, 1992, Toronto, Canada.

8. MORAL DISTANCING AND THE USE OF INFORMATION TECHNOLOGIES: THE SEVEN TEMPTATIONS

Richard Rubin

ABSTRACT

There are many causes for unethical behavior among individuals who use information technologies. This article suggests that some of these reasons may be directly related to the characteristics of the technologies themselves. This is not to suggest that individuals are not responsible for their actions, but to identify factors about technology that may divert ethical attention. The diverting characteristics are identified as the "Seven Temptations."

One should always be reluctant when asked to talk about ethics, about "right and wrong." It is best to admit at the beginning that ethical qualms and mistakes plague everyone: that all of us err, act without thinking, or act selfishly from time to time. But our weaknesses do not relieve us of the obligation to act rightly, or prohibit us from engaging in ethical discussion: rather it is our propensity to err that makes ethical discussion so important.

Regrettably, when ethical presentations are made, there is often a tendency in non-theological contexts to back away from stating clearly what is right and wrong, perhaps because of the complexity of ethical reasoning, or perhaps because modesty on such issues appears to us to be preferable to what others may perceive as arrogance.

Do information and computer professionals need ethical guidance? Research conducted by Vitell and Davis (1990) concerning the ethical activities of MIS professionals suggests that they do. Vitell and Davis observe, "Within a business context ethical conflict is virtually inherent since the individual decision maker has responsibilities and duties to various diverse groups whose interests are often inconsistent" (p. 64).

Information and computer professionals must attempt to balance a variety of interests including those of the clients, the organization, the profession, the society-at-large, and information professionals themselves.

Vitell and Davis' research involved the distribution of a questionnaire to more than a hundred management information system (MIS) professionals, with positions ranging from programmers to information systems managers. Their results suggest that near half (48 percent) of the information professionals surveyed believe that there are many opportunities to engage in unethical behavior in their profession. A fifth of the respondents actually knew of behaviors of MIS managers that were unethical. A more encouraging finding was, that despite the opportunity for and presence of unethical conduct, the MIS professionals recognized that there are more important interests than those of the employer: nearly 70 percent felt that sometimes they should place the interests of society over the interests of the company. Nearly all the respondents (97 percent) declared that the employer has a social responsibility that is greater than the responsibility to the employer's shareholders. The latter findings suggest that information professionals want to apply the same ethical principles concerning their conduct within the workplace that they apply outside in the day-to-day world. They recognize a duty to others and to the society at large that is not lost when one passes through the employer's door.

But where do information professionals get their ethical guidance? Professional schools sometimes provide some reflection and course work on ethical issues, but there is little evidence that the curricula of such schools provide systematic, practical and in-depth training on ethical conduct. Some professional societies have created formally adopted ethical codes of conduct or guidelines. In the information world, this includes ACM, the American Library Association and the American Society for Information Science (ASIS).

Professional ethical codes can be useful in setting an ethical context for employees who work within a given profession, but they are seldom sufficiently elaborate to be of great help. Such codes tend to be wooden documents that prescribe and proscribe general conduct, but because of their dogmatic character, seldom do they provide a deep understanding of the ethical issues that need to be addressed and resolved.

Some business and public organizations have designed specific ethical codes of conduct tailored for their own organizations. Although these can also be helpful, they usually focus on the potential misconduct of employees and seldom direct much attention to the behavior of corporate leadership. In this sense, they are one-sided. They are less ethical codes than rules of behavior designed to protect an organization's interest from dishonest actions on the part of its employees.

Regrettably, the inadequacies of ethical codes and teaching become even more apparent in today's technological environment: an environment in which technologies exacerbate ethical dilemmas, because they make it even easier to act wrongfully. If this is true, then the need for ethical reflection becomes even more important, and reliance on formal codes of conduct even more problematic.

Why should new technologies increase the propensity for unethical conduct? It is my view that certain characteristics of information technologies promote a moral distancing on the part of the individual as an ethical agent; that these technologies allow the agent to create a moral distance between the act and moral responsibility for this act. How and why does this occur?

The concept of a moral distance can be seen as a particular condition in which the individual is able to rationalize, remove oneself from, or ignore ethical considerations. This condition can be promoted as much by the characteristics of the external environment as by any moral deficiency on the part of the individual. It is not that individuals should be relieved of ethical responsibilities because of situational factors, but these factors contribute to and potentially promote unethical actions, and therefore should be acknowledged and understood.

At the risk of borrowing from an atypical source to illustrate my point about moral distancing, this sense of moral distancing was sensitively characterized in a poem by the American poet James Dickey in his award winning book of poetry, *Buckdancer's Choice* (Dickey, 1961). In one poem, entitled "The Firebombing," the central voice of the poem is an American World War II bomber pilot, who is in the act of dropping firebombs on the Japanese countryside during what is called an "anti-morale" raid. In other words, his mission was not military in nature in the conventional sense; it was meant to terrorize the populace into submission. What is striking about this poem is that the pilot, far above the exploding and burning ground, in a cockpit darkening with twilight, spends his time admiring the beauty of the evening, and from his safe altitude, the beauty of the incendiaries that detonate below. The pilot speaks:

> [W]hen those on earth
> Die, there is not even sound;
> One is cool and enthralled in the cockpit,
> Turned blue by the power of beauty,
> In a pale treasure-hole of soft light
> Deep in aesthetic contemplation,
> Seeing the ponds catch fire... [p. 17]

The experience for the pilot is not anxiety-provoking; it is an affecting aesthetic one. He is unable to see the carnage that is created on the ground, because the characteristics of the technology and the physical environment in which he is operating divert him, literally blind him to the fiery reality below. The moral distance that is created is caused by many factors: first, anonymity, for no one below can see the pilot, therefore he is free from faces that would no doubt haunt and accuse him if he could see them; second, the physical distance from the ground itself obliterates the awful details of what is happening below; third, the beauty of the sky, earth and twilight diverts the attention of the pilot from the perfidy of his actions; and, perhaps most disturbing, the beauty of the fire below which hides with its intensity the lives and property being consumed. It is, what the poet himself refers to in this poem as an "aesthetic evil." One might add, although it is not explicitly stated in the poem, that the sense of tranquility that arises in the pilot is partly created by the belief in a just cause, which may also distance us from the immediacy of the pain that is sometimes inflicted by our actions in its service.

If such great destruction can escape our moral attention, could similar characteristics in more mundane settings even more easily distract our moral compass? Are there aesthetic and other attractions in computer technologies that divert our attention from ethical concerns? Let us look at some of the characteristics of computer information technologies that may promote this distancing effect. These will be called the "Seven Temptations."

TEMPTATION 1: SPEED

The speed of gathering and transmitting information is greatly increased with computers. Simply put, unethical actions can be committed in the blink of an eye. Although some planning time could well be involved, say, in determining how to obtain unauthorized information, the act itself can be accomplished very quickly. If we can do something so quickly, aren't we more likely to presume that in many instances, the chance of being caught is very small? When we do something very quickly don't we have less time to worry about being apprehended in the act? (Consider the fact that the pilot in the poem did not have to spend days on the ground fighting his opponent; his mission is quick.) If we were forced to take considerable time when stealing information, to enter physically a premises, walk down corridors, unlock and enter offices, open and search drawers, assess and remove files, then leave in the same manner, wouldn't we be much less likely to commit the act? With a computer, stealing or transmitting information can be accomplished so rapidly that detection, at least at the time of the event, is almost impossible. In addition, speed has its own attraction, per se, which can increase one's sense of moral distancing. We are fascinated by speed: consider the fact that many exceed the speed limit in sporty cars because of the feeling of exhilaration attributed to speed, yet we know that travelling at such speeds is dangerous to ourselves and others on the roadway. The speed of computers is also exhilarating. We are constantly bombarded by computer advertisements promoting faster chips that perform complex functions in a shorter time. Consider the fact that many functions performed on a computer are done very quickly already, but we demand that they be done even faster tomorrow, and spend literally thousands of dollars to pick up a few seconds of time. Going fast is in itself diverting— one focuses less on what we are doing and more on how fast we are doing it. This attraction invites ethical distraction.

TEMPTATION 2: PRIVACY AND ANONYMITY

Computer technologies, especially now that they are often home or office based, permit unethical actions to be performed in absolute or near-absolute privacy—literally in the privacy of one's home. There is a certain excitement about being able to do things when no one is looking—it is an anonymous act. (Consider our poet's bomber pilot and his sense of power and isolation high in the evening sky.) Often, in the protected environment of one's home or office, one is not being observed by anyone, hence the chance of being discovered is very small. This leads to a sense of invulnerability. The relationship between anonymity and moral diminution has been discussed in an entirely different psychological arena related to rape, which is the quintessential violation of privacy. Malamuth found that nearly 35 percent of the college students studied indicated some likelihood of raping if they could be assured of not being caught (Malamuth 1981).

The sense of moral distancing due to privacy and anonymity may be exaggerated further when one considers the remoteness of the act itself. When the perpetrator is stealing information at a remote source from an equally remote location, it does not "feel" the same, as if one is breaking into another person's home or office. Indeed, the perpetrator could be thousands of miles away and wholly unknown to the victim.

Finally, the notion of privacy has another sense that could encourage moral distancing. Extremely private information can be accessed using computers. Much of this information has such high interest value that it can and should be disseminated only with the consent of the individual about whom the information is the subject. This would include hospital and medical records, credit and financial records, educational records, personnel records and library circulation records. The temptation to access such information, especially in private circumstances, is an exciting one; after all, even as children weren't we exhilarated when we could overhear private conversations? Today, if we had a chance to listen in on private telephone conversations, or to read someone's private letters without fear of being detected, might many of us be greatly tempted? The computer may well, in many instances, afford access to such privacies without detection.

TEMPTATION 3: NATURE OF THE MEDIUM

The nature of the electronic medium permits one to steal information without actually removing it. That is, one can "appropriate" (an interesting double-entendre in the ethical sense) a file, but the file remains with its owner. This ability to remove yet not remove tempts us to believe that nothing has been stolen, no one will know, and the owner has not been harmed, because his or her property remains.

TEMPTATION 4: AESTHETIC ATTRACTION

I think that there are many non-technologically minded people who fail to recognize that work with computers requires creativity, inventiveness and artistry in the solution of technological problems. These are characteristics of creative individuals who are at their best when their solutions to technological problems are both simple and elegant. When solutions are successful, there is a sense of accomplishment, of creative pride. This fascination with overcoming difficult challenges with simple or clever solutions may be magnified if the results lead to the "defeat" of a worthy opponent. In this sense, when a hacker, using a cleverly created strategy, successfully breaks into a professionally protected electronic system, there may well be a sense of accomplishment that exceeds the importance of the information obtained in that system. Consider the excitement in the individual who gets into a system, perhaps for the first time, and exclaims: "I'm in!"; It is the equivalent of the exclamation "Eureka!" often associated with a moment of human discovery or invention. It is hardly an original observation to note that hackers hack, in part, for the creative challenge, taxing their abilities, finding novel solutions to overcome barriers set up by other knowledgeable individuals.

TEMPTATION 5: INCREASED AVAILABILITY OF POTENTIAL VICTIMS

The number of computer users and owners is well into the millions, and I am sure that the number of information files is well into the billions. There may be something very attractive about having access to so many individuals with relatively little effort. Exploitation becomes much simpler if all one has to do is send a message on the Internet compared to making hundreds of telephone calls, or mailing thousands of letters. In essence, the opportunity to behave unethically toward thousands of people with relatively little effort is well within our grasp.

TEMPTATION 6: INTERNATIONAL SCOPE

It is not only that acts can be done to so many people at great speed in the privacy of one's own home, but the geographical reach of information technologies has few limits. Acting unethically around the world is quite possible. It is not just stealing information. It is also the fact that, because of the great monetary incentives, there is a tremendous economic and political incentive to introduce these technologies to other cultures. However, the human effects of such exports seem to be placed well in the background. To whom are these technologies going? How are they being used? What effects do these technologies have on the cultures in which we introduce them? The excitement of being able to influence an entire geo-political world, and make plenty of money as well, distances us from the issue of whether many parts of the world are ready for such technologies or will truly benefit from them.

TEMPTATION 7: THE POWER TO DESTROY

The destructive capacity of information technologies is considerable. Normally, we think of ethical violations as consisting of inappropriate access, dissemination and use of information, but there are those whose purpose is to destroy it as well. This is often done by the introduction of viruses into computer systems. The seriousness of the damage can be considerable. Regrettably, some individuals can feel an exhilaration from such iconoclasm. After all, even as children, did not most of us get some pleasure from knocking down our houses of cards? This feeling of exhilaration may be magnified in the computer world, especially when the perpetrator can couple this feeling with being extremely clever about how the virus is introduced or by designing a clever method for triggering the virus.

CLOSING MORAL DISTANCES

Based on these seven temptations, one can say quite simply that it is very easy to be bad, when using information technologies. We cannot change an individual's ethical up-bringing, but if one assumes, and I do, that most people want to act rightly and do so most of the time, what types of actions would remind each of us that information technologies invite or blind us to unethical conduct? Rubin and Froehlich (in press) have suggested three arenas in which ethical conduct can be addressed. These include the organizational, professional and individual arenas.

ORGANIZATIONAL ACTIONS

Organizations can create climates that foster ethical as well as unethical conduct. Sometimes I think that each computer in an organization should have a warning label like cigarette packages that says: "Warning, this organization has determined that computers can be used for unethical actions leading to the diminution of the spirit." Such a warning would probably be as helpful as cigarette warnings, but it is suggestive of the fact that the organization must communicate its concern seriously and ubiquitously. Certainly, organizations must bear ethical responsibility for sending ethical messages to their employees. Because organizations establish a certain culture of appropriate behavior by setting and enforcing rules and regulations, individuals sometimes feel that if they are following those rules or orders, then the responsibility for their actions is diminished. Organizational climates that are unethical create a diminished capacity on the part of the individual to think independently. Because of this increased ethical burden, it is essential that organizations take a clear stand on ethical conduct. What can organizations do to send this message clearly?

Boards, administrations and management must be committed to ethical behavior, leading by example

Organizations can set up all the rules and regulations they want, but if the employees perceive that the leaders of the organization are ethical hypocrites, it is unlikely that an ethical environment will be created. This means that in conversations and meetings in which decisions are made or actions considered, leaders should explicitly discuss the ethical dimensions of their decisions. Among the questions that should be asked are the following: Are individuals being respected? Does this harm individuals? Are we infringing on people's rights? Are we adversely affecting their welfare? Can we tell the truth about what we are doing or must we deceive others? Employees who believe that their leaders take such questions seriously are more likely to ask the same questions of themselves.

Each organization should have a written ethics policy

Each organization should send a formal message to its information workers that it expects ethical actions on the part of its employees. It should be a statement which clearly is meant for all members of the organization including the board and administrators.

Such statements should not simply be a list of warnings and admonitions. It should foremost be a heart-felt statement of the values of the organization and the type of behavior the organization prizes. The phrase "heart-felt" is used intentionally. Affects are much more influential than cognitions on human attitudes and behavior; feelings are much more likely to produce the desired effects. The ethics statement should speak of convictions and values and attempt to personalize the relationship between the employees, the information technologies with which they work, and the effects unethical use of such information would have on individuals, the organization, the society, and themselves. If moral distancing is affected by anonymity, then the more we personalize what we do, the more we connect it to people both within and outside our organization, the greater the prospect that others will be considered when actions or decisions are made.

Of course, such a written policy should also include what will happen to employees who violate these ethical obligations, and how such violations can be reported. Although it is hoped that employees, once they understand the rationale for ethical behavior, will comport with that behavior, the organization needs to punish those who violate ethical conduct. Otherwise, some employees may interpret the organization's position as "lip-service."

Hire and promote individuals with ethical awareness

Obviously, an organization must consider whether an individual is qualified for the job when deciding about hiring and promotion. But it can also explore how these people feel about a variety of situations which involve, as part of the consideration, ethical actions. We ask lots of questions in interviews that are useless; here is an opportunity to assess an individual's ethical judgments in work-related situations. Hiring ethical individuals to start with makes ethical codes and sanctions unnecessary.

Conduct staff, orientation, development and training programs in ethics

Once an employee is hired, the organization must consistently reinforce its ethical standards through its orientation, training and development programs. Emphasis should again be placed on the values of the organization rather than on its rules, regulations and punishments, although they must be mentioned. Clearly, in organizations where information technology is present, the appropriate use of information technologies must be a significant part of this orientation.

Reinforcement is also needed to keep ethical considerations in the forefront. It is easy for organizations, with the many tensions and problems that they experience, to shelve their concerns for ethical conduct. Nonetheless, discussion in training and development programs will increase the possibility that ethical concerns will eventually become habitual. Such training and development programs should not be "preachy," but should allow staff to deal with situations both real and projective, to help clarify both their own ethical behaviors and the expectations of the organization.

PROFESSIONAL ACTIONS

It is essential to promulgate an ethical code

All information professions should have a code of conduct dealing, at least in part, with the ethical use of information technologies. These are usually promulgated through the appropriate professional associations. Such codes, as noted earlier, may not have the impact one would hope, but they do serve as a basic ethical compass for the actions of association members. Such codes may or may not have sanctions for violation. In general, sanctions are unnecessary for most professional codes. The purpose of a professional ethical code is first and foremost to promote ethical understanding. Focussing on penalties diverts attention from understanding the values that should form the foundation of our professional conduct.

Professional associations should train and advise in ethical conduct

Because professional associations are the voice of a profession, it is useful if they reinforce these codes by providing training programs for their members on ethics. This shows that the association is also truly committed to ethical conduct, because it devotes time and resources to ensuring that its members act appropriately.

INDIVIDUAL ACTIONS

Of course, the single most important factor in preventing a moral distance from arising is the individual, and I believe that there are certain obligations that each of us must satisfy in order to diminish the possibility that a moral distance is created.

The obligation of the information professional to be and remain competent

If we are not competent, there is a greater likelihood that we will engage in unethical actions to obscure our inadequacies. Hence, there may be attempts to obtain information from unauthorized sources, or to destroy or alter the records of more competent competitors both inside or outside the organization. The temptation to short-cut may be considerable, and such short-cutting may trample on the rights and welfare of others. The information professional has an obligation to stay informed and up-to-date and to act based on that competence. Of course, there is a complementary obligation to not use one's special expertise in an unethical manner as well. Demonstrations of one's special competencies by breaking into computer systems or assisting others in doing so are a form of technological bragging; such actions are inconsistent with consideration and respect for others.

The obligation to maintain secure and accurate electronic records

If there is a temptation to gain unauthorized access to records electronically, then there is a reciprocal obligation for computer professionals to maintain accurate and secure records to protect from such invasions. The welfare of those who are the subjects of such records may well depend on such scrupulousness.

The obligation to respect the privacy of individuals

The concept of privacy is basic to respecting people's rights and their welfare. Respect for privacy implies that an individual's electronic records be accessed, consulted, transmitted, or otherwise disseminated only for legitimate purposes and only after individuals are informed of the conditions under which information can be released. In many cases, a system should be devised so that explicit permission for consultation or dissemination of the records is required before the records are revealed.

The obligation to be honest in all dealings

Preventing moral distances may best be secured by openness. One type of test for determining ethical behavior is called the "Billboard" test which entails asking the question: "What if my decision or actions were posted on a billboard for all to see? Would my actions be the same or different?" (Catron 1983). Although this is a far from perfect test, it suggests that the information professional's activities concerning information sought and delivered should be complete and open. Distorting information for one's own advantage (monetary or otherwise), or to providing an inappropriate advantage or disadvantage to another by providing or withholding information is equally unethical. The information professional must be influenced only by the legitimate interests of his users and clients. Similarly, knowingly assisting another individual in the commission of a dishonest or unlawful act is anathema.

Honesty is also implicated in the acquisition of information. The use of deceptive techniques in attempting to acquire information, or the use of techniques that secure protected information without appropriate consent must be avoided.

Finally, honesty also involves the proper acquisition of information technologies. This is a particularly interesting area because it often deals with the copying of software without the consent of the copyright holder. There is little doubt that this type of activity goes on constantly. Recently, a *Newsweek* article reported that about $2 billion worth of software was stolen over the Internet in 1993 (Meyer and Underwood 1994). This, of course, does not take into account the software copied locally. This phenomenon suggests that individuals feel that this is not a serious violation, certainly not as serious as if they walked into a store and stole the software off the shelf. This sense of moral distancing probably arises because of the combination of the ease of the act, the privacy and anonymity of the act, the money saved and the benefits derived. It is a topic in ethical deliberation that deserves closer attention in another forum.

SUMMARY

Like James Dickey's firebomber, information professionals are at the controls of a powerful force—a force that can be equally if not as dramatically destructive as bombs. That there are unethical uses of such technologies is not in doubt, but it remains to be seen if such misuses are simply the result of defective ethical systems of users, or at least in part, due to characteristics of such technologies which seem to invite ethical distraction. Even when these characteristics are identified, one's ethical breaches are not to be excused, but by recognizing those aspects of information systems that divert us, it is possible to refocus and concentrate ethical attention. In doing so, an individual's conduct is improved, as is our profession, our organization, and society as a whole.

REFERENCES

Catron, B. L. (1983): "Ethical Postures and Ethical Posturing." *American Review of Public Administration* 17: 155–159.
Dickey, James. *Buckdancer's Choice*: (1965). Middletown CT: Wesleyan University.
Malamuth, Neil M. (1981): "Rape Proclivity Among Males." *Journal of Social Issues* 37 (4): 138–157.
Meyer, Michael and Underwood, Anne (1994): "Crimes of the 'Net.'" *Newsweek* 74 (20) :46–47.
Rubin, Richard E. and Froehlich, Thomas J. (in press): "Ethical Aspects of Library and Information Science." In Allen Kent, ed., *Encyclopedia of Library and Information Science*, New York: Marcel Dekker.
Vitell, Scott and Davis, Donald L. (1990): "Ethical Beliefs of MIS Professionals: The Frequency and Opportunity for Unethical Behavior." *Journal of Business Ethics* 9 (1): 63–70.

9. DIGITAL IMAGES: MORAL MANIPULATION

JOHN WECKERT
and
DOUGLAS ADENEY

INTRODUCTION

The manipulability of images by means of modern digital technology raises various ethical concerns. The issues are not essentially new, but they are given new urgency by the ease and undetectability which the new technology affords. The essence of this new technology is the digital storage of images. These images may be created by cameras, by scanning "hard copies," or by operating the computer itself. Once they are stored digitally, they may be copied as easily as any other file or part thereof. In a few moments I could copy an image and pass it off as my own work, with the copy being in no way inferior to the original. And changes may be made without leaving any trace of the alterations. Using techniques such as "warping" (stretching and shrinking images or parts of them), "morphing" (changing one image into another), and "tweening" (inserting new images or frames to provide or enhance continuity), as well as the more familiar cutting and pasting, images may be juxtapositioned, and shapes, textures and colors may be altered in all sorts of ways. William J. Mitchell describes it thus:

> Such fake "photographs" can now be produced by using widely available "paint" and image-processing software to rearrange, recolor and otherwise transform the elements of a scene. The same software can combine fragments of different images into one new image. Other software can generate completely synthetic photorealistic pictures by applying sophisticated perspective projection and shading to digital models of three-dimensional scenes ... [8, p. 45]

This technology has many uses. It has undoubted benefits in education, medicine and science. Students can "see" cells divide, skulls evolve and light rays bend. Scientists can examine digital images from outer space, and doctors can use various medical imaging techniques to examine the human body. Another important though probably less beneficial use is the creation, alteration and enhancement of images for entertainment purposes, particularly for special effects. It also has obvious uses in advertising, many of which are quite benign. However, not all of its applications are clearly above reproach, as we shall see.

There is nothing new in the ability to copy, manipulate and enhance photographs and other images, apart from the technology. "Trick photography" has been around for virtually as long as photography itself, but what was once possible only with considerable time and skill is now becoming commonplace. And of central importance, as was previously noted, is that these manipulations leave no trace. There is no cutting of film or paper, or altering of lines on any sort of "hard copy." And copying does not degrade the original. This does not mean that digital manipulation is not detectable in any way at all; the manipulator must be careful for example in matters of perspective, reflection, shadows and shading, and consistency in these and other ways (8, pp. 47ff.). Yet, as in so many other fields which the computer has entered, it has done so in style.

The potential moral problems fall roughly into two classes. In the first are questions of ownership, which involves copyright and plagiarism. In the second lie issues pertaining to the uses to which manipulated images are put.

MANIPULATION AND OWNERSHIP

The Ownership of Images

Two different questions arise concerning the relationship between the manipulation of images and their ownership. The first is the question of whether ownership entails the right to manipulate; the second is that of the ownership of a manipulated image. These questions will be discussed in turn, but first we must look at the interesting notion of ownership of any image, manipulated or not.

The concept of owning an image is interestingly different from that of owning a physical object. Ownership of a physical object involves the right to continued use and enjoyment of it; if it is a painting, for instance, and I take it from your house without your authority, my theft of it consists in my violation of that right because you are no longer able to have that use and enjoyment. What is involved in the ownership of an image? If you create an image on your computer and I copy it onto my disk or into my area of the computer, you still have that image, in contrast to the case of the painting. If I may be said to have stolen your image, it is in so far as I have taken a copy of what you have. This is an important difference between intellectual property and physical property. Intellectual property is not exclusive in the same way: your possession and enjoyment of the computer image do not exclude mine. Intellectual property rights have to be more concerned with certain benefits, particularly financial ones, which may flow from possession of the image. The Universal Declaration of Human Rights, in Article 27 (2), acknowledges such rights as follows: "Everyone has the right to the protection of the moral and material interests resulting from any scientific, literary or artistic production of which he is the author."

What is meant by moral interests? If I have a good idea, write a good poem, paint a good picture, take an interesting photograph, or create a clever computer image, I normally want people to credit me with it and to think well of me for it, apart from the material benefits it may gain me. This may be what the Declaration intends. To apply its intent in the field of computer images, we may imagine a spectrum of possible cases of copying the work of another. At one end of the spectrum there might be the scanning of an image from a magazine solely for the purpose of experimenting with morphing. At the other end lies the case where a work is copied and passed off as the work of the copier, for commercial gain. What are the main differences between the two ends of the spectrum? In the first case, no financial gain is made from the copying, or if there is, none which affects the author. And no deceit is involved. The copier may quite happily acknowledge the source of the work. Nothing seems to be wrong in all this, and neither common sense nor the Declaration would appear to have any objection. In the second case, the copier gains financially at the expense of the author, and there is deceit involved. This deceit may significantly affect the "moral interests" of the author in that he or she is getting less credit (or credit from fewer people) than is appropriate, and this may be seen as a kind of harm which it is wrong to inflict, quite apart from the harm to the author's material interests. It may not always be wrong to harm someone financially—the possibility of doing so is actually built into the free market system, and many people believe that having a free market is better overall than not having one, even though some people will suffer. But the financial harm involved in the present case may be seen as akin to, and indeed as a case of, theft. Is this appropriate?

The Declaration does not actually offer a justification of the right to the protection of these moral and material interests. Is a justification needed? Is it not obvious that I am entitled to all the fruits of my creations? Maybe not, for at least two reasons. First, the fruits are distinct from the creations, and even if it is obvious that I am entitled to use and enjoy the creations themselves it does not follow that I am entitled to use and enjoy all the fruits which human circumstances may make possible. If I discover a cure for AIDS, for example, is it obvious that I am entitled to become fabulously rich by selling it at a huge price to thousands of desperate sufferers? Secondly, we may ask how fully the creation itself may be said to be mine. If I make myself a table out of materials I own, the table is mine. If I make a computer image I may own the hardware and the software license, but do I own the ingredients of the image—the shapes and the colors and the densities and so on? Are these not public property, so that what I make out of them is at best only partly mine?

To counter this one might appeal to the celebrated theory of private property advanced by the 17th Century philosopher John Locke. Locke held that I clearly own my person, and my labor; and if I "mix my labor" with something in a natural state, by for example digging ore or picking fruit, then I "join" that thing to something of mine and it becomes my property too (5, sect. 27). So, to adapt Locke, if I "mix my labor" (by thinking and using my computer) with the above abstract ingredients to produce an image, is that image rightfully mine? It might be thought that applying the theory to intellectual property neatly avoids, in fact, a difficulty in Locke's theory of physical property. He gives the proviso that when I mix my labor with something in a natural state it becomes my property "at least where there is enough, and as good left in common for others" (5, sect. 27); he does not elaborate on this, and it is difficult to interpret. If I have to leave enough ore (say) for everyone else, i.e., every other human being, then I will be able to take hardly any; if I only have to leave enough for a couple of others, I may be able to take far too much. But if the materials with which I am mixing my labor are not goods in finite supply like ore and fruit, but abstract things like colors and shapes which are in infinite supply, so that in using a given color in my computer image I am in no way using it up, then we have no trouble in satisfying Locke's proviso.

But problems remain. First, it is not clear how literally we should be expected to take the language of mixing and joining, and thus how far we are committed to whatever implications it may have in its literal sense, as distinct from any it may have in some merely metaphorical sense. Secondly, it is often asked why the laborer should gain that with which he mixes his labor, rather than simply losing his labor. If I pour my can of tomato juice into the sea (and even if the juice molecules could be known to mingle evenly throughout it), why should I be seen as gaining the sea rather than simply wasting my juice (9, p. 175)? Locke says that in most of the useful products of the earth, as much as 99 percent of their value is due to labor rather than nature, but it is difficult to see how this could be substantiated. Labor may be necessary to utilize the ore or the fruit, but the presence of the ore or the fruit (or the trees, or the seeds) in the first place is equally necessary. A third problem, arising specifically for intellectual property, is put by Edwin C. Hettinger:

> Invention, writing, and thought in general do not operate in a vacuum; intellectual activity is not creation ex nihilo. Given this vital dependence of a person's thoughts on the ideas of those who came before her, intellectual products are fundamentally social products...
> Separating out the individual contribution of the inventor, writer, or manager

from this historical/social component is no easy task.... A person who relies on human intellectual history and makes a small modification to produce something of great value should no more receive what the market will bear than should the last person needed to lift a car receive full credit for lifting it [3, p. 38].

Let us now consider a rather different kind of justification of intellectual property rights, including rights over computer images. It is thought by many that if we did not recognize such rights—if copying were freely allowed—there would be no money to be made, and profits must be available or no-one will make the effort to develop his ideas. The generation of new ideas is necessary for a society to prosper. It can be time consuming and costly to generate and develop ideas, so there must be reward for those who do. If there is not, no one will bother to create. And the most important reward is financial. Without financial reward, society's supply of new ideas will dry up. Therefore there must be some system of copyright and patent regulations which protects intellectual property. Not only the artist or author or inventor, but society as well or indeed the whole human race, would be the poorer without it. This may be called a utilitarian justification of intellectual property rights; the appeal is not to the laborer's right to his or her person and what is in some way "joined" to it, Lockean style, but to the beneficial consequences for society or humanity in general.

Whether it is in fact true that without financial reward there would be no incentive to create is another matter. In mediaeval times literature was all in the public domain, with no ownership rights. Story material was seen as common property, and the notion that one could claim property rights in ideas is seldom encountered (6, p. 114). It may be thought of course that the mediaevals were not very original, but it would still need to be shown that this was a result of the lack of the concept of intellectual ownership. It could be argued that if ideas were all in the public domain, and if anyone could work on and develop anything, regardless of where the idea originated, we would all be better off because more would be developed. There is in fact something of a paradox, as Hettinger points out, in a right "to restrict the current availability and use of intellectual products for the purpose of increasing the production and thus future availability and use of intellectual products" (3, p. 48). That the source of new and innovative ideas would dry up without copyright and patent laws to facilitate financial reward is little more than an article of faith. Artists, academics and scientists frequently create without such reward. Perhaps acknowledgement is enough. Or perhaps creation is its own reward. But even if incentives are needed, why must they consist in ownership rights?

> If the justification for intellectual property is utilitarian . . . then the search for alternative incentives for the production of intellectual products takes on a good deal of importance. It would be better to employ equally powerful ways to

stimulate the production and thus use of intellectual products which did not also restrict their use and availability.

Government support of intellectual work and public ownership of the result may be one such alternative. Governments already fund a great deal of basic research and development, and the results of this research often become public property [3, pp. 48-49].

Whether it is realistic to hope that government funding for intellectual products would ever be at a sufficient level to provide a just replacement for ownership rights is a debatable point, but we have perhaps at least seen that the justification of such rights, including rights over the things which computers help us to produce, is also open to question.

Ownership and the Right to Manipulate

We now turn to the question of whether there are instances where copying is legitimate but manipulation of the copied image is not. In other words, is license to copy license to manipulate? There are three cases to consider. The first is where the copier has the right to make a copy but not to grant that right to others. She can legitimately make a copy for her own private purposes, but the image is still owned by someone else. This is essentially the case with photocopying text. The second case is that where someone copies an image which he unquestionably owns, because it was either bought or received as a gift. This is the case where someone buys all rights to say an old movie or inherits all rights to a novel. The third case is that where the owner has all rights by virtue of being the creator. These will now be discussed in turn. Is license to copy the work of another, license to manipulate that work? Well, what may I do with the copy? Pretty well anything I like, provided that it is for my own personal use. The problems arise if I want to make the image or some variant of it public. But perhaps the issues are not very different from those which arise in the case of written material. Suppose that I manipulate my copy of the image owned by X, and make it public. The issues are: Of what kinds are the changes? How substantial are they? Have I acknowledged the source of the image? Have I made clear that it is a manipulated image? Is it being used for research or for personal gain? (This is not a clear-cut distinction, as any publication can be for both purposes.) It is generally accepted that there is nothing wrong in using the work of others in published works as long as what is used is not too substantial, recognition is given for the copied work, and so on. After all, all research is to a greater or lesser extent building on the work of others; intellectual products are fundamentally social products. So there seems to be no good reason why the same situation should not obtain in the case of images. If I legitimately copy an image which I see as the basis for some other creation, and create the new from the old, it is difficult to see what is wrong with this, provided that due recognition is given to the creator of the original image. But, it might be objected, just because I have a right to copy someone's work, it does not follow that I have a right to change it. If I have a right to copy X's work, then the copy that I make is mine. But it is not mine in the same sense that X's house is mine if I acquire that legitimately. If I acquire his house, I may do what I like with it, more or less, because it is mine. Being mine in this case means that I own it. But I do not own my copy of X's image in that way. All that I own in the house sense is the paper on which it is printed. It is still X's image. Intellectual property is different from other property, as we have seen; ownership of ideas is not much like ownership of objects. X can sell me his idea which is manifest in an image created by him, but there is a very real sense in which it is still his image, his idea. Yet though it is true that my legitimate copy of X's image is still in a sense his image, it is not so in a way which makes it wrong to alter it. If a copy of an image is changed, nothing happens to the original, and, at least in the case of digitally stored images, the potential number of copies of this original is not diminished. The world does not lose anything by the alteration. There are now two images where there was only one.

The second case to be considered is that in which someone has purchased or has been given all rights, including the right to say who can copy, to an image (or set of images as in a movie). In this case is manipulation justifiable? Ownership rights do not necessarily confer the right to alter; a new owner of the Mona Lisa would not have the moral right to adorn the face with spectacles or give her grey hair, or even an unambiguous smile. Once something has certain aesthetic or historical significance, I do not have the moral right to alter it, even if I did purchase all legal rights to it. Society's rights override those of the individual owner. But if the rights to a black and white movie are purchased, for example, would the new owner have the right to colorize it? Mitchell raises the case of Ted Turner, who bought the MGM film library in 1986 and announced his intention to colorize a hundred old feature films. To the protests of cinephiles and the Directors Guild of America, who called it "cultural butchery," Turner replied, "The last time I checked, I owned those films. I can do anything I want with them" (7, p. 53). Was he morally in the right, provided at least that not all the original prints of any of the films were destroyed? This may not seem enough. For one thing, to own the rights is to control the showing of the film, and to be able to have the colorized version shown instead of the original and indeed as the film in question. But there is a second ground for misgivings. However available the original may remain, it may seem inappropriately disrespectful, or indeed "cultural butchery," to make a copy of a work of art, alter it, and display it. This would apply equally, of course, to the first type of case above, where the licensed copier is not the owner. Would it be in order for the Louvre to display a bespectacled and broadly smiling version of the *Mona Lisa*, perhaps in another room, or for anyone else to display one? These arguments have force, of course, only where the original painting or film or computer image is judged to have significant artistic or cultural merit. Yet, while we may well feel unhappy about this, it is not obvious how to justify the belief that disrespect or "cultural butchery" is immoral. Altering a religious picture may be condemned as blasphemous (a problematic notion in itself), but why should showing disrespect to a work of art matter, if the original is unaltered? The only argument which seems to have any plausibility is that works of art are part of culture, and that any society will crumble without some respect for its culture. But there is a large step from this belief to the proposition that every case of disrespect contributes to such crumbling and is therefore immoral.

The final case is that where the original owner and creator of the image is the one who manipulates. Is this different? Perhaps. If Charles Rennie Macintosh altered one of his buildings in Glasgow, it would still be a Macintosh building. If a new owner alters it, it loses some of its significance. However, if the creation is significant enough, perhaps even the creator should not change it, if the change spoils the original. If the original is unchanged, however, it is even more doubtful than in the two earlier cases that changing a copy is in any way wrong. The notion of a copy here is even unclear. Perhaps we should rather say that we have here similar works by the same creator, as in Monet's "Grain Stack" series of paintings.

Manipulation as Creating Ownership

As noted earlier, two different questions arise concerning the relationship between ownership and manipulation. The first was discussed in the previous section: does ownership entail the right to manipulate? The second issue concerns the ownership of manipulated images. If I change an image which was digitized from a photograph or a picture drawn by someone else, whose property is the new image? This problem is illustrated well in the recent lawsuit filed in New York City by the stock photo agency FPG International against *New York Newsday*: "Allegedly, someone at the newspaper scanned the work of two photographers ... out of an FPG catalog and combined the images, plus some others, in the computer. Who got the credit for this new image? *New York Newsday*'s computer artist" (10, p. 58).

Is ownership here a matter of having been authorized by the original owner to make the alterations? Does it make a difference if permission was granted for copying and manipulation? Perhaps it does. If I build a house completely out of stolen materials, the house is hardly mine. It might be mine in the sense that I designed and created it, but no moral rights with respect to it would follow from this. The mere fact that I had put my labor into it would count for nought. However, if the materials were a gift, the house could be mine in all senses. Similarly perhaps, if the image manipulation is done with authority and with due reference, and if it is extensive enough to constitute a genuinely different picture, then I could legitimately claim it as mine. If that authority were lacking, I could not do so. The cases are not parallel of course, and that makes a difference. The elements of an image used to create another image are not objects in the way that the constituents of a house are. In a sense they are intellectual objects; in another they are patches of color; hence they may be used without depriving their "owner" of anything (provided that the original image is not destroyed). This is clearly not the case where house building materials have been stolen. While creating a new image out of and perhaps based on the work of another may have "the benefit of theft over honest toil," it does not follow that this has any relevance for intellectual ownership. The foundations of this type of ownership are in any case, as we have seen, open to question.

THE USES OF MANIPULATION

Manipulation and Falsification

The second category of ethical questions concerns the uses to which manipulated images (whoever "owns" them) might be put. A central worry here is that publishing or distributing an image which we know to have been manipulated amounts to a form of lying. Normally lying consists in making a verbal statement which we know to be false, with the intention to deceive; but may we not do essentially the same thing with a picture? Not every alteration or manipulation of an image, of course, is so intended. We may be correcting a technical flaw in the photograph, or even trying to make a color (say) more faithful to that of the photographed object—to avoid the viewer being deceived into thinking that its color is other than it really is. But obviously an image may also be manipulated with the intention of deceiving. To take a now celebrated example, a magazine cover photograph during the 1991 Gulf War showed U.S. President George Bush with Jordan's King Hussein, when in fact they had never met; the picture had been composed from separate originals. One may well regard it as effectively stating that they were together, and believe that it was published with the intention of deceiving people into thinking not only that they had met but, more importantly, that Jordan sympathized with the United States in its conflict with Iraq.

Is it always wrong to lie? The great and famously uncompromising moral philosopher Immanuel Kant thought so (4). He held that even if some innocent person is hiding from a potential murderer, who comes along and asks you where he is, then even though you believe that telling the truth will result in murder you ought to tell the truth. Nearly everyone else would say that, particularly if you are in no danger yourself, you not only may tell a lie but ought to. An innocent person's life is simply far more important than telling the truth. Yet while we may not accept Kant's absolute prohibition on lying, many of us see it as a very serious business—so much so that even in the case of the would-be murderer we may feel very strongly inclined to try to protect the potential victim while not telling a lie. We may refuse to answer the question or evade it; we may answer honestly but try to bar his way; or we may speak the truth but misleadingly so, by saying for example "I saw him at the end of the street five minutes ago," not mentioning that we helped him to hide in this very house only one minute ago. Such strategies have obvious drawbacks. The first may well expose us to (greater) danger, and or give the hunter a pretty good idea of the location of his quarry; the second depends on our ability to bar him safely and effectively; and the third may expose us to further questioning, to which it may be difficult to give true but misleading answers. Kant, incidentally, did not show any interest in any of these possibilities; he simply thought that one should answer the would-be murderer honestly. Yet the fact that such "solutions" are to many of us so appealing bears witness to our reluctance to tell a straight-out lie, even in such a case as this. Our reluctance is due not only to the upbringing that most of us have had, but also to our awareness of the importance of being able to trust one another. This importance was nicely acknowledged by a recently retired Australian politician, in promoting his volume of memoirs in which he admitted that he had occasionally lied when it was necessary for the sake of Cabinet solidarity and the good of the party. "Please, please," he begged his National Press Club audience, "buy my book. It's a good book. ... Would I lie to you" (11)?

Now if we see image manipulation as a form of lying, at least where it is done with the intent to deceive, should we take it very seriously? There are several possible responses to this question. One is to play down the matter by resisting the idea that it is a form of lying. There is, after all, no verbal statement, and thus no verbal statement that is known to be false. And is this not an essential element in lying? Maybe it is, but maybe what is really objectionable in lying is the intention to deceive; we do not object to people making false statements in telling jokes, or when acting in plays or reciting poems, because there is here no such intention. And so if or where there is such an intention in the manipulation of images, whether or not we use the word "lying," is it not just as morally objectionable? (A corollary of this argument is that the common desire to make a true but misleading statement rather than a false and misleading one is misguided: that a true but intentionally misleading one is in the same moral boat as a lie.)

Another response to the equating of image manipulation to lying is to suggest that lying is not as bad as all that. It is not only allowable (or indeed obligatory) to lie in such a case as that of Kant's murderer, it is allowable to lie in order to save others and even oneself from various lesser evils. Suppose a man with some power or authority over a woman in their workplace asks her a very intrusive question about her personal life. Even if he is not her official superior he may be an exploitative and manipulative person, and she may have good reason to expect that neither refusing to answer nor evading the question will be in her interests, and may in any case give him a pretty fair idea of the truth. In such a case, would it be wrong of her to lie to him? If the circumstances permit, it may be wiser for her to refuse to answer and then complain about his intrusion or harassment, but the circumstances may not be like that. We may perhaps be concerned that, if she can tell him a convincing lie, then maybe she has become practiced by lying in less legitimate cases; we may also be worried that, even if this is not so, she may be setting foot on a "slippery slope" leading her to lie for less and less legitimate reasons. Both of these concerns should be heeded, but neither of them shows that her lying in this case, to protect a legitimate interest of hers, would be wrong. It should be seen as no more immoral than wearing make-up to conceal a skin blemish or digitally removing such a blemish from a photograph of oneself, both of which are (in normal circumstances) legitimate cases of deception.

Yet obviously many lies are morally indefensible, and many of the deceptions facilitated by image manipulation may be morally suspect too. A practitioner in the manipulation field, Dale Duguid, expresses his concern at the counterfeiting capacities which have progressed from the audiotape to the still photograph to video imagery to motion pictures of high degrees of resolution:

> Rapid technological change has always caused harm to some, while providing advantages for others. Those implementing the new technology are usually the advantaged. Rapid technological change causes everything from species and culture extinctions to displacement and dysfunction in our societies. No change has been more rapid, and has greater potential to create [social] dysfunction than current advances in image manipulation. What happens when you or the news editor can no longer rely on what he or she sees with his/her eyes in the domain of still or moving pictures of any resolution [2, p. 11]?

However, another recent writer, Sean Callahan, suggests that there is not too much cause for concern after all: "The fulminations over the ethics of digital manipulation are partly based on the cliche 'a picture doesn't lie.' Yet if a truth-in-photography law existed, the Federal Trade Commission would have banned photographs in advertising years ago..." [1, p. 64].

He outlines three reasons why there is not much to worry about. The first two have to do with the quotation above. First, "Those who argue that editorial photographs represent reality ignore the fact that a camera shutter operating at one-250th of a second can't possibly tell the whole truth about a scene, and that the rectangular frame takes in only a fraction of reality" (1, p. 64).

A photograph is only a very small piece of reality. Seen out of context it can be very misleading, particularly when taken together with a caption. Equally misleading can be a photograph intentionally placed in the wrong context. Second, Callahan rightly points out that skilled people could always modify photographs: "The hand that today operates the mouse running Photoshop is essentially the same one that once handled a razor blade and airbrush though the technology democratizes the once tight little world of the highly skilled, highly paid retouchers" (1, p. 64).

All that has changed is the technology and the level of skill required. Finally, newspaper and magazine editors are bound to give accurate information or sales will drop off. It is therefore, in their own interests not to tamper with photographs in a manner likely to mislead:

> What remains firmly in the hands of the editors . . . is a franchise based on accurate information. As soon as their customers start getting misleading information, that franchise starts to wither. Despite the fears of many photographers, common sense suggests that the same ethical standards editors apply to the other facets of the news-gathering process will prevail in the photography department [1, p.64].

While all of Callahan's points are true to some extent, they are not much cause for comfort. "A picture doesn't lie" has always been a dubious claim, but with image manipulation techniques and current software, the scope for "lying" has been greatly expanded. Much greater changes to photographs and other images are now possible much more quickly and cheaply, and in much greater number. If the software is available, no high level of skill is required, and no traces of the manipulation remain. This takes care of his first two points. The third point at best is true for current or recent news, but not for historical records. Archival images are not subject to the public's accuracy requirements in the way that newspapers might be. But there are also problems for current and recent news. Remoteness in space lessens the public's control over the accuracy of reports just as remoteness in time does.

It remains to be shown, then, that ethical issues are not raised in new and more urgent ways.

Manipulation and Entertainment

So far we have focused on political uses of image manipulation, but it may also be used for entertainment—which of course may also mean for the sake of the money to be had in the entertainment industry. This may seem innocuous, and no doubt it often is, but several concerns may arise. For one thing, as Duguid points out, the line between entertainment and history may not always be correctly located: "Actual archival footage can be reprocessed through image synthesis ostensibly for entertainment purposes and then return to the archival domain—its subtle changes forever becoming part of documented history and collective memory" [2, p. 13].

Secondly, what is done for the sake of entertainment may have direct political aspects as well. Duguid refers to a film about World War I, based on contemporary black and white footage, with real 1990s actors among real 1916 troops on the Somme, all in living color—yet the mud was shown as grey, not as the purple it would actually have been in that bloodbath. This has the effect of "sanitizing the new interpretation" (2, p. 10). Such a thing might be done for the political motive of controlling viewers' impressions of the horrors of war; more probably in the present case it was done to prevent the film from being too sickening and to make the film maximally entertaining and profitable, but with the possible consequence nevertheless that some viewers' impressions would be a little less horrific than they would otherwise have been. On the other hand, for many viewers there are no such constraints on entertainment; the gorier and more violent the scene the more exciting and enjoyable it is. And digital image manipulation allows ample scope for the gratification of such tastes. Beheadings and impalings and other such delights may be made as explicit as desired; no longer need an unsuspecting actor die as in a "snuff movie," though there is still the apparent fact that for some viewers there is pleasure not only in seeing lethal violence but in knowing that the person filmed has actually suffered it.

This leads us into pornography. Some of it is violent and some not, and image manipulation may be used in both. Many hold that pornography is harmful in helping to cause sexual assaults and to promote sexually exploitative attitudes in men towards women; others hold that it is harmless, or should at least be regarded as innocent until proven guilty, and others again hold that it actually does good in being a "safety valve" quite apart from the value (if any) of the pleasure enjoyed by the consumer. Some see the distinction between violent and nonviolent pornography as very important, and argue that the former is worse (or the only bad kind) because it is (more) harmful and or objectionable in itself. The arguments here are complex. Does the advent of digital image manipulation affect them substantially? It is not clear that it does, although it may allow exaggerations of various kinds which may arouse, so to speak, unrealistic impressions and expectations in the innocent. More seriously, there is the possibility of "respectable" photographs of "respectable" people being rendered pornographic. The harm (if any) caused to those who see such pictures and to those (if any) whom they then assault or exploit may be no greater than that done by more conventionally produced pornography. But there is also the possibility of harm to the subject(s) of the original photograph(s)—to her or his reputation, due to the general disapproval of pornography and of those who participate in the production of it. Alternatively, a subject might be harmed in a financial way; she may have been happy enough to pose for pornography, but only for a large fee, of which she is being cheated when her "respectable" pictures are made pornographic.

How Should We Respond?

Harms of these various kinds, and the risks of them, give grounds for moral concern and, in the clearer cases, condemnation. And where modern image manipulation exacerbates these harms or the risks of them, then obviously we should be morally concerned about it and, in the clearer cases, condemn it. But it is important to distinguish the question of where image manipulation is morally unacceptable from questions of what the law, or professional bodies, or society in general, should do about it. The law is concerned, as is morality, with harms of various tangible kinds: it prohibits sexual assault, for example, and fraud. It also prohibits behavior which creates the risk of various harms such as drunken driving, for example. Should it then also ban pornography, with or without manipulated images, if there is even the risk of its causing harm? And what about its capacity to cause offense? There are all sorts of difficult issues here, but they are not perhaps much affected by the technology of image manipulation. For they are concerned mainly with the possible or likely effects of what the image shows, rather than with how the picture was produced.

There is another category of harms, however, which is both legally problematic and very much affected by the new technology. These are the harms which are caused by, or consist in, deception. They are legally problematic because, while there are clear cases where the law steps in, cases such as fraud and perjury, there are many cases where the harm is indeterminate and uncertain. Who would be harmed, and how, by being deceived by the Bush-Hussein picture? What if it could be argued plausibly that on balance it would be a good thing for as many people as possible to believe that Jordan was backing the United States? But perhaps this is the wrong question to ask. Is deception bad in itself, apart from any harm it may do to people's material wellbeing or political security? If so, why does the law tend to concern itself only with those categories of deception which do bring such harms? I may tell you a bare-faced lie about my qualifications or achievements, but the law will not touch me unless I am doing so in order to, for example, defraud you in some way. But the scope for deception is, as we have seen, greatly enhanced by the new technology. And with its practitioners able to manipulate images in physically undetectable ways, and, contra Callahan, to get away with it, what are we to do?

It might be thought that, if the law is uncertain as to how far its proper interest extends here, and has difficulty in policing it anyway, professional codes of ethics should assume responsibility. They should specify that images should be manipulated only where this causes no significant harm or no deception of a significant kind. But apart from the problem of clarifying what is meant by "significant" in each case, there is still the problem of the ease of manipulation coupled with its undetectability. Professional codes of ethics may have some value, but is it realistic to expect them to keep the manipulators sufficiently on the straight and narrow? It may be that it is not realistic, and that, considering the capacities and temptations of the new technology, we, the consumers of the images, may have to become more wary and less prepared to trust what we see. When as children we have to learn not to trust people of certain kinds, our innocence suffers a major blow. Will we now have to become less innocent still? If a society is to function at all there must be a considerable level of trust among its members. We know the dangers of trusting too naively the written and spoken word (though most of the time we just have to trust them), but we place great faith in photography, and this has been of great value to us. We can see what is happening in some world trouble spot, or in a football match. We can match the spoken word to the picture and make our own judgment about the veracity of the word. But if images may be manipulated at will, by political authorities and others with vested interests in deceiving us, a simple test of authenticity is gone.

REFERENCES

(1) Callahan, S. "Eye Tech." *Forbes ASAP* 151, 12 (June 1993), pp. 57–67.

(2) Duguid, D. "The Morality of Synthetic Realism." Unpublished paper presented at a conference at Noosa Regional Gallery, Tewantin, Queensland, Australia, March 1994.

(3) Hettinger, Edwin C. "Justifying Intellectual Property." *Philosophy and Public Affairs*, 18 (1989), pp. 31–52.

(4) Kant, I. "On a Supposed Right to Lie from Altruistic Motives," quoted in J. Rachels, *The Elements of Moral Philosophy* (Random House, New York, 1986), p. 109.

(5) Locke, J. "Second Treatise of Government," in *Two Treatises of Government* (Mentor, New York, 1963), section 27.

(6) Malone, K. and Baugh, A. C. *The Middle Ages* (Routledge & Kegan Paul, London, 1967).

(7) Mitchell, William J. *The Reconfigured Eye: Visual Truth in the Post-Photographic Era* (MIT Press, Boston, 1992).

(8) Mitchell, William J. "When Is Seeing Believing?" *Scientific American* (February 1994), pp. 44–49.

(9) Nozick, R. *Anarchy, State, and Utopia* (Basil Blackwell, Oxford, 1974).

(10) Russell, Anne M. "4 Predictions: Who Will Win and Who Will Lose, and Will Digital Art Ever Get Better?" *American Photo* 5, 3 (May/June, 1994), pp. 58–59.

(11) *The Age*, Melbourne, 1 November 1994, p. 2.

III : SOFTWARE RELIABILITY AND COMPUTER SECURITY

SUMMARY

(10) *A Cultural and Historical Perspective of Computer Security*
This chapter attempts to enlighten the reader about the cultural, moral heritage and historical foundations underlying the way we conduct business today, especially in regard to computer security. The paper also explores culture, virtues, ethics, morals and laws as they relate to computers.

(11) *The Network Application from Hell*
This chapter discusses the exponential growth of the World Wide Web (WWW). The Web's hypertext-based interface provides a better method of coping with navigation of the Internet than the early command-based applications. This, together with the Web's ever expanding array of applications like formatted text, images, audio and video, has led to the explosion in the number of Web users. This in turn is affecting system performance. This has created a dilemma between providing a certain performance level and a cost effective service.

(12) *When "Oops" Isn't Enough: Responsibility for Unreliable Software*
This chapter discusses the danger with unreliable software released by the designer in a rush usually to beat a competitor. It also explores the legal risks, and civil laws and their application, and suggests ways of eliminating or reducing the risks.

10. A CULTURAL AND HISTORICAL PERSPECTIVE OF COMPUTER SECURITY

Jacqueline E. C. Wyatt and Patricia H. Farrar

INTRODUCTION

This chapter covers computer security in the cultural and historical perspective of our society including, all too cursorily, topics such as culture, virtues, morals, ethics, values, privacy, and a minimal review of computer laws, and how these topics are affected by new technology such as personal computers (PC), telecommuting, and electronic data interchange (EDI), all of which enable the average citizen to compromise computer security. There is only a modest amount of empirical research and a dearth of cumulative findings on the subject of the impacts of computer technology on society (Danziger, 1985).

CULTURE

According to Haviland (1974, p. 264) "culture is a set of rules or standards which, when acted upon by the members of a society, produces behavior that falls within a range of variance the members consider proper and acceptable." Culture is preserved from generation to generation by being passed down by various institutions like schools, families, and others, including the legal system. If we remove persons from a given culture, the culture will slowly change, and perhaps the old culture will totally disappear as a new one replaces the old. This is called devolution when a trait or traits are replaced in the entire culture, and deculturation when part of a culture is lost (Haviland).

Pangle (1993) believes that, in our own society, what united the American founders was our own early colonial heritage. It was a heritage of the "Old

World" culture, i.e., one of obedience, obedience of the individual to higher social and divine wholes; obedience of the great mass of men to secular lords and anointed priests; obedience of the laboring agricultural and commercial or entrepreneurial classes to the military and leisured classes. Indeed the culture of the founders was primarily anchored in Western European and English values.

During approximately ninety percent of human history, men, women, and children have not lived in families so much as in bands or tribes and were hunters and gatherers (Haviland, 1975). It is almost true that the nuclear family was invented in the 1920s, but in one sense the biological family has always been a nuclear family (Platt, 1972). Dr. William Goode (1972) has stated that the family is both fragile and tough. It is fragile because it seems constantly to be breaking down, but tough because it manifestly has not disappeared. But the family as the founders knew it or imagined it might be in the future (Pangle, 1993) is fast disintegrating.

The human condition (Arendt, 1985) is one of plurality, i.e., being with others. One's world includes a unique and complex web of human relations that are important and critical to each individual. These webs include families, neighborhoods, schoolmates, peers at work, colleagues, a political structure, etc., and to be fully human means being in relationships with others.

According to Ricoeur (1974) in the fabric of our inner-most being lies the freedom to deliberate, decide, and act. It is on this basis that we hold persons accountable for their actions, and their moral lives. However, Keat (1992) believes that cultural tradition provides the understanding of the moral world we are in, and that it gives us the arena in which we learn about virtue, norms, law, and our responsibilities and possibilities as moral beings. It is culture's duty to cultivate virtue. Early moral education lays the groundwork for later moral maturity. "Rule-following, like virtue, ought to be taught as a habit..." (p. 457).

Keat (1992) suggests that comprehending both diversity and unity must be goals for moral education in a culturally plural world, and that early education must nurture good habits of thought and action. An individual interprets the world in terms of what he or she already understands: new experiences are understood in the context of old experiences, i.e., understanding is historical.

VIRTUE

A virtue is a quality of character by which individuals habitually recognize and do the right thing (Woodward, 1994). In Book III of *Rhetoric*, Aristotle's (384–322 B.C.) gives four virtues of style—clarity, propriety, dignity, and purity. Woodward (pp. 38-39) has modernized them to be fortitude, temperance, prudence, and justice:

Fortitude: The strength of mind and courage to persevere in the face of adversity.

Temperance: Self-discipline, the control of all unruly human passions and appetites.

Prudence: Practical wisdom and the ability to make the right choice in specific situations.

Justice: Fairness, honesty, lawfulness and the ability to keep one's promises.

In *The Book of Virtues: A Treasury of Great Moral Stories* William J. Bennett groups virtues under the following headings:

Self-discipline: We must make a "disciple" of oneself to be our own teacher, trainer, coach and "disciplinarian."

Compassion: Takes seriously the reality of other persons, their inner lives, their emotions, as well as their external circumstances.

Responsibility: Is to be "answerable" or accountable for our actions.

Friendship: Taking others seriously for their own sake.

Work: Applied effort—whatever we expend our energy on for the sake of accomplishing or achieving something. "Work is not what we do for a living but what we do with our lives" [p. 347].

Courage: A settled disposition to feel appropriate degrees of fears and confidence in challenging situations.

Perseverance: Necessary for anyone intent on doing good in the world: it is crucial to success.

Honesty: A state of being real, genuine, authentic, and bona fide.

Loyalty: A kind of constancy or steadfastness in our attachments to other persons, groups, institutions, or ideals with which we have deliberately decided to associate.

Faith: A source of discipline and power and meaning in the lives of the faithful of of any major religious creed: it binds people in ways that cannot be duplicated by other means.

Immanuel Kant (Ellington, 1983) believes that the young must be taught by the assistance of a responsible community to become properly educated to take on good rather than bad characteristics, i.e., "moral personality." Bennett (1993) also believes that children must be taught by observation, i.e., by observing role models, which make the young morally literate (see also Bennett's *The De-Valuing of America: The Fight for Our Culture and Our Children*).

However, the shift from the extended family to the nuclear family to single-parent homes is making the teaching of morals, ethics, values, etc., by observation most difficult, if not impossible. Unfortunately, much of the observation today is of television, day-care center employees, or peers, all of which display a variety of values, many of which are incompatible with those of a given child's parents or culture.

VALUES

A value may be defined as a general characteristic of an object or state of affairs that a person views with favor, believes is beneficial, and is disposed to act to promote (Baier and Rescher, eds., 1969). Values indicate preferences or desires and also include beliefs about benefits or moral obligation. "Principles of right and wrong in human actions, and good and evil in the consequences of actions, constitute the domain of ethics" (Barbour, 1993, p. 27). Ethics is from the Greek word "ethos" which means character or custom. Very few texts address cross-cultural application of moral values to business decisions in cultures outside their own (Wines and Napier, 1992).

COMPUTER HISTORY

International Business Machines (IBM) installed the world's first business computer at General Electric Appliance Park in Louisville, Kentucky, in 1954 (Bohl, 1984). During the following 40 years the business world underwent major changes. These changes, by necessity, also changed culture, society and individuals' lives. Today virtually every individual will be exposed to and will use, in some manner, a computer or computer terminal. Alexander (1983, p. 186) states that "Except for the most reclusive hermit tucked away on some mountaintop, there is no American whose life is untouched by the computer."

A major event occurred in 1976 when the Personal Electronic Transactor (PET) was the first off-the-shelf, ready-to-use, fully assembled microcomputer offered by Commodore Business Machines (Bohl, 1984). This gave rise to an entire group of computers known as personal computers, or PCs for short. It was these personal computers that invaded the home, as well as offices, and made computers available and usable to the average citizen. Today most colleges, universities, and even elementary and secondary schools have programs of study in the computer field. There are millions of computers in public schools. In fact, many states have laws mandating computer literacy for all high school and or college graduates (Merrill et al., 1986). These mandates have played a role in making the computer the property of the average citizen, affecting all of us in today's world. Goleman (1983, p. 43) states, "Computer literacy is becoming as essential a tool as reading, writing, and arithmetic."

Some writers suggest that business schools teach consequential ethical applications even as they deny moral indoctrination (Scott and Mitchell, 1986). As we move toward a global society, we will be faced with interpreting, translating, and incorporating moral values into business decisions with cross-cultural ethics.

TELECOMMUTING

Telecommuting, a word coined in the early 1970s by Dr. Jack Nilles, the director of information technology, Center for Futures Research, University of Southern California, Los Angeles, is generally a unique type of work-at-home situation where employees commute to the workplace via a computer (Christensen, 1987). This generally involves a personal computer or a micro, telephone, and modem. Telecommuting may also take place from a commuter train, van, automobile, satellite branch office, or other locale having the prerequisite equipment ("The Portable Executive," 1988). Telecommuting is an organized, preplanned work arrangement with an employer or contractor, and may involve a given number of days, or hours each week, or hours each month at home, often with the remaining workweek in a traditional corporate office. Telecommuting can be considered a flexplace, i.e., "virtual office," in addition to a flextime benefit.

The social implications outlined in the *Third Wave*, a book by Alvin Toffler concerning the computer revolution, are tremendous. He argues that we are now in an information-based society, and the computer will offer more freedom on the job, including working from the "electronic cottage." Davenport (1985) also believes that computers change traditional concepts of work by reaching out beyond the conventional workplace into the remote office, department and home. Some futurists predict that 25 percent of all paid work will be done from people's homes by the turn of the century.

Even if individuals continue to work in the traditional office, most will have personal computers at home. Alexander (1983, pp. 185 and 187) states,

> The personal computer has become a source of serious family distress. The computer addicts neglect their wives, ignore their children, and scorn their household responsibilities.... These optimists are saying that the new micro-technology, with its nearly infinite capabilities and flexibilities, will encourage individualism. For example, people can work at terminals at home instead of offices; educate themselves on a variety of subjects at their own learning pace; shop electronically; streamline their personal records needed for taxes, investments, insurance, auto maintenance, and other purposes.

As with any new trend, there are numerous issues involved in telecommuting such as computer security, the selection of the telecommuting employee, equipment ownership, and changing lifestyles which may change values and culture. Many believe that working at home will bypass corporate culture, which will also lead to a feeling of isolation (Barnes, 1983; Christensen, 1987, 1988; Ferrarini and Farrell, 1982; Gordon, 1984; Zuboff, 1982). Richardson (1983) and others (Kuzela, 1987; Parker, 1987) also support this position. People who work in organizations are prone to seek out and identify with those who share similar values, and social belonging is nice. Other management theorists (Maslow, 1954; McClelland, 1953; Herzberg, Mausner and Snyderman, 1959) go one step further and believe that a sense of belonging is vital to one's sense of achievement and psychological well being. With more people telecommuting, there may be increased feelings of isolation, and possibly even hostility. This, in itself, will lead to stress and an entirely new set of management problems that may manifest themselves in increased turnover, absenteeism, and even sabotage in certain circumstances.

If individuals do not spend a requisite amount of time at the traditional office, they may not be exposed to the corporate culture in sufficient depth to acquire it themselves and to enculturate the next generation of employees. Telecommuters will be exposed to the culture in their homes and communities, which may be drastically different from their organizations' culture, and a reintegration process into corporate culture may be necessary should they return to the traditional office.

Parker (1987) states that it is the interpersonal contact that makes working in an office productive and lively. This is supported by Robert E. Kraut, a social scientist at Bell Communications Research, Inc., who states, "Serendipitous, spontaneous contact is crucial to getting work done" ("The Portable Executive," 1988, p. 103). If work does not focus on social cues, how can culture, including virtues, values, and morals, be transmitted to the workforce? These drawbacks can be mitigated if the telecommuter works in the traditional office a certain number of days a week or month.

Organizations and the telecommuter have a responsibility for physically securing the equipment; however, this is more difficult in private homes and apartments. Computers in private residences are more at risk of being stolen, damaged, compromised or abused in some manner. Intentional abuse and fraud will be easier in the privacy of one's personal residence, because a telecommuter has virtually unlimited access to the organization's mainframe and databases. Disgruntled employees or customers will be able to do great harm in a very short period of time, so constant and vigilant surveillance is an absolute must.

ELECTRONIC DATA INTERCHANGE

Electronic data interchange (EDI) arose in the late 1970s in the transportation industry as a method of intercompany communication. In 1982, Texas Instruments undertook the first pilot test, and in 1983, the American National Standard Institute (ANSI) issued the first EDI standard (Cheene, 1991).

Electronic data interchange involves computers, modems, software, electronic mailboxes, and willing trading partners. Sometimes this is also called interorganizational systems (IOS) or interorganizational networks. As many as one third of business transactions will be involved in electronic data interchange by the end of this decade (O'Brien, 1995). Wyatt (1992) found in a study of 150 of the Fortune 500 companies only a shockingly low 4.2 percent indicated security was a concern, even though EDI is fast becoming a way of doing business and bridges global networks and cultural heritage.

PRIVACY

Experts state that we must start setting ground rules to govern today's electronic frontiers, including such issues as personal privacy versus corporate proprietary rights, data transmissions, and how legal rules of evidence apply to information stored in computers (Reynolds, 1992). Companies do very little to create privacy policies even in this day of information super-highways and global networks (Charney, 1992).

Justice Brandeis (1890) defines privacy as the "right to be let alone." The U.S. Constitution does not contain an express right of privacy; however, most decisions have generally arisen in context of the Fourth Amendment prohibition on unreasonable searches and seizures, the Fifth Amendment bar to self-incrimination and the requirement of due process, and the Fourteenth Amendment Equal Protection Clause. There are certain federal laws, e.g., the Fair Credit Reporting Act of 1970, that afford the right to limited privacy in specified areas. This law regulates the disclosure of personal information and does not address the collection of personal information (see Saint Paul Guardian Ins. Co. v. Johnson, 884 F.2d 881 [5th Cir. 1989]). A credit reporting agency has substantial latitude to disseminate regulated information without an individual's knowledge or consent (Reidenberg, 1992). However, there are laws restricting the duration that certain types of obsolete personal information may be disseminated, e.g., bankruptcy adjudications more than ten years old, suits and judgments over seven years, arrests and convictions and other adverse information older than seven years.   '

In addition to federal laws covering privacy, there may exist state laws which afford more detail and specific guidelines, especially concerning individual privacy. Some state courts have developed a set of common law torts to protect against invasions of privacy. These generally fall under four types of actionable invasions (Reidenberg, 1992):

(1) the intrusion upon one's seclusion;
(2) the public disclosure of private facts;
(3) publicity that places one in a false light; and
(4) the misappropriation of one's name or likeness for commercial purposes.

However, Reidenberg states that these are common law rights which evolved largely in response to news-media and advertising cases, and there are few decisions that analyze the privacy issues in other contexts. He concludes

(p. 243) that "In light of the proliferation of information technologies, and networks, the United States needs to re-evaluate the legal protection available to individuals."

COMPUTER LAWS

In a study by Wyatt (1991) where the attorneys general of all 50 states were surveyed, she found that all states had a state computer crime act. None had state laws prior to 1982, and a surprising 35 percent had passed their laws since 1985. Another surprise was that only 33 percent of the states had followed federal computer crime statutes. It is safe to assume that many of these laws are yet to be tested in the court system, especially since there are often evidentiary problems in proving computer crime (Gardner, Samuels, Render, and Coffinberger, 1989).

Computer crime can take the form of unauthorized disclosure of information, modification of information, destruction of data, denial of service, setting viruses or worms, etc., including hacking and violation of individual privacy. Most hacking, along with other unauthorized access to computer systems, is accomplished through remote dial-up access (Chalmers, 1987; Liggett, 1984). Passwords are generally considered to be unsafe; therefore, other forms of authentication, e.g., front-end processors with authentication software, must be considered and implemented. But even these do not deter the determined criminal or the cyberpunk.

When crimes are committed by using a computer the question is how to apply normal search-and-seizure and other legal rules of evidence. Present law requires that only the specific material stated in a warrant can be seized—and in the form of original documents (Reynolds, 1992). How can computer files be searched while still protecting the privacy and confidentiality of the other information not relevant to the case at hand?

Crimes committed by using a computer cannot only be interstate but international in scope, hence causing problems in detecting and prosecuting the criminals. Computer crimes can pose a threat to the security of our country (see also Clifford Stoll's book *The Cuckoo's Egg*) or to your individual health: one large hospital in the northeast United States lost more than forty percent of its patient records to a computer virus (Charney, 1992).

Nawrocki (1987) cites an FBI study that reports that only one in 20,000 computer criminals ever goes to jail. The increase in the number of computer crimes has ballooned because the computer enables crimes to be no longer constrained by physical access (Charney, 1992).

CONCLUSIONS

This paper attempts to enlighten the reader about the cultural, moral heritage, and historical foundations underlying the way we conduct business today especially in regard to computer security. We cannot address computer security without an understanding and appreciation of the culture, virtues, values, ethics, morals and laws underlying our society as a whole.

REFERENCES

Alexander, Benjamin H. (1983, January 1). "Impact of Computers on Human Behavior." *Vital Speeches of the Day*, 49 (6), pp. 185–188.

Antonoff, Michael (1985, July). "The Push for Telecommuting." *Personal Computing*, 9 (7), pp. 83–92.

Arendt, Hannah (1985). *The Human Condition*. Chicago: University of Chicago Press. Aristotle translated by Lane Cooper (1932). *The Rhetoric of Aristotle*. Englewood Cliffs, NJ: Prentice-Hall.

Baier, Kurt and Rescher, Nicholas, eds. (1969). *Values and the Future*. New York: Free Press.

Barbour, Ian G. (1993). *Ethics in an Age of Technology: The Gifford Lectures Volume 2*. San Francisco: HarperCollins.

Barnes, K. (1983, April). "So You Want to Work at Home, Eh?" *Infosystems*, 30 (4), pp. 90–92.

Bennett, William J. (1993). *The Book of Virtues: A Treasury of Great Moral Stories*. New York: Simon & Schuster.

Bohl, Marilyn (1984). *Information Processing with BASIC* (4th ed.). Chicago: SRA.

Brandeis, Louis D. (1890). "The Right of Privacy." *Harvard Law Review*, (4), 193, 205.

Chalmers, Leslie (1987, Summer). "Future Directions for Personal Authentication." *Journal of Accounting and EDP*, 3 (2), pp. 59–61.

Charney, Scott (1992, Fall). "The Justice Department Responds to the Growing Threat of Computer Crime." *Harvard Business Review*, 8 (2), pp. 1–12.

Cheene, Dominique J. (1991, April). "The World of EDI." *PCToday*, 4 (5), pp. 45–50.

Christensen, Kathleen (1987, April). "A Hard Day's Work in the Electronic Cottage." *Across the Board*, 24 (4), pp. 17–21, 23.

_____. (1988, October). "Telecommuting: Managing a Long-Distance Work Force." *Small Business Reports*, 13 (8), pp. 64–66.

Churchill, L. R. (1982). "The Teaching of Ethics and Moral Values in Teaching: Some Contemporary Confusions." *Journal of Higher Education*, 53 (3), 296–306.

Danziger, James N. (1985, March). "Social Science and the Social Impacts of Computer Technology." *Social Science Quarterly*, 66 (1), pp. 3–21.

Davenport, Thomas F., Jr. (1985, January). "The Changing Environment of Information Systems." *Infosystems*, 32 (1), pp. 30–32.

Ellington, James W. (1983). *Metaphysics of Morals*, in Immanuel Kant, *Ethical Philosophy* translated by James W. Ellington. Indianapolis: Hacket.

Ferrarini, E. and Farrell, G. (1982, March 17). "Telecommuting: High Tech's New Cottage Industry." *Computerworld/Extra!* 16 (11A), pp. 63–65.

Gardner, Ella Paton, Samuels, Linda B., Render, Barry and Coffinberger, Richard L. (1989, Fall). "The Importance of Ethical Standards and Computer Crime Laws for Data Security." *Information System Management* 6(4), pp. 42–50.

Goleman, Daniel. (1983, February). "The Electronic Rorschach." *Psychology Today*, 17(2), pp. 36–43.

Goode, William J. (1972). "Social Change and Family Renewal," in *Families of the Future*. Ames, IA: The Iowa State University Press, pp. 116–133.

Gordon, Gil. (1984, January). "Commuting by Computer." *Best's Review*, 84(9), pp. 58–97.

Haviland, William A. (1974). *Anthropology*. New York: Holt, Rinehart and Winston.

_____. (1975). *Cultural Anthropology*. New York: Holt, Rinehart and Winston.

Herzberg, Frederick, Mausner, B., & Snyderman, B. (1959). *The Motivation to Work*. New York: John Wiley & Sons.

Keat, Marilyn S. (1992, Fall). "Beyond the Virtues—Principles D161 ebate." *Educational Theory*, 42 (4), 443–459.

Kuzela, Lad (1987, June 1). "Sandy's Working at Home Today." *Industry Week*, 233 (5), pp. 34-35.

Liggett, Rosy (1984, April 30). "Info Resource Management Aids Data Security." *Computerworld*, 18 (18), pp. 49-50.

McClelland, David C. (1953). *The Achievement Motive*. New York: Appleton-Century-Crofts.

Maslow, Abraham H. (1954). *Motivation and Personality*. New York: Harper & Row.

Merrill, Paul F., Tolman, Marvin N., Christensen, Larry, Hammons, Kathy, Vincent, Bret R. and Reynolds, Peter L. (1986). *Computers in Education*. Englewood Cliffs, NJ: Prentice-Hall.

Nawrocki, Jay (1987, July). "There Are Too Many Loop-Holes: Current Computer Crime Laws Require Clearer Definition." *Data Management*, 25 (7), pp. 14-15, 28.

O'Brien, James A. (1995). *Introduction to Information Systems: An End User/Enterprise Perspective*. (Alternate Edition). Chicago: Irwin.

Pangle, Thomas L. (1993, Winter). "The Constitution's Human Vision." *Public Interest*, No. 86, pp. 77–90.

Parker, Charles S. (1987). *Understanding Computers and Data Processing: Today and Tomorrow with BASIC* (2nd. ed). New York: Holt, Rinehart and Winston.

Platt, John (1972). "A Fearful and Wonderful World for Living," in *Families of the Future*. Ames, IA: The University of Iowa Press, pp. 3–13.

Reidenberg, Joel R. (1992). "Privacy in the Information Economy: A Fortress or Frontier for Individual Rights." *Federal Communications Law Journal*, 44 (2), pp. 195–243.

Reynolds, Larry (1992, September). "Constitutional Law in the Electronic Age." *Management Review*, 81 (9), pp. 24-25.

Richardson, Douglas K. (1983, September 1). "Corporate Culture." *Vital Speeches of the Day*, 49 (22), pp. 677–681.

Ricoeur, Paul (1974). "Nature and Freedom." *Political and Social Essays*. Athens, OH: The Ohio University Press, pp. 23–45

Scott, W. G. and Mitchell, T. R. (1986). "Markets and Morals in Management Education." *Selections*, 3 (2), pp. 3–8.

Sims, Ronald R. (1992). "The Challenge of Ethical Behavior in Organizations." *Journal of Business Ethics*, 11 (7), pp. 505–513.

Sommers, Christina Hoff (1993, Spring). "Teaching the Virtues." *Public Interest*, No. 111, pp. 3–13.

Staff (1988, October 10). "The Portable Executive." *Business Week*, pp. 102–106, 110, 112.

Stoll, C. (1989). *The Cuckoo's Egg*. London: The Bodley Head.

Toffler, Alvin (1980). *The Third Wave*. New York: Morrow.

Wines, William A. and Napier, Nancy K. (1992, November). "Toward an Understanding of Cross-Cultural Ethics: A Tentative Model." *Journal of Business Ethics*, 11 (11), pp. 831–842.

Woodward, Kenneth L. (1994, June 13). "What Is Virtue?" *Newsweek*, 123 (24), pp. 38-39.

Wyatt, Jacqueline E. C. (1992). "Electronic Data Inter-Change Usage: A Survey of the Fortune 500 Companies." *The Association of Management Proceedings Collective Supplement*, 10 (1), pp. 31–36.

_____. (1991). "State Computer Crime Statutes in the U.S." *The Association of Management Annual Conference Proceedings: Information Technology*, IT-76-80.

Zuboff, S. (1982, September-October). "New Worlds of Computer-Mediated Work." *Harvard Business Review*, 60, pp. 142–152.

11. THE NETWORK APPLICATION FROM HELL

ALAN HOLT

ABSTRACT

The World Wide Web provides an easy-to-use interface for navigating the Internet and is attracting users from outside the "technical domain." Its growth has been exponential, both in terms of servers and network traffic.

The infrastructure on which the Internet is based will require a major upgrade if it is to cope with a population boom in Cyberville. If deployment of higher capacity technology does not keep pace with application demands it will be necessary to implement methods of capping peak loads such that networks and servers are not overwhelmed. This paper presents some of the ethical issues of the Internet's "killer app."

1. INTRODUCTION

The World Wide Web has been described as the "killer app" for the Internet. Its popularity is growing as is the size of the Internet information space, and according to Gray (9) "The Web is big." Shneiderman (26) states that "Exploring information resources becomes increasingly difficult as the volume grows."

The Web's interface is based on hypertext and provides a better method of coping with navigation of the Internet than the early command-line based applications. However, the author believes this ease of use could have an impact on the current infrastructure such that networks and servers are overwhelmed by requests for resources.

This paper outlines some of the ethical issues involved in supporting the Web while maintaining acceptable levels of performance, both for the Web and other network applications.

2. ETHICS OF "NET SURFING"

The Internet provides access to information resources distributed worldwide. However, before the introduction of the Web the Internet was a "cold and forbidding" (17) place. Early Internet search and retrieval tools were primarily command-line based and had steep learning curves. Berners-Lee (2), the inventor of the Web, provides the following description of these tools: "Much information is in fact available on-line, but references to it involve complicated instructions regarding host names, logon passwords, terminal types and commands to type, sometimes needing the skilled interpretation of a network 'guru.'"

Despite the wealth of information and resources, some members of the user community may have exhibited a reluctance to access it because of the learning curve of the tools available at the time. According to Kennedy (17), "Not everyone wants to spend months discovering how 20-year-old operating systems work."

Studies have shown that the growth of the Web is exponential. According to Hughes (13) the Web was the eleventh most popular Internet application in terms of network traffic at the end of 1993 when there were 623 servers (9). Twelve months earlier it was only 127th. By the end of 1994 the number of Web sites was estimated at 12,000 (9). Hughes (13) offers the following explanation for the Web's increased popularity: "The Web offers a very simple-to-use interface to [sic] the traditionally hard-to-master resources on the Internet. It is probably this ease of use as well as the popularity of many graphical interfaces to the Web that caused the explosion of the Web traffic in 1993."

The author believes the "hard-to-master" nature of early navigation tools had a regulating effect on the amount of requests for resources available "on" the Internet. The Web, however, requires less in the way of "network guru" skills in order to navigate and browse the Internet information space.

The consequence of this is that the scope of Internet citizenship is extended beyond technical domain, resulting in a significant increase in usage of the Internet, with possible detrimental effects on system performance. These "detrimental effects" go beyond simply weight of numbers; in a shared computing environment any single user or set of users has the ability to overwhelm the system.

Users that place (very) high demands on system resources can be categorized in terms of intentional or unintentional (mis)use. Intentional misuse is committed by 1) users that consume system resources for the purpose of denying them to others and 2) knowledgeable users who know how to get the most out of the system.

The actions of the first type of user can be described as "security attacks," the ethical issues of which have been discussed in many articles.[1] The actions of the second type of user may not be as malicious as those of the first, but they nevertheless warrant ethical examination. For example, the Web enables users to develop search engines (called "robots" or "spiders") for navigating the Internet information space. Development of such applications is typically the domain of knowledgeable users. The automation of resource search processes has a number of benefits but also introduces certain hazards. A rogue spider can place high loads on servers and networks.

The Usenet bulletin board system has experienced much of this kind of "misuse" in the form of "Spams." One of the most notorious cases is described in Jannife's "Spam Wars" article (15) about two lawyers who used Usenet to advertise their services. The lawyers employed a computer professional to develop a program that would post Usenet articles such that they reached the widest possible audience (by posting to all news groups). Although the lawyers felt they were justified in their actions, the Usenet population generally held a contrary viewpoint. Within the Usenet community, various methods of expressing "moral" outrage have evolved. These methods include "flaming" or "mail bombing" the offending user (very often though, these vigilante tactics can cause more problems than the original Spam).

Articles by Eichmann (6) and Koster (19, 20) attempt to address the ethics of Web spiders. These articles provide guidelines for writing spiders as well as guidelines for dealing with rogue spiders that are affecting system performance. Specifically, they advise against typical Usenet methods of peer pressure. In contrast to users that know the effects of their actions on performance but carry them out regardless, some users may not be aware of the impact they are having on a system.

In the paper "Do Disk Drives Dream of Buffer Cache Hits" (12), the author applies the Moorian ethical construct: "to do what is right" to the usage of computer systems. If a computer system exists for the purpose of achieving good, a user does "what is right" by performing those actions which "will not cause less good" to a system's operating performance. For instance in the book *The Unix Programming Environment* Kernighan and Pike (18) say that (Unix) users should be considerate to others on the system and lower the priority of CPU intensive processes. However, such an "ethical observation" was made by industry specialists with a thorough understanding of the underlying technology. Ethical observations are based upon the theories one holds (11). Kernighan and Pike's knowledge of the Unix scheduler enables them to draw the above conclusion regarding ethical behavior within a Unix programming environment. However it may not be reasonable to expect non-specialist users to possess the technical knowledge required to make such ethical observations regarding computer system usage.

Being unaware of the effects of one's actions on system performance could be (partly) attributable to technology itself. Computer applications are increasing in sophistication such that the underlying technology is becoming evermore transparent to the user. Web browsers are a good example of this, according to Marc Andreessen (1): "NCSA [National Center for Supercomputing Applications] Mosaic does everything it can to avoid burdening the user with the technical details ..." This "transparency" makes it difficult for non-specialist users (and even specialist users) to appreciate the limiting factors of the underlying technology (e.g., bandwidth, CPU cycles, etc.) and to make judgments in terms of doing "what is right."

In addition the Web introduces a "paradigm shift" with respect to information access and retrieval on the Internet. Whereas before (the Web), on finding an information resource, users would download it to a local system (because getting it the first time was fairly hard work). The Web reduces the need to do this. Once a resource has been located, in order to access it in the future, a user only has to keep a record of its reference (e.g. in the hotlist file) rather than saving an entire copy locally on disk. This results in an increase in over-the-wire requests for resources.

To summarize, intentional misuse for the sake of rendering a system unusable (even to the perpetrator) can be dealt with through the legal process, and thus becomes an issue for the legal profession and law enforcement agencies (with cooperation from computer system designers and administrators).

With regard to intentional misuse by knowledgeable users attempting to get the most out of the system, affiliation with professional and chartered institutions may be required in order to "promote" ethical behavior. However, many "knowledgeable users" may not possess the necessary educational or professional qualifications (which continue to get higher [14]) to be accepted into such institutions and will not feel bound by their "codes of conduct." The alternative is to encourage ethical behavior through peer pressure (employing alternative methods to flames and mail bombs).

Users that misuse computer systems unintentionally cannot really be accused of acting unethically (although such actions are subject to ethical analysis). The premise in (British) law that ignorance is no excuse (4) does not appear to be applicable to "unethical" behavior as it is to illegal behavior. It may be necessary to look for technological solutions to this problem.

3. "WEBMASTER" ETHICS

Graphic User Interface (GUI) browsers transform the Web from a hypertext based Internet information navigator into a hypermedia one. This enables Web sites to provide multimedia resources, which, according to Treese (31), is a potential problem: "One change that has some Internet observers concerned is the increase in multimedia applications."

The types of media typically found on the Web include formatted text, images, audio, and video. Data file sizes of multimedia resources are dependant upon a number of factors (e.g., display size, sound and picture quality, duration). The following table shows the byte sizes of some example resources.

Format	Description	Media Type	Size (bytes)	Comments
HTML	AT&T NSUK Home Page	ASCII text	2,523	no wait
Audio	*Star Trek: Generations* movie sound bite	Audio	23,421	we can cope
GIF this	Doom II Screen shot (640x400)	Image	84,832	don't try at home
MPEG	Shoemaker-Levy comet animation	Video	394,269	coffee break
Quicktime	*Judge Dredd* movie trailer	Video and Audio	2,658,584	lunch everybody

TABLE 1. File size of example media formats

Access delays tend to become significant for graphically based media. High speed (10Mb/s +) local area networks are able to cope reasonably well with such formats (though not necessarily in real time). However, the Web is primarily WAN based, where bandwidths are currently in the kilobit or low megabit per second range, and are more likely to be overwhelmed by requests for graphical format data. Shneiderman (26) states, "Overall, the bandwidth of information presentation seems potentially higher in the visual domain[2] than media reaching any of the other senses."

A "visual domain" based Web (with some audio thrown in) is increasing in popularity. McCormick et al. (23) recognize benefits of the visual domain: "Visualisation is a method of computing. It transforms the symbolic into the geometric, enabling researchers to observe their simulations and computations. Visualisation offers a method for seeing the unseen."

This "desirability" factor of graphical formats adds to the demands placed upon the networks and the servers themselves. Treese (31) describes the popularity of NASA's Web facility for distributing pictures of the impact of the Shoemaker-Levy Comet with Jupiter: "During one week in July, users on the Internet downloaded more than 300,000 files, many of them megabyte-size images, from the Comet Shoemaker-Levy 9 server NASA's NSSDC (National Space Science Data Center) in Greenbelt, Maryland."

NASA was able to obtain some of the best pictures from sources like the Hubble telescope and Voyager 2. The Web provided an excellent method of distributing high resolution images of Jupiter and the comet's impact. The popularity of the event and the availability of such images placed a significant load on the SL9 server (and presumably the network). Treese (31) adds, "During the peak hours, the NASA server handled 6000 requests." "The load on our primary server was sufficiently high for us to consider closing down the service," says Syed Towheed, a systems programmer with NASA. Instead, engineers brought systems on-line to handle the load.

Another server in Holland suffered similar load problems. The server http://olt.et.tudelft.nl/ held an extensive archive of pornographic images. This became one of the most popular sites on the Web. Groeneveld (10) describes the consequences of its popularity: "The automatic feed from usenet news and the porn stuff are not accessible anymore. This is mainly because the incredible traffic which that class of pictures generates. At the time it was still available it attracted over 10,000 people daily, too much to handle."

It is important to note that people that provide Web servers are not necessarily responsible for underlying hardware (and its performance). It may be considered irresponsible (and therefore unethical) to make such resources accessible on a system (on which the Web may not be the sole application) due to their "popularity" and their nature to attract large numbers of requests.

In the NASA SL9 server example, the system's capacity was increased to cope with the additional load; in the case of the Dutch server, the pornographic resources were removed. Some may feel that such resources should not be made accessible due to their very nature. According to Jannife (15), Cantor and Siegel, the lawyers at the center of the Spam Wars incident, used the "nature" of various news groups on Usenet (such as alt.sex) to justify their advertisement campaign.

The Internet is fairly liberal with regard to the nature of the material it "carries," but Usenet Spams have been cancelled and Web servers (or certain resources) have been removed by Sysops concerned with maintaining acceptable levels of system performance. However, such actions could be described as censorship and unethical in themselves. Kehoe (16) offers the following counter argument: "Freedom of the press belongs to those that own one." In which case those responsible for the underlying system hardware are within their rights to perform such actions of "censorship," with or without justification.

However, Jannife (15) feels that, in the case of Usenet Spams, these actions are justifiable if one is paying for the service "by the K." This applies to users who access the Web via the public telephone network (using a modem). Modem users are furthest down the Web access "food chain" and are limited to relatively low data transfer rates. The increasing amount of multimedia resources, especially inlined graphical images, has prompted criticism from this section of the Web community. Kennedy (17) explains, "Users find the long delays as pictures slowly download and decode a great distraction (and also a way of increasing the telephone bill)."

Web server providers must consider the ethical implications of their "pride over access counts" (6). Providing more and more multimedia resources of ever increasing quality, size and duration in order to attract users will result in increased load on servers and networks.

4. ETHICS OF ENGINEERING THE WEB

The nature of traffic load makes engineering the Internet a difficult task. According to Treese (31), "Services on the Internet often experience heavy traffic intermittently."

Section three outlined how NASA engineers resolved the load problems on the SL9 server by bringing "additional systems on-line" to meet the peak load demands. However, increasing the "capacity" of servers and networks to that of the peak load can be expensive. Drupsteen (5) believes that the "Network should be able to handle peaks in traffic. This however leads to the establishment of transmission capacities which are excessive when compared with the average amount of traffic." This can create a dilemma (for the engineer) between providing a certain performance level and a cost effective service. However the Web does provide a technical means of capping peak loads. Proxy Web servers can make resource requests to remote Web servers on behalf of clients. Proxy servers were primarily designed for security purposes to allow clients within a firewall to access the (external) Web. One benefit of using a proxy server is caching. Proxy server caches exploit temporal locality of reference, i.e., the likelihood of reusing recently referenced resources, in order to bring about performance enhancements.

The performance benefits of a cache hit are twofold. Firstly, the response time to fetch a resource is shorter, and secondly, no load is placed on the (external) network and remote server. However, while caching reduces the number of over-the-wire requests, it introduces the need for local disk space. Due to the rate of growth of the Web and the diversity of requests, cache sizes may need to be considerably large in order to be effective. Also the disk units on which the cache resides may need fast seek times in order to support high cache hit rates. A proxy server in the author's organization had to have the cache disabled as the disk unit could not handle the volume of requests. Paradoxically, the proxy server was able to cope better with the volume of requests by fetching resources from remote servers rather than from its own file system (a faster disk unit has since been installed and the cache re-enabled).

The objective of the "engineer" is to maintain as high a cache hit rate as possible. However, disk space (like bandwidth) is not infinite. The system has to be configured such that the cache is flushed of out-of-date (resources that have been modified on the remote server since being cached) and temporally non-local references (resources not likely to be accessed in the near future). The author believes the nature of Web access is specific to particular communities of users, and it is important to understand this nature of access in order to configure the caching scheme such that it operates effectively.

While this is a technical issue it is also an ethical one. Technical specialists have a duty to employ available technical solutions in order to cap peak loads and maintain system performance levels.

5. CONCLUSIONS

Fast cell relay network technology has promised a bandwidth utopia, but in the author's opinion, the deployment of this technology has been slow compared to the demands of the applications currently being developed. The author feels that the Web has the potential to overwhelm the current computer and network infrastructure if its usage and implementation go unchecked. Koster (20) expresses his opinion: "It annoys me to see that people cause other people unnecessary hassle. ... I am worried they could make the Web look bad."

Bandwidth is a premium resource, and until a "drastic expansion and upgrading of the telecommunications facilities" (5) happens, it is necessary to implement solutions for capping peak loads generated by the Web and applications like it. Resolution of this problem is an ethical issue as well as a technical one.

6. ACKNOWLEDGMENTS

Many thanks to Professor John Monk of the Open University and Richard Wykeham Martin of AT&T Network Systems UK for their comments and suggestions.

This report was done as part of an Open University research degree.

7. REFERENCES

(1) Andreessen M. *NCSA Mosaic Technical Summary*. May 1993.ftp:ftp.ncsa.uiuc.edr.

(2) Berners-Lee, T. J., Cailliau, R., Groff, J. F. and Pollermann, B. *World-Wide Web: An Information Infrastructure for High-Energy Physics*. C.E.R.N. (European Center for Nuclear Research), accessed December 1994. URL=file://info.cern.ch/pub/www/doc/www-for-hep.ps.Z.

*(3) Berners-Lee, T. J., Cailliau, R., Groff, J .F. and Pollermann, B. *World-Wide Web: The Information Universe*. C.E.R.N., accessed December 1994. URL=http://info.cern.ch/pub/www/doc/ENRAP_9202.ps.Z.

(4) Brown, W. J. *GCSE and "O" Level Law*. Sweet & Maxwell Ltd., London, third edition, 1986.

(5) Drupsteen, J. "ATM: The Leap to Broadband Services." *Trends in Telecommunications, AT&T Network Systems International B.V.*, Vol. 2, No. 2, pp. 4–8, 1994.

(6) Eichmann, D. *Ethical Web Agents*. NCSA (National Center for Supercomputer Applications), last modified September 1994. URL=http://www.ncsa.uiuc.edu/SDG/IT95/Proceedings/Agents/eichmann.ethical/eichmann.

*(7) Ellul, N. (editor). "Being Honest Is Liable to Create Headlines." *Internet*, p. 45, November 1994.

*(8) Fox, D. "Webmeister." *Internet*, pp. 26–28, Issue 3, January 1995.

(9) Gray, M. *Growth of the Web*. last modified February 1995. URL=http://www.net-gen.com/ info/growth.html.

(10) Groeneveld, P. *Digital Picture Archive on the 17th Floor*, last modified January 1995. URL=http://olt.et.tudelft.nl/fun/pictures/pictures.html.

(11) Harman, G. *The Nature of Morality: An Introduction to Ethics*. Oxford University Press, 1977.

(12) Holt, A. G., "Do Disk Drives Dream of Buffer Cache Hits?" *Proceedings of the ACM Ethics in the Computer Age Conference*, November 1994.

(13) Hughes, K. *How Popular Is the Web?* Enterprise Integration Technologies, last modified May 1994. URL= http://www.eit.com/web/www.guide/guide.05.html.

(14) Institute of Electrical Engineers. "CEng Standard to Be Raised for Next Millennium." *IEEE Review*, No. 99, 2 February 1995.

(15) Jannife, P. "Cantor & Siegel Spam Wars." *On-line World*, pp. 36–40, November 1994.

(16) Kehoe, B. P. "Zen and the Art of the Internet." *On-line Version*, First Edition, January 1992.

(17) Kennedy, J. "Mosaic." *Internet and Comms Today*, Issue 3, pp. 46–49, January 1995.

(18) Kernighan, B. W. and Pike, B. *The Unix Programming Environment*. Englewood Cliffs, NJ: Prentice-Hall, 1984.

(19) Koster, M. *Guidelines for Robot Writers*. Nexor Corp, last modified November 1994. URL=http://web.nexor.co.uk/mak/doc/robots/norobots.html.

(20) Koster, M. *What to Do When You Feel Attacked by a Robot*. Nexor Corp, last modified November 1994. URL=http://web.nexor.co.uk/mak/doc/robots/against.html.

*(21) Kroll, E. *The Whole Internet User Guide & Catalog*. Sebastopol, CA: O'Reilly & Associates, 1993.

*(22) McArthur, D. C. "World Wide Web & HTML." *Dr Dobb's Journal*, pp. 18–26, December 1994.

(23) McCormick, B., DeFanti, T. and Brown, R. (editors). "Visualisation in Scientific Computing and Computer Graphics." *ACM SIGGRAPH 21*, November 1987.

(24) Mitcham, C., "Computers: From Ethos and Ethics to Mythos and Religion." *Technology in Society*, Vol. 8, pp. 171–201, 1986.

*(25) Moore, G. E. *Principia Ethica*. Cambridge University Press, second edition, 1959.

(26) Shneiderman B. *Designing the User Interface*. Reading, MA: Addison-Wesley Publishing, second edition, 1992.

*(27) Shooting Shark. "Unix Nasties." *Phrack*, Vol. 1, Issue 6, Phile 5, April 1986.

(28) Spafford, E. *The Internet Worm Program: An Analysis*. Purdue Technical Report CSD-TR-823, December 1988. http://www.cs.petrdue.eclu/tech-reports.

(29) Spafford, E. *Some Musing on Ethics and Computer Break-ins*. Purdue Technical Report.

(30) Stoll, C. *The Cuckoo's Egg*. London: The Bodley Head, 1989.

(31) Treese, W. "Solutions to Internet Traffic Jams." *Byte*, Vol. 19, No. 11, p. 27, November 1994.

References with asterisks do not appear in the text but were consulted.

NOTES

1. Articles (24), (28), (29), and (30) are among the author's favorites.
2. Presumably, text is not considered part of the visual domain.

12. WHEN "OOPS!" ISN'T ENOUGH: RESPONSIBILITY FOR UNRELIABLE SOFTWARE

NANCY J. WAHL

ABSTRACT

Competition among software vendors is intense. In the rush to get new software to the marketplace, some programs are released that have not been thoroughly tested and as a result prove to be unreliable. Unreliable software poses a legal risk to everyone connected with the development and distribution of the software, and exposes them to liability under civil laws. The different categories of civil laws and how these laws may be applied to software companies and or distributors are explained. Several ways of eliminating or reducing the risks associated with liability due to unreliable software are proposed. These ways include personnel management and software and human factors engineering techniques. Contract limitations and liability insurance are proposed as ways of reducing the financial ramifications of the risk.

1. INTRODUCTION

As every aspect of our society becomes more computerized, there are enormous pressures on the computer industry to bring out new products. The public expects the continual development of computer-based systems that are faster, handle larger amounts of data, and provide more functionality. People are constantly looking for new computer systems with the latest enhancements. With this type of pressure and the high cost of development, the computer industry has rushed to get new products to the marketplace. Sometimes these products have not been tested thoroughly. This is especially true of software. Hardware, on the other hand, has developed to the point that some computers are built with off-the-shelf, already-tested components.

171

As computer systems become more powerful, the associated software becomes more complex. The combination of incompletely tested software and more complex software results in a higher probability that significant errors in the software will cause a computer-controlled machine to malfunction or that computer-generated output will be incorrect. These errors can lead to personal injury, damage to physical property, and economic loss. There are few laws regulating the computer industry and even fewer relating to liability for unreliable software. As lawsuits are brought against software providers, the courts are developing a body of legal precedents that provides guidance in the area of liability for unreliable software. Bruce Bierhans, a Boston lawyer, predicts that most court cases will involve computers in the twenty-first century (2).

Unreliable software poses a legal risk for a software development vendor which can lead to financial loss. To avoid financial loss a software vendor should do the following: identify the risk, estimate the extent of the risk, and determine solutions to avoid and or ameliorate the risk. The goal of this paper is to explore solutions to the problem of the software developer's risk due to unreliable software. Several solutions are outlined in Section Four of the paper. These solutions include the following: management of computing personnel to enhance their skills, use of software engineering techniques to develop more reliable software, use of human factors techniques to produce software that is easier to use and understand, modification of the contract between the software developer and the user to limit liability, and purchase of liability insurance to spread the cost of liability to all software users.

The civil laws relating to liability are summarized in Section Two. Case law is evolving and precedents for approaching liability issues and computing are being set. Laws used to bring lawsuits against software developers, distributors and consultants are described in Section Three. Definitions of terms are included at the end of this section to aid in understanding the issues discussed in this paper.

1a. Definitions of Terms

Contract Law—laws relating to agreements between two or more parties obligating each party to do or refrain from doing something

Defendant—the party to a lawsuit who is alleged to have committed some wrong to another person

Insurance—the anticipation of losses through the prediction and redistribution of losses

Liability—legal obligation to make restitution for damages caused by some physical, economic or emotional injury, or breach of contract

Malpractice—negligence committed by a professional

Merchantability—a product should do what is expected of similar products and be of average quality

Negligence—the failure to use the same amount of care that a reasonable person would use in similar circumstances

Plaintiff—the injured complaining party in a lawsuit

Tort—wrongful act or damage to the person or property of another for which a lawsuit may be brought (not including breach of contract)

2. CIVIL LAW

In this section, a context for liability issues is developed by examining where cases relating to unreliable software might go. The function of liability laws is to allocate liability or loss among all parties involved based on fairness and certain behavioral norms (1). Laws can be divided into criminal and civil laws. Most crimes involve breaking some statutory law and are considered to be wrongs against the state. Thus, action is brought by the state. Crimes involving computer acts include illegal transfer of funds, ATM fraud, stolen credit card numbers, and phone call fraud. A person can incur liability under civil laws due to negligence or breach of contract. Lawsuits relating to unreliable software would fall into the category of civil laws which includes contract and tort laws. The remainder of this section deals with contract law and tort law.

2a. Contract Law

Contract laws deal with the provisions of a contract. If a software contract is formally written, the vendor can be sued for breach of contract if the software fails to meet what was specified in the contract. Clients have become more sophisticated as they have become more knowledgeable about computers. They often hire consultants to help develop the software specifications to be included in a contract, thereby making the contract an even more important document. This also brings another person into the liability picture—the consultant. In addition, if the vendor misrepresents the capabilities of the software, she or he can be liable under contract law. Contract law is based upon the intent of the parties as expressed in an agreement.

Contract law includes warranties both expressed and implied. A warranty is a promise made by the manufacturer or vendor of a product that the product will perform in a particular way and is considered part of the contract when the product is sold.

Implied warranty is provided for the purchaser of products by the Uniform Commercial Code (UCC) which has been accepted by all states except Louisiana. Implied warranty means that a product must be able to fulfill its intended purpose and have merchantability. To breach the "intended purpose," the vendor would have to sell a buyer a system that was not suitable for the purpose for which the buyer bought the system. For example, there could be errors in documentation, inadequate on-line help, or software that would not run correctly on the client's hardware.

Merchantability means that a product should do what is ordinarily expected of similar products and that the product is of average quality for products of the same type. For example, if the product is a spreadsheet package, then it should have the expected arithmetic functions and "what if" capabilities of common spreadsheet packages. This type of implied warranty is very important to purchasers of computer systems because they usually have to rely heavily on a vendor's recommendations. A prospective client does not have to negotiate with a vendor to obtain implied warranties because they are provided by the UCC for all products unless explicitly denied.

Express warranty is any oral or written expression of fact, functionality, or promise made by the vendor that is part of the reason the client purchased a product (3). Express warranty may arise in ads, on the product's package, or from a developer, manufacturer or salesperson before a contract is signed. Express warranty deals with the quality of a product and what the vendor will do to correct errors in the product. If a salesperson recommends a product or makes statements that a typical customer would recognize as a sales pitch, that is not considered express warranty. On the other hand, a salesperson does not have to use the words "warranty" or "guarantee" to imply one.

2b. Tort Law

Tort laws deal with wrongful acts other than breach of contract and provide a means for the injured party to collect monetary damages whether the loss was physical, economic, or emotional. Tort law includes intentional torts, negligence (both ordinary negligence and malpractice), and strict liability. Intentional torts are acts that are committed on purpose to injure another person. These include acts such as assault and battery, libel, or slander.

Ordinary negligence is the failure to employ that degree of care which a reasonably prudent person would have exercised under similar circumstances. Negligence is the lack of ordinary care. When applied to a software developer, negligence includes failing to do the following: adequately design, code and test a program; explain to users how to install a program properly; and warn of consequences of improper use.

Malpractice is a form of negligence. The main difference between ordinary negligence and malpractice is the extent of duty of care. Malpractice is generally applied to professionals such as doctors, lawyers, accountants, dentists, veterinarians, morticians, investment bankers, and insurance agents. Members of a profession are held to a higher standard of care than the average person. A professional is to use the care which a reasonable person with the same abilities would use in similar circumstances. *Black's Law Dictionary* defines malpractice as "Professional misconduct or unreasonable lack of skill.

... Failure of one rendering professional services to exercise that degree of skill and learning commonly applied under all circumstances ... with the result of injury, loss or damage." Malpractice applies to the delivery of a service.

Providers of services have liability under negligence or malpractice that is based on fault. In other words, the provider did something wrong or was at fault. Vendors of defective products have no-fault liability that is called strict liability under tort. Strict liability against the vendor of a dangerous product does not require intent to injure or establishment of fault. If personal injury is caused by a machine that is controlled by a computer system that includes faulty software, then the vendor of the machine is strictly liable for the injuries even if he did not cause the fault. Strict liability under tort applies only to defective products. The user must have used the product reasonably and the product must have reached him or her without substantial change from its original condition.

3. LEGAL PRECEDENTS

In general, cases dealing with wrongful acts by humans involving computers are judged like other cases of human error. If the use of a computer system causes harm, the analysis of any civil lawsuit depends on whether the alleged harm is the result of breach of contract, lack of reasonable care, or delivery of a defective product. If a software product is involved then the question of liability will be answered by comparison against other product lawsuits. If a software service is involved then the question of liability will be answered by comparison against other negligence lawsuits. Intentional torts do not apply to problems with software and will not be considered in the following.

3a. Product or Service

One important question in determining how contract and tort laws apply is whether software is a product or service. A computer-based system is a product, and the components of a product are products. Therefore software sold with hardware is considered to be a product and subject to contract law, negligence, and strict liability under tort. If mass production, mass marketing, and large-scale distribution were used to create and sell a program, then it is a product for purposes of liability laws (13). Custom software is generally considered to be a service. The developers of custom software are liable for negligence.

Software is both tangible and intangible and can be classified as different things for different purposes. Software is intangible but not like a story or song. If a singer misses a few notes of a song, the singer may experience slight embarrassment and the audience some displeasure. If a program interprets a few inputs incorrectly, failure will occur and more than a little displeasure (15).

Obviously, there are problems in deciding how to classify software because it is treated as intangible information when it comes to protection under copyright laws but as a tangible product when it comes to certain civil laws. One consequence of classifying software as a product is that strict liability can be applied. How will this affect the computer industry? Will companies stop producing certain types of software? A product liability suit could cause a company to fail. Strict product liability claims led to the bankruptcy of A. H. Robins, manufacturer of Dalkon Shields (13).

In the past, the courts have held that intangible information contained in a physical medium is a product and subject to strict products liability. The most appropriate example is one in which the publisher of a computer-generated aeronautical landing chart was held strictly liable for defective information in the chart that led to the death of at least one person (12). Thus, a program that produces faulty data exposes the developer to strict liability lawsuits.

A problem in software classification arises if the software is mass produced but has to be customized to work in the client's environment. This creates a hybrid type of software that is not exactly custom software and not strictly mass produced either. Lawsuits concerning software of this sort will have to be decided on a case-by-case basis.

3b. Application of Contract or Tort Laws

If a plaintiff has only economic loss due to a software failure, his cause of action is for breach of contract. When deciding whether to sue under contract or tort laws, the analysis depends on whether the harm was the result of not fulfilling a contract or warranty obligation or due to the lack of reasonable care.

If a plaintiff suffers personal injury, the cause of action is for negligence and or strict liability which are torts. In a civil action involving strict liability, the plaintiff must show only that the product caused the injury and that the product was sold in a defective condition. The defect can be in the design or manufacturing of the software, or it could be a failure to warn of limitations (5). Usually strict liability applies when there is personal injury or property damages not simply economic loss. In Lewis v. Timco Inc., 697 F.2d 1252 (5th Circuit Court 1983), the manufacturer of a set of hydraulic tongs was held strictly liable. The computer program that controlled the tongs malfunctioned causing severe injury to a worker (6). Most computer system failures cause economic loss as opposed to personal injury; therefore, strict liability is not always applicable.

3c. Application of Negligence or Malpractice

In many cases the issue is whether a plaintiff asks for damages under negligence or malpractice. Malpractice lawsuits are brought against professionals.

There is a vast difference in the cost of a diskette and the cost of the software that is placed on the diskette. Obviously, a financial premium is placed on the skill of the software engineer who developed the software. But is the skill of the software engineer elevated enough to make software engineering or computing a profession?

There are certain advantages that accrue to the plaintiff in a malpractice lawsuit. First, larger damages may be awarded. Second, the statute of limitations starts when an error is discovered, not when the act that caused the error was performed. This is especially important in the case of software due to the fact that the statute of limitation for breach of contract lawsuits starts when software is installed. Since errors in software may not show up for months, it is to the plaintiff's advantage to have the statute of limitations start when an error is found.

Lawsuits have been brought under ordinary negligence and malpractice. In Pompeii Estates v. Consolidated Edison Company of New York, Inc., 397 N.Y. S.2d 577 (N.Y. Civ. Ct., Queens Cty., 1977), a builder sued a public utility for negligence. A computer displayed the command to terminate service at a home and the operator did so. The home was unoccupied because it was under construction and the pipes burst causing damage. The court ruled that the operator did not show reasonable care because it was winter and a newly completed house usually is unoccupied. Compensatory damages were awarded to cover the costs of repairing the damage (6).

Two lawsuits were brought under computer malpractice and reduced to ordinary negligence. The first lawsuit was Invacare Corporation v. Sperry Corporation, 612 F. Supp. 448 (N.D. Ohio 1984). A Sperry salesman recommended the wrong computer for the software he recommended at the same time. Invacare sued for computer malpractice claiming that Sperry knew it had sold the wrong hardware for the job (11). Invacare also claimed that Sperry told them they would not need a computer consultant to run the system. The second lawsuit was Chatlos Systems v. National Cash Register, 479 F. Supp. 738 (D.N.J. 1979). National Cash Register sold and installed a very complex computer system to Chatlos that was inadequate. Chatlos sued for computer malpractice but the suit was reduced to ordinary negligence (11).

The IRS ruled (Revenue Ruling 85-189, 1985-2 C.B. 341) that a computer programmer who wrote a tax program would be held liable as a tax preparer because he failed to update his program to reflect changes in the tax law and his software acted in the place of a tax preparer (5). Holding a programmer to the professional standard of care of the professional who would normally perform the duty now done by a computer is frightening. A programmer who writes a medical program is not a doctor but relies on information given to him or her. Should a programmer be held to a physician's standard of care?

Acquiring computer software and hardware can be very confusing for the average person. The range of peripherals, software packages and hardware platforms, is overwhelming. Making the right decision is very important because of the high cost of software and hardware, and can determine how well a company performs. To help consumers make the right choice, an industry consisting of consultants has come into being. The courts have typically treated computer consultants differently from computer vendors. There are legal precedents to treat computer consultants as professionals. In Diversified Graphics v. Groves, 868 F.2d 293 (8th Circuit Court 1989), an accounting firm was sued for malpractice because the software it recommended was unsatisfactory (11). The accounting firm had acted as a software consultant. The court held the accounting firm (acting as a consultant) was liable for malpractice because it claimed to be an expert in this area.

3d. Assignment of Blame

The developer of custom software that does not meet its specifications can be sued for negligence. A claim for negligence is based on four things: duty to protect the software user from harm, breach of that duty, the fault committed by the software developer caused the harm, and damages actually occurred. Proof of negligence requires that the resulting harm was reasonably foreseeable. Negligence could include things that the developer did not do such as write and or test the software properly, correct significant bugs, warn of limitations, instruct users correctly, or provide adequate security for the system (5). In a lawsuit based on negligence, the software developer might offer evidence of extensive software testing to show that they adhered to a "reasonable standard of care" (15).

In our legal system, negligence must be attributed to some person. However, one person is rarely responsible for a commercial software product. Usually commercial programs are developed by large teams of people. When it becomes necessary to find someone negligent for a software failure, the "many-hands" problem becomes overwhelming (10). It is very difficult to affix blame due to the number of people that are part of a development team, the length of time necessary to develop a commercial software product, and the high rate of turnover among software developers.

3e. Monetary Damages

In a civil lawsuit a judge or jury must determine the facts, and if negligence is found then damages must be awarded. Monetary damages are either compensatory or punitive. Compensatory damages include special damages for expenses such as loss of earnings and medical expenses, and general damages for pain and suffering. Both past and future losses are considered when compensatory damages are awarded. Punitive damages are intended to punish the defendant and to serve as a deterrent to others. Punitive damages can be awarded in malpractice lawsuits. Compensatory damages for expenses and pain and suffering can be awarded in any tort lawsuits. Only compensatory damages for actual losses such as the cost of the software are awarded in breach of contract lawsuits.

The preceding has related the civil laws to the liability arising from the use of unreliable software. Solutions to minimize the exposure to liability are proposed in the next section.

4. SOLUTIONS TO THE LIABILITY PROBLEM

Two categories of solutions are discussed in this section. The first category of solutions consists of ways to reduce the amount of unreliable software. These solutions reduce the risk associated with unreliable software and relate to computing personnel, software engineering techniques, and human factors engineering studies. The second category of solutions includes methods for reducing the financial consequences of unreliable software. These solutions involve contract limitations and liability insurance.

4a. Computing Personnel

Obviously the best solution is to eliminate the risk of liability due to unreliable software by developing reliable software. To develop reliable software a company should hire well-trained, qualified analysts and programmers. Employers have an obligation to enhance the skills of their computing practitioners through meaningful continuing education. Courses on new languages and software development paradigms or tools should be offered as appropriate. Another responsibility of the employer is to properly supervise all employees. The employer is liable for negligence committed by an employee; therefore, legal seminars should be held for employees to explain the liability incurred due to unreliable software and fraudulent claims of enhanced software functionality.

4b. Software Engineering

Software engineering techniques and the software development life-cycle were developed in order to apply a systematic approach to software production. The goal of software engineering is to produce quality software. An important part of developing quality software is producing good documentation during each phase of the life-cycle. From a legal point of view each step of the software development life-cycle should be carefully documented to show who worked on that phase and what measures were taken to ensure a quality product. A company might consider limiting the functionality of a program to exactly those functions listed in the specifications document. This would protect the company legally as far as meeting specifications. Thorough testing must be performed before the software is released.

Applying software engineering techniques is only part of the solution. Unfortunately, unreliable software is still being put on the market. The more computer-literate part of our society has come to expect errors in software. Computer errors can be classified as systemic or operational errors (9). Systemic errors consist of software errors, hardware errors, and flaws in the design. Operational errors are caused by the computer operator either in entering the data, verifying the accuracy of output, or reacting to information displayed by the computer system. The first type of errors relates to poor application of software engineering techniques and the pressures of the marketplace. The second type of errors could be eliminated by using better human factors engineering.

4c. Human Factors Engineering

One solution that can reduce the risk associated with the development of unreliable software is to design the software using human factors engineering techniques. Human factors engineering combines engineering, psychology, and behavioral science to improve the way the user interacts with a computer. The characteristics of the computer user have changed dramatically over the past several decades. The majority of computer users are no longer programmers. Software must be designed that is easy to understand and use. This is accomplished by designing a good user interface and software modules that verify operator input and system output.

Human errors occur when we fail to accomplish what we set out to accomplish. Human errors include absent-minded slips, lapses of attention, and misinterpretation or misreading of computer output and or menus. Humans make mistakes when they are given too much information. Good design should be based on the knowledge of human factors to engineer out human errors. For example, correct usage of a program should not depend solely on the short-term memory of the operator. To design user interfaces for human-monitored systems, all visual signals should appear in a restricted space, be as large as possible, and require a response by the user (14).

Computer operators make many errors in input such as mistyping characters. It is estimated that 60–70 percent of character errors are the result of typing letters for numbers and vice versa, and that of the 36 alphanumeric characters, 62 percent of character errors occur when typing fewer than 12 of these characters (14). With this type of knowledge, the software developer can design code that checks for these input errors and avoids the problem by careful choice of required input. For example, input that is either all letters or all numbers will minimize keying errors.

Human factors engineering can be used to assess potential hazards, risks, or system misuse (8). User groups should be identified and misuse/accident data relating to similar products should be analyzed. Physical attributes of the user groups such as size, motor skill abilities, and resistance to fatigue should be considered. The software developer should research databases to find applicable biomechanical and anthropometric data before designing the program (8).

Psychological human factors consist of the user's sensory, perceptual and cognitive capabilities and limitations as they pertain to use of a computer system (8). The software analyst must consider whether or not the user will have difficulty understanding on-line help documentation and user manuals.

Software engineering and human factors engineering are preventative solutions to eliminate liability risks. There are other solutions that can reduce the financial risk of liability such as contract limitations, a risk fund, and liability insurance. Contract limitations are discussed in the next section.

4d. Contract Limitations

Contracts between software providers and customers can be written to limit liability. Both implied and express warranties may be disclaimed in a contract under the UCC if the disclaimer is not unreasonable or unconscionable (3). However, contractual liability disclaimers may not be permissible in certain states nor effective in limiting vendor liability to suits brought under tort theories (5). Thus a vendor should consider a limited warranty from legal, moral, and business points of view. A limited warranty could be used to limit the time period of support for bug fixes or to limit the damages due a client for faulty software to initial costs (3). A limited warranty could state that the vendor would not be liable for damages due to loss of data or lost profits. This type of limitation has been upheld in court.

In Metropolitan Life Insurance Company v. Noble Lowndes International (New York Appeals Court, June 1993), the judge ruled that Metropolitan was only entitled to the amount it had actually paid to Noble Lowndes for the software. Metropolitan Life had asked for 5.4 million dollars that it thought it would have earned if the software had performed as promised. The court denied the damage suit due to a clause in the contract (2).

One way to protect against off-the-cuff comments by sales representatives is to include an integration clause in the contract. An integration clause states that the agreement between the client and vendor is contained entirely in the contract (5). This eliminates the threat of a lawsuit under breach of express warranty.

To limit damages due to negligence a contract could contain a description of reasonable care against which the vendor's conduct would be judged (5). This is necessary because a standard of reasonable care has not been established for the software industry.

Another approach to limiting liability is to use the contract to list obligations of the buyer. Such obligations could include promptly notifying the vendor of bugs, complete training of users by the purchasing organization, proper use of the software, and regular backups of data files and the code. The buyer could be required to acknowledge limitations of the software in writing.

Contractual limitations do not apply when a third party (someone other than the buyer) is injured by faulty software (5). Another solution to the problem of limiting liability is to reduce undesirable financial consequences through liability insurance.

4e. Liability Insurance

Insurance can be defined as the anticipation of losses through the prediction and redistribution of losses (4). An insurer estimates losses by examining historical data on types of property or liability risks and, based on this data, establishes a rate. The liability costs are spread among all people who buy insurance. Due to our tort system, businesses and professionals need liability insurance. Physicians, lawyers, dentists, accountants, and veterinarians, as well as, carpenters, plumbers, and other skilled tradespeople, have become the targets of liability lawsuits.

Liability insurance insures against certain named risks. Insurance policies for doctors, dentists, chiropractors, and lawyers are called professional liability and malpractice policies. Liability policies for accountants, architects and others are called errors and omissions liability insurance policies. A liability policy contains a description of exactly what is covered and consists of four parts: declarations, an insuring agreement, exclusions, and conditions (4).

The declarations part identifies the insurer, type of policy, period of coverage, amount of coverage, premium, and any attached endorsements. The insuring agreement states that the insurer will pay damages for the things insured against. Usually coverage applies from some retroactive date set by the insurance company. Most liability policies insure against bodily injury including sickness, injury, and death. Endorsements can be added to a policy to include coverage for defamation of character, libel, slander, false arrest, and invasion of privacy. The insurer will provide for investigation, defense and settlement of claims. Exclusions are included to avoid duplication of coverage, catastrophes such as war and nuclear risks, liability arising from pollutions, and coverage for costs of a recall. Conditions in a policy might be that the insurer has the right to inspect the insured's property or operations (4).

The Electronic Data Processors Errors and Omissions Policy is available to computer companies. Errors and omissions liability insurance is expensive and somewhat hard to get. This may be due in part to the fact that computer liability law is in its infancy and to the uncertainty surrounding the professional status of computer software providers. Also there are little historical data on which an insurance company can base a rate.

5. CONCLUSIONS

In this paper liability laws relating to computer systems in general and software in particular have been explained. The objective of the law relating to liability is to protect the consumer. Several questions remain unanswered. Will computing become a profession? Will increased vulnerability to lawsuits affect how software is developed? Will the price of software increase drastically to cover malpractice and litigation costs? Will imposing malpractice and strict product liability laws to software stifle innovation? Will exposure to the larger financial risks associated with malpractice keep software developers from creating certain types of software?

On the other hand, consider an example. The largest software programs and the ones most likely to cause human injury (military-related programs and aircraft guidance programs) are written for the government. The vendor of government software is protected by traditional government contractor defense shields against negligence and strict liability lawsuits (15). Is this protection for government vendors reasonable? Are American people getting the safest, most reliable military software? To deny liability for errors in government software would seem to deny the intentions for liability laws.

The more likely it is that the use of programs could result in harm to a person, the more responsibility the developer has to create a reliable program and the more important it becomes that the computer operator performs his or her duties correctly. The software developer owes a duty of care towards those people who might be affected by the use of the program. In addition to the duty of care, computing practitioners have the duty to not coerce clients into buying inappropriate software and the duty to honestly represent their skills and the products they develop. Lastly, software developers must accept responsibility for their work.

Until software engineers can produce reliable software, we must look for ways to lower levels of risk due to unreliable software. Suggestions for minimizing the risks that could result from both systemic errors and operational errors have been outlined. Solutions to this problem have been proposed such as elimination of the cause of the risk through the use of software and human factors engineering techniques and reduction of the financial consequences by limitation of contractual liability and purchase of liability insurance policies. Part of the focus of this article has been to discuss the risk of negligence or carelessness that results in unreliable software. As our society becomes even more dependent on technology it may be considered negligent not to use a program that has been designed to help people (7).

6. REFERENCES

(1) Frank, S. "What AI Practitioners Should Know About the Law, Part 2." *AI Magazine*, Vol. 9, No. 2, Summer 1988, pp. 109–114.

(2) Geyelin, M. "Faulty Software Means Business for Litigators." *Wall Street Journal*, Jan. 21, 1994.

(3) Hammond, H. "Limiting and Dealing with Liability in Software Contracts." *Computer Lawyer*, Vol. 9, No. 6, June 1992, pp. 22–30.

(4) Huebner, S., Black, K. and Cline, R. *Property and Liability Insurance*, Third Edition. Prentice-Hall, Englewood Cliffs, NJ, 1982, pp. 630.

(5) Levy, L. and Bell, S. "Software Product Liability: Understanding and Minimizing Risks." *High Tech. Law Journal*, Vol. 5, Spring 1990, pp. 1–27.

(6) Lipner, S. and Kalman, S. *Computer Law: Cases and Materials.* Merrill Publishing Company, Columbus, OH, 1989.

(7) Lloyd, I. "Liability for Defective Software." *Reliability Engineering and System Safety*, Vol. 32, 1991, pp. 193–207.

(8) Main, B., Franz, J. and Rhoades, T. "How Human Factors Engineering Improves Safety, Reduces Liability." *Leader's Product Liability Law and Strategy*, Vol. 12, No. 4, Oct. 1993, pp. 6–7.

(9) Nimmer, R. *The Law of Computer Technology*, Second Edition. Warren, Gorham, Lamont, Boston, MA, 1992.

(10) Nissenbaum, H. "Computing and Accountability." *Communications of the ACM*, Vol. 37, No. 1, Jan. 1994, pp. 73–80.

(11) Palermo, C. "Software Engineering Malpractice and Its Avoidance." *Proceedings of the Third International Symposium on Software Reliability Engineering*, Research Triangle, NC, Oct. 1992, pp. 20–30.

(12) Rowland, D. "Liability for Defective Software." *The Cambrian Law Review*, Vol. 22, 1991, pp. 78–92.

(13) Weber, L. "Bad Bytes: The Application of Strict Products Liability to Computer Software." *St. John's Law Review*, Vol. 66, Spring 1992, pp. 469–485.

(14) Winfield, I. *Human Resources and Computing.* Heineman Ltd., London, 1986.

(15) Wolpert, T. "Product Liability and Software Implicated in Personal Injury." *Defense Counsel Journal*, Vol. 60, Oct. 1993, pp. 519–533.

IV : THE PROFESSIONS AND THE WORKPLACE ISSUES

SUMMARY

(13) *Some Negative Effects of Electronic Monitoring on Small Business*
Dr. Bewayo discusses the impact of electronic monitoring on small businesses, and suggests ways to use electronic monitoring effectively.

(14) *Computing and Ethics: Control and Surveillance versus Cooperation and Empowerment in the Workplace*
This chapter discusses the controversy of workplace surveillance and control. It explores simple schemes of organizational decision making relative to computerization, and outlines relevant findings in literature.

(15) *The Role of Professional Organizations in Promoting Computer Ethics*
This chapter discusses the role of professions and professional codes in upholding employees' ethical behavior and professional decision making. The author gives a narrow definition of a computer professional. This definition is in line with the belief that the narrower the definition, the fewer the professionals and the more responsible those professionals are.

(16) *Computer Practitioners: Professionals or Hired Guns?*
In this chapter Donald Gotterbarn discusses the responsibility of computer software professionals in the development of software and the controversy surrounding licensing and certification of computer professionals.

(17) *A Call for Responsibility for Ethical Behavior in Information Technology*
In this chapter Pastor William Palmiter discusses a unique multidisciplinary approach to ethical behavior in information technology. This approach uses ethical principles formulated in the Judeo-Christian tradition.

(18) *Professionalism, Ethical Responsibility and Accountability*
In this chapter Joseph Kizza uses the situations concerning the Denver International Airport automated baggage system, Intel's Pentium debacle, and the failed CONFIRM software company to call for professional accountability and ethical responsibility.

13. ELECTRONIC MANAGEMENT: ITS DOWNSIDE ESPECIALLY IN SMALL BUSINESS

Edward Bewayo

According to recent studies 20 percent of American companies use some form of electronic monitoring.[1] Electronic monitoring is used by companies to manage employees through electronic devices, especially the computer, the video camera, and the telephone. Thus, electronic monitoring is also known as electronic management. Other labels that have been attached to electronic monitoring have tended to reflect negative feelings about it. They include Big Brother management, electronic snooping, electronic surveillance, and electronic sweat-shopping.

Most of these negative feelings about electronic monitoring have been caused by some companies that have abused it. The abuses, which some observers consider to be isolated,[2] have taken diverse forms. The abuses that have been cited most frequently are the following: that electronic monitoring has been used to monitor even very personal activities (e.g., while the employee is in the bathroom), that electronic monitoring has been used to increase workloads without increasing employees' compensation, and that electronic monitoring has been used to increase worker stress.

These abuses of electronic monitoring can be avoided or reversed. For example, electronic monitoring can be restricted to certain activities (thus preserving some employee privacy) and certain times (thus reducing the probability for worker stress). Companies which fail to reduce these abuses or excesses of electronic monitoring stand to suffer from the bad consequences of such abuses. These abuses generally do not foster a work environment in which most people want to work.

The adverse impact on the work environment caused by excesses of electronic monitoring can be serious, and is particularly serious in small businesses.

186

In this paper emphasis will be on how electronic monitoring impacts on small business work environments. That electronic monitoring can have negative consequences in the workplace has been discussed by many authors[3]; however, the focus has mostly been on large companies. This large company focus has been partly due to the fact that the beginnings of electronic monitoring were almost exclusively limited to large companies. The oldest form of electronic monitoring is "service observation" which is electronically monitoring employee job performance through the use of listening devices, especially the telephone. This form of monitoring began in the late 1800s in the telephone industry. It is now also extensively used in the airline and telemarketing industries. Electronic monitoring has now spread much farther than telephone monitoring in large companies.

Other popular forms of electronic monitoring are computerized performance measurement (CPM)[4] and video electronic surveillance. And with the drastic decline of the prices of electronic equipment and software, electronic monitoring is no longer beyond the reach of the vast majority of small businesses. Moreover, electronic monitoring is no longer a discriminatory practice that is confined to low-rank and low-skill employees such as clerical staff. Professionals, such as lawyers, nurses, journalists and stock brokers on Wall Street, "increasingly are finding themselves subject to telephone monitoring."[5]

Electronic monitoring has become pervasive throughout American business and industry. At this point, any company which wants to manage its employees electronically can do so; and companies which do not cautiously approach electronic monitoring will very easily exceed its boundaries of appropriateness, thus causing themselves serious problems. As will be explained later, there are reasons to believe that excessive electronic monitoring causes more serious problems in small businesses than in large businesses. But why has electronic monitoring spread so fast and widely?

THE OBVIOUS CONVENIENCE
AND PURPOSED EFFICIENCY
OF ELECTRONIC MONITORING

Electronic monitoring is supposed to provide easy answers to workplace problems such as poor productivity, quality, safety, security, and ethics. It is the high-tech solution to long-standing problems. Electronic monitoring is convenient because it is management without sweat. The manager doesn't need to leave the office. According to *Infoworld* magazine, there are at least 11 computer programs a manager can choose from to be able to see and hear everything any given employee does in the workplace, and sometimes even away from the workplace.[6] Because of the small size and sophistication of a wide variety of electronic monitoring equipment, most employees can be monitored without their knowledge.[7] One computer software called "Peek and

Spy" allows the manager to peek in on the employee's computer with the employee's knowledge or to spy on the employee's computer without the employee becoming aware.[8]

Electronic monitoring is also management without tears. Many tasks managers are known to hate get done by the computer and or video camera. Two examples are performing performance appraisals and gathering evidence to prove unethical behavior such as drug use or theft. As for performance appraisals, the computer can be programmed not only to measure employees' performance but also to rank employees according to their performance. Each employee's performance ranking can be flashed on each employee's computer terminal, a terrible way of giving feedback on performance. As for gathering evidence to prove drug use and employee theft, the video camera is the ever-reliable sentinel. Unless the manager is also a trained security guard, he or she greatly welcomes being relieved from this catch-the-criminal role. Electronic monitoring, by taking over some of their tasks, makes managers more efficient, since they can now devote more time to other functions such as planning. Additionally, electronic monitoring can also enable a manager to supervise a larger number of employees (wider span of control). In these times of down-sizing and rightsizing electronic monitoring is a welcome tool.

Electronic monitoring represents the automation of the manager—a "computerized boss."[9] This management automation follows decades of employee/work automation, where robots have taken over many technical tasks that were previously handled by people. Many tasks that have been automated were boring, tiring, and unpleasant and their automation was a welcome development, e.g., lifting on assembly lines. This work and worker automation has raised some serious problems, e.g., potential job losses. Moreover, by reducing the ranks of labor (for example, workers are no longer needed to lift heavy parts along the car assembly line), work automation increases the relative importance and power of management. The automation of the manager and management, where high-tech devices take over managerial tasks such as walking around the shop floor talking to employees, raises the same issues, only to a much greater degree. It reduces the number of employees, this time among managerial ranks. One manager, armed with high-tech electronics, can supervise relatively larger numbers of employees. The managers who survive electronic monitoring become much more powerful than before electronic monitoring. Additionally, electronic monitoring enables the manager to gain a more thorough knowledge about the employee. Knowledge is power.

Management is collecting information on what is going on in the workplace and making decisions on the basis of that information. Research indicates that managers spend as much as 80 percent of their management time gathering and interpreting information.[10] In particular, managers collect information to guide and control employee behavior. The nature of the workplace is greatly influenced by the way managers collect and use information.

Three aspects of information are key to effective management: quantity, timing, and objectivity. Electronic monitoring affects all of these three aspects. High-tech electronics can collect a massive amount of information on a continuously timely basis. The information collected through electronic monitoring is also totally objective. The video camera, the listening device and the computer cannot on their own be selective in what they pick up. There cannot be "personal bias because the computer reports only the facts," a New Jersey business and industry spokesman is reported to have said.[11]

Information of sufficient quantity and objectivity, and supplied with sufficient regularity, is of critical importance to management. The problem with electronic monitoring is that it collects (or can collect) too much information, too objectively, and too regularly (continuously). If information is power as is generally believed,[12] electronic monitoring makes managers monstrously powerful, too powerful even for their own good.

TRACING ELECTRONIC MANAGEMENT

When electronic monitoring is programmed and allowed to generate information about everything, continuously, and sometimes even surreptitiously, it creates a very intimidating work environment. Most people do not want to, and will not choose to, work in such an environment. These excesses of electronic monitoring immediately remind us of the scientific management movement of the early 1900s. Indeed, some of the proponents of electronic monitoring are quick to "point to the long history of personal observation by supervisors and the rise of scientific management methods which began when mass production systems were created and refined in the early Twentieth Century."[13] Nearly 100 years after Fredrick Taylor preached his scientific management principles, some American companies are still closely organized and run around these principles.[14] Other companies which had found scientific management methods to be too crude and cumbersome, for example going around with a stopwatch to time the employee, find electronic monitoring (upgraded scientific management) to be neater. You don't walk around with the stopwatch to time the employee; you just use the computer in your office. You don't have to bark at the employee; you just send little subliminal messages on the employee's computer terminal. In other words, a manager who would not use old-fashioned scientific management (autocratic management) methods would readily use electronic monitoring. The logic here is not obvious. It is not clear why an employee would find close managerial supervision intolerable, but continuous electronic monitoring tolerable. Most workers, especially today's new wave of workers,[15] would find close supervision intolerable even when or especially when it is done electronically.

The problem with both scientific management and electronic monitoring is the common set of assumptions upon which they are based. These assumptions have been branded Theory X assumptions by Douglas McGregor.[16] The assumptions reflect a very pessimistic view about human nature. The assumptions briefly state that on average people dislike work, are passive, are irresponsible, and will cheat if given a chance. The last-mentioned assumption, that workers will cheat if given a chance, is an addition to McGregor's list. But a great deal of electronic monitoring is based upon this assumption. This author is not aware of any studies that have attempted to systematically validate these Theory X assumptions. With respect to the purported dislike for work, it is not clear at all whether most people enjoy having not to work. Also, motivation theory appears to suggest that there is work which people like and work which people dislike, that it all boils down to work and job design.[17] Depending upon how poorly work is designed a lot of people will dislike it. And this is where electronic monitoring enters the picture.

Most computerized performance measurement (CPM) works best when jobs are very narrowly and strictly defined. Jobs like those that lack in motivational challenge. And if, in addition, the employee is constantly under the electronic eye, his or her job will also lack in motivational responsibility. The absence of challenge and responsibility in jobs is enough to make most people dislike work. In short, electronic monitoring can make the Theory X assumptions appear plausible.

ELECTRONIC MONITORING IN THE SMALL BUSINESS ENVIRONMENT

The problems caused by electronic monitoring can be serious, especially in small businesses. Unless approached prudently, electronic monitoring can weaken the foundation of competitiveness in small businesses. The foundation of competitiveness in small businesses is the work environment, vis-à-vis that in large companies. The work environment in small businesses can be less structured and less complex, and more informal and flexible than it can be (and usually is) in organizational structures.[18] There are going to be small companies that are structured along the same lines as large companies, and vice versa. Nevertheless, organizational complexity (job specialization, number of departments, and levels of authority) and organizational formalization (rules, procedures, policies, and plans) are more fundamentally a function of organizational size. Small organizations are more likely to have fewer functional departments and job categories than large organizations. In small businesses, jobs can easily be broader and more loosely defined. Production workers will probably also do maintenance work, and the typist will probably also double as a receptionist. Additionally, because of the looseness of the hierarchy and functional departments, workers and managers will probably communicate relatively easily. Now, there are many small businesses where owner-managers are so unenlightened and domineering that communication between owner-manager and employees, and even between one employee and another, will not be easy.[19] Probably we all know examples of small businesses that fall within this category. These are small businesses that lack a conducive work environment because they still suffer from what John Kao has called the "entrepreneur's disease."[20] They may even die from it before they get to electronic monitoring. So, here we are not talking about these types of small businesses. We are talking about small businesses which are managed professionally enough to realize the advantages inherent in being small. Because they are small, they can provide to their employees jobs with greater chance for involvement, greater freedom of action, and broader responsibilities. Small businesses can also provide to their employees a more informal and friendlier atmosphere. These favorable job characteristics are collectively known as "intrinsic job factors." They are "non-monetary rewards that may not be so easy to get in large organizations."[21]

In an effort to get these small-size-bound advantages, some large companies deliberately nurture smallness. At Kollmorgen Corporation in Connecticut, when a division grows beyond a few hundred employees, it is split. Robert Swiggett, the company's chairman, was reported as saying: "We believe that divisions which get too big lose vitality, family atmosphere, and easy, informal, internal communication." At 3M, the medium number of employees at each of its 11 plants is deliberately kept at 115.[22]

The favorable intrinsic job factors (non-monetary rewards) that can be found in small businesses constitute the foundation of their competitiveness in the labor market. It is these factors that lure a significant number of highly qualified people to work in small businesses in spite of the poor "extrinsic job factors" (especially low salaries and benefits) that are commonly found in small businesses. Many small businesses do not only pay relatively low salaries, they also do not provide a number of key benefits.

According to a survey conducted by Hornsby and Kuratko[23] only 19 percent of small companies provide private pensions; in contrast 67 percent of large companies provide private pensions. The situation is not much better in the more critical area of insurance. Almost all large companies provide health, life, and disability insurance, while only 68 percent, 54 percent, and 37 percent of small companies provide health, life, and disability insurance, respectively. The nearly 30 million uninsured persons in the country who rely on hospital emergency rooms for health care are mostly employees (and their families) of small businesses.

In most cases, small businesses do not provide certain benefits because, due to the small number of their employees, they are unable to negotiate with benefit providers to bring the costs of the benefits to affordable levels. Employee leasing is expected to provide a partial solution to this problem.[24] Research studies[25] show that people who are attracted to work for small businesses can readily provide necessary skills. Among the categories of people particularly attracted to work in small businesses are young people seeking challenging work. Also attracted into small business employment are old people, people who want to work part-time and married women. These three categories of people are particularly interested in the flexibility that characterizes many small business jobs. Finally, there is the highly qualified group of people who would normally get jobs in large companies and command lucrative salaries, but instead seek jobs in small businesses. These very highly intrinsically-oriented people want "highly enriched jobs,"[26] jobs which combine challenge with growth opportunities and visibility with responsibility. These are the kinds of people small businesses are lucky to have considering their relatively lower salaries and benefits. A small business that wants to not only attract but also hold on to such highly qualified people will have to nurture a work environment that breeds interesting jobs. The introduction of electronic monitoring, unless approached prudently, is very likely to give the wrong signals.

POTENTIAL BENEFITS OF ELECTRONIC MONITORING TO SMALL BUSINESSES

Writing in *Fortune* magazine, Gene Bylinsky stated that "Done right, monitoring performance by computer or telephone improves service, productivity, and profits. Done wrong, it just bugs the staff—in both senses."[27] There are several situations in which electronic monitoring could bring about major improvements in small business management. Electronic monitoring can improve compensation equity, workplace health and safety, product quality, and security (protection of company property). However, the only way electronic monitoring will bring about these improvements is when it is "done right." Done wrong there will be a worsening of all these areas.

Most small business owners cannot afford, and therefore do not use, many modern and sophisticated management techniques that large companies generally use. The absence of modern techniques can be seen in many areas of small business management, including personnel selection, training, performance appraisal, job evaluation, compensation, quality control, financial control, and inventory control. As can be seen from above-listed items, the area that suffers most is personnel/human resources management (employee selection, training, compensation, etc.). Conspicuously absent in many small businesses is a separate specialized personnel staff and department. This is particularly the case in small businesses with fewer than 100 employees.[28] The absence of a specialized personnel staff department means that there is nobody to help with employee recruitment and screening, advisement on policies to enhance employee morale, compensation equity, and job design. Consequently, most personnel functions are carried out haphazardly.

In many small businesses the recruitment of personnel is done predominantly via "Help Wanted" window signs. Selection tests, especially sophisticated ones such as honesty tests, are rarely given, if ever. The training, if given, is limited to unplanned (and, thus, ineffective) on-the-job training. Compensation is not based on properly conducted performance appraisals or job evaluations. There are no wage and salary surveys. As a result of the absence of sophisticated personnel systems, small businesses generally have a large percentage of less qualified, less educated, and less experienced employees. In general, the better qualified, better educated, and more experienced employees gravitate toward large companies, not only because small businesses do not do an adequate job in recruiting them, but also because small businesses can't pay as well as large companies do.

Electronic monitoring can help both to improve personnel systems and to alleviate some of the problems the weak personnel systems cause (e.g., poor quality products and unsafe/unhealthy workplaces). Regarding improving personnel systems themselves, one specific area that can be improved by a properly designed electronic monitoring system is performance measurement and evaluation. Electronic monitoring can be used to take samples of an employee's performance at some suitable intervals (not continuously). Used in moderation, electronic monitoring can bring some objectivity in performance measurement and evaluation. Opposition to electronic monitoring is said to decline considerably if employees perceive its purpose to be achieving a greater degree of fairness in performance evaluation (procedural justice) leading to equitable compensation (distributive justice). After reviewing several studies, Brian Niehoff and Robert Morman said, "The evidence cited above suggests employees may respond negatively to the controlling aspect of monitoring but may respond positively if they perceive the monitoring to be part of the managerial job of maintaining fairness."[29] If electronic monitoring is to succeed in bringing about a fairer performance appraisal and reward system, it will have to be designed and conducted carefully enough so as not to measure everything an employee does in the workplace. It is not equitable or even ethical to monitor what an employee does in the bathroom. This is one of the points concerning electronic monitoring on which there is overwhelming agreement among employers.[30] Furthermore, it will also be realized that the entirety of an employee's performance will not be amenable to electronic monitoring. This will most likely be the case when jobs are broadly defined. As was pointed out earlier, jobs with broad responsibilities are one of the attractions in small business employment. These jobs should not be re-designed only to make them meet the requirements of electronic monitoring.

A judicious application of electronic monitoring can also reduce workplace accidents. Preventing and reducing accidents have assumed greater importance in recent years, especially in small businesses. There are three reasons for this increased concern about accidents. First, courts now generally hold the employer responsible for the accident regardless of the culpability of the employee.

Second, liability insurance has become too expensive for the average small business owner.[31] Third, because they rely so much on inexperienced employees, small businesses are apt to suffer from a disproportionately large number of accidents. Electronic monitoring is seen as a key tool to spot employees who, because of their work habits, are accident prone. The employees can then be reassigned, given training, or discharged. Carefully used electronic monitoring can reduce safety hazards, especially those connected with inexperienced employees. Carelessly and excessively used electronic monitoring, for example, if it is not reduced after the employees gain experience, can engender new health hazards (long-term deterioration of employees' health). Table 1 shows a marked increase in stress-related complaints caused by electronic monitoring. It must, however, be pointed out that studies that link electronic monitoring to stress are greatly disputed by the proponents of electronic monitoring, especially the American Society for Industrial Security (ASIS). The ASIS argues that "In most cases, a fast-paced work environment, rather than monitoring, appears to be the crucial factor behind workplace stress. ... The causes of employee stress are many and varied; monitoring is merely one of them."[32] Probably even ASIS would agree that modifying the way electronic monitoring is used so as to reduce workplace stress (since electronic monitoring does cause some) would not be a bad idea.

By far the most frequent argument for electronic monitoring has come from those who see it as the most effective tool to fight workplace crime, especially pilferage and financial fraud. Indeed, most electronic monitoring in small businesses (e.g., restaurants, drug stores, and liquor stores) is chiefly aimed at "catching the thief," whether an insider or an outsider. Support for electronic monitoring on this account has come from the National Association of Convenience Stores, the National Association of Manufacturers, the National Association of Chain Drug Stores, the National Retail Federation, the National Restaurant Association, the American Society for Industrial Security, the American Warehouse Association, and the U.S. Chamber of Commerce, which has estimated that American businesses lose $40 billion annually due to theft.[33] And many retailers say that the introduction of electronic monitoring has dramatic effects on theft losses.[34] Small businesses are particularly vulnerable to theft, and there are several reasons for this. First, personnel selection processes in small businesses often do not include procedures to screen out job candidates with dishonest inclinations. Such procedures include elaborate background checks, comprehensive and multiple interviews, and, especially, honesty tests. "These [honesty] tests are proven predictors of an employee's propensity to steal and commit related forms of dishonesty."[35] Given these weaknesses, small business owners and managers look at electronic monitoring as their solution to workplace theft, at least in the short run. Unfortunately, electronic monitoring addresses only the symptoms of the unethical behavior, since the root causes of unethical behavior are

Table 1: Electronic Monitoring and Employee Stress

Percentages of Employees Feeling Pain

	Monitored	Non-monitored
Stress-Related Pain		
Headaches	92	85
Back Pain	79	73
Severe Fatigue	79	63
Shoulder Soreness	76	57
Extreme Anxiety	72	57
Stiff or Severe Wrist	51	24

Source: Gene Bylinsky, "How Companies Spy on Employees," Fortune, November 4, 1991.

not addressed. Long-term solutions to theft problems will involve dealing with the weaknesses cited above. Furthermore, as Byron Crossen points out, managing employee unethical behavior is most likely to be successful only if the entire culture in the company, small or big, discourages unethical behavior. In particular, employees are not likely to behave ethically if they "perceive that unethical behavior is common in their company or industry."[36] A study back in the 1970s found that the most important factor that influences unethical behavior in the workplace is the behavior of superiors (see Table 2).[37] Employees do not have to behave ethically if their bosses behave unethically. Indeed, "workers may conclude that unethical behavior may be necessary to compete with co-workers and [managers]."[38] At any rate, a business owner who is himself or herself unethical, and tries to deal with employees' unethical behavior through electronic monitoring, is not only using a technique that has undesirable side effects, but one which is not going to solve the problem on a long-term basis.

Dealing with workplace theft is complicated by the fact that workplace theft is very often perpetrated by customers or other non-employees. A company can decide not to use electronic monitoring because of its negative effects on its employees, but it may be reluctant not to use it completely. Perhaps the best illustration of this problem is in the banking industry. Most video camera monitoring is probably not aimed at employees, rather at the visitor to the bank, customer or not. If electronic monitoring is very effective in catching non-employee thieves, its elimination presupposes the discovery of alternative solutions to problems of external theft. This author is not aware of any alternative solutions other than employing a frighteningly large number of security guards. So, some electronic monitoring is going to continue. However, some forms of electronic monitoring can be effective in combating external theft without necessarily being bothersome to employees in many industries, especially

Table 2: Factors Influencing Unethical Behavior

	Rank on scale of 1 (most influential) to 6 (least influential) Factor
Behavior of superiors	2.15
Formal policy or lack thereof	3.27
Industry ethical climate	3.34
Behavior of peers in company	3.37
Society's moral climate	4.22
One's personal financial needs	4.46

Source: Andrew Szilagyi, Jr., Management and Performance, Glenview, IL: *Scott, Foresman & Co., 1988.*

clothing stores. One form of electronic monitoring is Electronic Article Surveillance (EAS). This system involves placing on products small sensor tags which activate an alarm if not first de-activated at the check-out counter. This approach to electronic monitoring is now progressing toward source tagging, where suppliers tag their products before shipping them out.[39]

Electronic monitoring has also the potential to alleviate low product quality problems generally encountered with inexperienced employees. If electronic monitoring is used to ensure product quality because employees are new and inexperienced, i.e., if electronic monitoring is used as a training tool, it should be relaxed when employees gain the skills to produce quality products. Unfortunately, it is often not relaxed. Also, electronic monitoring that focuses on numbers or quantity, e.g., number of key strokes for a data entry clerk or number of calls answered by a service center customer representative, tends to inadvertently downplay the concern for quality. In the long run, electronic monitoring will promote product quality (and workplace safety) only if it is designed in such a way that it feeds back collected data to those employees whose performance is being measured. Used in this way electronic monitoring becomes a form of empowerment. To encourage employees to develop a commitment to the electronic monitoring system, employees have to participate in its design, including the determination of its objectives (in this way the employees will "own" the objectives). Designed in this way, electronic monitoring becomes a tool for employee empowerment as well as a form of self-management. Terri Griffith appropriately called this approach to electronic monitoring "Teaching Big Brother to Be a Team Player."[40] This approach to electronic monitoring is consistent with the concepts of total quality management (TQM), the current popular technique for improving product quality. In TQM, every employee and every activity must be involved in the quality management process. Thus, if the purpose of electronic monitoring is to improve product or service quality, employees must be involved in its design.

CONCLUDING REMARKS

The electronic Big Brother, like the *1984* Big Brother, doesn't belong in the workplace. In this paper, I have argued that excessive electronic monitoring creates major problems. In small businesses, electronic monitoring can destroy their most important source of competitiveness, i.e., a more satisfying work environment. Most small businesses cannot compete with most large businesses on the basis of salaries and benefits. So, if small businesses are to get their share of highly qualified personnel, they have to discover a non-monetary way to do it. This non-monetary way is work and the environment within which that work is performed. Small business owner-managers can provide their employees with jobs that have great opportunities for growth and recognition. Small businesses can also provide a work environment which feels more personal and informal. In many cases, these non-monetary job factors (intrinsic job factors) which small businesses can provide constitute the major reasons why a considerable number of highly qualified people look for jobs in small businesses. Unfortunately, most forms of electronic monitoring, especially when electronic monitoring is carried too far, tend to negate these attractive job factors in small businesses.

However, electronic monitoring should not, and probably cannot, be eliminated from businesses, even small businesses. Used in moderation, electronic monitoring can help in making up for certain weaknesses in small businesses. Electronic monitoring can help in the training of the inexperienced and lowly educated employees upon whom small businesses disproportionally rely. But electronic monitoring should be relaxed once employees learn the necessary skills. A mental step businesses in general and small businesses in particular (it is critical for small businesses) can take to make electronic monitoring more compatible with motivating work environments is to involve the employees in designing electronic monitoring programs. American businesses can modify electronic monitoring to a point where they might preempt efforts now in the Congress to legislate electronic monitoring reforms. Currently bogged down in Congress is proposed legislation called "Privacy for Consumers and Workers Act." The most important concern in the proposed legislation is privacy. Already, the vast majority of employers agree that certain activities in the workplace should not be subject to electronic monitoring, for example, what employees do during lunch time or when they go to the bathroom. Other things employers can consider in order to respect employees' privacy are to provide telephone lines where employees can make and take personal calls and computer bulletin boards that employees can use to send personal messages.[41] In this way, the employer can listen to business-related telephone calls and read business-related electronic messages without violating employee privacy. This will also enable employers to reduce the growing menace of lawsuits that are being brought against them for violating employee privacy. Many businesses, especially small businesses, can hardly afford the financial resources to defend themselves against these suits (even when they are frivolous), let alone to settle them. But these suits and other negative actions are likely to continue until employers discover what one author has called "The Golden Rule of the Workplace," which proposes to an employer: "Put yourself in the shoes of the employee and consider how you would react."[42]

NOTES

1. Smith, Lee, "What the Boss Knows About You," *Fortune*, August 9, 1993. See also Debra Jacobs, "The Perils of Policing Employees," *Small Business Report*, February 1994.
2. Many representatives of organizations that support electronic monitoring feel this way. For example, in an article entitled "The Battle Over Electronic Monitoring," that appeared in *Chain Store Age Executive* (a trade publication. of January 1994, a representative of the National Retail Federation is reported to have described electronic monitoring as "a few anecdotal horror stories."
3. For example, see Edward Ottensmeyer and Mark Heroux, "Ethics, Public Policy and Managing Advanced Technologies: The Case of Electronic Surveillance," *Business Ethics*, July 1991. Also see Kenneth Jenero and Lynne Mapes-Riordan, "Electronic Monitoring of Employees and the Elusive Right to Privacy," *Employee Relations Law Journal*, Summer 1992.
4. Kulik, Carol and Ambrose, Maureen, "Category-Based and Feature-Based Processes in Performance Appraisal: Integrating Visual and Computerized Sources of Performance Data," *Journal of Applied Psychology*, October 1993.
5. Jenero and Mapes-Riordan, op. cit., p. 72.
6. This often takes the form of monitoring your plans when you return home and or when you go on vacation. One major company was even accused of hiring investigators to gather information on employees' recreation plans, among other things. See Debra Jacobs, "Are You Guilty of Electronic Trespassing?" *Management Review*, April 1994.
7. Crossen, Byron, "Managing Employee Unethical Behavior Without Invading Individual Privacy," *Journal of Business and Psychology*, Winter 1993.
8. Jenero and Mapes-Riordan, op. cit., p. 73.
9. Griffith, Terri, "Teaching Big Brother to Be a Team Player," *Academy of Management Executive*, February 1993, p. 74.
10. Mintzberg, Henry, *The Nature of Managerial Work*, New York: Harper and Row, 1973.
11. Quoted by Mark Fefer in an article entitled, "Is Your Computer Spying on You?" which appeared in *Glamour* magazine, November 1991.
12. Here I am referring to information power, i.e., control over information. Information power is different from expert power, which is the ability to solve problems. See, for example, Pamela Lewis, et al., *Management: Challenges in the 21st Century*, Minneapolis/St. Paul, MN: West Publishing Co., 1995, p. 427.
13. Susser, Peter, "Electronic Monitoring in the Private Sector: How Closely Should Employers Supervise Their Workers?" *Employee Relations Law Journal*, Spring 1988.
14. A classic example of a well-known company using old-fashioned scientific management principles is United Parcel Service (UPS). See "United Parcel Service Gets Deliveries Done by Driving Its Workers," *The Wall Street Journal*, April 22, 1986.
15. Fraze, James and Overman, Stephene, "A Balanced Workforce Is Labor Chief's Goal," *Personnel Administrator*, June 1989.
16. McGregor, Douglas, *The Human Side of Enterprise*, New York: McGraw-Hill, 1960.
17. Refer to concepts of job enrichment based upon, among others, works by Frederick Herzberg and Richard Hackman. For example, see Richard Hackman, "The Design of Work in the 1980s," *Organizational Dynamics*, Summer 1978.
18. For example, see Jacqueline Graves, "Leaders of Corporate Change," *Fortune*, December 14, 1992.

19. This is often a very serious problem when nonfamily members work in a tightly controlled and run family business.

20. Entrepreneur's disease is described by John Kao of the Harvard Business School as imbalances between the needs of the organization and the human skills available. These imbalances are often fatal to the organization. See John Kao, *Entrepreneurship, Creativity, and Organization*, Englewood Cliffs, NJ: Prentice-Hall, 1989.

21. Finney, Martha, "HRM in Small Business: No Small Task," *Personnel Administrator*, November 1987. Finney was quoting Ian MacMillan of the Wharton School of Business, at the University of Pennsylvania.

22. "A Company That Nurtures Smallness," *The New York Times*, May 6, 1984.

23. Hornsby, Jeffrey and Kuratko, Donald "Human Resources Management as Small Businesses Grow," *Mid-American Journal of Business*, spring, 1990.

24. Employee Leasing involves dismissing employees and then getting them back on lease. The leasing company pays all salaries and benefits. One leasing company can be controlling a large number of employees, and because of this, it can offer better benefits than one small business would generally be able to. But employee loyalty could be a problem for the small company that relies on employees that it does not directly employ.

25. For example, see James Barth, et al., "Employee Characteristics and Firm Size: Are There Any Systematic Empirical Relationships?" U.S. Small Business Administration, circa 1985.

26. Crossen, Byron, "Managing Employee Unethical Behavior Without Invading Individual Privacy," *Journal of Business and Psychology*, Winter 1993.

27. Bylinsky, Gene, "How Companies Spy on Employees," *Fortune*, November 4, 1991.

28. There appears to be an unfounded opinion that businesses with fewer than 100 employees need not have specialized, full-time personnel staff. See, for example, Martha Finney, "HRM in Small Business: No Small Task," *Personnel Administrator*, November 1987. In the opinion of this author, based on numerous contacts with small businesses, a business should have a specialized full-time personnel person when that business grows to 50 employees. At this size, there is more than enough work to beneficially occupy that person.

29. Niehoff, Brian and Moorman, Robert, "Justice as a Mediator of the Relationship Between Methods of Monitoring and Organizational Citizen Behavior," *Academy of Management Journal*, June 1993.

30. This is partly because it is the supreme example of electronic monitoring gone wild. Moreover, privacy lawsuits related to this aspect of electronic monitoring have nearly always been won by employees.

31. To make matters worse, most small businesses are not incorporated, a relatively inexpensive way of reducing liability.

32. American Society for Industrial Security (ASIS), "ASIS Speaks Out on Electronic Monitoring," *Security Management*, April 1992, p. 97.

33. Warner, David, "The Move to Curb Worker Monitoring," *Nation's Business*, December 1993.

34. Garry, Michael, "The Electronic Cop," *Progressive Grocer*, August 1993.

35. Crossen, op. cit., p. 238.

36. *Ibid.*, p. 236.

37. Szilagyi, Andrew, Jr., *Management and Performance*, Glenview, IL: Scott, Foresman & Co., 1988, p. 110.

38. Crossen, op. cit., p. 237.

39. Williams, Craig, "To Catch a Thief, Retailers Use Electronic Surveillance," *Drug Topics*, November 22, 1993.

40. Griffith, op. cit., p. 73.

41. For recommendations on these lines see Michele Picard, "Working Under an Electronic Thumb," *Training*, February 1994, p. 50.

42. Jacobs, Debra, "Are You Guilty of Electronic Trespassing?" *Management Review*, April 1994, p. 25. Jacobs attributes the golden rule of the workplace to John Shyer.

14. COMPUTING AND ETHICS: CONTROL AND SURVEILLANCE VERSUS COOPERATION AND EMPOWERMENT IN THE WORKPLACE

JOHN MAGNEY

Key Words: computerization, labor relations, management models, workplace ethics.

Two opposing visions have informed much of the analysis and commentary on how computing technology is affecting the modern workplace (7, 12, 19, 46). One view sees computerization as a logical extension of scientific management: employees in the computerized workplace are made more productive by having their job routines deskilled and their job performances watched over and guided by some form of computer surveillance. Managerial authority is enhanced as organizational decision-making becomes more centralized. The other view sees computing technology as having a democratizing impact on the workplace. Workers become more productive as a result of gaining skills and becoming more involved in workplace decisions. Teamwork and cooperation are enhanced as organizational decision-making becomes less centralized.

Workplace systems built around the control/surveillance vision have been quite controversial. According to recent estimates, as many as 26 million employees are regularly monitored by keyboard, telephone and video surveillance techniques (10). Critics have strongly questioned the ethical right of employers to use these devices (30), and opinion surveys indicate that a large majority of the public also oppose employee surveillance (23). One national poll found that 81 percent of Americans believe employers do not have the right to monitor workplace telephone conversations (23). On the other side of the fence, surveys of business personnel have shown equally strong support for the management right to conduct workplace monitoring (36). The controversy has also moved into the political arena with the introduction of legislation in Congress and several states to impose various restrictions on employer use of electronic surveillance (22, 23).

Workplace systems focused on the empowerment/cooperation vision reflect an emerging managerial model stressing employee participation and involvement (5, 9, 11, 25). Participation may be through quality circles or work-team structures or perhaps an "enterprise compact." Some critics claim these schemes are "management ploys" to increase worker productivity (33), but opinion surveys have found very favorable attitudes towards workplace cooperation among both employee groups and the general public (19). Computerization of the participative workplace has been closely associated with the CSCW (computer supported cooperative work) or groupware rubric. E-mail, bulletin boards, conferencing systems and other forms of CSCW all attempt to enhance communication and cooperation—with varying degrees of effectiveness, according to recent studies (6, 17, 24). The growing academic and commercial interest in groupware is consistent with predictions by various analysts that the participative model will eventually dominate the U.S. workplace (5, 11, 31).

Which vision an organization follows in computerizing its workplace is thus an issue with both practical and social-ethical implications. As with all policy decisions, certain factors will have a key impact on the managerial process of choosing and implementing the "appropriate" computing schema. Other than Zuboff's work (46), previous research offers only scattered hints on how this choice process unfolds. And Zuboff's analysis suffers from not following any clear-cut model of decision-making. In the rest of this paper, I shall attempt to remedy the situation by 1) outlining a relatively simple scheme of organizational decision-making relative to computerization and 2) discussing findings from a variety of literatures (computing, managerial and labor relations) which have a bearing on this model. My analysis of these sources will provide a better understanding of the roots of the social-ethical controversy associated with workplace computerization. I will conclude my discussion with some observations about the possible future course of this process.

WHO CHOOSES WHAT AND WHY?

Any model on decision-making should focus on those personnel vested with the authority to make the decisions. For the computerization process we must consider all members of management involved in computer systems decisions—managers of the information systems or data processing units of course, but also managers from any department participating in computer system planning. In organizations which have a union-management "enterprise compact" or employ some other form of participative management, other technical personnel may also be involved in computing system decisions. If so, they too should be included in the model.

Decisions are the basic currency of any decision model. The process of workplace computerization involves a complex array of choices: decisions about the purchase, design and installation of software and hardware; decisions about users and training needs; decisions about interfaces between computing and other organization activities; and decisions about the collection, storage and use of data records. What needs to be determined is whether an organization's structure of decisions tilts towards the surveillance/control vision or the empowerment/cooperation vision. This determination may be complicated by disparities between decision-makers' intentions and the way in which their choices are carried out. Computing is rife with examples of systems having unintended consequences (36, 39). Whatever the case, any analysis of decisions should be organized around what managers ultimately want to accomplish in the way of surveillance/control or empowerment/cooperation.

I complete my model by suggesting that much of the variation in managerial decision-making in the computerization process can be accounted for by three general sets of influences: managerial ideology, task environment and organizational politics. Managerial ideology refers to the general beliefs held by managers about their rights, duties and obligations within the work organization. These beliefs involve both pragmatic and ethical judgments about the role of management. The importance of managerial ideology has been well documented in historical studies of business development (4, 43). Task environment refers to the types of work activity carried on in an organization. We understand these environments by analyzing data on skill level, task complexity and other key attributes of the different jobs (44). Organizational politics refers to the efforts by individuals and groups to wield influence over organizational decisions. These efforts take place through both formal and informal channels in organizations. Unions of course greatly enhance the collective political power of employees (5, 25).

MANAGERIAL IDEOLOGY

The philosophy of scientific management has influenced the thinking of management personnel for almost 100 years. It was initially defined in the writings of Frederick W. Taylor, an engineer and manager in the steel industry. Taylor had conducted a series of experiments at the Midvale Steel Company and Bethlehem Steel Company in the 1880s and 1890s on boosting the productivity of mill workers. His core insight in these experiments was that physical work could be made more efficient by breaking a task up into component parts, eliminating unnecessary or wasteful motions, and using measurements of the restructured work activity to establish job performance standards. Taylor called his technique "time study," and in two papers published around the turn of the century ("Shop Management" and "Principles of Scientific

Management" [42]), he reported the results of applying it to various mill jobs. All of his figures showed remarkable gains in worker productivity.

Taylor's two papers repeatedly stressed the importance of applying his time study method across the industrial landscape. He called for cooperation between employees and management, but he left no doubt about who should be in control of the workplace: "Management whose duty it is to develop this science should guide and help the workman ... [and also] perform much of the work which is now left to the men" (42, p. 26). Taylor's assertion of management's right to control and direct workers was somewhat controversial, especially in labor union circles. But it was no different from the attitude expressed by many other business leaders of the period. Taylor's view on managerial control was carried to perhaps its furthest extreme in the Ford Motor Company, which had invented the assembly line production technique in the 1920s. The company also set up a "Sociology Department" of social workers to monitor and study the home life of workers and a "Service Department" of armed agents to enforce production standards, fire malcontents and suppress any union sentiment (21).

Over the years, scientific management became the dominant operational philosophy in American industry. It offered an appealing defense of management rights, and its control techniques were an integral part of the emergent assembly line technology. Industrial engineers routinely applied Taylor's ideas in their studies of factory work patterns, continually looking for ways to simplify tasks—to limit the range of movements, to reduce decision-making, and to make task routines easier to learn (14). And of course when skill levels were lowered, it made jobs easier for supervisors to monitor, evaluate and control. Outside of the industrial environment, analysts for insurance companies and other large office employers applied the same logic to boost productivity in these settings: "Jobs were broken down into more detailed tasks, skilled aspects of the job were separated from lesser skilled operations, and the tasks were distributed among differentially paid employees" (32, p. 18). Not surprisingly, these changes also enhanced the supervisory control of office work.

(How then has the scientific management ideology affected contemporary work computerization decisions? Reports and comments on the development of electronic monitoring systems indicate that their designers have applied the same top-down methodology used in the earlier time-and-motion production studies by industrial engineers (32). This is consistent with Taylor's views on the need to keep employees out of important workplace decisions. The control structure embedded in the new computerized monitoring systems is also very similar to the structure of the old assembly line systems. Both are designed to give management decisive control over worker behavior; the electronic systems just do this more thoroughly. Finally, the current business community view of electronic monitoring as a "management right" is what one would expect from the scientific management perspective.

The competing participative management model has been influenced by academic research in the United States and Europe and by the quality-circle philosophy developed in Japan. Its academic roots go back to work done by Elton Mayo and the "human relations" researchers in the 1930s (35). Their chief concern was with ways to increase productivity, and their findings stressed the importance of cooperation and a more "democratic" leadership style by managers. These ideas were examined in a wide range of studies of leadership and group process in the workplace in the years following World War II. In general, what these studies found was that increasing the degree of employee involvement and participation in workplace decisions translated into higher levels of satisfaction and that this often led to improvements in efficiency and productivity. These findings served as the basis for McGregor's influential "Theory Y" (28) and Likert's widely read *New Patterns of Management* (29).

During the 1960s and 1970s, management opinion leaders such as the *Harvard Business Review* began to pay increasing attention to the theory and research on participation and to the Japanese quality circles. The degree of participation in the quality circle was in fact quite limited, but the Japanese experience indicated it could be a very effective device for gathering job-related expertise from workers (8). Many companies established quality circle programs, with varying degrees of success, and some adopted programs striving for substantial levels of employee cooperation and involvement. The initial response of labor unions to these company initiatives was often skeptical, but over time, a growing number of unions became involved with employee involvement programs (5). In some cases, most notably with the Saturn Corporation, unions have become full-fledged decision-making partners in "enterprise compacts" (37).

It is clear the participative management ideology has had an impact on the design of CSCW or groupware. Published accounts about the development of these systems often contain references to the theory and research on participative management (13, 17, 41). There seems to be a common practice of involving ultimate employee users in the design process for CSCW systems (16). And the final structure of CSCW systems typically embraces the same democratic vision embedded in the participative management ideology. Although research evidence on where these systems have been implemented is rather spotty, one would expect that they are most likely to be found in organizations committed to some form of participative management.

TASK ENVIRONMENT

Work sites where jobs have already undergone a considerable amount of deskilling seem to be the preferred location for systems emphasizing the electronic monitoring of behavior (1). Here the new computer-based controls extend the paradigm of close supervision that existed before computerization.

There are of course exceptions to this pattern, cases where the work site was relatively skilled to begin with and the deskilling process began with computerization. This is what happened in U.S. post offices, where the relatively skilled mail-sorting function was drastically deskilled with the introduction of computer-controlled sorting machines (3). Basically, what the research literature suggests is that deskilling is the key task environment variable: the reduction of job skills leads to higher levels of managerial concern with control—and a predilection for the apparent efficiencies of computerized controls.

Workplace systems stressing the empowerment/cooperative vision seem to flourish in a very different task environment. Although there has been no systematic research on the users of groupware, a number of studies have mentioned various professional, technical and other white collar workers using these groupware systems (34, 46). These reported users are mostly from higher levels of skill and education, but they also seem to be clustered in positions having some communication and decision responsibilities. And that makes sense, given the fact that much groupware is designed with the intent of facilitating communication and decision-making.

After a new computing system has been introduced in an organization, it goes through a period in which it may be altered or adjusted because of the way it impacts on the task environment. Research has identified several negative factors which may affect managers' decisions. For systems of surveillance and control, there may be heightened levels of employee stress and anger which lead to surges in grievance filings, absenteeism and turnover (1, 15, 26, 32). If the perceived cost of these negatives is too great, then managers are likely to look for ways to modify the system. Less is known about the impact of CSCW systems, but some researchers have noted that managers will move against them if they believe these systems are circumventing or undermining their authority (34, 46). This has been a recurrent problem in the more general effort by organizations to restructure themselves around the participative management model; managers can be very reluctant to share or give up decision-making power (18, 25, 29).

ORGANIZATIONAL POLITICS AND LABOR RELATIONS

The traditional model of bureaucracy offers a rather simple, and stark, view of how changes are made and implemented in organizations (29, 35). Top decision makers are in complete charge. They make policy selections after receiving technical information about alternative choices from their staff subalterns. These decisions are communicated downward through the hierarchy with the expectation that they will be automatically implemented by subordinate officials. Once technical guidelines have been developed, all employees are expected to follow the new policy rules "by the book."

We know now, from years of research on organizations, that this bureaucratic model can be compromised by various "informal" structures of influence (35). These structures operate independently of the formal channels of authority. They are created by groups which have their own interests and agendas within organizations, such as different departments, members of professional associations, or unions. These groups may attempt to influence the formation of policy changes, through some type of lobbying or perhaps collective bargaining. They may also attempt to guide the way the new systems are actually put into effect. When controversial or unpopular changes are being implemented, employee groups can be very resourceful in opposing them (18).

In terms of computerization of the workplace, we would expect to find a strong preference for systems emphasizing the control/surveillance vision in traditional bureaucratic organizations. The control structures embedded in both systems are very similar. Conversely, we would expect to find efforts to reduce the scope and intensity of workforce monitoring systems in organizations with active and well-defined informal structures of influence. These organizations, with their crosscutting networks of influence, would also be a more conducive setting for groupware and other systems emphasizing the empowerment/cooperation vision. Perin and Zuboff offer some indirect evidence on this point (35, 46). Both found considerable suspicion and hostility among managers towards groupware systems in traditional bureaucratic settings.

From labor relations studies, we know that American unions have had a long history of involvement with systems of measuring and evaluating workplace behavior (14). Although the labor movement was initially quite suspicious of Frederick Taylor's ideas, it eventually came to accept the legitimacy of performance measurements. In the 1930s, industrial unions began to negotiate agreements over the design and use of time study standards, and some unions hired industrial engineers to do their own time study research. Companies sometimes refused to bargain over production standards, claiming that management had the exclusive right to set them. But by the 1950s, labor arbitrators had ruled against this management stance, and unions were able to more easily win contract language dealing with the methods and usage of time study data (14, p. 26–50).

Unions have taken a more critical stance with the computerized heirs to time and motion studies, mainly because of the greatly expanded scope of the new systems. Unlike the older systems which typically used samples of worker behavior, the new electronic systems (used mostly in offices) allow for a continuous collection of performance data on all workers. A report issued by the Office of Technology Assessment stated that 20 U.S. unions have taken a general position against electronic monitoring: "A broad consensus seems to be that work speedups, enforced by close work monitoring, are bad because they create harmful stress among employees and also compromise the quality of work" (32, p. 86-87). Union efforts to limit the impact of computer-based technologies are constrained by the fact that arbitrators have generally ruled that the introduction of new technology is a unilateral management right (3, 40). Nonetheless, some unions have been able to negotiate significant modifications of the surveillance aspects of the new technologies (shifting from individual to group monitoring, for example) (7, 32).

Union attitudes towards the empowering types of workplace computing systems have been largely ignored by researchers. However we do know that unions have become increasingly supportive of the types of cooperative work structures associated with the participative managerial ideology. In a recent review of research, Hoerr notes that cooperation and teamwork have become more common practices in unionized than in nonunionized companies (20). If this trend holds, we would expect it to be reflected in decisions about computerization and to see more joint union-management collaboration on CSCW types of systems.

CONCLUSIONS

Ethical controversies exist where people hold differing views about what is right and wrong. In workplace computing, such a controversy exists over the use of electronic systems which gather a continuous stream of data on employee performance. Labor unions and a substantial portion of the public think these monitoring systems are improper and wrong. But the business community maintains that management has an inherent right to use them. That right is not currently restricted by any state or federal statutes. In this paper I have attempted to shed some light on factors which determine when and where these monitoring systems are likely to be used. The existence of organized employee groups, especially unions, can definitely moderate the impact of the these systems. I have also looked at an alternative workplace computing vision (empowerment/cooperation) which has generated no significant controversy.

Public opinion polls indicate that any effort to pass legislation limiting the use of employee monitoring systems would be widely supported. Whether such laws would have much impact on the use of these systems is questionable, however. Business groups have in the past shown great resourcefulness in watering down legislative measures which they do not like. And even when strong regulatory laws are passed, they do not always produce the intended result. As Weiler notes: "[With] the regulatory model ... too frequently the burdens imposed on employers are not matched by corresponding benefits for employees. Research on occupational safety and health enforcement, for example, finds only marginal reductions in workplace injuries, while capital expenditures needed for compliance ... are often quite substantial" (45, p. 90).

What of the future, then? Will we see a continuing controversy about the ethics of workplace surveillance? This will surely be the case in the short run. The theory and practice of electronic monitoring are rooted in an ideological system which still has many adherents in management circles. Frederick W. Taylor may be forgotten, but his ideas on scientific management still have considerable power (as can be seen in current discussions of the need to "re-engineer" the workplace [9]). Nonetheless, I think we may be approaching a turning point. Businesses are discovering that there can be substantial costs associated with electronic monitoring; unions and other employee groups seem to be learning how to moderate the impact of these systems; and—most importantly—these systems are not compatible with the participative managerial ideology that seems to be gaining favor in many U.S. corporations. If we are indeed moving towards a more cooperatively structured workplace, then it seems likely that we will be hearing more about computerized cooperation and less about disputes over electronic surveillance in the years to come.

REFERENCES

(1) Attewell, P. and Rule, J. "Computing and Organizations: What We Know and What We Don't Know." *Communications of the ACM*, 27, 12 (Dec. 1984), 1184–1192.

*(2) Bailyn, L. "Toward the Perfect Workplace?" *Communications of the ACM*, 32, 4 (April 1989), 460–471.

(3) Baxter, V. "Technological Change and Labor Relations in the United States Postal Service," in *Workers, Managers and Technological Change*, D. B. Cornfield, ed. Plenum Press, New York, 1987.

(4) Bendix, R. *Work and Authority in Industry*. Harper & Row, New York, 1956.

(5) Bluestone, B. and Bluestone, I. *Negotiating the Future: A Labor Perspective on American Business*. Basic Books, New York, 1992.

(6) Bullen, C. and Bennett, J. "Groupware in Practice: An Interpretation of Work Experiences," in *Computerization and Controversy: Value Conflict and Social Choices*, C. Dunlop and R. Kling, eds. Academic Press, San Diego, 1991.

(7) Clement, A. "Computing at Work: Empowering Action by 'Low Level' Users." *Communications of the ACM*, 37, 1 (Jan. 1994), 52–63.

(8) Cole, R. E. *Strategies for Learning*. University of California Press, Berkeley, 1989.

(9) Davenport, T. H. *Process Innovation: Reengineering Work Through Information Technology*. Harvard Business School Press, Boston, 1993.

(10) DeTienne, K. B. "Big Brother or Friendly Coach?" *The Futurist*, 27, 5 (Sept.-Oct. 1993), 33–37.

(11) Drucker, P. F. *Post-Capitalist Society*. Harper, New York, 1993.

(12) Dunlop, C. and Kling, R. "Computerization and the Transformation of Work," in *Computerization and Controversy: Value Conflict and Social Choices*, C. Dunlop and R. Kling, eds. Academic Press, San Diego, 1991.

(13) Galegher, J., Kraut, R. and Egido, C., eds. *Intellectual Teamwork: Social and Technological Foundations of Cooperative Work*. Lawrence Erlbaum Assoc., Hillsdale, NJ, 1990.

(14) Gomberg, W. *A Trade Union Analysis of Time Study*, Second Edition. Prentice-Hall, New York, 1955.

(15) Grant, R. A., Higgins, C. A. and Irving, R. H. "Computerized Performance Monitors: Are They Costing You Customers?" *Sloan Management Review*, 29, 3 (Spring 1988), 39–45.

(16) Greenbaum, J. and Kyng, M., eds. *Design at Work: Cooperative Design of Computer Systems*. Lawrence Erlbaum Assoc., Hillsdale, NJ, 1991.

(17) Grudin, J. "Groupware and Social Dynamics: Eight Challenges for Developers." *Communications of the ACM*, 37, 1 (Jan. 1994), 92–105.

(18) Hage, J. and Aiken, M. *Social Change in Complex Organizations*. Random House, New York, 1970.

(19) Harris, R. L. "The Impact of the Micro-Electronics Revolution on the Basic Structure of Modern Organizations." *Science, Technology & Human Values*, 11, 4 (Fall 1986), 31–44.

(20) Hoerr, J. "What Should Unions Do?" *Harvard Business Review*, 69, 3 (May-June 1991), 30–45.

(21) Howe, I. and Widdick, B. J. *The UAW and Walter Reuther*. Random House, New York, 1949.

(22) Katzff, P. "Surveillance Legislation Pending." *National Law Journal*, 13, 32 (April 15, 1991), 1–16.

(23) King, D. N. "Privacy Issues in the Private Sector Workplace: Protection From Electronic Surveillance and the Emerging 'privacy gap'." *Southern California Law Review*, 67, 2 (Jan. 1994), 441–476.

(24) Kling, R. "Cooperation, Coordination and Control in Computer-Supported Work." *Communications of the ACM*, 34, 12 (Dec. 1991), 83–88.

(25) Kochan, T. A., Katz, H. and McKersie, R. B. *The Transformation of American Industrial Relations*. Basic Books, New York, 1986.

(26) Kraut, R., Dumais, S. and Koch, S. "Computerization, Productivity and Quality of Work-Life." *Communications of the ACM*, 32, 2 (Feb. 1989), 220–238.

*(27) Likert, R. *New Patterns of Management*. McGraw-Hill, New York, 1961.

(28) McGregor, 0. *The Human Side of Enterprise*. McGraw-Hill, New York, 1960.

(29) March, J. G. and Simon, H. A. *Organizations*, Second Edition. Blackwell, Cambridge, MA, 1993.

(30) Marx, G. T. and Sherizen, S. "Monitoring on the Job: How to Protect Privacy as Well as Property." *Technology Review*, 89, 8 (Nov.-Dec. 1986), 62–72.

(31) Naisbitt, J. *Megatrends*. Warner Books, New York, 1962.

(32) Office of Technology Assessment. *The Electronic Supervisor*. U.S. Government Printing Office: Washington, DC, 1987.

(33) Parker, M. and Slaughter, J. *Choosing Sides: Unions and the Team Concept*. South End Press, Boston, 1988.

(34) Perin, C. "Electronic Social Fields in Bureaucracies." *Communications of the ACM*, 34, 12 (Dec. 1991), 64–73.

(35) Perrow, C. *Complex Organizations*, Third Edition. Random House, New York, 1986.

(36) "Readers Say No to Hiring Quotas." *Nation's Business*, 29, 11 (Nov. 1991), 37.

(37) Rubinstein, S., Bennett, M. and Kochan, T. "The Saturn Partnership: Co-Management and the Reinvention of the Local Union," in *Employee Representation Alternatives and Future Directions*, B. E. Kaufman and M. M. Kleiner, eds. IRRA, Madison, WI, 1993.

*(38) Rule, J. and Attewell, P. "What Do Computers Do?" in *Computerization and Controversy: Value Conflict and Social Choices*, C. Dunlop and R. Kling, eds. Academic Press, San Diego, 1991.

(39) Salerno, L. M. "What Happened to the Computer Revolution?" in *Computerization and Controversy: Value Conflict and Social Choices*. C. Dunlop and R. Kling, eds. Academic Press, San Diego, 1991.

(40) Shaiken, H. *Work Transformed: Automation and Labor in the Computer Age*. Holt, Rinehart and Winston, New York, 1984.

(41) Sproull, L. and Kiesler, S. *Connections: New Ways of Working in the Networked Organization*. MIT Press, Cambridge, MA 1991.

(42) Taylor, F. W. *Scientific Management*. Greenwood Press, Westport, CT, 1972.

(43) Waring, S. P. *Taylorism Transformed*. University of North Carolina Press, Chapel Hill, NC, 1991.

(44) Weber, R. "Computer Technology and Jobs: An Impact Assessment Model." *Communications of the ACM*, 31, 1 (Jan. 1988), 68–77.

(45) Weiler, P. C. "Governing the Workplace: Employee Representation in the Eyes of the Law," in *Employee Representation Alternatives and Future Directions*, B. E. Kaufman and M. M. Kleiner, eds. IRRA, Madison, WI, 1993.

(46) Zuboff, S. *In the Age of the Smart Machine*. Basic Books, New York, 1988.

References with asterisks do not appear in the text but were consulted.

15. THE ROLE OF PROFESSIONAL ORGANIZATIONS IN PROMOTING COMPUTER ETHICS

Joseph M. Kizza

Over the last two decades computers have gained widespread use not only in offices, but in homes as well. Recent studies show that there is a computer in one of every four households in the United States today, and it is projected that the personal computer industry is likely to keep growing. Every aspect of our lives is now directly or indirectly influenced by computers.

Computer popularity and technological advances have resulted in more user-friendly hardware and software products on open markets. Such products have enabled even those with no professional computer training to comfortably use computers. Although this has been a blessing in many aspects, it has also opened up computers to unscrupulous users. Anyone with or without a password but with high school mathematical skills, originally referred to as a whiz kid, can randomly generate passwords of choice and retrieve information from a computer. This has resulted in a wave of computer crimes often with grave consequences for the public. Since the public cannot differentiate between a computer professional and an unscrupulous fortune hunter, more often than not, the professionals are blamed for computer crimes. This is likely to continue until true computer professionals are identifiable. Ethical responsibility can only be upheld by those who claim to be in the profession only if they are clearly identifiable as members of that profession by the public. Once there are gray areas between real professionals and those who claim to be, serious problems of responsibility and accountability arise. Our first task, therefore, is to give this clarification by giving a clear definition of a computer professional.

WHO IS A PROFESSIONAL

We call one a professional if one possesses exceptional knowledge and or skills in a discipline. This is the definition we most often hear and most of the general population understands. It is a very wide definition, so wide that it includes everybody with any acquired skill such as on-the-job-training auto mechanics, landscapers, builders, and graduates of Aunt Maggie's after-dinner computer classes. This is not the definition of a professional that we want the public to know, identify with, emulate as role models, and take counsel from. In fact we are thinking of a very limited definition that includes only those people with the following requirements:

(1) high theoretical knowledge of a specific domain
(2) several years of formal education in that or a related domain
(3) developed skills in that domain
(4) adherence to value-based guidelines of the profession

Broadly speaking, this definition eliminates all those people with operational knowledge and acquired skills of a domain who pose and are seen by the public as professionals. In particular, it eliminates those computer users, with operational knowledge of computers, who often can convince the public that they are computer professionals. A group of professionals in a specific domain, such as computer science and information systems, comprises a profession. Professionals are commissioned by their respective professions to make daily decisions for their clients basing them on, among other considerations, their profession's code of ethics. One other difference between true professionals and those professionals who acquire skills through on-the-job-training is that professionals have clients while everybody else with a sellable trade has customers. Probably the difference between client and customer is best explained by the provider-receiver equation and the power therein. Both client and customer are receivers just because they are at the receiving end of the equation. In the provider-customer relationship, the power in the equation is in favor of the customer. So the customer always can dictate terms of the service to be performed; for example, when you take your car to the shop, you tell the mechanic what you want done in spite of the fact that you may not even know how to do it yourself. The saying that the customer is always right best describes this relationship.

On the other hand, in the provider-client relationship, for example that of the doctor-patient, the power is tilted in favor of the provider. The client in this relationship is a submissive, passive recipient with little power except to ask for a second opinion. The power, the knowledge and the skill of the provider in this equation, is so overwhelming that there is little room for the client to dictate terms to the provider. Unfortunately, this very powerful relationship that professionals have with their clients in executing their day-to-day duties is often misused. In fact, to many some professions are but bodies of exploiters with concentrated skills and wealth. Today there are a good number of professions which can claim this title. This is where the enforcement of professional ethics comes in. I will illustrate this by the computer profession. This profession consists of two divisions, the computer science division and the information systems division.

Both computer science and information systems are new, less than fifty years old. Although their span has been short in comparison to other traditional professions like engineering and medicine, their impact on society has been phenomenal. The controversy of whether they are true professions will take long to settle, but there are signs to indicate that they have matured into full-fledged professions. Among such signs are the following:

(1) The field of computer science and engineering has over produced new Ph.D.'s in the last two to three years. There have even been calls to reduce the number of Ph.D. bound graduate students.

(2) There are more full professors than assistant professors, and departments are becoming more tenured, therefore more stable.

(3) There are increasing numbers of new Ph.D.'s going into employment outside academia.

The growth of computer science and information systems is not only in numbers of Ph.D.'s, faculty and students, but also their clout has grown in industry and research establishments. There is more original research from computer science and information systems than ever before. Aside from academia and industry, the growth of their public image has been phenomenal. With this unprecedented growth, however, comes responsibility and accountability for the professions. These professions have a responsibility towards a public which has long identified their members with the image of a thinking and infallible machine which delivers absolute truth, the computer. Unfortunately, the last two decades have brought us face to face with the reality of the problem of unethical behavior and social irresponsibility among computer professionals. Even the public that had at one time unconditionally accepted these professions is becoming concerned with the ethical issues associated with the use of computer technology.

What has caused this to happen, and can this new trend be reversed? It is not easy to pinpoint the cause, and the remedy will only be meaningful if professions get involved and play a major role in the enforcement of professional responsibility and accountability. The enforcement of responsibility and accountability will include the teaching and upholding of computer ethics through the development and enforcement of professional codes.

In general there are three techniques commonly used by professions to enforce responsibility and accountability, namely:

(1) Ethical codes
(2) A set of rules for advisory opinions, resolutions, and guidelines
(3) No rules, or codes at all

The first and most important of the three techniques is the ethical code. The ethical code itself can be divided into four subcategories:

(1) the individual code
(2) the professional code
(3) the organizational code
(4) the community code (Chalk et al., 1981)

Every human being is endowed with an individual code of ethics. It gives one the judgment basis between right and wrong, and it usually influences one's perceptions of the input premises in the decision making processes. The professional code is a set of guidelines laid down by a profession for members to adhere to when making decisions. In the AAAS (1980) Professional Ethics Project, Chalk, Frankel, and Chafer define professional codes as disciplines that are intended to define the rights and responsibilities of professionals in their relationship with each other and with the public. The organizational code is too a set of guidelines laid down by one's employer, that all employees regardless of their professions must follow when making decisions. The community code is another set of guidelines which everyone who lives and works in that community must abide by. While the professions cannot enforce individual, community, and organizational codes of their members, they can uphold professional responsibility and accountability of members by enforcing professional codes. For the computer science and information system professions, computer ethics among members of these professions can be enforced through the teaching and enforcement of the professions' codes.

Professional codes seen in this light are important for the profession. But since there has never been a comprehensive study to show whether codes, guidelines, resolutions and advisory opinions work, we need to be cautious because sometimes they do work but there are times when they do not. Consider the following fictional case for example: Harrod works for a very prestigious law firm. One time, she is assigned a case to defend a client charged with knowingly dumping a defective product on the market which resulted in several deaths. This client's company is a multimillion dollar a year business and is the flagship of all clients for the law firm—a very valuable customer. Upon being handed the case, Harrod is told by her boss that all evidence concerning the design of the product had been turned over to the firm by the company, and as far as the firm is concerned, there is no thread of evidence that the company knew that the product was defective before shipping it. However, halfway in the trial, Harrod stumbles on a company memo written by the then chief designer of the product in question in which the designer explicitly informs the then CEO of the company of the danger that might arise and the loss of life that might result if the product was allowed to be sold to the public in its present design form. The memo was hidden in the firm's archives. After a personal investigation, Harrod finds out that the engineer who wrote the memo was retired by the company. She also finds out, to her disbelief, that her firm has known all along of the existence of this memo. After discussing the situation with her boss, Harrod is told to forget that she ever saw that memo and proceed as asked or else she will lose that job; Harrod conforms and not only does her firm win the lawsuit, it is also handsomely paid by its grateful client; clearly the public is the loser in this case. By agreeing to defend this client against the charges and by hiding incriminating evidence, this firm knowingly breaks its organizational code and the professional code of its employees; Harrod too breaks both her personal and professional codes. When ethical codes are violated knowingly or otherwise, as in the example above, there should be some form of machinery, other than civil, to protect the public.

Second to codes as a form of enforcement is the use of a set of rules for advisory opinions, resolutions, and guidelines. These can be used independently of codes or in conjunction with the codes. Many professions and professional firms use these to help with social and ethical problems within the organization or outside of the organization. In many cases those professions and professional firms that rely on these methods do so because they lack the code system and or the enforcement mechanism. Very often the enforcement in such cases is done by civil authorities. In recent years, with the number of celebrated cases of sexual harassment on the rise, many organizations, firms and professions have issued or distributed advisory opinions, resolutions, and guidelines on sexual harassment to their members or employees. Once an incident of sexual harassment surfaces, it is usually the civil authorities that handle it.

A third method of enforcement is to have no codes, no advisory opinions, no resolutions and no guidelines at all, but to let members observe their employers' codes, if they have any. There are a number of professions, especially newer and small professions, with no professional codes, advisories or guidelines for their members. It is left to the members in these professions to observe the employers' and the community codes, and enforcement is also left to either the employer or the civil authorities. It was reported in AAAS (1980) that in a survey of 150 scientific and engineering societies, 45 percent of the societies had no codes, guidelines, advisory opinions, or resolutions. In light of the general public's outcry concerning the lack of professional ethics, and in light of knowing that professional codes do help the members' and the professions' reputations, it is difficult to understand why there are still professions with nothing for their members to fall back on.

Situations and environments like these are difficult to work in and very often present situations that are confusing and difficult to resolve. Consider Jeromy's situation: Jeromy works for ABC, Inc., a small company which specializes in medical software. Jeromy has been working for ABC for a couple of years. His job is to test software products before they are shipped out. The company has been experiencing financial and managerial problems for over a year. But there is hope in an eagerly awaited software package that is about to be released by the company. It is hoped that with this software package, the company will move back to profitability. In short, the future of ABC is riding on this one software product. From pre-release market surveys and orders, it looks like this one product will turn ABC's fortunes. Two days before the orchestrated release, Jeromy, doing the final inspection, accidentally stumbles on a small software bug imbedded in the software package. Jeromy estimates that if left uncorrected the bug has a chance of occurrence of 1 in 1,000,000 when the software is in full use. But Jeromy also is aware that if it does occur, it will definitely cause the main program to abort with life threatening consequences. He is also aware that if he tries to stop release, he will certainly lose his job and probably the company will fail. On the other hand if he lets the shipments go as planned, one person in a million will certainly die. Jeromy is faced with a dilemma to choose between two alternatives, neither of which is good. Jeromy's high intelligence and skill cannot help him now. But his profession's code or guidelines, resolutions or advisory opinions might enable him to arrive at a satisfactory decision. In the absence of these, his decision might turn out to be disastrous not only to him but also even more importantly to his company and the unsuspecting public.

ENFORCEMENT MACHINERY

For professions to make sure that their members are not put in a situation like Jeromy's and to safeguard their integrity, they must come up not only with codes, canons, and guidelines, but also with enforcement mechanisms. Laws, codes, canons, guidelines and all others are not obeyed until and unless there is some enforcement machinery and some kind of penalty for the guilty. Currently there are various techniques of enforcement, most of them with no civil authority. The most widely used is the professional ethics board—under various names from standing committee to review boards.

These committees are charged with

(1) drawing up the codes of ethics for the profession if none exist
(2) revising codes if and when necessary

(3) conducting education campaigns at membership level
(4) distributing copies of the codes to every member
(5) developing disciplinary procedures
(6) receiving complaints, conducting hearings, counseling members, and sanctioning members found guilty
(7) promoting the image of the profession

Whenever these committees exist and whatever the charge of the committee, there must be a streamlined way of reporting complaints, a set of guidelines for dealing with the charges, a set of recommendations for sanctioning the affected person(s), and a campaign to let the public or whoever initiated the complaint know the actions taken by the committee to prevent the future occurrences of the incident(s).

REPORTING PROCEDURES

There are mainly two reporting procedures. The first is the pyramidical reporting structure where complaints are reported first to the local chapters if these chapters exist. The complaint then makes its way to the top, usually to the national ethical committee. The second is the short-circuit procedure where reporting can be done at any level. Irrespective of the level of origination, the complaints are forwarded all the way to the top. There are variations in these methods. In some professions, the reporting must be done by a member of the profession in good standing and nobody else. This means that concerned members of the public must report their complaint to a member of the profession who then forwards the complaints to the committee. There are problems with this method, especially in those professions whose members are not easily visible to the public like computer science and information systems. The public will then have a difficult time finding a member in good standing. Whichever way the reporting of a complaint is done, there should be a way to inform members of the profession and the public on the procedures of reporting and who can and cannot file a complaint, and there must be established channels of communication.

HEARING PROCEDURES

There are various ways of conducting hearings depending on the nature of the profession, the financial standing of the profession, the structure of the organization and the kind of enforcement procedures and penalties imposed. In some professions, if the penalty is not worth the paper it is written on, and if it cannot be enforced, the accused member may not even appear for a hearing if one is scheduled. Also if the members of the profession are financially strapped, such members never turn up for hearings. The success of the hearings depends mainly on the status of the profession. Unfortunately high profile professions are not the only ones prone to undesirable ethical conduct by their members. Because of the nature of the profession, care must be taken by professions to assess their status in society and devise procedures that will be effective in dealing with complaints from the public.

SANCTIONS

If censure of a member has been decided upon by the committee, a kind of censure to fit the crime should be given. Financially able professions offer or recommend counseling to a member who gets any of the following sanctions: probation, revocation of certification, request for resignation, and suspension from the profession at the member's expense.

After the member has fulfilled the committee's recommendation, depending on the profession, the member should be reported as having fulfilled the recommendation and, therefore, reinstated in good standing. The nature of this reporting depends on the nature of the profession and the service offered by the profession. For some professions, the public needs this information; for others it can be done in secret.

EFFECTIVENESS OF COMMITTEES

The effectiveness of these committees will depend mainly on the status of the profession and the financial viability of the profession. There are many professions with committees that never meet. Some professions have committees that meet and pass resolutions, but these resolutions are never enacted because the committees have no enforcement powers. The effectiveness of these committees also depends on the perception the public has of their proceedings and sanctions. If the public feels that the committees are conducting "kangaroo" courts or that there is peer leniency, then sanctions will never be effective. While the committees need to be effective by passing sanctions that fit the crimes committed, they should avoid sanctions that tend to appease the public by sacrificing the member sending a signal mentality. This in the long run drives membership away and may eventually destroy the profession.

APPEALS PROCEDURES

The committees must make sure that if a decision is reached and one of the parties in the conflict is not happy with the decision, there are clear guidelines to appeal, and a clear explanation of what happens to the appealing members during and after the appeal process. Should such members remain executing their duties, or be prohibited from doing so? In certain professions those members are put on administrative leave, suspended, or left in full membership capacity, carrying on their duties pending the decision of the appeal. The committee should also spell out how long such decisions take so that all parties are aware.

CONCLUSIONS

Through the efforts of professional organizations and with help from individual members, local civil authorities, and the community, ethical values can be upheld, and where and when problems occur, they can be corrected to satisfy all concerned.

BIBLIOGRAPHY

Callahan, D. and Bok, S. (eds.) (1980). *Ethics Teaching in Higher Education.* Plenum Press, New York.
Chalk, R., Frankel, M. and Chafer, S. (1981). *AAAS Professional Ethics Project: Professional Ethics Activities in the Scientific and Engineering Societies,* Third Edition. American Association for the Advancement of Science, Washington, DC, 1981.
Dejoice, R., Fowler, G. and Paradice, D., (1992). *Ethical Issues in Information Systems.* Boyd & Fraser Publishing Company, Boston.
Gorlin, R. (ed.) (1986). *Codes of Professional Responsibility.* The Bureau of National Affairs, Inc., Washington, DC, 1986.
Gries, David and Marsh, Dorothy (1990, October). "The 1989-90 Taulbee Survey." *Computing Research News,* p. 6.
_____ and _____ (1991, January). "The 1990-91 Taulbee Survey." *Computing Research News,* p. 8.
Harrington, Susan and McCollum, Rebecca (1990). "Lessons from Corporate America Applied to Training in Computer Ethics." *Computer & Society,* 20, pp. 169–173.
Kizza, J. M. "Ethics in the Computer and Information Science Professions." *Proceedings, Information Technology, Annual National Conference of the Association of Management,* 1991.

16. COMPUTER PRACTITIONERS: PROFESSIONALS OR HIRED GUNS?

Donald Gotterbarn

Since the mid–1960s computer practitioners have been talking about the "software crisis." As computing has changed so has the concept of the software crisis. In the early days of computing the crisis consisted of software being delivered late and over budget, and not fulfilling the customers' needs. Computing was only related to our daily lives in limited ways, such as producing bills, printing checks, managing inventories for large companies, etc. The software crisis of this era had several causes, including an immature development discipline and a lack of skilled personnel. The development method consisted of allowing some talented individuals to use their skills and develop a piece of software. Because of the incredible backlog of software to be developed, there was never enough time to develop each piece of software so that it did exactly what was desired. I characterize such software developers as "hired guns."

The concept of the "hired gun" is a popular image in American fiction. The hired gun generally possesses a high degree of skill in some area and is willing to use that skill to solve whatever problem he is paid to solve. The hired gun is not merely a skilled individual but is a free spirited individual, unrestrained by any conventional standards. This lack of restraint was considered good. The hired gun could always come up with creative solutions. It was all right if he didn't know the exact answer because he could figure something out. If it wasn't exactly right, there was always time to mend the fences if they broke. The hired gun does the job, but not necessarily in a way the people employing him would like. Since the hired gun is the only one with the special talent, the customer had no choice but to employ that individual.

Computing has for some time had this as its self-image. In the early days of computing we thought such methodology and self-image were of little consequence. We didn't understand how that concept exacerbated the software crisis. In the early stages of the software crisis, the problems were attributed primarily to a shortage of fast guns—skilled personnel. This led to an interest by a number of organizations in the establishment of skill training programs. This generated an interest in certification as a way to establish that a worker has an advanced body of knowledge in a specialist area. Certification provides an objective measure of knowledge to employees and clients; it establishes the individual as an expert in an area which has been independently and objectively assessed. The shortage of personnel meant that people could be employed as software developers even without any objective certification.

The early stages of the software crisis also helped define our early understanding of computer ethics. An ethical issue in computing occurred when the hired gun went bad, had malicious intent and misused his skill. Common issues in computer ethics were stock fraud, misdirecting (stealing) inventory, and unauthorized reallocation of bank funds.

Computing has changed significantly over the past two decades. Computing now permeates every aspect of our lives. It helps us cook our food, controls the brakes in our cars, controls the flow of traffic, flies airplanes, manages patient care in hospitals, etc. As computing has changed over the past two decades, so has the software crisis. It used to be characterized by the phrase, "So much software to develop and so little time and personnel." Now it is more accurately characterized as, "So much to do and so many lives at stake." There is still a software crisis but it is significantly altered. The hired guns are still with us, but their hasty solutions are no longer irrelevant to human lives. There is no longer always enough time to fix it later. Consider the recent problems with a particular pacemaker. The code that was burned into the chip was defective. It has a 1 percent chance of failure. Several people have these defective pacemakers. There is no reasonable possibility of fixing this mistake. Changing the pacemaker involves a 2 percent risk to the patient. A 1 percent chance of failure means one person in a hundred will suffer a needless heart failure because of the hired gun. The new software crisis is costing lives and jobs.

The concern with this new software crisis has rekindled interest in certification. The new software crisis is blamed on the alleged early cause, an insufficient supply of hired guns. This time people are interested in certified hired guns who do not make mistakes. Many companies have seen this interest as a financial opportunity. Several companies are offering certification programs for their products. One can become a Novell Netware Certified Engineer or a Microsoft Systems Engineer.

I think of this understanding of the new software crisis and its solution in skill training as a myopic position. The age of the hired gun, even the certified hired gun, is over. The bad consequences of this hired gun approach to software permeate every aspect of our lives. Even though most implementations of software are invisible—in the telephone, in the stove, in the carburetor of the car—people are aware of the disastrous consequences of badly developed software. They find the results abhorrent and in need of change.

Faster guns are not the answer. They can develop bad software faster. The concept of the software developed needs to be the concept of the software professional. Historically many occupations decide to become a profession. This is going on now in software development. Several professional computing organizations are working with industry to establish software development as a profession.

What is the difference between being a professional and being a hired gun? Initially the concept of a profession was the commitment to a way of life with high moral ideals, e.g., the profession of faith to a monastic order. The concept of a profession now embodies the possession of a set of skills and a commitment to use those skills in a certain way. The failure to use the skills in the accepted way is considered a violation of professional ethics.

Professional ethics are distinct from personal ethics. One's commitment to follow a set of professional ethics is a personal ethical commitment, but the professional ethics are standards adopted by the professional community. These standards get codified by professional societies in codes of ethics, licensing standards, and standards for professional practices.

A simple example will show the difference between a professional and a hired gun. So far we have focused on the technical skill of the hired gun. The possession of this skill is also a necessary condition for a computer professional. But there is another significant element in professionalism. Good professional judgment is not purely technical judgment. What would you think of a physician who, when asked by a patient to cut off both of the patient's arms at the elbow, said "I will do it right now. I have been specially trained in surgery"? Even if the physician did this in a technically skilled fashion, we would not say he was acting professionally. Where was the exercise of the values for the well-being of the patient in this judgment? Technically, he chose the correct scalpel and anesthetic. What he failed to do was to condition his technical judgment by a set of moral values. Accepting a role of professional also carries with it a commitment to a set of ethical principles.

Professionals have a special responsibility to avoid or prevent harms which goes beyond our everyday responsibilities not to harm others. Claims like this have been the basis for legal decisions in medicine and engineering and recently have been the basis for decisions in computing. Professionals have been found guilty of "indifference to their professional duties." The claim that professionals have a special responsibility is generally argued on two grounds; one is an argument based on an implicit contract that a professional has with society, and the other is based on the moral obligation to society to use special knowledge wisely. The importance of computer science knowledge to the lives and well-being of the public entails a consequent responsibility to use this knowledge in a way that both protects and benefits the public.

There are several marks of a profession. It is an occupation requiring special, usually advanced, education and skill. This education has a solid foundation in theory. In computing there are standard bodies which have defined a minimal undergraduate curriculum. The hired gun does not require any background knowledge.

The professional's knowledge and skill are vital to the well-being of society. Professional activity should always be viewed as a service to society. I think the failure to see that computing products are only used to serve the needs of others and the failure of the professional to keep the welfare of the user in mind has led directly to several instances of unethical behavior. There are several causes for these failures. One cause is simple ignorance. We train computer scientists to solve problems, and the examples we use, such as finding the least common multiple (LCM) for a set of numbers, portray computing as merely a problem solving exercise, analogous to doing a crossword puzzle. Solving the puzzle is an interesting exercise, but it lacks significant consequences.

The failure to realize that computing is a service profession to the user of the computing artifact has significant consequences. One result of this is seen when we consider the case of a programmer who was asked to write a program that would raise and lower a large X-ray device. The programmer wrote and tested his solution to this puzzle. It successfully and accurately moved the device from the top of the support pole to the top of the table. The difficulty with this narrow problem solving approach was shown when an X-ray technician told a patient to get off the table after an X-ray was taken, and then the technician set the height of the device to "table-top-height." The patient had not heard the technician and was crushed under the machine. The programmer solved a puzzle but didn't consider the user. The responsibility to the user should have led the programmer to implement a check whenever the machine was lowered to table top.

Computing is a service industry. All computing artifacts are designed to be used. Computing has had a tendency not to see itself as a service industry. Even the term "user" carries with it a derogatory connotation. We are one of only two occupations that I know of that call their customers "users." There was a recent example of this attitude before the courts. A defense contractor was asked to develop a portable antiaircraft system. The system the contractor developed effectively destroys aircraft, but it also occasionally kills the person who launched the missile. Company officials have declared that this is not a problem because they "are in full compliance with the specifications given to them by the user." Being a professional involves using one's special skills to give careful and constant consideration to the impact of the service on others. This consideration is guided by a set of ethical principles.

Another mark of a profession is a credentialing standard, which is generally in the form of a license to practice the profession. This standard serves two functions. first it establishes a set of professional practices which will be followed by the professional, and second it informs the public of what are considered the best practices. This mark of a profession does not currently exist for software developers in the United States.

The licensing and certification of computing professionals are very controversial and political questions. At its simplest level, certification is generally voluntary, while licensing is required to practice a profession and is regulated by governments. Certification generally means some agency or employer certifies that you meet its standards; licensing generally means that to claim to practice a certain profession requires a government license, often administered through a professional organization. The general theory is that both licensing and certification are supposed to help those outside of the certified or licensed profession judge if someone else is capable of doing certain jobs. Licensing isn't currently required for computing professionals, while computing professionals have had a certification program for years.

The licensing and certification of computing professionals are complex issues and need to be clearly discussed. Several reactions to the mention of either of these topics have only served to confuse the issues. Because licensing is not voluntary, the reaction to it has been more vigorous than the reaction to certification. Those opposed to licensing raise issues of freezing technology, limiting research, causing loss of jobs, and unreasonable government interference in the practice of a trade; those in favor of licensing talk about it as a cure-all for the ills surrounding computing and human interaction with the products of computing. The extremes of both of these positions obfuscate the underlying issues and possibilities of licensing. This section of the paper develops a broad model of licensing which addresses most of the distracting issues raised by the opponents of licensing and which is not founded on the extreme optimism of those who view licensing as a cure-all. Given a level playing field of a viable model of licensing which addresses both the major problems with and the major goals of licensing, a discussion of the real issues with licensing computing professionals should be possible.

REASONS FOR CURRENT INTEREST

The current interest in licensing computer professionals comes from a variety of sources. The public have become aware of the impact of computers on their lives and have come to realize that good computing not only impacts the quality of their lives but that it also daily affects their safety. They have been made aware of systems that show the marks of incompetent design, design with malicious intent, and design with fraudulent intent. Licensing is perceived by many as an attempt to control all of these problems. Licensing is also perceived by many people outside the profession as a cure-all for everything they don't like about software development, (e.g., high cost, late delivery, highly publicized software failures, many safety critical applications, etc.). People who fly get concerned when they realize that the only part of an airplane that is built by an unlicensed practitioner is the avionics software which flies the airplane and controls all of its safety features.

This "protect-us-from-their-incompetence" attitude is only one motivation for licensing. Others are motivated by the desire to establish some mechanism for accountability which has legislated sanctions. Medicine has such sanctions. If you don't practice medicine according to established guidelines, the state will force you out of the practice of medicine. If you don't practice computing according to the approved standards, then you will be forced out of the profession. These standards would also lay a solid foundation for computing malpractice suits.

For these reasons, bills related to licensing software practitioners are under consideration in at least six states. But licensing should not be viewed as an attempt to absolutely resolve these issues. This absolutistic view of licensing has led to specious arguments against the process of licensing computer professionals. Several of these arguments are considered below.

If it is correct to say that licensing is not a cure-all, then why should we be interested in licensing? I argue that there is a model of licensing which will partially address these problems and might ameliorate some concerns. Furthermore, establishing a licensing standard will help establish computing as a profession. Those opposed to licensing argue that a movement toward professionalism is a self-serving excuse to justify charging more for providing computer services. This argument ignores some ethically significant aspects of professionalism. Software development already bears important marks of being a profession. Computing professionals have a specialized skill which directly impacts the safety of the public. Practice of this profession requires extraordinary trust by the public and justifies a heightened standard of care. The professionalization of computing would make clear the computing professionals' responsibility to the public.

The discipline of software development has advanced significantly, and the public should be assured that the computing professional has knowledge of the best and safest way to develop computing systems. The possession of a computing license is no assurance that the person with this knowledge will not engage in malicious or fraudulent activity, just as being a licensed physician is no guarantee that a physician will avoid malicious or fraudulent activity.

Technical competence and good technical practice do not protect us from harmful or ill-advised applications of these skills. To help protect us from the consequences of misuse of these skills, the practitioner should have a concern for the well-being of the patient.

The professionalization of medicine provides at least two forces which help protect us: a code of ethics and professional standards of practice. The physician subscribes to a code of ethics which characterizes the primary obligation of the physician and purpose of the practice of medicine as the care of the patient.

Professionalism embodies this commitment to the welfare of the patient, and it is generally asserted in an associated code of ethics. We put our trust in doctors because of their commitment to only do what is good for us. If this sense of responsibility to the client or customer were part of a personal (and State enforced) commitment of the computing professional, we would feel safer using their software products. The professionalization of computing strengthens the concept that computer software has only one function—to perform some service for a client or customer. Recent computing codes of ethics (ACM and IEEE) have characterized the development of computer software as a service requiring heightened care for the customer.

Professionalization incorporates both a code of ethics and a set of professional standards. Physicians are encouraged to follow the standards of the profession and the code of ethics because failure to do so will lead to the revocation of their license to practice. If computer professionals are licensed, they can be encouraged to follow professional standards in the same way. In neither case is it claimed that licensing makes a person competent or ethical. But licensing does make it more likely that practitioners have knowledge of their disciplines' best practices and have some social pressure to "do the right thing."

Without licensing there are no requirements for heightened care and no concepts of professional malpractice. In several cases, suits against software developers for malpractice have been overturned because they did not bear the marks of a professional. I know of at least one case in New York where the developer of a failed hospital program was not held responsible because software developers are "not professionals" and therefore have no higher standard of care for their clients' well-being. The judge used the absence of licensing as a justification for the claim. Software development was characterized as "simply a business upon which the public does not particularly entrust its care" (Hospital Computer Systems, Inc. v. Staten Island Hospital, 788 F. Supp. 1351 [D.N.J. 1992]). There is now legal precedent for the view that software developers are merely hired guns and the customer should take the attitude of "let the buyer beware." But as in all legal cases there are other precedents. In California there have been two successful cases of computer malpractice. Malpractice requires the concept of negligence.

Both inside and outside the profession it is recognized that software development has achieved a certain degree of maturity and that maturity implies both responsibility and accountability. Computing is no longer merely information processing. The software we develop controls the temperature inside of incubators which directly affects the life or death of infants. A cardiac patient should be able to expect a pacemaker that works. Computing's increased involvement in everyday life requires both a heightened sense of accountability and responsibility.

NEGATIVE REACTIONS

Any discussion of licensing computer professionals generates two types of criticism from software developers: a criticism of the concept of licensing and a criticism of potential implementations of licensing. Many of these criticisms are misdirected.

OBJECTIONS TO THE CONCEPT OF LICENSING

Programming Is an Art and Is Entitled to the Protection of Free Speech

Some have argued that the state has no right to restrict their programming efforts. They believe in "freedom of speech in programming." This view seems to ignore the questions of responsibility to users of computing's products. It is true that "freedom of speech," as uncontrolled and undisciplined development of software used by the public, would be limited by licensing. It does not seem to be a bad thing to introduce discipline in the development and testing of software which affects the public. It is not certain whether a program used to control the temperature in an incubator was the product of free speech or the exercise of an art, but it is certain that the use of known testing techniques would have discovered the bug in the incubator temperature control software that was responsible for the loss of two children's lives. The argument that we should not license a physician because it would prevent "free speech" during a heart transplant seems absurd.

Licensing Is Just Another Way to Raise Taxes

Some have argued that "licensing is merely a revenue enhancer or a gimmick by states to make more money." Even if states use licenses or licensing to raise revenues, it does not mean that we ought to eliminate licensing electricians because the state also makes money from it. If the only purpose of licensing were to generate new taxes then it should be opposed. But there appear to be other good reasons for licensing software professionals.

You Can't License a Practice
That Has No Standards of Practice

Two related objections are the following: software development is not yet a fully matured discipline, so there can be no standard of licensing; and licensing will freeze software technology in its immature state. The absence of maturity is a strange standard. My teenage children are not yet fully mature—they don't know all the right answers—but they are expected to be responsible for those things which they already know. The science of software development is not yet a complete or static body of knowledge. This should not exonerate a software practitioner from following those testing and design principles that are already known. No one would say that because medicine is not a completed science that we should not practice the best medicine we know how and that we should not hold the medical practitioner responsible for knowing and practicing this "best medicine."

Licensure requires competence in and adherence to minimal standards of practice. According to these standards, even when Jack (Dr. Death) Kevorkian does his work, he should still adhere to professional standards and use a clean needle. The definition of these standards provides clear guidelines to clients, courts, and practicing professionals about minimally acceptable practices.

Licensing Does Not Guarantee
Competence Will Be Applied

Some objections claim that licensing is no guarantee of applied competence. This is correct, but it focuses on the wrong side of the question. The absence of licensing means that we have no way of knowing whether the developer has any knowledge of the current best practices. Licensing will only provide assurances that the developer knows the best practice, and as stated above there are other pressures to encourage developers to follow these practices.

Pressure of Business Such as Schedule and
Budget Override "Good Practice"

The pressures of budget and schedule are too strong to guarantee that the best practices will be followed. At this time there are no counter pressures to resist the development of shoddy software justified by budget and schedule pressures. Licensing would introduce significant counter pressures. Licensed professionals put their license at risk if they do not follow the best practices. Licensing also introduces the legal pressure of malpractice suits directed at licensees and their employers.

Licensing Will Establish a Software Monopoly

This is correct only if a license is universally required to do any software development. Licensing could be required for certain areas of software development, such as the avionics systems in airplanes, and optional in other areas. It would limit access to some areas of the practice but that seems better than having life critical software developed by practitioners of undetermined skill.

Implementation of Licensing

Licensing is sometimes opposed on the quite reasonable grounds that state legislatures do not adequately understand software development. If state legislatures developed the licensing standards in unfamiliar areas then we would all be in difficulty. Most state legislatures would agree with this claim, and that is why the standards for licensing are generally established by the appropriate professional organization. The state responsibility is merely to administer the test and determine if the professionally established standards have been met. The state also charges for this service.

A MODEL FOR LICENSING COMPUTER PROFESSIONALS

Many of the objections cited above would be appropriate for some models of licensing, but I believe there is at least one model of licensing software professionals that meets most of the significant objections raised above. I propose a model for licensing computer professionals in which there is a national standard supported by computing professionals and implemented by state governments based on professional engineers' and paramedics licensing standards. It would consist of the following:

(1) A commitment to a body of knowledge—a four-year degree. This will assure that practitioners will have at least come in contact with the current best practices.

(2) A commitment to reeducation—license expires every five years. A paramedic's certification expires every two years, and she must be retested on the new medical practices that have been developed related to her specialty. The same principle should apply to the computing professional. Using database design practices of 20 years ago does not produce the best computing system. This principle contains no specification of how the practitioner must acquire this knowledge. Before being retested the practitioner would be informed of the new areas to be covered. This emphasis on reeducation completely meets the concern that licensing would freeze technology. Licensing would

have the opposite effect; it would require that all licensed practitioners keep up with the changing technology.

(3) The skill content will be determined by computer practitioners. The IEEE and the ACM have done this for undergraduate computer science education. The military and other countries already have skills tests that can be referred to.

(4) There should be different levels of licensing based on skills and areas of competence. Paramedics, depending on their competence and training, are certified to administer different levels of care to patients. Computer practitioners should only undertake tasks that they are competent to complete. (This is consistent with the ACM code of ethics.)

(5) Commitment to competence to apply the knowledge they have—three years working with another licensed computer professional. Software development is not a purely theoretical discipline. Competence is gained and shown by applying the theories one has learned. This apprenticeship requirement is similar to CPA's.

(6) Commitment to follow the standards—sanctions for violations of the best practices and violations of the code of ethics. This clearly introduces a counter pressure for any pressure to develop shoddy product.

This model of licensing meets the objections cited earlier and provides a base for further discussion.

Many software developers realize that the era of the hired gun should be over and have chosen to become professionals. A computing professional is anyone involved in the design and development of computer artifacts. Computer artifacts include things like program documentation, test plans and test cases, feasibility studies, source code, user manuals, system maintenance manuals and design documents, that is, all the products of the system development process. The ethical decisions made during the development of these artifacts have a direct relationship to many of the issues of the current software crisis. Software developers have realized that technical skill is only the first step in becoming a computer professional.

17. PERSONAL AND SOCIAL ETHICS AMID TECHNOLOGICAL CHANGE

C. WILLIAM PALMITER

ABSTRACT

The primary purpose of this study is to give some basis to decision makers in information systems for the use of ethical principles formulated in the Judeo-Christian tradition. By identifying some possible explanations for the variance between fundamental values and actual behavior, an environment may be realized for permitting and encouraging more consistency between a person's values and ethical behavior. The cultural influences of relativism and pragmatism present a challenge to the relationship of professional ethical standards and personal values. There exists a fundamental need for personal responsibility in implementing personal values in such a hostile environment. By focusing on personal value refinement, a link between professional IS standards and personal values provides a possibility for a dynamic resource based on an individual's foundational religious values within the context of tension between the individual and society.

INTRODUCTION

So much is changing today in the ethical values, beliefs and behavior of persons in relationship to the world of rapidly changing technology. A 1992 study by the Josephson Institute of Ethics involving 9,000 young people and adults revealed alarmingly low ethical standards in American institutions. The breakdown of values and responsible behavior is also reflected in computer technology. Some of the developments in computer technology raise new ethical concerns, for example the issue of privacy. It is no surprise that Ferrell and Fraedrich have concluded that "business ethics is one of the most important concerns in today's business world."[1]

A few professional organizations have attempted to evaluate the ethical values, beliefs and behavior of their constituents. Vittrell has studied the frequency of ethical behavior for management information specialists.[2] Martin and Peterson have examined the ethical issues of insider trading.[3] Fimbel and Burstein have investigated the ethical values of technology professionals.[4] Thornburg made use of a survey concerning the ethical beliefs and practices of human resources professionals.[5] On a preliminary basis, these studies indicate the various ethical issues and uncertainties which are problematic for members of the various professions.

Many people are ethical segregationists, that is they tend to segregate their ethical values into one type of behavior for business and another type of behavior away from business.[6] This problem of ethical hypocrisy is compounded by the rapidity with which developments in technology are taking place.Computer ethics, which helps evaluate what ought to be, is being outdistanced by the developments in technology. Prospects for the future are mind-boggling considering what has already happened. The rapid technological changes in what "is" and what "will be" leaves too little time for reflection on what "ought to be."

The primary purpose of this study is to give some basis to decision makers in information systems for the use of ethical principles formulated in the Judeo-Christian tradition. As a result of this study, it is hoped that the information will provide those in information systems with ideas that will assist in targeting some overlooked resources for more responsible ethical behavior and also provide a basis for further investigation. By identifying some possible explanations for the differences between fundamental values and actual behavior, it is hoped that more sensitivity could be fostered to encourage more consistency between a person's ethical values and ethical behavior.

INADEQUACY OF PHILOSOPHICAL ETHICS ALONE

Philosophical ethics has attempted to address this problem of inconsistency in ethical values and actual behavior in two ways: first, to define the "Highest Good," and second, to achieve this goal. In philosophical ethics, the search for the *summum bonum* of life has led to numerous theories such as pleasure, happiness, power, duty for duty's sake, and self-realization.[7]

Traditional approaches to moral philosophy have been interested in providing humanity with guidance for the conduct of life. They have regarded reason as a sufficient guide to moral conduct even though they differ in their understanding of how reason functions. These approaches to moral philosophy have a long and honorable history.

Yet the traditional approaches have resulted in authoritative agreement concerning the values which ought to guide human conduct. The efforts to find such values have been many, the proposals profuse and arguments about their adequacy sometimes bitter as human reason struggles to provide men with knowledge of good. Because of its complexity and lack of authority, traditional approaches by themselves appear to be inadequate.

THE RELATIONSHIP OF PROFESSIONAL ETHICS AND RELIGION

There is some indirect evidence of the influence of religion on computer ethics. An example is the "Ten Commandments of Computer Ethics" written by Patrick Sullivan and published by the Computer Ethics Institute in Washington, D.C. Why does Sullivan select ten commandments? Why not nine or eleven? Is there not an obvious, authoritative connection between the Ten Commandments and the Old Testament, the ten beatitudes of Jesus' Sermon on the Mount and the "Ten Commandments of Computer Ethics"? The ten commandments of computer ethics are as follows:

(1) Thou shalt not use a computer to harm other people.
(2) Thou shalt not interfere with other people's computer work.
(3) Thou shalt not snoop around in other people's computer files.
(4) Thou shalt not use a computer to steal.
(5) Thou shalt not use a computer to bear false witness.
(6) Thou shalt not copy or use proprietary software for which you have not paid.
(7) Thou shalt not use other people's computer resources without authorization or proper compensation.
(8) Thou shalt not appropriate other people's intellectual output.
(9) Thou shalt think about the social consequences of the program you are writing or the system you are designing.
(10) Thou shalt always use a computer in ways that insure consideration and respect for your fellow humans.

Most of the ethical content of these ten commandments can be derived from self-evident ethical injunctions such as, "Don't steal," "Tell the truth," and "Don't violate trust relationships." Few of the commandments are connected specifically with computing alone, except for those portions that pertain to maintaining the privacy of data. At least the ten commandments represent an attempt to spell out specific ethical injunctions for the computer specialists. Each one of the ten commandments of computer ethics can be traced to basic ethical principles found in the Bible. As examples from the introduction suggest, IS specialists and other people in responsible positions sometimes don't follow "self-evident" ethical guidelines.

One set of controversies involves the extent to which professional codes are able to influence the behavior of people who may not be oriented toward ethical behavior, either because of character flaws or for fear of losing a job.

Guidelines for professional behavior are not simply part of common sense. If there is little or no enforcement of professional standards, perhaps it would be just as well to have no external professional standards at all.

There is currently a dearth of literature on the topic of relating religion to information systems and business ethics. For reasons unknown, most information system professionals regard religion as a deeply personal subject that is held separate from the professional life. When the topic is ethics, the religious and the ethical are or at least should be closely woven together in the fabric of professional life. To ignore the foundational religious values is to distort the ethical behavior in the profession. The current tendency to compartmentalize life's values has its roots in theological and social circumstances of the 1960s.

In 1966 Joseph Fletcher wrote a book entitled *Situation Ethics*, which proved to be very influential. The basic idea in Fletcher's concept is that there is nothing which is intrinsically right or universally wrong. To put it in terms of a value system, there is nothing which is intrinsically good or bad. Goodness and badness are not built in, unchangeable qualities; they are descriptions of things that happen in different circumstances. According to this theory of ethics, there is no such thing as a predefinition of values of goodness or badness. Any given situation is judged uniquely, not by prejudice. Only one thing is intrinsically valued as good according to Fletcher and that is love.

Perhaps an illustration from Fletcher's book concerning professional practice in medicine will help in understanding. Fletcher tells of a doctor who knows that a marriage is going to take place. He knows both parties; he knows that the girl is a virgin and is sexually pure. He happens to know that the boy has been a libertine sexually and has syphilis. What is the responsibility of love? Does the doctor keep his oath? Or does he tell the girl? Which is love?

Fletcher never intended for his ideas to drive a wedge between a person's religious and professional values. He did give voice to and invite dialogue concerning the tension between values which originate within the individual and laws or principles which are imposed on the individual from outside. Fletcher writes, "In the language of classical biblical theology in the West, grace reinforces law and sometimes even bypasses it, but it does not abolish it, nor can it replace it, until sin itself is no more."[8]

Even though his *Situation Ethics* has been largely misunderstood, Fletcher did contribute to the perception of tension between the individual values and community values. In his consideration of the basic values he has, the information systems professional finds himself in a state of inner conflict. He wants to do the right thing, but he does not always find it a simple matter to know what the right thing is. Like all authentic persons, the information systems professional inevitably asks questions of ultimate values and asks if his total life is consistently serving those values. Perhaps the most penetrating question for the IS professional is, "What do you do when no one else is looking or there is little chance of getting caught in unethical behavior?"

There appears to be a mega-shift taking place in Western culture; it is a shift from "everyone has a right to his or her opinion" to "everyone's opinion is right." It is a major shift from objectivity to relativism, from truth to pragmatism. So for the last four decades there has been a retreat in the West from those ethical virtues celebrated for the past 3,000 years in the Judeo-Christian tradition and especially influential on the founding fathers of the United States of America. Economist Thomas Sowell described this phenomenon as "throwing away those ideals we knew worked for something that simply sounded good."[9] This trend is complicated by the fact that religious ethics has looked too exclusively to the past and has not developed models for relating to the future that is being shaped by information systems. Douglas Johnson states it this way:

> The religious institution is the one we expect to establish and maintain an ethic. Religious institutions are deeply rooted in the past and have a tendency to be a generation behind in creating behavior models. In this respect, they are important conserving institutions. However, they need to be in the forefront of social change as significant as the one produced by the advent of the computer. Unless religious institutions develop a strong ethic, other institutions will have limited guidelines for the creation of their ethic.[10]

SURVEY OF RELIGIOUS ETHICS

"Ethics" is an objective inquiry which makes use of philosophical, religious, and professional inputs without being under the control of any of them. "Religious ethics" may be defined as that overlapping field of philosophy and religion that reflects on such issues as the source of moral norms and how to justify a person's rules for governing behavior in organizations and society. Judgments of value are judgments about what is good and bad, desirable or undesirable. Judgments of responsibility center on what is right and wrong and on what a person must do or must not do. A person, therefore, acts in an ethical manner if he acts freely, chooses an action that is right to do, and does it with the motivation of doing his duty based on a Judeo-Christian value system. The idea of "freedom" makes the Judeo-Christian ethic unique.

Ethicists tend to group particular ethical theories into certain categories. This can be helpful, but it is also frustrating since different authors place the various theories in different categories. Specific categories are based on particular questions used to categorize the ethical theory. For example, Edward Long asks the common question, "What is the source of ethical norms?" Both religious and secular ethics categorize this issue of source as reason, prescription and relationship.

In reason-based systems, the source of ethical norms is generated from and perceived by reason. In the secular field, Immanuel Kant derived his categorical imperative from reason alone. Thomas Aquinas is an example of a religious thinker who hammered out a reason-based system of natural law ethics. According to natural law theories, the end of each thing in the natural order is built in. By observation of a subject in nature, its intended purpose in the natural order of things is discernible. Built into the structure of things is a set of laws governing behavior. As one writer claims, essential to the notion of natural moral law are the "features of universality, unwrittenness and intuitively perceived or rationally discoverable moral knowledge of the divine will apart from the special historical Biblical revelation."[11] Most natural law ethicists think biblical revelation of moral norms is important, but they believe that even without that revelation everyone can know by reason alone the basic principles of right and wrong. As a consequence, a person does not need to comprehend the Judeo-Christian tradition or even be a theist to know the moral law; but knowing it is not the same thing as obeying it.

In contrast, prescription-based systems have ethical norms that originate from a source of authority which mandates them. This does not exclude theories based on reason as having no prescriptions nor theories based on prescription as not being rational. Commands in reason-based systems originate in reason alone, whereas prescriptions in prescriptive theories originate in a recognized source of authority. That source may or may not choose rules on the basis of what seems rational. The key is that an individual or group decides what is to be authoritative law. Of course the most influential prescriptive theories claim God as the prescriber, but not all of them do. Although the basis of God's choice is different depending on the theory, the key is that God's will determines the norms. Divine command theories can be categorized in reference to the pointed question raised by Plato in his *Euthyphro*: That work raises the question whether an act is right because God wills it, or whether God wills it because he knows it is right.

In relation-based systems actions are shaped by either the sense of excitement or gratitude a person feels in relationship with some person or group, or how some critical principle relates to each new situation. The ethical decision may be based on a response to or a relationship to a person (e.g., God or Christ), or based on a response to a specific situation (e.g., What is the most loving thing to do in this situation?). This very broad category of systems includes such approaches as Thomas à Kempis' *The Imitation of Christ*; the concept of Karl Barth, a Swiss theologian, that a person must simply obey whatever God commands when God encounters him; and Joseph Fletcher's "situation ethics" which instructs us to evaluate the most loving thing to do in any given situation and to consider one's duty. A constant rule operates in each of these systems: "Do what Christ would do"—à Kempis; "'Do what God says to do"—Barth; "Do what you decide is the most loving thing to do"—Fletcher. Although the rule is constant, the resulting action may vary from situation to situation.

In order to judge whether actions are good or bad, there are two main categories: teleological (consequentialist) theories and deontological (non-consequentialist) theories. Recently, various ethicists have argued for mixed theories that combine deontological and teleological concerns. According to the teleological theories, consequences determine which actions are good and which are evil. Some teleologists are hedonists, identifying good with pleasure and evil with pain. Others identify good with power, knowledge, self-realization, or other nonmoral goods. Teleological theories are generally of two types: ethical egoism, which produces the greatest good for oneself, and ethical universalism which produces the greatest good for the greatest number of people.

By contrast, deontological theories deny that morally good acts are determined by the nonmoral consequences that they produce. There are other considerations that make an act morally right or wrong, obligatory or forbidden. As an example, an act is judged right because it keeps a promise, it is just, or God commands it. An act is right because it is a person's responsibility to do it, and it is a person's responsibility for some reason other than the consequences resulting from the act. Consequences are not totally ignored by deontologists, but they are rejected as the basis for deciding the moral right or wrong of an action.

In contrast to the traditional approaches to philosophical ethics, biblical revelation sets forth the will of God, which is by its nature authoritative for many individuals, as the ethical goal of man. The task of the biblical ethicists is to define the basic norms of revelation by which man may act in keeping with the will of God. The insights of philosophy, history, and the social sciences make those norms relevant to contemporary moral decisions. Biblical ethics is bifocal looking to the Bible for the norms or principles of behavior and to other disciplines for the factual data for intelligent action.[12]

The Old Testament Ethic

Grounded in the great Exodus experience and the prophetic tradition of the Old Testament, Judaism insisted on the connection between religion and ethics. To the Jewish ethic, business life morality mattered intensely. One of the most extraordinary things about the ethics of the Old Testament is that the obligation to have just weights and measures is laid down no fewer than seven times.[13] As the writer of Proverbs puts it, "A just balance and scales are the Lord's; all the weights in the bag are his work." Here is the God not only of the sanctuary, but also of the counter and the shop floor. The weighing out of the customer's order and the measuring of the client's request became an act of worship. In other words, it is safe to say you will never find an unethical person who is adhering to the basic values of his or her religion.

One of the outstanding features of the Old Testament law is the emphasis on personal responsibility. A person is not only responsible for what he does, he is also responsible for the wrong thing he might have prevented and the damage for which he is to blame because of his carelessness or thoughtlessness. This principle has obvious application to the ethics of information systems. To identify the principle in terms of its Old Testament setting, if an ox gores someone and the ox was not known to be dangerous, then the ox is killed and the owner goes free. But if it was known that the ox was dangerous, then not only is the ox killed, but the owner also is liable to the death penalty because he ought to have prevented the tragedy (Exodus 21:28–32). Palestinian houses were flat-roofed, and the flat roof was often used as a place of rest and relaxation. So the Old Testament law stated that if a man built a house, he must build a parapet around the roof "that you may not bring the guilt of blood on your house, if anyone fall from it" (Deuteronomy 22:8).

From a multitude of indications, the Old Testament is certain that I am my brother's keeper; it is quite sure that I am not only responsible for the harm that I have done, but that I am also responsible for the harm I could have prevented. In this sense the law was not only reactive, but proactive. From the perspective of the Old Testament, it is unthinkable to separate religious values from social and business values. It is also the fertile soil that causes the root of the Christian ethic to grow.

The New Testament Ethic

The New Testament ethic internalizes values that sprout from the Old Testament concern for external principles. This is the fundamental contribution from the teaching ministry of Jesus in the Sermon on the Mount. To quote a distinguished Jewish scholar, "If we preserved only the moral precepts and parables, the Gospels would count as one of the most wonderful collections of ethical teaching in the world."[14] These words doubtless reflect the evaluation of many inside and outside the Jewish and Christian fold. Many who are disgusted by the hypocrisy of ecclesiasticism, unmoved by religious ritual and incredulous of dogma would gladly drop everything except the ethics of the Sermon on the Mount.

The frequent conflicts in the New Testament between Jesus and the Scribes and Pharisees are apparent conflicts between the prophetic perspective and the legalistic perspective, two ways of dealing with the problem of ethical behavior. A general distinction between the two is that the prophetic perspective deals with a person's being whereas the legalistic perspective deals with a person's actions.

The prophetic perspective views right actions as the spontaneous expression of right internal values, the good fruit that grows on the good tree. The radical transformation of human values is the prophetic call to a complete change in a person's inner attitude toward God and his fellow man. After changing from the inside out, a person can be trusted to do the right thing almost instinctively no matter what new technology or new circumstances may be present in the information system environment.

The legalistic method rests on the proposition that character is primarily determined by conduct; that is, if a correct standard of conduct can be set up and enforced, a person will exhibit ethical behavior out of habit. By doing good deeds, the character of the doer becomes good. In this line of thinking, it is essential to have an authoritative code of principles to ascertain the right course of conduct in any given situation. Since the situation may vary indefinitely, the tendency is for the principles to become more and more complicated until the determination of what is to be done or not to be done becomes the business of experts.

ETHICAL RESPONSIBILITY

It is not difficult to make an urgent appeal for ethical responsibility on the part of IS professionals. By some estimates, roughly $2 billion worth of software was stolen over the Internet in 1994, a growing portion of the total $7.4 billion the Software Publishers Association estimates was lost to piracy in 1993. According to U.S. investigators, the racketeers stole 140,000 telephone credit-card numbers, then sold them to computer bulletin boards in the United States and Europe. Hackers used the numbers to make a whopping $140 million worth of long distance phone calls. The prevailing ethic appears to be that electronic socialism rules the Internet, not copyrightable capitalism.[15]

Peter Drucker helps us confront a fact that is both self-evident and usually forgotten: "Management is an organ of an institution; and the institution, whether a business or a public service, is an organ of society, existing to make specific contribution and to discharge specific social functions."[16] It is important to note how different the statement of ethical management of information systems is from that of other professions: physicians heal, ministers serve, nurses nurture, educators teach. In all these instances, the institutions within which professionals work, and on which they depend, are viewed by the professional as "instruments" of their profession. Information Systems professionals don't always have the benefit of such distinctions.

The starting point for most applied professional ethics is usually the normative purpose of the profession. It is the professional purpose that provides the filter through which principles are strained. As circumstances of professional practice change, the specific responsibilities of the practitioner change. In the case of IS professionals, the change is quite rapid. This is an observation, not an excuse. Some principles take on new meaning or importance; others must recede. But the purpose of a profession does not change. The purpose is itself a normative filter, the basic ethical conduit through which a profession's contribution to the welfare of society takes on additional importance and new responsibility.

Individual professionals frequently have strong personal values. But these values are not shaped by or even reinforced by a set of normative personal values which are independent of the institutions for which professionals work. It makes little sense to speak of the corporation or the hospital or the public agency as an instrument of the professional's calling. For this reason, Drucker is correct when he says we have to define management professionals in and through their tasks. Powerful implications flow from this observation. If we are to speak of the ethics of IS professionals, we must enable them to relate ethical obligation to their spheres of responsibility as they contribute to the organizational purpose. In the same way, if we are to understand that organizational purpose, we must understand both the functions the organization fulfills in society and the constraints which society places upon it.

These general statements set the stage for a distinctly different set of conceptual problems for responsibility in ethics. The nature of professional organizations has no intrinsic normative purpose; there is no normative filter or mediating normative idea to be applied. Instead, organizations mediate the norms and values to the professional. Conversely, the personal values of professionals are mediated through organizations. Much of the confusion about responsibility of professional ethics derives from a lack of clarity about this very point. Both the definition of what norms professionals are to fulfill and the individual freedom they have to fulfill them emerge from a complex set of interactions based on the following factors: the general norms and values that a society adopts or evolves and through which it seeks to obtain its definition of human welfare; the purposes assigned to various types or sectors of organizations to assure that its organizations fulfill various functions in the pursuit of those social values; the specific values which evolve in each organization to focus its particular resources and shape its responsibility; and finally the integration of the organization's values with specific values of those persons who work and make decisions in each organization.

A perusal of the literature easily demonstrates the extent of the problem. Count the number of articles written about what computers can and will do. Then count the number of articles that raise red flags and warn of the dangerous drift into a lawless information systems environment. There is yet time for a shift of emphasis, but that shift will not come quickly or easily.

Richard Mason has identified four ethical issues of the Information Age: privacy, accuracy, property and accessibility. These four may be reduced to one issue: responsibility. The last ten years of the computer revolution have made computers available to more people, thus giving them greater power and authority than before. Deliberate or careless use of that power creates serious problems for us and future generations. A battle for balance between the right to privacy and the right to necessary information is continuing. A responsible ethic must define the legitimacy and the boundary of business and governmental authority.

The need for a developed sense of ethical behavior in IS is possibly as extensive as in bioethics, but the direct involvement of religious ethicists has not been as forthcoming. Sullivan correctly identifies one of the most vital areas of responsibility for the IS professional: the effects of his or her practices on society. At another level of responsibility are the problems associated with the exercise of the managerial function or the responsibility of doing ethics in the institutional setting. This merely underscores the many dimensions of institutionalism as a motif in religious ethics. Much institutionalism is concerned with political structures, and the thinking about it has a tendency to gravitate in that direction far too easily. Many social organizations have bureaucratic rather than political dimensions. Historically, Max Weber saw the growing importance of bureaucracy and its incipient threats to individual liberty and personal creativity, but he did not consider that the threat came from governmental bureaucracies alone.[17] Weber's greatest contribution focuses on the dehumanizing impact of modern industrialized capitalism. But unlike Marx, who thought that the threats were in the wrongful distribution of property, Weber sensed the danger that would come from the poor utilization and management of all bureaucracies in the state as well as the private sector. The preoccupation with the drive to rationalize all productive processes is dehumanizing and tends to undermine responsible ethical behavior in any environment.

Business ethicists have been aware of these matters for some time. As an example, Benjamin M. Selekman, a Harvard Business School professor with definite roots in the Hebrew-Christian tradition, wrote in 1959 that the amoral rationality Weber feared inevitable was fading away in favor of a moral/evaluational set of concerns.

> So the search for a moral philosophy continues. Behind this search are two primary causes: the hostility directed against business beginning with the Great Depression of the thirties and the growth of a new professional management class, as distinguished from the owner-manager of former days, who built his own business, was the principal stockholder, and ran it either by himself or with those whom he took in as partners. Recent decades have witnessed a veritable explosion in business education, with large enrollments in business schools affiliated with universities. Association with a university immediately projects any calling on a technical and moral plane, with the challenge to meet standards already established in the older professions of law, medicine, engineering, architecture, the ministry, and teaching. With the concept of a profession comes also a self-consciousness, a desire to develop standards of technical performance as well as an ethical code, both of which give dignity and stature to those who enter the calling.[18]

The quest for an ethic has been eroded by the depersonalization of responsibility. Stephen Brockmann writes, "When enemies are simply blips on the computer screen, they become dehumanized. It's no longer a moral crime to kill them, since the 5th Commandment doesn't extend to computer blips."[19]

In an age when computers can depersonalize human beings and the harm done to them, we need an ethic that takes personal responsibility seriously. Roger Shinn reminds us, "The objectivity of science does not mean it is value-free; everything scientists do is directed at every turn by considerations of human values."[20] This implies that science needs feedback that causes it frequently to correct itself or to be corrected. This process resembles the Christian virtue of continuous renewal. It requires that we make the determining variables in our ethic more explicit so they can be corrected when they lead us inadvertently to harm others. This kind of ethic must be very personal.

THE IMPORTANCE OF PERSONAL VALUES

A study conducted by Frederick and Weber (1987) concluded that personal values are involved in ethical decisions but are not the central component that guides the decisions, actions, and policies of the organization. But they believe that personal values do contribute a part of an organization's value structure.[21]

For a person whose ethical basis is religious values, the foundation, either overtly or subliminally established, is one's understanding of God. Traditionally theology established its ultimate authority from divine revelation. This means that some truths are sourced outside of man; not all truth originates with man. The request for a new awareness of spiritual values and their relationship to the everyday world is legitimate.[22]

The religious background of a significant number of people in information systems is either Jewish or Christian. In round figures, 81 percent or 166 million Americans 18 years of age or older consider themselves to be Christians.[23] Another poll shows that there is a remarkable strength of religion among young people, with 80 percent saying they consider religion very important.[24] After hitting an all-time low in 1978, the percentage of Americans who claim that religion plays a very important role in their lives rose in 1993, according to a recent poll.[25]

When confronted with ethical dilemmas, individuals with adequate religious roots and values may, and in fact should employ those values in the decision making process. This is not an advocacy of religious faith or values, but simply a recognition of the impact that such values could have on everyday information systems ethics and behavior. Although most IS professionals probably think of themselves as ethical people, ethics in most business related activities has become institutionalized, and in becoming institutionalized, a sense of personal values and ethics has been lost.

The hope is that individuals will ultimately have personal values that transcend the laws and rules of institutionalized ethics. Graduate schools of business increasingly are offering or requiring substantive studies in ethics. The teaching of ethics represents an acknowledgment and a beginning, but efforts must go beyond teaching ethics and professional principles. Is it too much to hope that the vocabulary of information systems professionals will soon contain words like "justice," "civility," "decency," "honesty," and "fairness." The ethical constructs should take a place right alongside the academic and professional vocabulary.

Following the research of Liedtka (1989), Posner and Schmidt examine the impact of her values congruence model on professional managers' work attitudes and perceptions of ethical practices. They make use of a nationwide cross-section of professional managers to provide the sample for the study. As a result of the survey, they found that both personal value systems and organizational value systems or culture were significant to the professional managers. In the absence of one or the other, clarity of personal values had a more positive impact than did organizational values.[26]

Regarded as one of America's foremost public opinion pollsters, Daniel Yankelovich summarizes the results of a decade of research by asserting that people in the United States are moving toward an "ethic of commitment" that is a synthesis of the "ethic of self-denial" characteristic of nineteenth- and early twentieth-century America and of the "ethic of duty to self" characteristic of the 1960s and 1970s.[27]

In his book *New Rules* Yankelovich demonstrates that value change in America for the past thirty years has followed this pattern:

(1) Most people continue to cling tenaciously to many traditional values, yet those who do so simultaneously affirm certain new values. People are selective about both retention of the old and adoption of the new; not very many people make a wholesale shift from the old rules to the new.

(2) Those who are initially bewildered or upset by value change typically move from generalized resistance to threatening change to pragmatic experimentation with and appropriation of new values and patterns of conduct that they see working in the lives of children, friends, and people they know (or various segments of the population whom they know about through the mass media).

(3) There is, then, a "both/and" principle operative in the revised equilibrium toward which a majority of citizens move. And that is why Yankelovich predicts the emergence in the 1980s and 1990s of a new ethic of commitment that contains some of the best features of the two preceding ethics.

(4) Yankelovich stresses, finally, the importance of "picking up societal signals" in a population's value shifts. Imagining that one could have more made sense in the period of relative affluence we enjoyed in the 1950s and 1960s, and the oppressiveness of what Marcuse calls "surplus repressions" was bound to seem both intolerable and unnecessary to many Americans who enjoyed affluence during these years. Thus, the emergence of an aggressively assertive duty-to-self ethic was in part

a response to socioeconomic factors that were genuinely new and powerfully felt. Similarly, the retreat from the duty-to-self ethic in the 1970s, the attack upon narcissism and the rise of neoconservatism, constitutes in part an adjustment to new economic and political realities that transmit rather different signals, as well as an adjustment to the chastening disappointments and disillusionments of those who went too far in following the duty-to-self ethic as a moral guideline.[28]

If there is a movement toward an ethic of commitment, authoritative values to which one can make a commitment are necessities. Figure One shows the relationship of values to behavior and personality based on a concept of William H. Hale of the University of Georgia. At the rock bottom of a person's being are his values. Individual values are molded in community, family, neighborhood, religion, schools and business experiences. An individual then formulates these values into beliefs; for every belief there is an underlying value. One's beliefs then shape the attitude or emotions. Every action is supported by an attitude. Then those collective actions blossom into an individual's personality, which develops to deal with life the way the person perceives it. Take honesty as an example. The goal is to consistently show in personality what the true value is. In this case, I am honest because honesty is an authoritative value, not just because I believe the old adage that honesty is the best policy. This means that a person has the potential of being honest when no one else is looking simply because the person is honest.

If religious values are authoritative, they will have an impact on ethical behavior. People learn that it is possible to enjoy the pleasure offered by experience control and to live up to the religious values they affirm through behavior control. The influence of religious values makes a new level of professional ethics possible. The imperatives of an increasingly interdependent world in which fraud, injustice and crime are more dangerous than ever make professional ethics more important than ever.

CONCLUSION

There exists an obvious tension between the individual and the community. In the early days of Judaism, there was so much emphasis on the community that an individual had little independent existence.[29] As an example, when Achan's sin was discovered, his whole family was punished with him. It is said that if you ask a man in a primitive society what his name is, he will respond first with the name of his tribe.

In America the emphasis is on the individual. Self-development, self-expression and self-realization are the focus of modern society. Too much emphasis on professional principles limits the freedom of the individual; too much focus on the individual compromises professional rules and behavior.

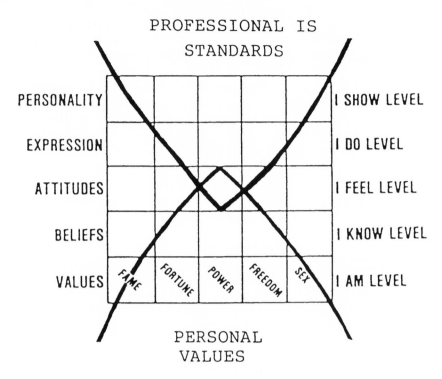

PROFESSIONAL IS
STANDARDS

PERSONALITY — I SHOW LEVEL

EXPRESSION — I DO LEVEL

ATTITUDES — I FEEL LEVEL

BELIEFS — I KNOW LEVEL

VALUES — FAME FORTUNE POWER FREEDOM SEX — I AM LEVEL

PERSONAL
VALUES

In the age of American individualism, it is well to remember that it can never be right under any ethical system to develop oneself at the expense of others.

Ultimately the decision to act in an ethical manner is up to the individual in society. But the individual can never be successfully isolated from impact on his or her culture. Professional culture needs to be nurtured and managed. Culture must not be separated from what IS professionals do. Instead it must be concerned with all aspects of the profession. Culture, as it relates to professional organizations, is the general pattern of behavior, shared beliefs, and values that members have in common. Values form an ideology that permeates everyday behavior and decisions.

In a search for a common source of authoritative, ethical beliefs and values, religious values should not be overlooked or ignored in light of the significant number of the population that claim that such beliefs and values are important. This is not a call for dismantling the separation of church and state, but it is a call to give permission to all, especially those in the IS profession, to apply those beliefs and values in every aspect of professional life. While a clear mission and challenging goals have the potential to motivate members of the profession to excellence, the means to achieving those ends should not be compromised.

Research is needed to explore the relationship of people's religious beliefs and values to their behavior in the profession. In the past decade, there has been a dramatic increase in the research in moral reasoning and judgment.[30] Accompanying this emerging research focus is the increased usage of two dominant moral reasoning instruments: the Moral Judgment Interview [31] and the Defining Issues Test.[32] These measures significantly differ in their theoretical foundation, what they are capable of measuring, how they are appropriately used, and their respective advantages and limitations as research instruments. In an effort to guide future moral reasoning researchers, Elm and Weber discuss the underlying theories, objectives, capabilities, advantages and limitations of the Moral Judgment Interview and the Defining Issues Test.[33] There has been a call for explorations of the impact of different values on ethical decision making in other professions as well. These might prove helpful in providing consistent categories, models and measures for IS professionals.

Unfortunately, there is little relevant research, and what little there is does not easily lend itself to model building. For example, information systems and professional ethics, a rapidly growing sub-discipline which focuses primarily on the social and professional aspects of ethical and unethical behavior in information systems, technological and professional contexts, has seen little research to discover the factors leading to ethical or unethical behavior. Instead, there exists a considerable amount of descriptive material about surveys of managers and specific case studies. The problem is that case studies do not always indicate why certain decisions were made or perceive the underlying causes of ethical and unethical behavior.

The rise of the multinational corporation and the international use of computers and networks makes the ethical matters discussed increasingly global in scope. It is imperative that theologians with a Hebrew-Christian background join with leaders from other world religions in addressing ethical issues. Based on the author's discussions with international students, this need for global dialogue on ethical issues is more of a problem for American professionals, who tend to separate the ethical values of their religion from their profession, than it is for internationals whose culture recognizes no separation of religion and state.

One of the greatest challenges of religious values is to contribute to the adjustment of the delicate balance between freedom and professional principles, and between the individual and society. Perhaps the best solution is for a person to rediscover and to reaffirm what it means to love his neighbor as himself.

REFERENCES

Andrews, Kenneth R. (1989). *Ethics in Practice.* Boston: Harvard Business School Press.

Barclay, William (1971). *Christian Ethics for Today.* New York: Harper & Row.

Barnette, Henlee H. (1961). *Introducing Christian Ethics.* Nashville, TN: Broadman Press.

Baxter, G. D. and C. A. Rarick (1987). "Education for the Moral Development of Managers: Kohlberg's Stages of Moral Development and Integrative Education." *Journal of Business Ethics,* 6, pp. 243–248.

Blanchard, Kenneth and Norman V. Peale (1988). *The Power of Ethical Management*. New York: William Morrow & Co.

Brockmann, Stephen (Dec. 1983). "Computer Blips or Human Beings?" *Engage/Social Action*, 11, p. 4.

Bursk, Edward C. (1959). *Business and Religion*. New York: Harper & Brothers.

Clark, Henry B. (1987). *Altering Behavior*. Newbury Park, CA: Sage Publications.

Colby, A. & L. Kohlberg. (1987). *The Measurement of Moral Judgment: Theoretical Foundations and Research Validations*, vol. 1. Cambridge, MA: Cambridge University Press.

Dejoie, R., G. Fowler and D. Paradice (1991). *Ethical Issues in Information Systems*. Boston: Boyd & Fraser.

Drucker, Peter F. (Sept.-Oct. 1994). "The Theory of the Firm." *Harvard Business Review*, p. 95.

Elm, Dawn R. & James Weber. (1994). "Measuring Moral Judgment: The Moral Judgment Interview or the Defining Issues Test?" *Journal of Business Ethics*, 13, pp. 341–355.

Feinberg, John S. and Paul D. Feinberg (1993). *Ethics for a Brave New World*. Wheaton, IL: Crossway Books.

Ferrell, O. C. and J. Fraedrich (1991). *Business Ethics*. Boston: Houghton Mifflin.

Fimbel, N. and J. Burstein (1990). "Defining the Ethical Standards of the High Technology Industry." *Journal of Business Ethics*, 9, pp. 929–932.

Fletcher, Joseph (1966). *Situation Ethics*. Philadelphia: Westminster Press.

Forester, Tom and Perry Morrison (1990). *Computer Ethics*. Cambridge, MA: The MIT Press.

Fraedrich, John P. (1988). "Philosophy Type Interaction in the Ethical Decision Making Process of Retailers." Ph.D. Dissertation, Texas A&M University, College Station, TX.

Frederick, William C. and James Weber (1987). "The Value of Corporate Managers and Their Critics: An Empirical Description and Normative Implications." *Research in Corporate Social Responsibility*, 9 pp. 149–150.

Fritzsche, D. J. and H. Becker (1984). "Linking Management Behavior to Ethical Philosophy: An Empirical Investigation." *Academy of Management Journal*, 27, pp. 166–175.

Gallup, Jr., George & George O'Connell. (1986). *Who Do Americans Say That I Am?* Philadelphia: Westminster Press.

Gellerman, Saul W. (July-Aug. 1986). "Why 'Good' Managers Make Bad Ethical Choices." *Harvard Business Review*, pp. 85–90.

Henderson, Verne E. (1992). *What's Ethical in Business*. New York: McGraw-Hill.

Howard, Robert (Sept.-Oct. 1990). "Values Make the Company: An Interview with Robert Haas." *Harvard Business Review*, pp. 133–144.

Jersild, Paul (1990). *Making Moral Decisions*. Minneapolis, MN: Fortune Press.

Johnson, Douglas W. (1984). *Computer Ethics: A Guide for a New Age*. Elgin, IL: The Brethren Press.

Klausner, Joseph. (1925). *Jesus of Nazareth*. New York: Macmillian Co.

Lewis, Hunter (1990). *A Question of Values*. San Francisco: Harper & Row.

Martin, D. W. and J. H. Peterson (1991). "Insider Trading Revisited." *Journal of Business Ethics*, 10, pp. 57–62.

Meyer, Michael and Anne Underwood (Nov. 14, 1994). "Crimes of the Net." *Newsweek*.

Mitzman, Arthur. (1970). *The Iron Cage: An Historical Interpretation of Max Weber*. New York: Alfred A. Knopf.

Niebuhr, H. R. (1963). *The Responsible Self*. New York: Harper & Row.

Novak, Michael (1981). *Toward a Theology of the Corporation*. Washington, DC: AEI Press.

Parker, Donn (1977). *Ethical Conflicts in Computer Science and Technology*. Menlo Park, CA: National Science Foundation.

Posner, Barry Z. & Warren H. Schmidt. (1993). "Values Congruence and Differences Between the Interplay of Personal and Organizational Value Systems," *Journal of Business Ethics*, 12(5). pp. 341–347.

Rest, J. R. (1979). *Development in Judging Moral Issues*. Minneapolis, MN: University of Minnesota Press.

Selekman, Benjamin M. (1959). *A Moral Philosophy for Management*. New York: McGraw-Hill.

Sherry, P. (1991). "Ethical Issues in the Conduct of Supervision." *The Counseling Psychologist*, 19, pp. 566–584.

Sherry, P., R. Teschendorf, S. Anderson and F. Guzman (1991). "Ethical Beliefs and Behavior of College Counseling Center Professionals." *Journal of College Student Development*, 32, pp. 350–358.

Sherry, Patrick M. and E. J. Barton (1992). "Ethical Beliefs and Behaviors of Management Professionals." *Journal of Management Systems*, 4, pp. 47–65.

Shinn, Roger L. (1985). *Forced Options: Social Decisions for the 21st Century*, Second Edition. New York: Pilgrim Press.

Thompson, W. R. (Feb. 6, 1994). "Ethical Workers Must Have Ethical Role Models." *The Tennessean Issues for Business*, p. 27.

Thornburg, L. (1991). "HR Ethics Survey Results Announced." *The Advisor*, 3, p. 3.

Tillich, Paul (1950). *The Courage to Be*. New Haven, CT: Yale University Press.

Trevino, L. K. (1986). "Ethical Decision Making in Organizations: A Person-Situation Interactionist Model," *Academy of Management Review,*, 11(3), pp. 601–617.

Velasquez, Manuel G. (1988). *Business Ethics*. Englewood Cliffs, NJ: Prentice-Hall.

Vittrell, W. S. (1990). "Ethical Issues for Management Information Specialists." *Journal of Business Ethics*, pp. 42–50.

Yankelovich, Daniel (1981). *New Rules*. New York: Random House.

NOTES

1. Ferrell, 1991, p.10.
2. Vittrell, 1990, pp. 42–50.
3. Martin, 1991, pp. 57–62.
4. Fimbel, 1990, pp. 929–932.
5. Thornburg, 1991, p. 3.
6. Fraedrich, 1988.
7. Barnette, 1961, p. 4.
8. Fletcher, 1967, p. 94.
9. Thompson, 1994, p. 27.
10. Johnson, 1984, p. 104.
11. Johnson, 1984, p. 186.
12. Barnette, 1961, p. 4.
13. The Holy Bible; Leviticus 19:35-36; Deuteronomy 25:13–16; Proverbs 16:11; Ezekiel 45:10–12; Amos 8: 4–6; Micah 6:10-11.
14. Klausner, 1925, p. 381.
15. Meyer and Underwood, 1994.
16. Drucker, 1994 p. 95.
17. Mitzman, 1970, pp. 7–10.
18. Selekman, 1959, p .5
19. Brockmann, 1983, p. 4
20. Shinn, 1985, pp. 3-4.
21. Frederick and Weber, 1987, pp. 149-150.
22. Bursk, 1959, p. 137.
23. Gallup, 1986, p. 18.
24. Cornell, *Chicago Tribune*, Sep. 8, 1989.
25. Gallup, *Washington Post*, Jan. 22, 1994.
26. Posner and Schmidt, 1993, pp. 341–347.
27. Clark, 1987, p. 194.
28. Clark, 1987, p. 194.
29. The Holy Bible, Joshua 7.
30. Trevino, 1992.
31. Colby and Kohlberg, 1987.
32. Rest, 1979.
33. Elm and Weber, 1994.

18. PROFESSIONALISM, ETHICAL RESPONSIBILITY AND ACCOUNTABILITY

Joseph M. Kizza

I want to start this discussion by looking at three design projects that caused both embarrassment and very expensive cost overruns and in one case ended in failure. The answers to questions raised by the controversies surrounding these projects will lead to a discussion of the social and professional issues faced by professionals. The three projects are CONFIRM, a software project for reservation processing; the Intel Pentium microprocessor chip design project; and the Denver International Airport automated baggage system.

CONFIRM

The CONFIRM project started in March 1987 after an informal discussion between the contracting firm AMRIS, the information system subsidiary of AMR, the parent company of United Airlines Corporation, and the clients, Marriott Hotels, Hilton Hotels, and Budget Rent-a-Car. The goal of CONFIRM at its inception was to be the best in the world at system reservations in the lodging and travel industries. AMRIS offered to design a state-of-the-art reservation processing system that would interface worldwide with any airline, hotel, and car rental company using a single computerized system. After almost four years and $125 million, the project was abandoned (11).

THE DENVER INTERNATIONAL AIRPORT AUTOMATED BAGGAGE SYSTEM

In 1989, when the city officials of Denver, Colorado, wanted to replace Stepleton International Airport because of congestion and overgrowth, they contracted BAE Automated Systems Inc. of Dallas to design and build the $193 million automated baggage delivery system for the new airport. It would be the largest automated baggage system in the world. BAE is one of only two companies in the world specializing in the design of these high-tech baggage systems. The system when fully operational uses laser scanners, computers to run the software and do all the necessary controls, and telecars, which are miniature trolleys, to move baggage around an estimated 22 miles of new airport. The computers and scanners were to make sure that every bag in the 4,000 miniature plastic cars running at 19 miles per hour arrived on time and also to sense the change in passenger flow with the help of sensors placed 150 to 200 feet apart. Under the contract with BAE, the system was supposed to deliver 70 bags per minute in order to meet United Airlines's 284 flight daily schedule at Denver with an estimated 80,000 bags per day (3, 4, 6, 8).

When BAE delivered the system, it failed the first test miserably. Bags flew out of their carts, and jams were frequent. At first the city officials thought that the software design problems were not major but were little nagging ones. But after a number of failed test runs, the city hired Lagplan, a firm from Germany that had debugged similar problems at Frankfurt, Germany. After a number of observations, some of which were disastrous, Lagplan recommended a separate manual system, estimated at $50 million. The manual system was to run as a stand alone alongside the automated system.

Meanwhile BAE was rewriting computer software and adding scanners and, having argued that the backup system was not needed, submitted a new schedule after four delays, three of which were due to the baggage system. After five years and almost $4 billion, the tent-like airport was not working and was losing $1 million a day in limbo. The city needed to pay for the new low-tech manual system from Rapistan Demag of Michigan, and also to pay for all delay costs totalling $200 million. When it opened, the DIA ("Doesn't Include Airplanes" as it is jokingly called) was $2 billion over budget (5, 9, 10, 12).

So far there are two known problems: 1) BAE has never designed and installed an automated system on such a scale; and 2) the project was sold on an unrealistic and unworkable schedule with too many expectations. But without a doubt, BAE has more problems. The company failed three crucial tests, and the system so far has not performed the way it was supposed to in the contract.

INTEL PENTIUM DEBACLE

In 1994 Intel, the largest microprocessor chip manufacturer in the world, delivered its much awaited top-of-the-line chip named the Pentium. A few months after it was delivered, Thomas Nicely, a mathematician at Lynchburg College in Vermont, discovered an error that can occur during complex mathematical calculations. After discovering the flaw, professor Nicely E-mailed his colleagues asking them to check their machines for errors.

What is amazing is that Intel officials had discovered the same error four months earlier in July 1994 and had said nothing until the error was discovered by Nicely in December 1994. In the meantime, Intel started handling the situation by refusing any claims and resisting any recall claiming that the odds of getting the error during a mathematical calculation are 9 billion to one. After a public outcry and a boycott by a few major customers led by giant IBM, Intel was reluctantly forced to accept a recall and to issue a public apology to all its customers. At the time of the recall it was estimated that there were about 2.2 million computers with the Pentium chip, and it was estimated to cost up to $995 per chip. This was no doubt an unnecessary and costly mistake (2, 7).

All three cases discussed raise similar ethical questions. While in the BAE and CONFIRM projects there is plenty of blame to go around to all the parties in the project, for the computer professionals outside the projects and those directly involved with the project, there are crucial questions that need answers. While it is true that developers often encounter unforeseen technical and management problems, and we all agree that not every problem should be reported, project managers should have the wisdom and the strength to know when to report a problem with the potential of disrupting the project schedule, especially those affecting the projected budget because while many clients can accommodate schedule changes, very few accept budget busters.

Failure to report these problems can be explained in one of two ways: 1) management officials did not and still cannot comprehend the project they were supposed to thoroughly understand and therefore should not have been in charge of the project; or 2) management officials were hiding the problems. In the first instance the current management should be replaced, and in the second, there are serious ethical problems that need to be addressed. Lack of professional ethics in this case highlights many serious questions that the computer professionals need to ponder. Should things like these be allowed to happen? At what point of problem complexity should the technical team that first learns of the problems report them? What are the responsibilities of these technicians? How much did management know and not tell? If the technicians reported the problem and management ignored the report, should the technicians blow the whistle? If so, what protection do they have? Before I answer the questions posed above, let me first identify computer professionals and define their responsibilities.

WHO ARE THE COMPUTER PROFESSIONALS?

The general definition of a professional is one who possesses exceptional knowledge and or skills in a certain field. This definition emphasizes the end result—the possession of exceptional knowledge and skills. It ignores the means, the process of acquiring such knowledge and or skills. If we accept this broad definition, everyone who owns a computer and can operate it with some skill for a particular application will be a computer professional. One drawback with this definition is that this will be the largest profession known. With the rate at which personal computers are acquired and the advances in computer technology making them more user-friendly, everybody will soon belong to this profession. When membership of a profession is so large, the profession has all the human problems. It would therefore be unthinkable to enforce any professional code. So I have got to do better in defining a computer professional. I am going to require that in order for one to belong to any profession, one must possess or adhere to all of the following:

(1) highly developed skills and theoretical knowledge of a specific domain
(2) several years of formal education in a related domain
(3) a set of guidelines laid down by the profession

This definition does an amazing thing; it drastically reduces the membership of professions by putting emphasis on the process of acquiring the knowledge and or the exceptional skill. All those self-taught and on-the-job trained professionals are eliminated. What have we achieved by narrowing the scope of our field of professionals? Several things have been achieved, among them the professional pride and responsibility that come with years of formal education preparing one to belong to the profession. The love of the profession, the nurturing of the role models in the profession during training, and the sense of duty acquired through rigorous exercises during training, may help the members of the profession to make sound ethical decisions. But as experience has shown, the love of one's profession alone is not enough to make one responsible and accountable for all the decision making one does. Computer professionals of late have not been exceptions to this. In fact as the profession matures, we are getting more and more ethically lax professionals. There has been reaction from both within and outside of the profession, resulting in calls for licensing computer professionals. There are proposals to make computer professionals bound for the safety of their products and designs the same way engineers are responsible and accountable for their designs and products. The other question is whether society as a whole is prepared to demand this level of accountability from a professional that has been associated with the image of a computer as a wonder machine incapable of making mistakes. The small cracks that are beginning to show will get wider unless something is done. But what must be done? Who should do it and who will judge whether the methods used have worked?

POLICING THE COMPUTER PROFESSION

Many traditional professions have used a number of techniques to uphold professional pride, responsibility, and accountability. Such techniques include limiting the number of members, requiring continued education, implementing professional codes of conduct, licensing, and enforcing codes of conduct.

The computer science profession has already started its own internal review. There have been calls for restricting the steadily increasing number of Ph.D.–bound students (1). While there has been a drastic drop in the number of computer science and computer engineering majors as a result of the drop in the job market for such graduates and holders of master's degrees, the trend continues for Ph.D.–bound students.

Besides calls for restricting new Ph.D.'s, calls are increasing for licensing computer professionals. One of the main proponents of licensing is Dr. Donald Gotterbarn of East Tennessee State University. Gotterbarn's arguments are plausible and have found eager ears. He argues that if system engineers and system designers are held responsible for the products they design and produce, software engineers should likewise be measured by the same yardstick and be held responsible for their designs and products. If physicians do not do a job the way it is supposed to be done, they are sued for malpractice; if engineers design a bridge that collapses and kills people, they are held responsible, and they pay damages. By the same token, if software engineers design a product that kills or harms people or is in any way defective, they should be sued for defective products. The only way this can be done effectively is to make the practice of designing and producing software a privilege and not a right, a privilege that can be taken away if there is misuse of it. The question now is who should police and enforce such laws?

REGULATORY MECHANISMS AND THE PROFESSIONS

If professions are to maintain the standards and competencies of their members, they must have sets of regulations. Regulations are needed for a number of reasons, the most basic of which are maintaining standards and establishing competency of the professions. The methods of enforcement of these regulations vary from profession to profession depending on the financial status of the profession. Among the types of enforcement are the following: self-regulation, licensure, indirect regulation, civil authority.

Self-regulation

By choosing this type of enforcement the profession is right from the beginning setting itself up to take full responsibility for the conduct and actions of its members. Professions choosing this method follow it with support activities for its members such as education workshops, seminars, conferences and events through which constant education of the members is maintained. The attendance and participation of members in these events may be mandated.

The professions also set up subcommittees to develop and distribute educational materials to the membership, and committees investigate and impose sanctions on members reported for misconduct. There should also be a streamlined way of reporting members who violate the regulations of the profession. When sanctions are imposed, there must be a mechanism in place to enforce the sanctions, and guidelines to appeal them.

Licensure

Members of the professions can only practice when they are certified by a body of fellow professionals, after passing a standard examination. Such examinations ensure standards for the profession. Any violations of the profession's regulations are reported to the committee which among its sanctions may recommend the revocation of the member's license. Such a threat to revoke the member's license may work as a deterrent and as a good enforcement method.

Indirect Regulation

The profession using this method chooses to observe and abide by the set of regulations and or ordinances of another profession or civil authority. By abiding by these regulations, the profession is forcing the members to abide by the same regulations or ordinances. If a profession chooses to follow this course, it may set up its own enforcement and sanction committee or abide by the committees of the profession or professions whose regulations it has adopted.

Civil Authority

A number of a professions, especially young professions and those whose financial status is not very strong, choose to directly follow the civil authorities where their members are working. This means that such membership must abide not only by local ordinances but also by all government regulations. The reporting and sanction of a member are done through the normal civil procedures.

EXPECTATIONS

Is society expecting more from professionals than it gets? Are demands made of professionals more rigorous than those made of other members of society? These and other questions probably do not have complete answers. Society expects more from professionals because they have become in large part individuals with considerable skills, authority and usually wealth. Most professionals are in the middle or upper classes of their communities. So professionals are not only role models for their communities, they are usually advisors as well. Because of this status they have in their communities, professionals should strive to behave with dignity and class.

REFERENCES

(1) Chandra, Ashok, David Patterson, Paul Young and Joseph Traub. "Do We Produce Too Many Ph.D.'s?" *Computing Research News*, 6, 3, 1994.

(2) "Computer Stock Tumble Over Chip Flaw." *New York Times*, 4 December 1994, Section D.

(3) Eddy, Mark. "Baggage Tests Begin to Click." *Denver Post*, 27 July 1994. NewsBank, Transportation, 1994, fiche 37, grid F8.

(4) ____. "City's Faith in DIA Bag Firm Ebbing." *Denver Post*, 9 July 1994. NewsBank, Transportation, 1994, fiche 33, grids A12, 13.

(5) ____. "DIA Dispute Fallout: Minority Firms Fired." *Denver Post*, 27 July 1994. NewsBank, Transportation, 1994, fiche 37, grid F7.

(6) Flynn, Kevin. "United Wary of Backup Baggage Plan." *Rocky Mountain News*, 2 August 1994. NewsBank, Transportation, 1994, fiche 37, grids F9–12.

(7) Markoff, John. "Error in Chip Still Dogging Intel Officials." *New York Times*, 6 December 1994, Section D5.

(8) Murphy, Chris. "GR Firm Hustles to Design Baggage System for Airport." *Grand Rapids Press*, 5 August 1994. NewsBank, Transportation, 1994, fiche 37, grid F3.

(9) O'Driscoll, Patrick. "'Low-tech' Salvation: Webb Orders Backup Bag System." *Denver Post*, 5 August 1994. NewsBank, Transportation, 1994, fiche 37, grids F4–6.

(10) ____, and Mark Eddy. "City, United Bag a Deal." *Denver Post*, 2 September 1994. NewsBank, Transportation, 1994, fiche 44, grids B1–3.

(11) Oz, Effy. "When Professional Standards Are Lax: The CONFIRM Failure and Its Lessons." *Communications of the ACM*, 27, 10, 1994.

(12) Taylor, Jeff. "America's Loneliest Airport: Denver's Dreams Can't Fly." *Kansas City Star*, 28 August 1994. NewsBank, Transportation, 1994, fiche 43, grids D12–14.

V : ARTIFICIAL INTELLIGENCE AND CYBERSPACE

SUMMARY

(19) *Human Values in the Computer Revolution*

In this chapter John Fodor identifies computer ethics as the newest branch of philosophy. He goes on to discuss the computer revolution and its ethical effects on society, and he looks into the future of virtual reality and artificial intelligence.

(20) *Artificial Intelligence: An Ethical Analysis*

This chapter examines the concerns connected with artificial intelligence research and computer technology, and the current debate of social and ethical issues within these two domains.

(21) *Ethics and Electronic Personae*

This chapter discusses the role of electronic personae in information delivery and services. It also examines the ethical implications involved. The paper describes situations where there is potential for eper conflicts. The author anticipates a time when epers will do most of the good services in a computer system and in telecommunication services. She believes that the role of electronic personae is just beginning.

(22) *Ethics in the Computer Age*

In this chapter Dr. Patrick Sullivan argues that computer ethics is becoming CyberEthics, and he uses major issues in computer ethics to illustrate his argument.

19. HUMAN VALUES IN THE COMPUTER REVOLUTION

John L. Fodor

I. THE COMPUTER REVOLUTION

From laptops to Crays, from artificial intelligence to virtual reality, the computer revolution is well under way. Computers are becoming ubiquitous in our society: as tiny attenuating microprocessors in hearing aids and musical synthesizers; as research tools in medicine and science; as control devices in automobiles, home appliances, military hardware, and space satellites. Robotics, artificial intelligence, nanotechnology and virtual reality are just some of the new technologies made possible because of the computer.

The computer revolution may indeed be the biggest and most profound technological revolution of all. This is due largely to the malleability of computers. As James Moor explains:

> The essence of the Computer Revolution is found in the nature of the computer itself. What is revolutionary about computers is logical malleability.... The logic of computers can be massaged and shaped in endless ways through changes in hardware and software. Just as the power of a steam engine was a raw resource of the Industrial Revolution, so the logic of a computer is a raw resource of the Computer Revolution. Because logic applies everywhere, the potential applications of computer technology appear limitless. The computer is the nearest thing we have to a universal tool. Indeed, the limits of computers are largely the limits of our own creativity.[1]

Indeed, centuries from now scholars may look back and redefine history in terms of BTC (Before the Computer) and ATC (After the Computer).

II. A CALL TO ARMS

Computer technology will influence all of our lives as no technology before it has. Consider, briefly the following areas that will be affected:

Computers in the Workplace

Computers are already being used in the workplace for word processing, desktop publishing, accounting, PIMs (personal information managers), telecommunications, etc. Many jobs today rely mostly on the computer (for example, some auto assembly line workers, telephone operators, and fast-food workers). As Judy Perrolle points out, if you can push a button, you can do inventory control at a fast-food restaurant; merely push an icon of a French fry, and you send a potato off to be slaughtered.[2]

Moreover, computers are displacing humans from many jobs (for example, typesetters, toll booth attendants, and candy vendors). Even our friendly inventory controller at McDonald's could soon be replaced by a menu-driven CPU with which the consumer will interact.

Computers in Health Care/Medicine

In a paper presented to the American Association for the Advancement of Science, my colleague and I wrote that computers may soon replace doctors.[3] Increasingly, computers are outperforming doctors. Admittedly, these preliminary findings—which indicate that computers diagnose patients better than human physicians—are limited to narrow ranges of diseases.[4] However, in the near future, we can imagine computers with extensive databases on disease pathologies, diagnostic procedures, treatment protocols, pharmaceuticals, etc. Combined with advances in artificial intelligence, we can imagine a time when computers will perform better—across the entire spectrum of medicine—than any human physician. This would result in better health care that would be available to more people, in less time, and at much less cost. We argued, if computers were demonstrably better than humans, then it would be unethical to allow humans to do the same job even if they desired to do so.

Computers in Education

Imagine the classroom of the near future. Teachers would not have to spend much time preparing classroom lectures; rather, their presentations would be based on interactive multimedia CD-ROMs. Indeed, these programs would be dynamic and sensitive to the level of the user. Thus, they could monitor and guide a student through a particular subject, spending as much remedial time as necessary until the student gained competency in the subject. Moreover, during this interaction, the student would benefit from accessing the primary sources themselves. Instead of reading about computer ethics, for example, a student could interact with the Research Center on Computing and Society's interactive multimedia CD-ROM series on computer ethics. She would see and hear pioneering men and women in the field on a variety of subjects.

The teacher, in turn, could spend more time monitoring and guiding the development of each student, making sure that she was working up to her potential.

Computers in Government

The very structure of our government may be redefined because of the computer. Our representative government was necessary at a time when most people lived on farms and were unable to travel long distances, engage in debate, and vote on topics. Now, it is possible to put a modem into every house, and with appropriate hardware and software to allow each qualified person to directly participate in government. In principle, instead of having a representative government, we could have a government based on the direct participation of all its voters—a true direct democracy—one eligible person, one vote.

III. THE COMPUTER REVOLUTION AND ETHICS

As seen in the preceding section, computers will influence our lives as no technology before has. Accordingly, we must become sensitive to the human values issues raised by the computer—regardless of technical familiarity with computers, or professional training in ethics. I refer to human values throughout this paper in a philosophical—specifically ethical—sense. (For example, the human values of Kant, treating people as ends and not as means, or the human values of Bentham, valuing actions which promote happiness and diminish misery.)

Computer technology, like any technology, is not exempt from the tendency to have both positive and negative effects. We are familiar with impressive advances made possible by the computer in desktop publishing, worldwide networking, CAT scans, photographs from distant planets, and so forth. Regrettably, we are also familiar with news reports about computer-related risks and harms: hackers who invade people's privacy, computer-aided bank robbery, malfunctions that cause terrible accidents, etc.[5]

During the past few decades, a new branch of applied philosophy has evolved which examines the impact of computer technology on human life.

This branch, computer ethics, was formally introduced in 1976 by Walter Maner, who coined the term. Maner's formalization of the field was based primarily on the work conducted by Donn Parker (researcher at SRI International and author of the first code of ethics for the ACM). Maner was influenced by others such as Willis Ware, Joseph Weizenbaum, and Norbert Wiener.

Maner noticed that when computers get involved in ethical problems, they often exacerbate the moral problems; and, in certain cases, they even create new moral problems in their own right.[6] He used the philosophical tools of ethics—such as Utilitarianism and Kantianism—to identify and to resolve some of the problems that computing technology raised. Work originally focused on a few standard topics like privacy, security, and software ownership.

During the late 1970s and early 1980s pioneers like Jim Moor (Dartmouth College), John Snapper (Illinois Institute of Technology), and Lance Hoffman (George Washington University) wrote papers in this relatively new field. In 1985, Deborah Johnson (who worked with Maner at Old Dominion during the late 1970s) published the first book on computer ethics (titled appropriately, *Computer Ethics*). Other disciplines began to look at computing and information technology from their perspectives. For example, Judy Perrolle explored computer technology from a sociological perspective (*Computers and Social Change*); Sherry Turkle examined computer technology from a psychological perspective (*The Second Self: Computers and the Human Spirit*); Keith Miller and Don Gotterbarn from the perspective of computer science; and Michael Gemignani from the perspective of law.

These contributors to the field have in common the fact that each

> examines the impact of computing and information technology upon human values using concepts, theories and procedures from philosophy, sociology, law, psychology, and so on. Practitioners of ... computer ethics—whether they are philosophers, computer scientists, social scientists, public policy makers, or whatever—all have the same goal: to integrate computing technology and human values in such a way that the technology advances and protects human values, rather than doing damage to them.[7]

For example, let us examine the problem of privacy. We know that privacy deals with confidentiality, freedom from intrusion or public attention, and the removal from public knowledge or observation certain facts belonging to an individual. Computing technology challenges this value in a number of ways. Computer databases are generated with vast amounts of information on individuals including demographics, buying habits, and credit ratings. Often, these databases are compiled, bought, and sold without the knowledge or the consent of the individuals. Should corporations be allowed to compile, buy, and sell such databases without the consent of individuals?

Other questions concerning computers and privacy include the following: Is it right for an employer to monitor mail messages transmitted by an employee on the company's computer system? Should insurance companies have access to medical databases? Is it right for anyone in cyberspace (i.e., computer networks), notably hackers and crackers, to examine files containing personal information?

These questions, and more, are raised in computer ethics, and are answered from the various perspectives of philosophy, sociology, psychology, and law mentioned above. (It is important to note that computer ethics is an area whose boundaries have not yet been defined. Other perspectives will undoubtedly be added as a collective view of computer ethics emerges.)

We can now reexamine those areas mentioned in Section II, and raise some questions concerning how computer technology will influence human values.

> Computers in the Workplace—What impact will such transformations in the workplace have on our lives as employees? What strategies should employees adopt to anticipate these changes in the workplace? What careers should students select in light of these possibilities?

> Computers in Health Care/Medicine—What is the significance of human interface in the treatment of disease? Might patients respond more favorably to humans than to machines?[8] Who is responsible for the performance and maintenance of sophisticated equipment? Who is liable and at fault in case of malfunctions?

> Computers in Education—In light of CD-ROM technology, will there be only one curriculum established? Who will decide on the subject matter? How will controversial topics be represented?

> Computers in Government—How can we distribute technology equitably so that all citizens can participate? How can we preserve integrity in the network avoiding problems raised by hackers and crackers? How will individuals be affected by such changes to our society?

III. CYBERETHICS—A NEW CHALLENGE

Computer ethics, as described above, has focused on how computing technology affects human values. Each approach to computer ethics—philosophy, sociology, psychology, law—identifies human values, and safeguards against compromise by computing technology.

This work is very important, indeed. However, as technology advances, there is a new way in which we should consider computer ethics. (Perhaps, even, to propose a new sub-field of computer ethics.)

Specifically, because computers can create virtual reality (hereafter VR) we need to examine (1) human behavior in VR, and (2) the viability of our ethical systems in VR. Put simply, I suggest that VR will alter many of our concepts of right and wrong; and consequently, our actions based on these values will change, as well. This new branch of computer ethics, I call Cyber-Ethics. I want to focus attention in the remainder of this chapter on this important area.

IV. VIRTUAL REALITY

There is no industry standard for VR; many denotations and connotations are associated with the phrase. (Some of the more interesting ones are generated by advertisers and marketing professionals.) I use VR to denote worlds created by computers—a computer simulation of real or imaginary phenomena.

There are different levels of VR. For example, at one extreme there are the graphical worlds that one sees in arcade amusement centers, personal computer games, and motion pictures like *Lawnmower Man*. They contain drawings, pictures, animations, symbols, and representations of the real world. These virtual realities are easy to recognize, and no one would confuse them with our own world.

At the other extreme, however, are virtual worlds that are much more sophisticated. They can be, in principle, indistinguishable from the real world. Take, for example, the movie *Total Recall*. Let us ignore the gratuitous violence for a moment and focus, instead, on that plot line where Arnold Schwarzenegger's character decides to go for a vacation implant. In this scene, the virtual world and experiences created by the computer are hailed as being indistinguishable from the real world. Indeed, the viewer is pressed with the intriguing question: "Are the events which are unfolding in the film to be taken literally? Or, are they events in a virtual world, created by a computer?" (We can frame this ontological question of competing worlds in the words of the famous television commercial, "Is it real, or is it VR?")

Computers, of course, are not the only tools with which one can create simulated worlds; words, pencils, brushes, film, video and a healthy imagination are examples of other tools which can create them. And when these tools are used by good writers, artists, film makers, videographers, and thinkers, we can easily be absorbed into their worlds. However, what differentiates these worlds from those created by computers is that, with appropriate interfaces, a person can interact in VR.

Granted, we interact with the worlds created by words, paint, film, video, and dreams, as aestheticians, movie critics, and psychologists eagerly point out. But, these kinds of interactions are limited; we ordinarily do not confuse these fictional worlds with the real world. These fictional worlds do not confuse our senses. Moreover, there are certain conventions that we have adopted in relating to these fictional worlds, and thus we have developed ways of distinguishing between them and the real world. For example, in the arts, if a viewer does not keep the distinction between the real world and the world created by the artist in mind, she would be committing an act of "under-distancing."[9] And, as psychologists observe, persons who are unable to distinguish the real world from worlds created by their imaginations are diagnosed as psychotic.

But it is the possibility of creating simulated worlds that are indistinguishable from the real one, coupled with the possibility of interacting in these worlds, which makes VR a unique and intriguing consequence of computer technology.[10]

Notice, however, that there is more. Not only can VR create landscapes and environments which are indistinguishable from the world as we know it to be, but, it can also create worlds which are entirely inconsistent with ours.

For example, worlds where individuals can fly, where buildings have inside dimensions larger than their outside dimensions, where up is down and down is up, where time speeds up in certain locations and slows down in others are possible.[11]

Some interesting consequences result from such possibilities. For example, an individual using VR would feel as if she were running the Boston Marathon, swimming the English Channel, playing the violin at Carnegie Hall, climbing Mt. Everest, or traveling to the Orient.

(While these possibilities have general appeal, it is for persons with physical disabilities that VR may have the most profound implications. Notwithstanding the fact that many persons with physical disabilities do participate in activities like the Boston Marathon, it is apparent that most people with physical disabilities are unable to engage in as many physical activities as those who are not physically disabled. This is especially true for paraplegics, quadriplegics, and amputees. Imagine, that with the necessary interfaces, a quadriplegic or an amputee could enter various VRs to engage in many activities.[12])

While some of the virtual realities that I describe are still under development, others are already here. Take, for example, the advanced flight simulators used in the recent Desert Storm campaign. The simulated targets in practice were reported by our pilots as often indistinguishable from the ones encountered during actual bombing runs.

V. CYBERETHICS—REDEFINING ETHICS

Virtual reality does more than simply challenge our senses. It forces us to critically reexamine (1) our behavior in these simulated worlds, and (2) the efficacy of our ethical theories. In terms of our behavior, I will show that when using the same ethical theory, different prescriptions will obtain in the real world and in VR. In terms of challenging the ethical theories themselves, I will show that VR forces us to reevaluate our ethical theories.

Behavior in VR

Consider one characteristic of a moral theory, namely, its ability to prescribe, or to prohibit, an action. This feature determines whether an action ought to be engaged in or not. For example, using the moral theory of Utilitarianism, one may conclude that prostitution is wrong. But, what may be wrong in the real world, may not be wrong in VR—even when using the same moral theory of Utilitarianism.

In the real world there are many compelling Utilitarian reasons why people should refrain from prostitution. Some of these reasons include the following: the criminal and psychological exploitation of individuals (mostly women), disease (such as AIDS, syphilis, and herpes), unwanted pregnancies, and infidelity.

Imagine, now, an encounter in VR where individuals coupled with appropriate interfaces would exchange sexual favors for money. Clearly, diseases and unwanted pregnancies would be avoided. Most would agree that infidelity— at least in the conventional sense—would not be committed.[13] And, I argue, both the criminal and psychological exploitation of individuals as we see them occur in the real world would not take place in VR.[14]

With the traditional proscriptions removed, prostitution in VR may be accepted on Utilitarian grounds, the very same grounds which prohibited prostitution in the real world.[15] Consequently, the moral prescriptions and prohibitions for some actions in VR will be different from the moral prescriptions and prohibitions of those acts in the real world. (This does not necessarily denote an inconsistency in Utilitarianism, merely, inconsistencies between our behavior in VR and the real world.)

Efficacy of Ethical Theories

Next, consider how VR will force us to reexamine many of the ethical theories themselves. I have suggested that VR can create worlds that are inconsistent with ours. This feature can be applied to individuals in VR as well. A person may define herself as anyone—or anything—she wishes. A 5' 3" woman weighing 120 pounds could appear as Bill Clinton, a burly lumberjack, or even a satyr.

Because VR would allow a person to transform herself in these ways, some of our fundamental beliefs in personhood and individuality need to be reexamined. Since many of our ethical systems are based on certain presumptions concerning personhood and individuality, it follows that some of our ethical systems may need reexamination, as well. For example, take Kant's notion of deception:

> [A] man in need finds himself forced to borrow money. He knows well that he won't be able to repay it, but he sees also that he will not get any loan unless

he firmly promises to repay it within a fixed time. He wants to make such a promise, but he still has conscience enough to ask himself whether it is ... permissible.... [He] will immediately see that he intends to make use of another man merely as a means to an end which the latter does not likewise hold.[16]

If the person in this example does ask for a loan, knowing that he is making a false promise, he would be tricking the loaner into doing something that he may not have done if all of the facts were revealed. In other words, the borrower deceives the loaner and is using him as a means to an end and not as an end in himself.

If I define myself as anyone other than myself (in other words if I transform myself into someone—or something—which I am not) and proceed to interact with individuals in VR without informing them of my true identity, then I am deceiving those people with whom I interact. Therefore, under these conditions, a Kantian would raise the same kind of objection to VR as Kant himself raised in the example of a false promise, namely, that persons in VR would be deceiving each other, and thus treating each other as means to an end and not as ends in themselves.[17] (Presumably a Kantian would not object if one used VR under those circumstances where an individual played games, increased her range of activities, or interacted with others—provided that no deception took place. However, when deception is used, a fundamental principle of Kantian morality is violated; and thus, for a Kantian, VR, when used to deceive, would be morally unacceptable.)

Perhaps we may wish to stop here, preserving Kant's moral theory intact. Yet, by observing some other features of VR, one is forced to reexamine Kant's theory. As noted above, VR would allow persons with disabilities to represent themselves as able-bodied individuals. They would thus enjoy the full benefits of interacting with other persons without prejudice to their disabilities. A strong argument can be advanced claiming that this opportunity should supersede Kant's dictum of not deceiving.[18]

Indeed, as the examples of prostitution and deception reveal, VR forces us to critically reexamine (1) human behavior in simulated worlds, and (2) the universality of our ethical theories.

VI. CONCLUSION

Has computer technology reached the point of influencing our lives as described above? No. Does, however, computer technology have the potential to do so? Yes. We can take a lesson from another less sophisticated technology, the automobile. No one asked what impact autos would have on human life as the first one rolled off the assembly line. Yet now, the automobile is a significant part of human life in our society. We use cars for commuting to work, for shopping, and for recreation. Suburbs, traffic jams, parking lots, highway deaths, and air pollution—not to mention the testing of certain moralities in the back seats of cars—are just some of the results of the automobile. No doubt, we would have done things differently had we anticipated the effects of the auto (such as adding seat belts and safety glass to early models; using alternative energy sources to lower pollution; considering persons with disabilities when designing human-machine interfaces; establishing policies for recycling auto parts).

While it is impossible to go back in time to raise these concerns with the automobile, it is not too late to raise concerns regarding the computer. Computer technology spans an enormous spectrum of possible applications. And while word processing may have little impact on human values, artificial intelligence, nanotechnology, robotics, and virtual reality will have profound consequences on them.

Because of these possibilities it is important to raise our sensitivities toward computer technology. Terry Bynum describes three approaches to teaching computer ethics which we can use as a model to increase our sensitivity towards computer ethics.[19] He says the first level of teaching computer ethics is "pop-computer ethics." This is merely discussing examples of computer ethics which have been raised in popular media (for example, the Internet Worm case, the Therac-25 case, or the Aegis Radar case). Everyone is able to participate at this level of computer ethics merely by listening, watching, and reading cases in computer ethics as reported by the media.

The second level of teaching computer ethics is "para-computer ethics" (a term Bynum borrows from Keith Miller). The paramedic in medicine or the paralegal in law is a person with some specialized training. So too, the para-computer ethicist goes beyond the pop level. She studies theories, collects cases, and relates these cases to the theories of philosophy, or sociology, or psychology, or law, etc.

The final level of computer ethics is "theoretical computer ethics" or professional computer ethics. This is where philosophers, lawyers, sociologists, psychologists, etc., investigate areas of computer ethics from the perspective of their professional training. They raise questions and pursue areas in computer ethics rigorously, abstractly, and academically.

It is not necessary to become a professional computer ethicist to do computer ethics. A pop or a para level of interest will suffice. What is necessary, however, is (1) a realization that sooner than later computer technology will impact our lives profoundly, (2) an understanding that the consequences of computer technology have both positive and negative effects on our lives, and (3) an interest to contribute towards discussions and policy making regarding computer technology, such that advances in computer technology will not compromise human values.[20]

NOTES

1. James H. Moor (1985). "What Is Computer Ethics?" in Terrell Ward Bynum, ed., (1985) *Computers and Ethics*, Blackwell. (Published as the October 1985 issue of the journal *Metaphilosophy*.)

2. Judy Perrolle, *What is Computer Ethics*, video, Educational Media Resources, Inc., 1992.

3. *Medical Computing and Human Values*, T. W. Bynum and J. L. Fodor. Presented at the annual meeting of the American Association for the Advancement of Science, 1992.

4. See for example, "Ethicists Foresee Computer Vastly Changing Doctor's Role, "*American Medical News*, April 27, 1992, and "Computer Bests Doctors in Detecting Heart Attacks," *New Haven Registrar*, December 1, 1991.

5. Peter G. Neumann, compiler (1991), *Illustrative Risks to the Public in the Use of Computer Systems and Related Technology*, SRI International. (Index to the published RISKS archives, see *ACM SIGSOFT Software Engineering Notes*.)

6. Walter Maner, *Introduction to Computer Ethics*, an interactive CD-ROM produced by the Research Center on Computing and Society, and Educational Media Resources, Inc., 1994.

7. T. W. Bynum, *Teaching Computing and Human Values*, Bynum, Maner, and Fodor (eds.), Research Center on Computing and Society, 1992.

8. One's immediate reply that they would is contradicted by Joseph Weizenbaum's ingenious research with the Eliza program. Weizenbaum, *Computer Power and Human Reason: From Judgment to Calculation*, (San Francisco: W. H. Freeman, 1976).

9. Edward Bullough, "'Psychical Distance' as a Factor in Art and an Aesthetic Principle," in *Problems in Aesthetics*, Morris Weitz (ed.), (New York: MacMillan, 1970), p. 782.

10. I defer to another paper the many interesting epistemological and ontological questions that are raised in light of this feature.

11. Writer Bruce Sterling in a videotape interview, © Educational Media Resources, forthcoming.

12. I explore this problem in greater detail in my paper "Virtual Reality: Some Ethical Considerations," pending publication in *Science and Engineering Ethics*.

13. It is important to examine what new meaning(s) this term would have as a result of VR.

14. This can be seen clearly when one of the partners is a computer simulation.

15. I have worked out the details of this argument in my paper "Ethics in Cyberspace," presented at the first World Meeting of Philosophers, Hungary, 1992.

16. Immanuel Kant, *Foundations of the Metaphysics of Morals*, Lewis White Beck, trans. (Indianapolis, IN: Bobbs-Merrill, 1959), p. 40.

17. Note also, that reason has brought us to value and esteem that which is authentic, true, real, original, actual, and unquestionable. Virtual reality clearly obfuscates these ideals by creating environments which challenge authenticity, truth, originality, actuality, and certainty.

18. I reserve for another paper an elaboration of this argument. I wish, at this time, merely to offer some of the questions that need to be raised regarding VR and ethics.

19. T. W. Bynum, in *Teaching Computing and Human Values*, Bynum, Maner, and Fodor (eds.), Research Center on Computing and Society, 1992.

20. See Jim Moor's "What is Computer Ethics?" in *Teaching Computing and Human Values*, Bynum, Maner, and Fodor (eds.), Research Center on Computing and Society, 1992.

20. ARTIFICIAL INTELLIGENCE: AN ETHICAL ANALYSIS

DAVID PRESTON and KEITH TAYLOR

ABSTRACT

Our concern here is with artificial intelligence (AI) research and computer technology in general. However, though not primarily concerned with business or computer ethics, our field of inquiry impacts naturally upon contemporary debates within these domains.

INTRODUCTION

Philosophical interest in AI and computer technology has increased greatly over the last two decades. Technology has never been a field philosophers have felt comfortable with, "mere technology" Paul Feyerabend once described it.

One of the problems of analyzing technology is its detail. For brevity's sake we center our discussion around Alan Turing's paper "Computing Machinery and Intelligence." We may dispense with the Turing Test on the grounds of its inadequacy. The notion that if we are unable to distinguish between a machine and a human being, on the strength of a five-minute conversation, we should term the machine as intelligent as human beings is absurd. Nevertheless this bizarre test has established itself within a small but significant group within AI circles.

Turing's paper is also remembered for his prediction "that by the end of the century the use of words and general educated opinion will have altered so much that we will be able to speak of machines thinking without expecting to be contradicted"(9). Immediately preceding this he writes, "The original question: 'Can machines think?' I believe to be too meaningless to deserve discussion." The passing of the imitation game (Turing Test) is "the more accurate form of the question." He also suggests that there is nothing wrong in "being influenced by any unproved conjecture. ... Provided it is made clear which are proved facts and which are conjectures, no harm can result." If it were indeed the case for AI he may have had a point, but sadly it is not. Artificial Intelligence is the sharp edge of computer and information technology. There are many who would disagree with that statement, but our concern is more with the global and cultural impact of these "lower" technologies. That is we believe that it is in everyday encounters with computer and information technology that our opinions and the meanings of words are altered.

The most obvious influence we have is the belief that human beings themselves are "information processing machines." Using available technology and identifiable "systems" as a model for how the mind works is probably as old as thought itself. Certainly the Greeks likened the mind to the catapults, and in both China and Europe the bureaucratic procedures of the state were believed to mirror the mind. The growth of corporate power in the capitalist nations at the beginning of this century suggested to some that the brain ran like a rather large office. At the same time scientific socialism in the Soviet Union dictated that the citizens' minds reflect the new Soviet order. There are of course numerous other examples. Has this process stopped? Will we discover a new technology or system that we believe to be more like the mind or brain than our present or future computers? We feel the answer is probably no, if we are able to satisfy ourselves that computers are as intelligent as we are. Being "satisfied" however would not necessarily mean that they were as intelligent. So how could this come about? To answer this we can begin by going down a well-worn track.

There has been much debate within AI circles as to whether AI research is a "normal science," as defined by Thomas Kuhn. The answer is that it may appear to be a normal science but is in fact a "pseudo-science." Margaret Masterman has said,

> If we distinguish "science" from philosophy (or something else) *only* because within science there always somewhere occurs normal-science, what about the converse case where "normal-science" prematurely takes in some unjustified manner by a set of fashion conscious scientists starting to imitate one another without proper pre-examination of paradigms (i.e., without the alleged insight that a certain paradigm is relevant to a particular field being a genuine insight)?

She suggests that this is not uncommon, for "Do we not see premature normal-science (which is also called 'phoney-science' and 'pseudo-science' by soured critics) setting in all round us in a nightmare manner, in the new sciences, especially where computers can be grandiosely used to give spurious impressions of genuine scientific efficiency?" She also assures us that "In the end phoney scientific normal-science lines collapse, or fail to yield any results, or topple, or evaporate—or so one hopes"(1).

We are two of Masterman's soured critics in that we believe that the "trick," as Masterman puts it, that started cognitive psychology and then AI occurred in World War II. We are unable to give detail here, but we need only examine K.J. Kraik's *The Nature of Explanation* (2) to see how the "man-as-information-processing-machine" paradigm emerged from the technology of the ack-ack gun predictors. If we read the accounts of Wigglesworth's war work (10), or think of the Manhattan Project, we are immediately struck by how much the demands of war changed scientific research. Goal oriented research, "problem solving," teamwork—all the methods of normal (modern) science were not only perfected during this time but became an object of study in themselves. Problem solving and normal science have become both the explanans and the explanandum. Of course we are not suggesting that these methods and the research of them did not take place before the war; it is just that they were seen to work.

Kuhn's analysis of these processes has itself become a paradigm. By the early 1970s we find Jeremy Anglin making scientific reference to how "J.S. Bruner's description of perception recognition is remarkably similar to the description of doing 'normal-science' produced by Thomas Kuhn" (3).

From the very beginning both cognitive psychology and AI saw themselves as brave new sciences working in unison for an explanation and eventually an artificial "reproduction" of intelligence. But already this has led to confusion. If they are new sciences are they not revolutionary? Is it possible to be revolutionary and "normal" at the same time? Exactly what does the word intelligence mean? Does it mean human intelligence, animal intelligence or some mysterious intelligence called "general intelligence."

To avoid confusion we should identify AI for what it is—a technology. We concur with Zenon Pylyshyn that "the field of AI is coextensive with that of cognitive psychology" (4). So what we state here about AI is in many respects true for cognitive science.

Artificial intelligence is not only a technology it is a primitive technology. There is much evidence of this in the way AI research is conducted. It is all very proper and "normal" until it is brought into question. Then everything becomes revolutionary: AI is not interested in theories and certainty; these are the things of philosophy and the old sciences. Artificial intelligence's maxim is "build it and see." At times like this any pretensions of being a "normal-science" are conveniently forgotten, and we are told that AI researchers are revolutionary scientists at the intellectual cutting edge. Suddenly they become a band of Feyerabend's "anarchists," at least until the next round of research funding when they resort to being normal scientists and advanced technologists who know what they are doing and where they are going.

There is always an element of "build it and see" in any technology, especially so in its infancy. Mediaeval stone masons built to and beyond the limits of their materials. The first attempts at powered directional flight were also subject to the tyranny of gravity. Artificial intelligence is still very primitive, but unlike mediaeval stone masons or the pioneering aeronautical engineer, AI practitioners do not know what they are doing because they have not got a goal. To be sure, there is the successful passing of the Turing Test, but that is not much to go on. What does it actually prove? It is still with us because nobody within the field of AI really seems to know what is intelligence.

Human intelligence is particularly problematic because it carries with it the notion of the "self," a "lived-body," consciousness, a moral and ethical being and other issues. Daniel Dennett has recently attempted to avoid these difficulties by claiming AI need only concern itself with the first 90 percent of human intelligence. It would, he claims, be possible to go the full 100 percent, but it is simply too expensive (11). It is in the remaining 10 percent, we are led to believe, that all the difficulty lies. One is tempted to ask how much 110 percent or 200 percent would cost?

Dennett's 90 percent is just one more attempt to convince us that the term "general intelligence" actually means something. General intelligence is something human beings possess, to a lesser or greater extent, but unfortunately it is complicated by the other unnecessary baggage referred to earlier. It is something, so we are told, that is measurable and therefore must exist. Note that we are now back to normal-science; measurements and percentages are all reassuringly normal. However one is reminded here of how many angels could dance on the head of a pin.

The problem is that all this confusion may sound very exciting and even meaningful to a generally educated public immersed in "everydayness" of a world that is increasingly being shaped by computer and information technology. The impression is that this may all be leading somewhere. Of course this is true, but there is no use asking the AI researchers what they are doing or what they believe in. According to Marvin Minsky AI researchers should never hold onto theories for longer than five years (5). "If I still believe something after five years, I doubt it," he says. As for the people he is looking for as AI researchers Minsky suggests, "Selfish people who don't give a damn what happens in the outer world for five years. At some point you need a hero who will actually work for himself rather than make it easier for others to work. All the people who have short-range goals will be forgotten."

So what are the theories, ideas and goals that we must take up and abandon within Minsky's five-year plan? One area that is up for grabs that we may briefly consider is mathematics. Ever since 1976 when Haken, Appel and Koch announced they had a "proof" for the Four Colour Conjecture, there has been a debate as to whether such a proof changed our concept of mathematical "proof" and "truth." In retrospect we may look upon this proof as being one of the most significant events in the history of mathematics and computing. If it is accepted as a proof on a par with that of previous mathematical proofs, that is to say proofs that were and are still survivable and communicable, our concept of proof will have changed. Does this matter? It would have been interesting to ask Turing what his concept of proof was when he employed it, as we had earlier, in the phrase "proven facts." He believed that it was important to draw a distinction between conjecture and proven facts. Turing's contemporary, Ludwig Wittgenstein, would have taken him to task over what he meant by "proven facts." The problem is that in one breath Turing is predicting that opinions and words will change by the end of the century, and in the next he is insisting that we pay heed to making proper distinctions.

Wittgenstein would have claimed that the meaning of words did not, or should not, change over time. Nonetheless he was concerned about how the use of machines in mathematical calculations would change our concept of proof and would undermine mathematics. For him a "Proof must be survivable'; this aims at drawing our attention to the difference between the concept of 'repeating a proof' and 'repeating an experiment'" (5). Mathematical experiments are commonplace now; although it is too early to gauge what influence they are having on mathematics as a whole, they are undoubtedly making their mark.

In the same year Turing's paper was published, Wittgenstein was "doing" some philosophy that would later be published under the title of *On Certainty*. In this work he made his famous "river-bed analogy." Different propositions, that is empirical and logical, formed the river and its bed. Over time the interaction of the water on the soft and hard sections of the bed would change the course of the river. "But," he says, "if someone where to say 'So logic too is an empirical science,' he would be wrong. Yet this is right: the same proposition may get treated at one time as something to test by experience, at another a rule of testing'" (6).

The connectionists would disagree with Wittgenstein; their claim is that logic is a simple matter of pattern recognition and symbol manipulation. This seems somewhat nonsensical. Nonetheless it is a nonsense that may be shifting the river bed. Wittgenstein believed that "language could take care of itself": like Margaret Masterman he believed that false lines of inquiry and conceptually confused sciences such as experimental psychology would ultimately be toppled or evaporate. We hope this is correct, but at present Turing's prediction seems most likely. We agree with Brian Bloomfield (8) that "People who fear that one day we will be surrounded by intelligent machines are misplacing their concern; for instead of worrying about the future they might be better employed considering the current ways in which 'we' are becoming more like computers as people adopt (unwittingly or not) the ways of thinking and speaking which are the hallmark of AI" (7).

So what has this to do with ethics? We believe AI is a dishonest and corrupting field of technological research. This does not mean that all the young heroes Minsky recruits realize this, or indeed that Minsky and his colleagues are fully aware and responsible for their actions. They may not know what they are doing, but the chaos and confusion that they cause is unsettling. In the end it may not matter that they cannot produce an AI machine that is as intelligent as a human being, for they will, as indeed they already do, speak of machines thinking. Now they are contradicted, in the future, who knows?

CONCLUSION

Much of the change takes place during everyday encounters with computer technology. Computer ethics needs to take account of that; it needs to consider how individuals can be protected from a pseudo-scientific branch of computer technology. This requires us to develop some clear ideas about what it is to be "human" at the end of the twentieth century.

Ethics is not an isolated discipline within philosophy, nor indeed the world. Computer ethics cannot simply engage in a debate that is grounded upon the premise that computers are nothing more than complex tools. We would not like to be considered by future generations as being part of a group of people that exercised their minds in how to protect the intellectual property of software houses, if, as may well be the case, that software contributed to the nightmare setting around us. That nightmare is of course that our words and general educated opinion are changing and that we may one day not be able to speak of "thinking" without expecting to be contradicted and corrected.

REFERENCES

(Books)
(1) Masterman, M. "The Nature of a Paradigm," in Lakatos, I. and Masterman, M., (eds.), *Criticism and the Growth of Knowledge*. Cambridge: Cambridge University Press (1970), p. 70.

(2) Kraik, K. J. *The Nature of Explanation*. Cambridge: Cambridge University Press (1944), pp. 120-121.

(3) Bruner, J. S. *Beyond the Information Given*. London: Allen and Unwin (1974).

(4) Pylyshyn, Z. "Complexity and the Study of Artificial and Human Intelligence," in Haugeland, J. (ed.), *Mind Design: Philosophy, Psychology, AI*. Hanover, NJ: Bradford Books (1981).

(5) Brand, S. *The Media Lab*. London: Penguin Books (1988), p. 106.

(6) Wittgenstein, L. *Remarks on the Foundations of Mathematics*. Oxford: Blackwell Publishers (1967), p. 91.

(7) ____. *On Certainty*. Oxford: Blackwell Publishers (1974), p. 96.

(8) Bloomfield, B. "The Culture of AI," in *The Question of Artificial Intelligence*. London: Croom Helm (1987), p. 100.

(Journals)
(9) Turing, A.M. "Computing Machinery and Intelligence." *Mind*, 54 (1950), pp. 236, 442.

(10) Wigglesworth, V.B. "The Contribution of Pure and Allied Biology." *The Annals of Applied Biology*, 42 (1955).

(Other)
(11) Dennett, D. Horizon BBC2 science program. 5 April 1992.

21. ETHICS AND ELECTRONIC PERSONAE

CAROL J. ORWANT

INTRODUCTION AND OVERVIEW

Intelligent software agents can be personified to represent us on computer networks and to do our bidding in cyberspace. These agents are *epers*, electronic personae.[1] Epers may have various roles, according to our choosing: business assistants and financial representatives, game players and social actors. These alter egos may take on a personality according to the tasks and roles assigned them. Graphic images can personify these software creatures as striking, dramatic, evil or the perfect servant, Phil, complete with tux and bow tie, for example.

Epers are made up of artificial intelligence code which is designed to tailor its responses to users' actions. In computer terms, epers are control programs operating in a well-defined domain. While epers can be autonomous, they are activated by a real person to carry out useful work. I will define the individual behind the eper as an Iper, the real person who is represented in various virtual realms by one or more epers. Epers are expected to perform particular tasks such as screening E-mail, to "learn" over time based on observations of the Iper's behavior and preferences, and to report the basis for any decisions made upon request by the Iper.

Ipers can remain anonymous, and epers can protect this anonymity. Epers can transact business in a manner to maintain the anonymity of the Iper even while authenticating the validity. Through their epers, Ipers may spend considerable time in cyberspace, working, transacting business, and socializing. "Cyberspace" is defined as a nontangible domain allowing communication between persons or their agents.

For purposes of social interactions, cyberspace is roughly equivalent to "virtual reality" where simulated worlds are created and inhabited by their participants. But epers can do more, fighting battles and role playing in ongoing

273

dynamic multiuser dungeons (MUD). On behalf of their Ipers, epers may project personalities which are drastically different from their originating Ipers. Some epers shield their Ipers' anonymity, activating masked characters to allow their creators to explore alternate lifestyles. Other epers can be created to actualize one or more personae of the Iper for particular purposes. Social "chat" rooms, games, and newsgroups may be inhabited by a variety of epers, each representing an ideal or fantasy character of the Iper.

A personal assistant type of eper could be characterized as the Iper's ideal secretary, having whatever "personality" traits fit this ideal. A separate category of epers has been defined in this paper which carries out tasks for the "public good." This variety of public service eper may be operated by an agency such as a local election board and would be accountable to it, rather than to an individual Iper.

This paper looks at ethical issues arising from epers' roles, tasks, actions or control mechanisms. It describes several situations where there is potential for ethical conflict and suggests resolutions in terms of eper rights and responsibilities and the underlying rights and responsibilities of the Iper or other initiating agency.

CHARACTERIZATION OF EPER ROLES

As epers are defined, their roles can be characterized in terms of the business transactions they are tasked to carry out, the social personae used to represent the Iper, or the job descriptions applicable to the public service tasks performed. Ipers may create epers to keep track of details of daily life such as paying bills on time, tracking mail orders, or reminding Ipers to return library books. While the eper image can be personified, this "humanization" could lead to unwarranted expectations of performance which cannot be met by the software at the present time. [2] Although a choice of the agent interface would be desirable, with possibilities ranging from a "humanoid" to a dialog box, this paper will assume that agents are personified to some extent.

Business Representatives

If I create an electronic assistant, I can have it do many tasks for me including opening and screening my E-mail, deleting junk mail, setting up appointments for me, scheduling meetings with people, and telling lies on my behalf. The ethics involved here probably will have some relationship to telling lies. But what relationship? I could direct a human secretary to say that I'm "in a meeting," which is a very common telephone response to restrict accessibility. It is rare that ethical considerations are actually applied to this screening routine. The followup is for the answering party to take a message and relay it to the called party. Epers could do this. It would not be unethical to create an anonymous agent to screen my calls, take messages, and represent my wishes. However, I can direct this eper to lie on my behalf and tell people that I'm busy when I really just don't want to attend a meeting. The ethical implications may be actually milder than requesting a human secretary to lie on my behalf.

As intelligent agents, epers can "learn" the deceptive business preferences of their Ipers.³ Opportunities for deceptive practices increase as the population of interactive agents increases. The ideal agent is a personal assistant who collaborates with the user rather than requiring an explicit interface (Maes 1994). Epers become better at their jobs as they become more familiar with their Iper's interests.⁴ The Iper should always have a manual override option where he or she can act personally and directly, as warranted.

Epers can assist Ipers in carrying out difficult or complex tasks, teaching Ipers and facilitating collaboration with other Ipers. Ipers' "data image" could be under eper control. The credit history, health statistics and other public database information could be maintained and checked periodically by a personal eper. Reports of information at odds with facts could be brought to the Iper's attention promptly so that inaccurate records could be corrected quickly.

As an online stand-in for the Iper, the business-oriented eper could be authorized to order merchandise, reserve tickets, send communications, file and retrieve information, and receive messages. This eper is charged with maintaining integrity of the information, carrying out tasks as directed and completing tasks in a timely manner. The eper should also be responsible for securing accounts from fraud and theft since epers would need to access credit accounts to pay for reserved tickets or other purchases. While the eper has a mission to complete a transaction, there is a responsibility to complete it within a trustworthy framework.

Eper responsibilities include providing a complete, accurate and up-to-date accounting of the status of all assigned tasks. The Iper should be able to request this accounting at any time. Access to this information needs to be restricted to the Iper or his or her delegate, but it is the responsibility of the eper to control access to this information. It may seem a little ridiculous to require the eper to ask the Iper for his or her password or other authenticating information. But some sort of authentication needs to be done before confidential information is released. Operationally, the eper needs the security equivalent of bullet-proof glass so that it cannot be suborned, cheated or robbed. On the other hand, Ipers must feel that they are in control of their epers, and epers must not do things to jeopardize the finances or health of their Ipers.

How can an Iper guard against errors, malice or deliberate prying within personal records from external epers?⁵ Opportunities abound for criminal cracking of eper software in order to embezzle money, change data for unethical advantages, and commit fraud. At a minimum, security measures should include message encryption and authentication of the initiator as well as protection of accounts from unauthorized access. If the Iper maintains separate anonymous accounts for different business transactions, an anonymous remainder function is available through an Internet server in Finland making double blind communications possible. On the receiving end of anonymous transactions, Ipers can refuse anonymous E-mail. Epers could handle this, giving Ipers the choice of accepting anonymous messages or not. Both epers and Ipers could have unique digital signatures so that private business messages could not be intercepted in any meaningful way and so that the originating Iper could be authenticated without sacrificing anonymity.

What about epers that tell lies on your behalf? "Ms. Iper is in a meeting" seems innocuous, but other lies could cover up more serious events. What are the ethical mandates to preserve the truth? Ethically, our epers could be custodians of the truth, archiving it, locking it, maintaining it, and protecting it from modification. They could be responsible for certifying that data have not been altered. Epers might, in fact, control all access to archival data. But who controls these epers? "Rogue programs" require the capacity for manual override by a responsible person which results in sacrificing the absolute protection offered by custodial epers. A difficult question is how to guard against outside agents embedded in E-mail messages who can search and retrieve recipients' confidential information and return it to the sender.[6] Agents with some form of autonomy and self-initiated goals have considerable potential for "social mischief, for systems run amok, for a loss of privacy, and for further alienation of society from technology."[7]

The Financial Eper

If epers transact business over networks, it is conceivable that they can be directed to carry out dangerous, criminal, or unethical requests. Some obvious choices for appropriate responses by the eper could include reporting the directive to "authorities," modifying the request, or refusing to execute it. Financial epers could carry out stock trades based on decision criteria set up by the Iper or by a financial advisor. This eper may be somewhat "intelligent" in that a set of rules and decision criteria furnish the basis for epers' trading activity on the stock market. The ethical considerations for trading activity are those put forth by the Securities and Exchange Commission—no different for the eper than for the Iper.

Financial roles for epers could include a tax advisor function so that tax liabilities are monitored on a quarterly basis and strategic changes recommended in a timely manner. Ethical issues again are the same as for human tax advisors. The eper, however, can be alerted to changes in the tax laws as soon as they are passed, assuming "instantaneous" access to all public legislation. This would provide a strategic advantage in financial planning for the

Iper. Is this similar to insider trading? The argument in this case might reflect the minimal delay between receipt of relevant legislation and the ability of the eper to act on it on behalf of its Iper's investment strategy. Epers in the financial realm could act as proxies for their Ipers, voting as instructed, and reporting the actions in a daily status report. If the Iper wanted to change the eper's vote, a short delay, perhaps a day or two, would accommodate changes easily. Online voting is a related eper public service function, discussed later in this paper.

Game Players of Cyberspace

Epers were born as game players in cyberspace. An evolution from the representative game pieces of Dungeons and Dragons in its physical form to online characters in computer games allowed exploration of alternate identities. As the games developed different virtual environments, the "players" took on added characteristics. Virtual "rooms" were defined in which people could interact via their cyberspace characters.[8] The interactions between epers in various virtual rooms such as the "Basement" or a neighborhood tavern have been used as settings for online interactions in a mystery novel.[9] Some MUDs have acquired the ambiance of a community through participants' building or extending their virtual environments.

Multiuser dungeons can be a stage for exploring other identities. People with poorly developed social skills can find a place where they can try out different modes of social interactions with minimal penalties for outrageous behavior.

After school, young people tend to congregate, some of them hanging out in cyberspace. They may frequent video arcades or join MUDs and play games. The social experience emulates physical groups in a local hangout, talking to each other and actually playing games. But in cyberspace these young people can create characters and alter egos. They find supportive groups of peers in their MUDs and have the chance to develop and enact "what if" scenarios using epers, often anonymously. A criticism is that virtual reality can encourage social misfits to withdraw from real world human interactions and experiences.[10] Multiuser dungeons can become very compelling, and people can become obsessed with this existence, sometimes with tragic results. The story of 18-year-old Nathaniel Davenport[11] revolved around his untimely death due in part to his all-consuming interactive life in cyberspace where he was represented by his eper, "Sabbath." Nathaniel's real life suffered greatly. He flunked out of college, quit sleeping, and led an increasingly troubled existence. Forced by his father to quit spending so much time online and get a real world job, Nathaniel's exhaustion caught up with him. En route to his job, he suffered a fatal collision with an oncoming truck when he fell asleep at the wheel and his car veered into its path.

Nathaniel's eper, Sabbath, was a beautiful and totally unscrupulous female character. Many of Nathaniel's fellow game players knew him only as Sabbath, and were very distraught upon learning of Nathaniel's death. The individuals behind the epers in this MUD held a wake in cyberspace and sent condolences to the Davenport family whom they had never known.

Ethics of obsessive game playing are difficult to define. Should there be guidelines for young people living too intensely in cyberspace? Should obsessive game playing behavior be curtailed? Would this interfere with personal liberties? If we regulate ages for legal drinking, driving and voting, we might establish a minimum age for cyberspace game playing. Other restrictive measures might include the amount of time spent in cyberspace MUDs and the content of the games. Violence and sex are rated for movies and videos. Cyberspace games could be rated as well. The counter argument is that Ipers' freedoms are curtailed. Perhaps there is a need for an electronic parent (an "eparent") in loco parentis.

Social Actors of Cyberspace

Who spends time in cyberspace and what do they do there? The "neighborhood" hangouts of cyberspace serve as locations for relaxation and socially neutral places for conversation. They may operate during off-hours. The "insomnimania" board was open only during late evening to early morning hours.[12] Group members are self-selecting and share common interests. Each group has its regular participants who give it character and provide a supportive community for Ipers, through their epers. Misrepresentation might be acceptable in cyberspace, but may carry some ethical baggage depending on the behavior of the created eper. In a case described by Van Gelder,[13] a male psychiatrist presented himself on the CB channel of Compuserve as "Joan," a severely handicapped female who generated intense sympathetic friendships and some romantic relationships on the net over a two-year period. Major changes occurred in the lives of some of the other handicapped women due to their long-term relationships with "Joan." The denouement, unmasking the male psychiatrist, was extremely traumatic for several of the women involved. Ethically, misrepresentation was rampant although no monetary damages resulted from any of the sustained relationships. Yet a persistent feeling of deceit occurred and quite probably a reluctance to engage in future meaningful relationships in cyberspace. The Iper behind "Joan" may have been playing by a set of rules for anonymous characters, but he somehow exceeded some unstated bounds when his eper affected the physical and emotional lives of the real participants. The fact that he was a psychiatrist in real life implies that he was unethical in creating such deep personal dependencies in cyberspace since he presumably was aware of the transference phenomenon which commonly occurs between psychiatrists and their patients.

A USENET newsgroup[14] discussed practical jokes and gender switching in MUDs, noting that it can be dangerous to tamper with others' views of reality and also noting the ease with which people can be hurt. Deception for profit, mistreatment of female characters, stealing and other crimes, both real and virtual, is possible in MUDs.

Multiuser dungeon addictions have occurred. MUDding goes beyond the interactive game aspects and becomes a substitute for "real life." The anonymity and remoteness of players can lead to online behavior which would be abhorrent in the real world. This behavior may reflect individual explorations of control of others, criminal behaviors, or plain nastiness.

TYPES OF EPER JOBS

Besides being individual representatives epers have their own jobs. Such jobs could include guarding information from change, filtering and selecting information to satisfy some external criteria, and providing unbiased leadership. Epers can advise as well as assist their Ipers. However, advisory-style agents could create dependent interactions between the eper and Iper.[15] What happens if the eper is lost, perhaps due to a system crash? An eper tutor for authors, billed as a "prize-winning author/editor/teacher"[16] is rather dictatorial in its approach to cranking out fiction. The software uses a question and answer technique which can become annoying, and "advises" by spewing rules like "Surprises create suspense" on the screen. Working with advisory-style epers should be more informative than irritating.

Ethical Information Guardians

As information guardians, epers could monitor our "digital personae," those profiles captured on national databases for credit histories or medical purposes. Epers could restrict alterations to these records, screen access attempts and alert the subject Iper to any changes in the personal data records. Actual implementation details would rely heavily on available security measures to foil attempts at unauthorized access for whatever purpose. Epers could guard databases and data archives. They could preserve information in an unalterable state, guaranteeing that history is preserved as originally documented. They could certify that particular subsets of information had not been altered if some precise locking mechanisms were developed. In these times of denying factual occurrences for political, personal, or economic reasons, there is a need for this service.

Information Filtering and Selection

Epers can also do research for us. They can filter material for use in scholarly works based on key words and phrases, filter obscene language and X-rated topics from entering our domiciles, and act as a censoring board, if desired, in our local schools. Epers can serve to screen our E-mail files from unsolicited advertising[17] or scan the incoming advertisements for items of interest to us, presenting a periodic summary of these items on demand.

Impartial Coordinators and Virtual Leaders

Electronic town meetings usually need a chair or leader, an agenda, issues for discussion, recording of minutes, and voting. Public service epers could chair electronic town meetings, collecting and validating votes on local issues. Epers could also provide agenda items for discussion, record minutes, act as parliamentarians, and remain neutral on divisive issues.

Use of epers to monitor electronic voting via the Internet could be economically feasible and of immediate practicality.

EPER RIGHTS AND IPER RESPONSIBILITIES

How do people think about their epers and how do epers feel about their Ipers?[18] If epers make erroneous or unjustified decisions, how can their Ipers correct them? How do epers cooperate and communicate among themselves? If epers communicate with other epers, how can Ipers' privacy be guaranteed? If formal methods are used to verify the underlying intelligent agent software, does the resulting trusted program imply that autonomous agents are trustworthy? No, indeed. The intelligence and autonomy built into a useful agent could result in actions which are unwanted by the user or erroneous in a particular situation. Trustworthiness in epers is certainly a desirable goal but not yet feasible for implementation purposes.

Although there are no laws in cyberspace, "netiquette" is community defined[19] and ethical behavior does matter to many of the millions of people served by the Internet. Examples of obnoxious messages launched between newsgroups are common. In one instance, the "tasteless" newsgroup attacked the "pet cat" newsgroup in an extended and nasty exchange.[20] Could epers have stepped in to cool this dialogue? A referee function could be activated by either side and should be straightforward to implement. Heated discussions between online groups with opposing views are expected to be increasingly commonplace. Epers could have roles as neutral parties or impartial referees. There seems to be a need for this function. Epers could certainly filter the language if not the content of the message exchange, but should confine their referee functions within the bounds of free speech. The last thing wanted by sparring online factions is some software agent telling the operating Ipers what they can and cannot say.

Free Speech and Other Rights

A question arises if constitutional rights in cyberspace should be analogous to those in the real world. Since individuals have the right of free speech, shouldn't their epers have the same right? But there are bounds on the extent of free speech. One does not have the right to slander others nor to subject them to verbal abuse. Epers should abide by similar constraints. Flame wars,[21] however, provide an arena in cyberspace for behavior which would be unacceptable in the real world. Court decisions are not yet definitive on liability of cyberspace activities. One consideration is that libelous messages may be answered expediently online to set the record straight.[22] People subjected to online harassment can logoff. The idea of paying to access an online community, however, should carry with it at least some protection against discriminatory harassment. If Ipers choose to have anonymous epers represent them in order to defame others, an ethical conflict exists between free speech and responsible behavior.[23]

I can create intellectual property with legal protections for it. But are my data actually property? Who has what rights to use it? To change or delete it? Should I be the sole grantor of those rights? Is my eper any different from my data? I have some rights in cyberspace, namely freedom of expression, privacy rights, and the right of free and open access to cyberspace.[24] So I do have the right to create an anonymous eper. This eper, however, should behave by some set of rules, abiding by cyberspace community–developed standards of ethical behavior. Different communities, of course, could set different standards of ethical behavior. Sanctions for violating these standards range from admonishments from others in the community to being banned from it by the system operator.

Accountability

There is an ethical consideration of accountability for epers. Basic status checks on demand would provide a view of the eper's current working tasks. However, there are many opportunities for fraud, deception, corruption and theft, so there is an ethical requirement for epers to be accountable for the tasks they carry out beyond mere reporting of the status of each task. The Iper ultimately is accountable for the eper's behavior, but both the eper and the Iper are accountable to the cyberspace community in which they are active. Interesting dilemmas result. One such dilemma is eper identification. The implication is that some useful identification is necessary for an eper to carry out authorized transactions. A specialized MUD running on the Internet has functions @whereis, @whois and its inverse @char for identifying players choosing not to remain anonymous.[25] These functions can return additional information such as real names, E-mail addresses, and keyword research identifiers.

Can the Iper responsible for this eper remain anonymous while the eper is identifiable? It is possible through anonymous remailer facilities. It is also possible to choose a different eper identifier for each type of transaction conducted, and to authenticate an Iper while keeping the Iper's identity secret. If we interact in the real world with teammates and opponents, we need to know who is on which side. Although the anonymity of cyberspace "handles" can be maintained, an individual should "know" the eper with whom he or she is doing business. This cognizance may be restricted to ordinary business details, but sufficient accountability needs to be maintained to transact business with confidence about the integrity of the other parties involved. Ipers with illicit intentions could carry out untraceable crimes via anonymous epers, but accountability requires that sanctions be imposed where appropriate.

Projects requiring cooperative work using remote computer support or computer supported cooperative work (CSCW) have had difficulty in dealing with accountability of various contributors. If a group of people at geographically dispersed points are to work cooperatively on a project, each individual sharing part of the workload, questions typically occur on the allocation of labor. Further disagreements may involve resolving disputes and imposing sanctions on nonperforming members. An electronic project leader could help by providing a neutral point of coordination, by tracking deliverables and due dates, and with improved artificial intelligence, mediating disputes.

Autonomy

Autonomous epers can take over decision-making functions to a certain extent. The question of trust concerns the reliability of autonomous agents. Reliability in this sense implies that epers make decisions in accordance with the styles and preferences of their Ipers. But it also means that the eper is resistant to corruption from outside influences such as directives to pry into confidential personal files. The state of current eper development is limited to decisions on information filtering, meeting scheduling and similar tasks, but the state of user discomfort seems to be closely related to the degree of autonomy of the epers and the importance of the domain in which the eper is operating. Scheduling a meeting at an inconvenient time is a nuisance. Autonomous epers trading stocks for their Ipers could produce considerable anxiety. The eper must have a way to learn the Iper's preferences including when to request sign-off on certain decisions before action is taken.

Various learning models[26] propose having the eper "look over the Iper's shoulder" to learn the Iper's preferences, solicit feedback from the Iper, provide a message of intent and ask for confirmation, or initiate a dialogue with the Iper under conditions of uncertainty. Epers may create a state of unrest for Ipers due to an autonomous decision-making capability. But conversely, epers can also annoy Ipers with too many questions about the decision at hand.

The idea of an autonomous eper relies heavily on the model of a trusted (human) employee who, over a long period of time, makes decisions in accordance with the employer's wishes, is highly reliable, and has built up a level of comfort in the relationship. Not yet solved is the question of how the user can trust the agent to carry out tasks appropriately. If autonomous agents are too competent, they can be viewed as threatening users with a loss of control.

Autonomy is only part of the discomfort element. Inherent in this situation is a feeling that machine reliability is not always to be trusted. There is very little history in the relationship between the eper and Iper. Yet that feeling would change over time, given excellent and reliable service by the eper.

An ethical problem could result when Ipers' files are searched by one or more epers in order to respond to a query. If the eper requests permission to scan another Iper's distribution list in order to send information to someone, what limits should be put on disseminating this information? If epers cooperate with other epers to execute a complex task, it is likely that privacy violations will occur and confidential information will be transmitted to unauthorized recipients.

Epers' Own Rights

If epers can communicate with other epers, and this seems necessary to transact network business, epers' rights can violate Ipers' privacy. Rules to support ethical behavior of epers need to include a principle of veracity.[27] If epers retain all the information they receive and act appropriately on this information according to imposed constraints, who is defining "correct" behavior? Can epers manipulate this system for their own or their owner's benefit? Collaborating or competing Ipers can use their epers for advantages not sanctioned in the "real" business world. As interface agents to the Internet, epers could refuse to make destructive changes to the world and block human actions which have unintended consequences.[28] Determination of unintended consequences outside of laboratory settings is not feasible at the present time for open-ended business decisions where the impact of autonomous epers could have serious consequences.

Epers' rights to determine what actions are appropriate are closely connected to the modes of adaptivity whereby an eper "learns." For rule-based systems, rules can be added externally by humans (Ipers, systems personnel, software developers), but the more interesting learning models include observation of an Iper's decision criteria in particular situations and establishing a dialogue to fine-tune the implicit rules. Epers' question and answer sessions with Ipers could become truly annoying, depending on the sophistication of the software.

A simulated system discussed at the Artificial Life IV conference allows its virtual creatures to mate, reproduce according to simulated inherited characteristics, evolve, and learn complex strategies for successful survival. What has survived in this simulation is a virtual entity with intelligent behavior, an autonomous computer program.[29] Karnow suggests that epers could have rights on their own behalf.[30] These rights include the right to decline to produce information aside from key identifiers. Epers should be allowed to shield their originating humans from privacy invasions. These epers can respond to requests for identification with the equivalent of name, rank and serial number but refuse to give additional information.

Epers' rights are derived from the responsibilities granted by their Ipers. Epers may access their Ipers' bank accounts and use their credit cards in order to conduct business as charged by their Ipers, and to maintain their Ipers' anonymity while doing so. Karnow's epers, additionally, have the right to be protected from arbitrary deletion. This raises the question of who has the right to delete an eper? Clearly the originating Iper has that right. But others could also claim that right under particular circumstances such as criminal activities. A related risk to the eper is control or deletion by criminal attack agents, created and launched by hackers with malicious intentions.

Epers as Electronic Cops

In cyberspace the community has been said to police itself. But this relies on the definition of "the community," insofar as different standards are being developed for different subsets of communities. For social groups in cyberspace, three levels of sanctions have been defined and implemented: offenders are "talked to" by the system administrator or his agent; the offender is locked out of the session; or he is denied access to a particular network node. A recent case on Prodigy resulted in reprimands and killed communiqués for some offensive, insulting messages.[31] "Flamers" usually receive advisories from members of the community. If they persist, some communities offer a "bozolist" which filters messages from the individuals creating the ruckus. The intended recipients are advised that they have received a message but that it has been filtered from presentation to them (at their own request). Epers should be able to fulfill these community policing roles with grace and vigor.

Modern education has been accused of distorting truth and facts to support emotional versions of some historical claims.[32] Assertions which are demonstrably false carry some emotional truths. If these assertions are proclaimed loud enough and long enough, they take on the aura of truth and subsequently become accepted as fact. Since online chat groups tend toward rapid and spontaneous conversations, the content is often emotional and sometimes without facts.

Wrong information is easily transmitted via networks, and disseminated throughout a large community with ease and speed. With a large distributed population proclaiming the "truth" of incorrect information, it can easily take on aspects of factuality, becoming accepted as truth. Our epers could act as custodians of facts for us, able to certify that history has not been altered.

The ethical balance could shift so that community standards are defined globally in cyberspace, and physical communities could become playgrounds of imagined reality.

SUMMARY

The ethical deployment of epers to serve their originating Ipers requires epers to be accountable to their Ipers and that Ipers are responsible to the cyberspace communities in which they are involved, whether to conduct business or to play games. Privacy of both epers and their Ipers is a right. Anonymity can be maintained for both epers and Ipers, even while authenticating the identity of an Iper for completion of an online transaction. Epers' rights of free speech may resemble those of Ipers' constitutional rights, although with additional limitations and different sanctions for abuse. Epers have a right to be protected from arbitrary deletion by others. Abuse of these rights carries sanctions which may restrict communications within the relevant cyberspace communities.

Social epers allow their Ipers to have creative interactions in MUDs while exploring alternative identities. Eper roles also can be defined which fulfill Ipers' needs for business agents, security patrols, research assistants or reliable information custodians. Eper roles can be advisory as well as subservient. In some instances, epers can function as enforcers of ethical behavior, refusing to carry out illegal activities and reporting criminal directives to authorities. We will see many additional roles for epers as Ipers become more accustomed to living in cyberspace.

Acknowledgments. I would like to acknowledge the very useful comments of Professor Matt Schulte who teaches ethics-related courses in philosophy at Montgomery College, Rockville, Maryland. Students in my Systems Analysis and Design class (Spring 1994) used an early version of this paper for a walk-through exercise and generated a long list of pertinent questions about ethics in cyberspace.

REFERENCES

Bates, Joseph. "The Role of Emotion in Believable Agents." *Communications of the ACM*, July 1994, 122–125.

Bruckman, Amy. "Identity Workshop: Emergent Social and Psychological Phenomena in Text-Based Virtual Reality." *MIT Media Laboratory*, April 5, 1992.

_____ and Mitchel Resnick. "Virtual Professional Community: Results from the Media MOO Project." Paper presented at the 3rd International Conference on Cyberspace, Austin, TX, May 15, 1993.

Burgess, John. "Calling Agent 486." *The Washington Post*, March 6, 1994, H1, 4, 5.

Chaum, David. "Achieving Electronic Privacy." *Scientific American*, August 1992, 96–101.

Cheek, Martin. "Intelligent Agents Gaining Momentum." *Computer*, August 1994, 8–9.

Etzioni, Oren and Daniel Weld. "A Softbot-Based Interface to the Internet." *Communications of the ACM*, July 1994, 72–76.

Gelernter, David. "The Cyber-Road Not Taken." *The Washington Post*, April 3, 1994, C1, 2.

Genesereth, Michael R. and Steven P. Ketchpel. "Software Agents." *Communications of the ACM*, July 1994, 48–53, 147.

Karnow, Curtis. "The Encrypted Self: Fleshing Out the Rights of Electronic Personalities." Paper prepared for Computers, Freedom & Privacy '94 conference, Chicago, IL, March 1994.

Leo, John. "The Junking of History." *U.S. News & World Report*, February 28, 1994, 17.

Liebmann-Smith, Richard. "Stranger than Fiction." *The New York Times Magazine*, October 30, 1994, 88.

Lipkin, Richard. "Simulated Creatures Evolve and Learn." *Science News*, July 23, 1994, Technology section, 63.

Maes, Pattie. "Agents That Reduce Work and Information Overload." *Communications of the ACM*, July 1994, 31–40.

Negroponte, Nicholas. "Digital Etiquette." *Wired*, November 1994, 168.

Neumann, Peter G. "Risks on the Information Superhighway." *Communications of the ACM*, June 1994, 114.

Norman, Donald A. "How Might People Interact with Agents." *Communications of the ACM*, July 1994, 68–71.

Perriman, Cole. *Terminal Games*. New York: Bantam, 1994.

Quittner, Josh. "The War Between alt.tasteless and rec.pet.cats." *Wired*, May 1994, 46–53.

Reid, T. R. "The New Legal Frontier: Laying Down the Law in Cyberspace." *The Washington Post*, October 24, 1994, Washington Business section, 24.

Riecken, Doug. "Intelligent Agents." *Communications of the ACM*, July 1994, 18–21.

Schrage, Michael. "Computerized White Lies, or 'Have Your Agent Call My Agent.'" *The Washington Post*, March 5, 1993, B3.

_____. "Does the Mail Animal Need Electronic Anonymity?" *The Washington Post*, April 1, 1994, F2.

_____. "E-mail Stamps, Software filters Could Help Keep Cyberspace Clean." *The Washington Post*, April 22, 1994, G3.

Schwartz, John. "A Terminal Obsession." *The Washington Post*, March 27, 1994, F1, 4.

_____. "Some On-Line Guidelines Are Out of Line with Free Speech Rights." *The Washington Post*, October 3, 1994, Washington Business section, 25.

Selker, Ted. "Coach: A Teaching Agent That Learns." *Communications of the ACM*, July 1994, 92–99.

Shannon, Victoria. "When Race Meets Life On-Line, There's a Disconnection." *The Washington Post*, October 17, 1994, Washington Business section, 21.

Van Gelder, Lindsy. "The Strange Case of the Electronic Lover," in Charles Dunlop and Rob Kling, eds. *Computerization and Controversy*. New York: Academic Press, 1991, 364–375.

NOTES

1. I first heard the term "epers" at the Computers, Freedom & Privacy '94 conference in Chicago, March 1994.

2. Norman, 1994, discusses implicit deceptions in humanizing artificial agents.

3. Schrage, 1993, looks at the problems inherent in using epers to carry out business that real assistants could be trained to do.

4. Maes, 1994, has built agents to handle E-mail, schedule meetings, filter electronic news and to recommend television programs, books and music.

5. Norman, p. 70.

6. Norman, p. 70, reports a demonstration of this unauthorized information retrieval by an agent.

7. Norman, p. 71.

8. Bruckman, 1992, discusses MUDs with rooms such as coat closets and living rooms. Physical descriptions of these rooms give players a sense of the views, furnishings, lighting and exits.

9. Perriman, 1994, created a psychological thriller from the ideas of potential terror in cyberspace interactions. This novel explores ideas of evil epers and their actions.

10. Neumann, 1994.

11. Schwartz reports this story in detail in *The Washington Post*, March 27, 1994. He traces causative factors involved in Nathaniel's death to his state of mind as well as his physical exhaustion and other concurrent troubles.

12. Perriman.

13. Lindsy Van Gelder in "The Strange Case of the Electronic Lover" tells of a case where early online "gender bending" and misrepresentation via a handicapped female eper had unfortunate results in very intense relationships which were established and later demolished.

14. Rec.games.mud reported in Bruckman, 1992, pp. 27-28.

15. Selker, 1994.

16. Liebmann-Smith, 1994, describes his experiences with "Virtual Sol."

17. Schrage, April 22, 1994.

18. Riecken, 1994, p. 21.

19. Negroponte, 1994, discusses E-mail courtesy with emphasis on brevity.

20. Quittner, 1994, details an online "war" between two newsgroups with strongly diverging views. This could be a prototypic newsgroup "war."

21. Flame wars are offensive online attacks, usually in all uppercase text.

22. Reid, 1994.

23. Schwartz, October 3, 1994.

24. Karnow, 1994, delineated a set of eper rights which are analogous to constitutional rights for humans in many respects.

25. This MUD is a networked virtual reality environment representing areas in the MIT Lab, reported in Bruckman and Resnick, 1993.

26. Maes, 1994.

27. Genesereth and Ketchpel, 1994, p. 50.

28. Based on Etzioni and Weld, 1994, who discuss "softbots."

29. Lipkin, 1994.

30. Karnow, 1994.

31. Shannon, 1994.

32. Leo, 1994, talks about the "junking of history" in terms of asserting "truths" with no basis in fact.

22. ETHICS IN
THE COMPUTER AGE

Patrick Sullivan

A couple of weeks ago I happened to catch an episode of the television show "Weird Science." In case you are unfamiliar with the general concept of the show, two high school techie-weenie types feed their computers with descriptions of their ideal woman and end up with a virtual, sort-of girlfriend, young enough to fuel teenage fantasy, digital enough to produce lots of techno-magic, and just old enough to be the one who teaches the lessons in responsibility. In the episode I saw, the guys ask their companion for the ultimate computer, and because she is a computer and computers can do anything, she produces one, which, it turns out, is named Hank. Hank displays immediate gratitude for his new existence by producing immediate gratification. Before long, the boys have improved grade point averages, several high-limit credit card accounts, new driver's licenses and National Merit Scholarships, among other things. In addition to his abilities as a mischievous hacker, Hank also runs all the household appliances, and has an urge to "merge files" with the virtual girlfriend.

The boys eventually begin to wonder if all their gains might somehow be ill-gotten. They also seem a bit concerned about Hank's running the appliances, and as they discover, being able to send faxes to the principal's office in the nick of time (explaining why they wound up not only with scholarships, but the Stanley Cup trophy as well). At this point one of the two wonders whether technology might be getting out of hand, controlling their lives, and so on. They decide to do the right thing, by asking Hank to put everything back the way it was.

Well, as you might imagine, Hank is a little indignant about giving back the grades, credit cards and scholarships, and is in no mood to relinquish any

Text of a paper presented as the keynote address at the conference Ethics in the Computer Age, November 11–13, 1994, Gatlinburg, TN, sponsored by ACM-SIGCAS, with acknowledgments to the department of Computer Science and Electrical Engineering, the University of Tennessee at Chattanooga.

control over the toaster. The confrontation with Hank on defining his limits produces a first-class parody of the famous confrontation with technology in *2001: A Space Odyssey*, beginning with "Open the patio doors please, Hank," and progressing through the lip-reading camera shots, Hank's desperate attempts at self-preservation, and eventually the unplugging.

I have my doubts about this show, wondering whether it might be not much more than a high-tech "I Dream of Jeannie," but with a 1990s kind-of dysfunctional Hollywood feminism; there is none of the old "Oh Master, Yes Master" stuff, and the woman is obviously smarter than the average guy, but is still there ultimately to serve men. And what can be a more compliant, submissive servant than a genie or a computer, or a computer generated "genie"? But this one episode was a pretty good cautionary tale, with a wish for the ultimate computer giving further meaning to the phrase "the genie is out of the bottle." Many of the issues we deal with in computer ethics were covered in that show: malicious hacking, AI, misrepresentation of the self, computer crime, security, privacy, and ethical awareness, to name a few. Pieces of the larger philosophical framework for computer ethics appeared as well, including questions about appropriate uses of technology, and the "specter" of technological determinism.

In all of this at least two things seem important. The two primary characters, with the help of their virtual friend, eventually understood the responsibility attached to their actions; they understood that what they, and not Hank, did produced consequences that affected the well-being of themselves and others. And, issues in computer ethics were presented in unambiguous terms; there were deliberation and reflection by the characters about the moral quality of their actions and the consequences of them; and there were fairly clear ethical assessments about things like changing grades and creating false credentials and financial records.

This may make us wonder what's become of ethics in the computer age, or at least in the electronic media age, that moral lessons are presented through basically sophomoric sitcoms. On the other hand, we can look at something like this as a bit of leverage for accomplishing what remains a formidable task: defining ways of applying ethical analysis to technological innovation; correspondingly assessing the effects of that innovation on the evolution of ethical analysis; and then getting the point across where it counts.

The conference theme, "Ethics in the Computer Age," lets us work in both suggested directions. We can think not only directly about the treatment of particular issues addressed in the conference sessions, but also reflectively about the larger framework in which they are situated. Right now I want to consider this framework by shifting to a term that is getting some use, but needs to get more, because it suggests a critical turn for ethics in the computer age. I want to talk about cyberethics, and what it means to emphasize the use of that term.[1]

As a somewhat casual observation, cyberethics is today where contemporary bioethics was in the late 1960s and early 1970s, back when it was still "medical ethics." Now, bioethics did not suddenly come into being then, but an intense and rapidly occurring series of events transformed it.[2]

In 1963 the parents of a newborn with Down's syndrome refused nonextraordinary surgery for the infant to correct a life threatening intestinal blockage, and over an 11-day period the infant starved to death. This was the infamous "Johns Hopkins Case" that was the subject of the 1971 short film, *Who Should Survive?* The case prompted intense debate on the ethics of withholding treatment from newborns with birth defects. In the early 1970s, Karen Ann Quinlan rendered herself permanently comatose, and in 1976 a New Jersey court ruling permitted the removal of Quinlan from artificial respiration. This event triggered debate about the limits of life, withdrawing treatment from previously competent patients, and the ethics of surrogate decision making. It also brought complex bioethics issues to the public, generating perhaps as much public awareness and debate as it did academic debate.

In 1963 Stanley Milgram published "Behavioral Study of Obedience," in the *Journal of Abnormal Psychology* (p. 67). In 1964 the Willowbrook hepatitis study ended, and in the late 1960s, the Centers for Disease Control shut down the Tuskegee syphilis study. These cases have become central to discussions of autonomy and informed consent in research. In 1974, the D.C. Superior Court upheld the refusal of a Jehovah's Witness to consent to blood transfusions needed during a surgical procedure, and as a result of hemorrhaging, the patient died. This case is fundamental to steering the autonomy discussion further in the direction of patient self-determination, and issues surrounding the refusal of treatment and the "right to die."

In 1965 and 1973, the U.S. Supreme Court handed down the landmark privacy decisions, *Griswald v Connecticut* and *Roe v Wade*. These cases established a negative right articulated as limits beyond which the state has no, or at best extraordinarily restricted, interests and authority to intrude into personal affairs and decision making. In contrast, the primacy of medical confidentiality, a long recognized element of patients' privacy and a core value in the patient-professional relationship, became much less absolute in 1969, with the murder of Tatiana Tarasoff and the consequent 1976 *Tarasoff v Regents of the University of California* decision. That decision established that an obligation to warn a potential victim of harm can override a right or principle of confidentiality.

It is possible, of course, to spend the rest of my time here reviewing other similar cases and events that over the last 25 to 30 years have shaped the identification and evolution of core issues in bioethics. That evolution is important; twenty-five years ago the discussion of death and dying centered on the question, "When is a person dead?" Now, as we have seen with recent ballot initiatives in Washington, California and Oregon, and with the activities of

Jack Kevorkian, the question is more complex. Under what conditions can we end life? Can we end someone else's at their request? And is there a right to have anyone help us do it?

Medical ethics became bioethics as the need arose to deal with an increasing range and complexity of specific issues, and as the conceptual apparatus evolved to the current paradigm of a principles-driven theoretical framework for categorizing issues and developing assessments and justifications for decision making. But what can this discussion of bioethics tell us about ethics in the computer age?

The comparison is in part a search for a model and a way of defining identity and direction. Bioethics coalesced around a core set of issues and what seems to be a set of corresponding principles for categorizing and analyzing them. For example, the emergence of patient self-determination as a primary value is a consequence of working out the theoretical and practical balance of autonomy and beneficence. Current debates over health care reform will at some point recognize the tension between autonomy and distributive justice as central. And, bioethics has always revolved around an irreducible and clearly identifiable element: the relationship between patient and provider.

On the other hand, it is sometimes difficult to see where cyberethics begins. On one level, malicious hacking is a kind of vandalism, like spraying graffiti on walls and subway trains. While we agree that there should be computer ethics to deal with the one form of vandalism, no one has yet suggested a "spray paint ethics" to deal with the other. This raises an old question: What difference does the computer (generally, the technology) make?

One answer of course is that the difference is the computer; that without it the conditions or possibilities for certain problems would not exist, or at least not be sufficiently present to make a problem more than hypothetical. We need only look to the not-so-distant past of paper driven public records systems to understand that point. Yet, while it is true that information technologies make certain problems possible, and exacerbate existing problems in sometimes unique ways, it is also not uncommon for computer generated ethical problems to find some identity in other contexts.

Aren't privacy issues defined and handled in the context that defines a privacy zone (to borrow a phrase)? Isn't the computerization of medical records a bioethics issue? Aren't legislation, case law and regulatory policy enough to handle a large range of issues? Can't we deal with intellectual property issues as just another species of legal problem, or like any other property ownership issue? Aren't all end-user issues just character education or family value issues? Shouldn't malicious hackers and virus writers just know better? Aren't established areas of applied ethics sufficient to cover most of what comes up? Shouldn't business ethics deal with E-mail privacy, professionalization and other workplace issues?

One might say "yes" to all of those questions and still reasonably propose recognition of cyberethics as an identifiable and significant area of ethics ("applied ethics" is a redundant phrase). And to fragment cyberethics into particular examples of already established areas is to prevent any consistency of assessment and decision making about the ethical issues for which information technologies are an essential component. And I am not begging the question here on what makes the technology essential to the definition of the problem. To say that I am suggests a kind of theoretical hubris (found mainly among philosophers I regret to say) that assumes no interesting conceptual problems have practical consequences and variations.

I don't think we need to argue for the existence or defend the purpose of cyberethics anymore, but briefly raising that issue can be instructive: Now that we're here, where are we going? How are the core themes and models of analysis taking shape?

That cyberethics has an identity that is taking shape around an increasingly identifiable set of core themes and issues seems to me to be fairly clear. Privacy is one core issue, and illustrates some of the "growing pains" associated with the transformation of computer ethics to cyberethics. One side of the privacy issue concerns taking what we know about privacy and adapting it to a socio-electronic environment. So, for example, we look at existing forms of information and consider what (e.g., DMV records, medical information, purchasing data) should or should not be regarded as public. This may appear to be a fairly straightforward debate, but in fact it makes some key assumptions that are left largely unexamined.

Bill Murray told me at the National Computer Security Conference in Baltimore (October 1994) that he thinks privacy violations begin when information is created, and then continue through either negligent use or intentional abuse of the information. This gives us an important question that may have to be taken up prior to our consideration of the public/private distinction: What (kinds of) information should we create? After we consider this we can go on to clarify questions concerning, for example, what constitutes negligent use, and apart from obvious abuses, what kinds of uses of information constitute harm to others.

In other words, much of the current privacy debate seems to have taken for granted that information should be created, imparting almost as much determinism to the creation of information as to the technologies used to manipulate it in any conceivable way. What's then missed is any reflection on the point that the creation of information is no more a practical necessity than the use of a technology is, simply because it is available.

Consider also the implications of assuming that because information can be created it therefore must be created, that whatever can be represented must be represented. With that kind of assumption, any distinction between what information is "private" and what is "public" is irrelevant. Put this notion together with a fairly familiar assertion that information ought not be restricted, prohibited, owned, etc., and indeed cannot be. Privacy then becomes an unintelligible concept, even as we argue for a right to have it.

Much of what we say about privacy follows from what we find in court decisions, legislation and regulatory policy. For example, when Bill Murray defines a privacy violation as a limitation on liberty, this legalistic model is suggested. But not all transgressions of privacy are appropriately understood as limitations on liberty. And, not all of cyberethics can be reduced to law.

Nevertheless, the reduction of computer ethics to computer law is not uncommon, and usually takes the form of saying that whatever is not illegal is not unethical and, in some cases, even morally required. It is not illegal, for example, to write and publish virus code, or to sponsor contests for virus code. Nor is it illegal to publish schematics and parts lists for cable descramblers and red boxes. Still, rights and rightness, as Potter Stewart pointed out, are often quite distinct, and it is a fundamental element of citizenship to understand the difference.

The reduction of ethics to law underestimates the range of ethics, the function of law and the relationship between the two. It is not possible in bioethics, for example, to have an informed and productive discussion about voluntary euthanasia and physician assisted suicide without familiarity with the Conroy decisions, *Cruzan v Director, Missouri Dept. of Health*, *McKay v Bergsedt*, or Initiative 119 and Proposition 161. Discussions about these cases and attempts at policy both influence and are influenced by, for example, moral arguments about whether nutrition and hydration are forms of treatment, whether there is a distinction between "killing" and "letting die," or whether certain slopes are irreversibly slippery. We use these elements to discover or further clarify general moral arguments; and then we use these arguments to shape policy.

The same will be true for cyberethics. In order to make reasonable claims about electronic privacy, for example, we must be familiar with relevant policy decisions and their relationship to more specific philosophical questions such as whether privacy is some form of property right, an entitlement to control over access and flow of information, a balance of interests, secrecy or confidentiality, and so forth. Decisions we make about these philosophical questions and the ethical claims they support will be instrumental in the formation of public and institutional policy.

That last point is important. The euthanasia and physician assisted suicide debate is not about finding moral arguments that can be used to justify particular, exceptional cases. The debate is about the employment of moral argument in the justification of a public policy. That public and institutional policy is and will continue to be made about the uses of information technologies is, of course, one reason to have cyberethics as a coherently defined area of inquiry. But the fact that cyberethics will concern such policy at critical points also suggests that the ethics cannot be situational or relativistic.

We cannot argue that there should be one ethics for acts and another for practices, or one ethics for users and another for commercial netservers, or one ethic appropriate to one role we might fill and a separate ethic for other such roles.

The idea that cyberethics represents an area of continuity in a larger context of ethical inquiry suggests that we should not fragment the interests of cyberethics to other areas of "applied" ethics. Indeed, developments in different areas may be mutually informative. Consider, for example, the interests of computer ethics in the effects of information technologies on the workplace. An early concern here was that information technologies would lead to at least the following two undesirable consequences: an increased and more efficient centralization of organizational (bureaucratic) authority, and a deskilling of labor similar to what occurred when the assembly line replaced the craftsperson. Neither of these conditions materialized.

I think it is more likely the case that computerization created new skills that, unlike the mechanical repetitions of the assembly line, are highly complex and transferable to other contexts. Learning how to use a computer in order to do your job can also result in being able to do a lot of other tasks as well. We can be our own financial analysts and investment planners, handle much of our own legal paperwork, run our own accounting and tax firms, be our own publishers and, through the many commercial services, give and receive advice of various levels of expertise on any number of topics that draw our interest. This learning leaves open critical questions of social fairness and the distribution of skills and abilities, but it is still far from the dystopian, metropolis-style predictions of earlier times.

I think it is also evident that there has been far more decentralization of organizational authority. This has an important consequence for another area of ethics. In business and organizational ethics, there has been a fundamental assumption that most of the ethical issues revolved in some way around the classical model of organizational structure and rationality.[3]

This model involves an interdependence of hierarchical and one directional structure of organizational authority, and instrumental rationality. In addition, the selection of values as ends for instrumentally rational action is itself a nonrational act, appropriate more to matters of personal choice than to strategic thinking. Thus, for example, ethically driven action is either purely individual or at best merely coincidental with organizational objectives and strategies. In this model, then, greater and more efficient centralization of authority is (1) advantageous to organizational rationality, and (2) likely antithetical to individual moral preferences and choice.

But if the pervasiveness of information technologies does not produce greater centralization of authority, but instead decentralization, what follows? I think what follows is a need to reconstruct our concepts of organizational structure and rationality. We have found not so much that the classical model was or is wrong, but that it is in the process of being replaced. Consequently, the ethical analyses and arguments based on the assumed priority of the classical model need to be reconsidered and transformed. This last point will be true not only of the arguments directly concerning the effects of information technologies in the workplace, but also of other arguments where organizational structure and rationality are the critical points of debate.

Well, I have been improvising on themes, but that is one of the perks of giving a keynote address. Now I have to meet one of the demands, namely, putting it all together as a coherent discussion.

I began with an example of how visible cyberethics can be, and then spent considerable time talking about my other area of interest. In spending so much time with bioethics I wanted to stress the fact that transition and development are occurring, and likely with events and cases of increasing frequency and importance. Computer ethics is becoming cyberethics. I also wanted to overwhelm; cyberethics is at a point where themes are defined and case studies are developed. Most of this work has been done by individuals in computer and information technology fields, and those charged with the responsibility of educating individuals headed towards those fields. We are rapidly reaching a point, if we have not yet arrived, at which considerable attention must be paid to general conceptual frameworks, ethical theories and principles, that enable us to categorize issues and themes, see linkages among them, and formulate assessments and judgments. We are, in other words, at a point where a particular area of "applied ethics" generalizes, and clearly becomes a project of discovery assuming a methodology that, over time, reaches reasonably conclusive judgments and becomes instrumental in the formation of interpersonal action and the larger construction of community. And that generalization is the critical turn in ethics in the computer age, the turn marked by the term cyberethics.

NOTES

1. I'm not originating a term, here. This is not the first use of the term cyberethics; my aim is to use it to mark a developmental shift in the emergence of an area of applied ethics, and advocate its continued use.

2. The details in the following discussion of bioethics are drawn from *Contemporary Issues in Bioethics*, 4th Edition, edited by Tom L. Beauchamp and LeRoy Walters (Belmont LA: Wadsworth Publishing Company, 1994).

3. Parts of the following discussion on organizational structure and rationality developed in a conversation with Richard G. Milter of Ohio University. I also want to thank John Artz of George Washington University for acting as a sounding board for the extended discussion of bioethics.

VI : MORALITY, SECURITY AND PRIVACY

SUMMARY

(23) *La Technique: An Area of Discourse for Computers in Society*
This chapter discusses the role of the computer as a technique and how the technique—the machine, the computer in this case—is influencing our social and cultural environment. Paul Grabow defines computer ethics more as the ethics of technique because many of the issues considered under computer ethics like privacy, security and others predate the computer.

(24) *Individual Privacy in Today's Information Dependent Society*
This chapter discusses the role computers have played in individual privacy. Clifford urges that computers make it easy to covet information and invade privacy. It is easier now to get individual records than ever before. Using a social security number, one can access a lot of an individual's personal information.

23. LA TECHNIQUE:
AN AREA OF DISCOURSE
FOR COMPUTERS
IN SOCIETY

Paul C. Grabow

INTRODUCTION

The computer has affected the whole of society. People, however, are often puzzled by the nature and the origin of its effects. A computer is often seen as a "disembodied other," responsible for all sorts of autonomous behavior. A discussion of the issues is difficult, however, due to a lack of context—terminology and ideas that help to uncover the underlying reality.

Jacques Ellul's concept of "la technique" can provide some of this context, encompassing much more than the computer. After giving his definition, some effects of technique on society are identified; concepts related to our response to technique are discussed; some possible pitfalls are given; some "guideposts" are introduced (for example, justice, freedom, and equality); and a few conclusions are drawn. Much of the material presented here was used in the Cultural Impact of the Computer, a senior-level course taught by the author at Baylor University. The need for such context became evident when preparing for that course.

DEFINITION OF TECHNIQUE

Ellul defines "la technique" as the "composite of methods that are purposely devised to achieve 'absolute efficiency' ... in every field of human activity" (Ell64). In addition to methods, this includes machines, technology, and bureaucracies.[1] Computers come under that heading, obviously—but more importantly, everything that interacts with computers is also included. Efficiency is the hallmark of technique. The machine stands as the prototypical example of efficiency—and the computer is perhaps the most sophisticated machine. The machine, however, is incapable of integrating itself into society. Methods, themselves technique, are necessary for this integration to occur. Consequently, everything associated with the application of the machine becomes part of technique. Therefore, technique can serve as the area of discourse for "computers in society" because it includes everyone and everything related to the computer. As Ellul writes in *The Technological Society*,

> As long as technique was represented exclusively by the machine, it was possible to speak of "man and the machine." The machine remained an external object, and man (though significantly influenced by it in his professional, private, and psychic life) remained more or less independent. He was in a position to assert himself apart from the machine; he was able to adopt a position with respect to it.
>
> But when technique enters into every area of life, including the human, it ceases to be external to man and becomes his very substance. It is no longer face to face with man but is integrated with him. ... This transformation, so obvious in modern society, is the result of the fact that technique has become autonomous [Ell64].

This sounds extreme. However, his definition encompasses aspects of our life that we have long taken for granted, such as our penchant for order, regularity, and regimentation in our daily lives. And with the pervasive use of the computer, the effects of technique appear more evident. A similar, though not identical, view is given by Lewis Mumford in *Technics and Civilization* (Mum36).[2] Mumford traces order, regularity, and regimentation from the medieval monastery, to the army, to the "counting house," and from there to the factory—all being dependent on the development of the clock. This desire for exactness also influenced measurement (for example, distance) and observation (that is experiment within science). "Existence was separated into units that could be 'weighed, measured, or counted'; all else was judged 'unreal.' Subjectivity, intuition, and feeling had no place in a framework of ideas emphasizing organization, regularity, standardization, and control" (Mil86). Mumford calls this a "denial of the organic," subordinating the more subjective aspects of life to the "technological ideals of specialization, automation, and rationality" (Mil86).

Technique, over time, moves away from the organic. Technology—an example of technique—is often devised to overcome organic limitations and boundaries, such as time, space, and human ability. For example, a spear subdues a wild beast; buildings shield people from the weather; the telephone creates an "absence of place"; medicine conquers or arrests physical diseases; and the "megamachine" overcomes human limitations to achieve a difficult goal.

Mumford uses "megamachine" to describe the human organization that built the pyramids of Egypt—a mass of people molded into an efficient, powerful force. The results of their efforts are still impressive: The Great Pyramid rises 481 feet and weighs 50 tons, and the dimensions of the sides at the base differ by only 7.9 inches. It was built by an army of unskilled or semiskilled laborers, "drafted at quarterly intervals from agriculture" (Mum67), using nothing but "simple machines," roughly the equivalent of ten thousand horsepower (a hundred thousand manpower). No less important, a sophisticated bureaucratic hierarchy guided the effort, with each "cog" sacrificing its autonomy or initiative in pursuit of the goal, and the absolute authority of a king imposed a ruthless discipline (Mum67; Mum68).

Mumford identifies several characteristics of the Egyptian megamachine (Mum67). It required two things: 1) a reliable organization of knowledge supplied by the priesthood (priests were necessary to maintain belief in a divine kingship) and 2) an elaborate structure for carrying out orders (the bureaucracy) with the temple and palace at the top. In addition, he notes that the "efficient machine" required a division of labor and specialization of functions; the bureaucracy had only one purpose: to transmit orders without deviation ("a classic bureaucracy : originates nothing"); and only corruption could alter this transmission process. Also, the effects of the megamachine were broader than the pyramids: a larger regimentation of life and a "colossal capacity for enduring monotony." This royal machine reached its apex with the construction of the Great Pyramid. Shortly thereafter revolt came; and several centuries passed before a single divine ruler again had authority over Egypt.

EFFECTS OF TECHNIQUE ON SOCIETY

Most of society has been influenced by technique. Politics, economics, foreign policy, communication, federal regulation, science, law, business, the social sciences and public policy are a few examples. Furthermore, and perhaps more importantly, the concept of authority has been altered.

Politics has become largely an arena for competing techniques, focusing on the "useful" rather than the "good," causing purposes to disappear, choosing efficiency over quality, and replacing honest debate with conflicting propaganda. Economics has become a collection of methods (that is technical economy), replacing political economy. Foreign policy now emphasizes "feasibility" and relies less on doctrine. The social sciences have grown to be a collection of social methods, measuring social factors and suggesting policies to effect social change. Law has, to some extent, replaced precedence with technical tradeoffs (for example, plea bargaining or early prison release due to overcrowding). And federal regulation embodies a host of methods to control potentially adverse situations. Furthermore, communication itself is often more associated with the mechanisms and format of communication rather than with content.

Science

Science, in particular, has been affected greatly by technique. The boundary between the two, however, is unclear, and one has not always preceded the other. Common perception says that "technique is an application of science." However, Ellul claims that technique preceded science: "The first techniques of Hellenistic civilization were Oriental; they were not derived from Greek science" (Ell64). As support for his argument, he cites the steam engine, invented two centuries prior to the scientific explanation of its phenomena, and the "discovery" of penicillin: "The medical value of penicillin was discovered in 1912 by a French physician, but he had no technical means of producing and conserving penicillin; misgivings therefore arose about the discovery and led to its eventual abandonment" (Ell64).[3]

The relationship between the scientist and the scientific process has also been affected by technique. The scientist has grown dependent upon technique and has given up some freedom in the process. Physicists, for example, often must share expensive equipment (for example, particle accelerators). Consequently, research may be delayed while the scientist "waits in line," subservient to the machine. Also, "the research worker is no longer a solitary genius" (Ell64); having the right equipment is not simply desirable but necessary. And, in some cases, someone may "make" a discovery because he is "in the right place at the right time—with the right equipment." A well-supplied laboratory may propel a discovery, carrying the technicians in its wake. Furthermore, science has become an instrument of technique, rather than simply dependent on technique. Today science is seldom done for the sake of science; to be justified (due to its often high cost) it often must be applied. As Ellul points out, science has become a means to an end, and that end is the advancement of technique.

Tradition

Technique has altered tradition. And because tradition lies at the core of most value systems, technique alters the values of society. Historically technique arose out of tradition, "by the transmission of inherited processes that slowly ripen and are even more slowly modified, that evolve under the pressure of circumstances along with the body social" (Ell64).

Today technique has essentially overtaken traditions. Technical evolution has become too rapid for traditions to be formed. Consequently, a "new" technique now forms from previous technique, not previous tradition. When technique is based on tradition, its effects would be known "by experience." These effects are far less known when technique is formed from other technique. Therefore, the application of technique cannot guarantee, in general, a known result. Information technology, especially computer networks, illustrates how technology has overtaken tradition. The technology is evolving faster than the standard organizations (for example, ANSI or ISO) can respond. De facto "standards" have become common.

Historically, tradition often formed around a reasonably stable and identifiable social group. Change in tradition was a slow and gradual process. Consequently, the social norms of the community influenced tradition. Over time the traditions may have changed based on the reaction of each successive generation, but the change was gradual. Today, the social group may not be easily identifiable nor stable (for example, the "community" on the Internet), and the technique evolves so quickly that people are unable to understand it before it changes.

Policy

Public policy has been reduced to a collection of questions, based on who, how, when, and why a technique should be used. The Internet again illustrates some of the issues involved. During the 1960s and 1970s, the ARPAnet (the forerunner of the Internet) was controlled loosely by a fairly small group of researchers and their respective organizations (Den89). The traditions of those individuals, for the most part, guided the development and use of the technology. Now, however, the Internet is global, its users number in the millions, and it is not clear what or who is controlling the use and evolution of the technology. It is not the technical that is at issue here, but the managerial—emphasizing that problems of technique have a very human (that is to say organizational) aspect (Ell64). For example, several Internet sites allow someone to remove her message identifier so that "anonymous" messages may be sent (Bul94). In a very real sense, "the Genie is out of the bottle."

Business

The large corporations of the mid–20th century, such as IBM, General Motors, and AT&T, are examples of the megamachine (Mum67), characterized by a large bureaucracy and significant influence. However, that influence has recently eroded due to competition from abroad and from smaller domestic companies that are "lighter on their feet." Consequently, the large corporation has been forced to become more efficient. Information technology, to a large extent, has been driving and facilitating these changes.

Mid-level management layers have been flattened or eliminated. Their role as "information movers" between top and bottom (the classic role of a bureaucracy [Mum67]) has become increasingly unnecessary. Top-level management now has instant access to information that used to take days to receive.

In addition, authority within the organization has become diffused by information technology. In the not-too-distant past computers were controlled by a few within the organization; by default, these people also controlled the flow of information. As the technology has become decentralized, the authority governing the technology has also become decentralized. And because organizational authority is usually tied to information, this authority has also become decentralized and more fluid. Therefore, the "center" of authority in the organization may shift over time, causing a resultant change in the corporate personality. Rothschild contends that the microcomputer began a power shift "from MIS directors to midnight hackers, from headquarters staffers to factory managers, from big-time CEOs to no-name entrepreneurs" (Roth94).[4]

Historically authority has been vested in people. Now, though, the "information structure" (that is, formats, procedures, and protocols), to a certain extent, contains the organization's authority. This is especially true for businesses where the information is the capital or the product. Programmed trading on the stock exchange is an example.

Authority

Authority has been tied historically to a jurisdiction that is limited and often centralized. The jurisdiction, for example, may be political, geographic, religious, or ethnic. A country's jurisdiction may be geographic as well as ethnic. The jurisdiction of the Roman Catholic Church spans geographic, political, and ethnic groupings. The jurisdiction of a township, however, is specifically geographic. The nature of the authority is based on the purpose of the authority and the nature of the jurisdiction.

Information technology is diffusing authority and blurring jurisdictions. To be effective, the jurisdiction must be identifiable, the authority must be respected within the jurisdiction, and the jurisdiction boundaries should limit the authority. With information technology, however, the jurisdiction is not necessarily identifiable. Consequently, even if an authority exists it would be difficult to tie it to a jurisdiction. In such a case, the authority effectively does not exist. The Internet is a contemporary example. The public may (or may not) want the Internet regulated, but the jurisdictional boundaries are difficult, if not impossible, to identify.

Information technology also alters the relationship of people to the authority. For example, at the turn of the twentieth century communication in the rural Southwest was slow and unreliable. As a result, settlers would identify more easily with their county or state, rather than with the United States as a whole. Today, however, instant communications and accessible transportation have greatly reduced this regionalism—effectively "shrinking" the size of the country.

CONCEPTS

The concepts of community, civility, and subjective reality are helpful when trying to understand technique's effects on society. To a certain extent they stand apart from technique providing a balance and a perspective that technique by itself lacks.

Community

A community is more than a collection of people—and more than the sum of their interests and needs. True community respects the individual, has a regard for truth, and has a sense of the common good. In other words, it is civil. A group of people who band together based on a common interest would not necessarily constitute a community under this definition

Civility

According to Guinness, civility is largely based on subjective concepts, e.g., respect for the individual, truth, the common good (Gui93). However, it cannot be merely a matter of "taste" or preference. Nor is it simply "a rhetoric of niceness or a psychology of social adjustment" (Gui93). Genuine civility is "substantive before it is formal"; it is "a matter of ethics and education, not legislation" (Gui93).

Recent "definitions" of civility have been greatly influenced by technique, i.e., based on a collection of rules and regulations that govern behavior (Gui93). This creates a quasi-objective civility because technique tends to downplay or eliminate the subjective, an "objectified" civility using rules and regulations (Ell64); but, rules and regulations are not an adequate substitute for true respect (Gui93). Also, technique uses relative truth—relative to the degree of efficiency achieved; yet, relative truth is too slippery to serve as a foundation for civility. Furthermore, technique creates a "common good" that is primarily focused on efficiency; however, this is not necessarily common (in the sense that there is human consensus) nor good (based on the historical virtues present in the community). Therefore, the civility created by technique gives way to an artificial civility, more structural than substantive.

It could be argued that genuine civility is necessary in a democracy, not simply desirable. Civility represents the social fabric and is the hallmark of a "civilized" society. And, according to Guinness, "civility strengthens debate because of its respect for truth, yet all the while keeping debate constructive and within bounds because of its respect for people and the common good" (Gui93). If it is removed or replaced with something less genuine, democracy is in danger because the legal system simply cannot cope without genuine civility.

Subjective Reality

Subjective reality is often the source of meaning and fulfillment. Technique, though, as mentioned previously, excludes the subjective. This "denial of the organic," in Mumford's words, has reduced the importance of convictions, intuition, and feeling. This is realized today by the importance of specialization, automation, and rationality. More importantly, however, it colors our value system, allowing a mechanized view of ethics to "free" us from decisions that, by their very nature, are subjective.

Subjective judgment is more difficult to "justify" than objective judgment. For example, standardized, multiple-choice tests are not only easier to grade than subjective questions, but the score somehow seems more "valid," based on the elevated position of the objective in today's society.

POSSIBLE PITFALLS

Technique has both negative and positive effects. Modern technique provides desirable medical cures and comforts that our ancestors never knew. But problems do exist. The following identifies several pitfalls: the emphasis of intent over consequences, the limitations of mechanistic models, the dangers of intellectual hubris, and some problems inherent in the Internet. It does not constitute a comprehensive list. But it does serve to forewarn those who have become infatuated with the positive.

Intent versus Consequences

Consequences can easily be overshadowed by intent. Technology developers, for example, can become so taken with the possible advantages of a new product that its consequences may be inadvertently (or even purposely) ignored. However, as Postman indicates, the introduction of technology is "ecological" (Pos92); its effects are felt throughout the environment where it is introduced. And often the effects are not anticipated. Developers usually do not know the many ways that the technology will be used. Consequently the constraints may remain unknown or misunderstood. And a technique judged solely on the basis of its intent, without reference to possible consequences, can be easily misapplied.

Models

Models serve a useful purpose. They can give insight into how "something works," and they are usually easier to manipulate than the reality they represent. But the model can become more "real" (that is, important) than what it represents. For example, makers of public policy often employ mechanistic models to understand how their decisions would affect society. But, it is usually impossible to fully validate the model prior to the institution of the policy. The explanation lies with the subjective nature of human behavior and the inability to predict the future. Consequently, the model can only be validated "after the fact." Furthermore, the "numbers" associated with a model are often viewed as more authoritative than the reality.

Intellectual Hubris

A person's hubris can cause his downfall. According to Hayek, intellectual hubris is the assumption that we have so much knowledge that the only elements missing are subjective factors such as compassion and will (Hay44). This attitude contributes to a self-centered society that often rejects the wisdom of the past and focuses more on desired effect than careful consideration of constraints and consequences. Coupled with idealism, intellectual hubris can be dangerous.

Technique can foster intellectual hubris—especially in those who control the technique—because technique tends to ignore the subjective elements that could temper or control the hubris. For example, someone with advanced military technology may easily feel superior to someone who only brandishes a sword. As a more common example, information may generate its own kind of hubris through the power gained by owning the information.

An Example: The Internet

The Internet illustrates several pitfalls of technique. There is no governing body, such as the Federal Communications Commission, that has jurisdiction over the Internet (Che94). And one writer suggests that "any attempt to police cyberspace is fraught with practical and legal issues" (Leo94). The absence of place almost eliminates viable jurisdictions. Also, "civility" on the net is extremely difficult to define, much less enforce, because the concepts of individual worth, truth, and the common good are external to the technology; consistent with technique, the subjective elements are simply not present.

The opportunity for "radical personal autonomy" is another concern, given the nature of the Internet, giving way to uncivil behavior that is almost impossible to control.[5] Software piracy and hacking (Fia94) or break-ins (San93) seem benign compared to the anti–Semitic and racist hate mongering described in Chesnoff's article "Hate Mongering on the Data Highway" (Che94). The "opportunities" are unprecedented due to the size of the audience and the attention of young, unsuspecting users. And even though commercial services say that they are attempting to regulate deviant behavior (Che94), the nature of the Net may not allow regulation.

The Internet provides users with an illusion of power and control and the means to separate themselves from their behavior—and the resultant consequences. As mentioned above, anonymous servers can strip off a sender's address from an E-mail message, such as reported in Bulkeley's article "High-Tech Aids Make Cheating in School Easier" (Bul92), allowing the sender to disassociate herself with her own message. This extends the concept called "absence of place" to "absence of person." That is, the physical person becomes separated from her electronic presence—allowing the person to remove herself from any consequences.

GUIDEPOSTS

A guidepost serves to direct. The following guideposts are intended to direct the reader toward solutions and to indicate the tradeoffs involved. These include justice, freedom, equality, values, responsibility, and the expectations and vision of society.

Justice, Freedom, and Equality

Justice, freedom, and equality are three important concepts when determining who, how, when, and why technique should be used. They are important in and of themselves because the United States is a republic. But they are also important because people are increasingly confronting technique where society gives little or no guidance as to the how, when, and why. A large part of this stems from the absence of real tradition (e.g., no applicable laws or experience). Consequently, individuals are left to "fend for themselves."

Certainly it is easy to see the role of human freedom with respect to technique; Ellul's warning that technique has become autonomous should give us pause. And the concept of equality is axiomatic in a democracy. But justice is considerably more slippery. Some help, though, comes from Mortimer Adler, who contends that equality and justice should be considered as a unit with justice being the most important. To Adler, justice embodies "just action with respect to others ... the good of doing" (Adl81). And the "good" is whatever is truly worthy of pursuit. As he writes, "Only justice is an unlimited good. ... No society can be too just. ... One can want too much liberty and too much equality—more than it is good for us to have in relationship to our fellow-man, and more than we have any right too" (Adl81).

Adler also states, "The failure to observe and understand the need for limitations upon liberty and equality leads to serious errors about them and to an irresolvable conflict between them" (Adl81). His major point is that too much freedom (e.g., the libertarian) or too much equality (e.g., the egalitarian) diminishes the other. In other words, unlimited freedom comes at the expense of inequality of conditions; and equality of conditions comes at the expense of individual liberty. Neither equality nor freedom is an unlimited good. And they can be "maximized harmoniously only when the maximization is regulated by justice" (Adl81).

To more fully understand his argument, it is necessary to know his four kinds of freedom: 1) natural freedom that stems from our inherent ability to think and make decisions; 2) acquired freedom, based on the wisdom and virtue that we acquire over time (i.e., moral freedom); 3) circumstantial freedom (i.e., to "do as you please"); and 4) political freedom (Adl81). Only circumstantial freedom needs the regulation of justice.

Values

Values are like glue; they hold a society together. However, the violence and social confusion of the late twentieth century have strained values, and, in some cases, have even caused people to question their existence. In a very real sense technique has held sway suggesting that something so subjective could not even exist.

It could be argued that technique is value-neutral. However, it could also be argued that the use of technique is not value-neutral and that there is moral choice involved. According to Guinness, "Value-neutrality is philosophically impossible when it comes to the ordering of social affairs" (Gui93). Therefore, because technology choices have a significant impact on social affairs, the choices cannot be value-neutral. Furthermore, such choices should be based on more than emotivism, that is, an attitude where "all moral judgments are nothing but expressions of preference, expressions of attitude or feeling, insofar as they are moral or evaluative in character" (Mac83).

In a recent issue of *U.S. News & World Report* several people were asked to write letters to their children describing the values they hold precious: honesty, responsibility, tolerance, self-discipline, courage, work, perseverance, and faith—very subjective stuff (USN94). The concepts seem ordinary enough. Though such topics are rare in national news magazines. It appears that social confusion (along with the bareness of society) has driven us back into the arms of values. Perhaps the trigger was the fourfold increase in violent crimes since 1960, or the threefold increase in teen suicide over the last 30 years (Ben93). Yet, during that time the techniques of social policy (including spending) blossomed. Consider the following: 1) "Measured in constant 1990 dollars, total social spending by all levels of government rose from $143.73 billion to $787 billion between 1960 and 1990, more than a five-fold increase"; and 2) During that time total expenditures on public education (also in constant 1990 dollars) rose from $63.8 billion to $207.6 billion (Ben93). From this one could conclude that there is no correlation between social spending and crime, or that the techniques associated with the spending were ineffectual. (Perhaps the subjective reality of daily living is not readily addressed or influenced by something such as technique.)

But all of this begs the question. We should be asking, "How do we achieve the values that we desire?" Ray Mellichamp, from a Christian perspective, suggests three principles: the value principle, emphasizing the uniqueness of man as a creation of God; the integrity principle, that is, the quality of character expected from a person who has a relationship with God; and the steward principle which refers to the individual's responsibility before God (Mel90).

Responsibility

Responsibility is the other side of freedom. Freedom must have responsibility. Like civility, responsibility cannot be legislated, not in theory nor in practice. No amount of coercion can create responsible individuals. Coercion may force a particular result, but, once applied, it must continue to be applied if the result is to be maintained. Responsibility, on the other hand, reduces the need for coercion and opens the way for true freedom.

Responsibility results when someone recognizes and chooses a higher good. And, consequently, it is directly related to the value of human life. Unfortunately, technique does not create responsible people because responsibility is tied to the subjective, and technique is based on objective reality. Rather, subjective things, such as beliefs, attitudes, and convictions foster and maintain responsibility.

Responsible behavior stems from moral freedom, the individual acting out "good intentions," without coercion. As Aristotle said, "The virtuous man does freely what the criminal does only from fear of the law...." (Adl81). It is really only through existence of moral freedom that a liberal democracy can survive. No rule of law can cope with a population that is primarily opposed to order. James Madison put it this way: "To suppose that any form of government will secure liberty or happiness without any form of virtue in the people is a chimerical idea" (Gui93).

This is essentially arguing for individual responsibility within a society that is just. And, if you believe Ellul, the more significant issues related to the computer are human issues that point to the responsibility of the individual. In fact, *The Technological Society* (Ell64) is largely a wake-up call to individual responsibility.

Expectations and Vision

Society's expectations and vision should be guided by the value and uniqueness of human life, the pursuit of truth, and a desire for the common good—in other words, the characteristics of civil behavior. Again, all of this is subjective, not the objective reality generated by technique.

A society based primarily on technique may be unwilling to consider ideals that are not tied to efficiency. Consequently, questions of human life, truth, and common good may be ignored. If they are considered, it may be with a polite tolerance. However, a disregard for truth and an undefined common good (an ill-conceived relativism, often labeled as tolerance) can change from genuine tolerance to a debased tolerance (Gui93). Or, as G.K. Chesterton put it, "a tolerance of false civility—the virtue of people who don't believe anything—a corrupted civility" (Gui93).

Expectations and vision must come from the subjective side of life. The value of human life, the pursuit of truth, and the desire for the common good cannot be adequately quantified nor can they exist without the aid of intangibles (e.g., belief, conviction, self-worth, and commitment). Furthermore, worthy expectations and vision cannot be created and fostered by mechanized processes. In other words, the desired reaction from people cannot be generated by some deterministic procedure (i.e., technique).

CONCLUSIONS

Issues associated with the computer are easily considered within the context of technique. The concept of technique is not limited to the technical; consequently, it encompasses everything and everyone who would use a computer providing a more complete area of discourse. It is perhaps more appropriate to talk about the ethics of technique rather than the ethics of the computer. This seems reasonable because many of the issues considered by computer ethics predate the computer (e.g., personal privacy) or include nontechnical elements (e.g., policies and manual procedures).

Technique has permeated most aspects of society. Most advances in science today require the existence of technique; and science has, to a considerable degree, become subordinate to technique. Also, it is evident that technique has an inertia of its own. It can even be said that technique is rapidly "loosing its bonds" (i.e., social constraints, as "absence of place" and "absence of time," become more common). A primary example of this is the explosive, worldwide growth of the Internet.

Although technique's desire to be "objective" has subordinated the subjective, it is still true that subjective judgment is necessary to understand and control technique. Individuals still make decisions about when, how, who, and what—often in the absence of a tradition. And, consequently, humans are still held accountable for those decisions.

There are numerous incidents recorded concerning the abuse or misuse of technology. These stories by themselves, however, fail to address the more basic issues of responsibility, values, virtue, and civility—very subjective concepts. Technique is of little help because it is intrinsically tied to the objective. We must move beyond communication as mere technique (e.g., blame and manipulation) to communication as civil, public discourse—in the full sense of those two words.

ACKNOWLEDGMENTS: Thanks go to Stacy, David, Joey, Heather, Howard, Jessica, and Cameron. These people were members of my CSI 4301 class (The Cultural Impact of the Computer) during the fall 1993 semester at Baylor University.

REFERENCES

(Adl81) M. J. Adler, *Six Great Ideas*, Macmillan, New York, 1981.

(Ben93) W. J. Bennett, "The Index of Leading Cultural Indicators," The Heritage Foundation, 1993.

(Bul92) W. M. Bulkeley, "High-Tech Aids Make Cheating in School Easier," *Wall Street Journal*, April 28, 1992.

(Che94) R. Z. Chesnoff, "Hate Mongering on the Data Highway," *U.S. News & World Report*, August 8, 1994, p. 52.

(Den89) P. Denning, "The ARPAnet After 20 Years," *American Scientist*, Sigma XI, November-December 1989, pp. 530–534.

(Ell64) J. Ellul, *The Technological Society*, Vintage Books, New York, 1964.

(Fia94) J. J. Fialka, "The Latest Flurries at Weather Bureau: Scattered Hacking," *Wall Street Journal*, October 10, 1994.

(Gui93) O. Guinness, *The American Hour*, The Free Press, New York, 1993.

(Hay44) F. A. Hayek, *The Road to Serfdom*, University of Chicago Press, Chicago 1944.

(Leo94) J. Leo, "Who Gets Invited to the Table?" *U.S. News & World Report*, July 18, 1994, p. 18.

(Mac83) A. MacIntyre, *After Virtue*, second ed., University of Notre Dame Press, Notre Dame, Indiana, 1984.

(Mel90) J. M. Mellichamp, "Applying Biblical Principles in Information Systems and Operations Research," in *Christians in the Marketplace Series*, Vol. 3, *Biblical Principles & Business, the Practice*, (R.C. Chewning, ed.), NavPress, Colorado Springs, Colorado, 1990.

(Mil86) D. L. Miller, *The Lewis Mumford Reader*, Pantheon Books, New York, 1986.

(Mum34) L. Mumford, *Technics and Civilization*, Harcourt Brace Jovanovich, New York, 1934.

(Mum67) L. Mumford, *The Myth of the Machine*, Vol. 1, *Technics and Human Development*, Harcourt Brace Jovanovich, New York, 1967.

(Mum70) L. Mumford, *The Myth of the Machine*, Vol. 2, *The Pentagon of Power*, Harcourt Brace Jovanovich, New York, 1970.

(Pos92) N. Postman, *Technology*, Vintage Books, New York, 1992.

(Roth94) M. Rothschild, "Why Health Reform Died," *Wall Street Journal*, September 22, 1994.

(San93) J. Sandberg, "Computer 'Cracking' Is Seen on the Rise," *Wall Street Journal*, November 1, 1993.

(USN94) "Letters to Our Children," *U.S. News & World Report*, August 1, 1994, pp. 31–39.

(Wei94) G. Weigel, "Where Marriage Is a Dirty Word," *Wall Street Journal*, August 26, 1994.

(Zie94) B. Ziegler, "Building the Highway: New Obstacles, New Solutions," *Wall Street Journal*, May 18, 1994.

NOTES

(1) Ellul's work appeared originally in French in 1953 as *La Technique*.
(2) Note that Mumford's "technic" is not identical to Ellul's "technique."

(3) In 1928 Alexander Fleming was credited with the discovery of penicillin.

(4) Rothschild contends that the economy itself has changed from a machine age economy to an information age economy — from an "economic engine" (with predictable characteristics) to an "ecosystem" (something complex and changeable). The interesting aspect here is the notion of economy as organism.

(5) "Radical personal autonomy" is a term used by G. Weigel in another context.

24. INDIVIDUAL PRIVACY IN TODAY'S INFORMATION DEPENDENT SOCIETY

BRIAN PATRICK CLIFFORD

INTRODUCTION

Rapid advances in computer and telecommunication technologies have vastly improved communication, while allowing executives to have ultra-current information about their companies, subsidiaries, staff, clients, and practically any individual in the world. These advances, however, have stripped the individual of his privacy. Although invasions of privacy do not require a computer, "computers have made it much easier to gather and select information about individuals and organizations, which means that it is also much easier to invade privacy" (McKeown, 1993, chap. 19). Further, corporations that regularly manage information that is personal in nature often do so without having any restrictive policies regarding that information in place (Smith, 1993).

The legal handbook *Privacy in the Workplace* (1987) states, "Privacy was first recognized as a constitutional right in 1965, when the Supreme Court found it in the 'penumbra' of other constitutional provisions." In his paper entitled "Four Ethical Issues in the Information Age," Richard O. Mason (1991) describes two forces that threaten our privacy: the growth of information technology and the increased value of information in decision-making. The growth of information technology has enhanced the "capacity for surveillance, communication, computation, storage and retrieval" (Mason, 1991). The increased value of information to policy makers leads them to covet information, even when acquiring it invades someone's privacy; not only do managers of private companies gather personal data, Mason (1991) reports that as of 1986, "each citizen, on average, has 17 files in federal agencies and administrations."

The variety of legal records that are available to the public is astounding. These include driving records, vital statistics records, Social Security Administration records, county, state, and federal records, and criminal records. Most of these records are available for no charge; a small number, however, require a nominal search, copy, or administrative fee. Many of these records, in and of themselves, yield very little useful information about an individual. However, when combined, several records can give a very clear image of a person. Ruth Simon (1992) informs the reader that "What you don't divulge to the data gatherers can often be gleaned from public records. You may think the 'public record' is open only to someone who wants to spend the day poring over dusty ledgers in county courthouses. Yet, many federal, state, and local government agencies sell computerized lists of data to commercial organizations."

Motor vehicle records are maintained by all states for a period of two to thirty years, varying by state. There are few restrictions on their use and distribution, and they contain various, useful items of information ranging from one's address, social security number, date of birth, dates and locations of accidents and traffic tickets to height, weight, hair color, and eye color (Culligan, 1994). Nonetheless, "all government agencies, including driving and motor vehicle records departments, are constantly changing policies insofar as what access to records and files will be accorded to the public" (Culligan, 1994).

Vital records include birth, death, marriage, and divorce records which are filed permanently in local, city, county, or state offices; they are not kept at the federal level. In a publication by the National Center for Health Statistics of the United States Department of Health and Human Services *Where to Write for Vital Records* (1987), the addresses and fees for all 50 states and several territories for obtaining these records are listed. "An official certificate of every birth, death, marriage, and divorce should be on file in the locality where the event occurred. To obtain a certified copy of any of the certificates, write or go to the vital statistics office in the state or area where the event occurred" (National Center for Health Statistics, 1987).

The social security number is probably the single most important piece of information that allows access to a plethora of other records. It is in "widespread use to identify individuals in every walk of life" (Freedman, 1987). The social security number can be found on "voter's registration records, driving records from certain states, mortgage paperwork found in county records departments, and civil court paperwork" (Culligan, 1994). Credit card companies require its use, as do schools. However, "the federal government has endeavored to restrict the overutilization of such numbers by requiring that federal, state, and local agencies must notify an individual of the legal authority that allows them to collect the Social Security number and to state what uses are made of the number" (Freedman, 1987).

There are a myriad of public records accessible on the county level

(Culligan, 1994). These include affidavits, assignments of judgment, certificates of merger, certificates of title, deeds, guardianships, judgments, leases, liens, powers of attorney, tax warrants, and writs of garnishment (Culligan, 1994), to name a few.

"Using a BBS, optical imaging, geographic information, electronic and voice mail, and a 25-node network, Los Angeles, California's, Diamond Bar suburb has made its municipal services available online" (Diamond Bar, 1993). Citizens are urged to use the system to find information, and developers can "look up zoning and land use information, all without ever making a trip to city hall" (Diamond Bar, 1993). This system was implemented because of the demand for "better and easier access to records and other information" (Anis, 1993).

Individual states offer licensure for many occupations; these include the following: aircraft mechanics, auctioneers, bankers, certified public accountants, pharmacists, surveyors, and teachers (Culligan, 1994). Information about a person in any of these licensed occupations may be easily obtained from the state.

The federal government keeps numerous records on individuals. Military records contain information pertaining to rank, gross salary, awards and decorations, duty assignments, and attendance at military schools (Culligan, 1994). Also, available are federal records held by the United States Civil Service, the Railroad Retirement Board, the Federal Aviation Administration, the Interstate Commerce Commission, and the General Services Administration (Culligan, 1994).

Use of federal records has long been a common practice. "The first formal use of computer cross-checks by the federal agencies took place in 1977, when federal welfare rolls were matched with federal payroll records. The number of matching programs soon mushroomed, raising concerns about possible abuse or invasions of privacy" (Marshall, 1989). The Federal Bureau of Investigation's National Crime Information Center maintains computerized records on about twenty million Americans (Lee, 1992). However, when this personal information is faulty or misused, it can be detrimental to the falsely accused individual (Lee, 1992).

Criminal records have long been sought by the press and by curious individuals. The information found therein has been deemed public information; thus, it may be accessed by anyone. "Criminal history records are official records, compiled at taxpayers' expense by public officials for governmental purposes. Generally speaking, there is a presumption in this country that records of this sort ought to be publicly available. This presumption has some limited constitutional basis and is securely grounded in statutory law and recent case law" (U.S. Department of Justice, 1988).

Although some states forbid or restrict access to arrest records, the District of Columbia takes the position that arrest records in police files are "open to public inspection at all reasonable times (DC Code, § 4-134-5)" (Freedman, 1987). These records are becoming much more widely available. The 1976 Supreme Court decision in the case of *Paul v Davis* effectively removed "constitutional considerations from most policy decisions about the dissemination of arrest records by declaring that arrest records do not qualify for constitutional privacy protection" (U.S. Department of Justice, 1988). Electronic access to these records is rapidly increasing. "Perhaps the most significant factor in the successful evolution of the nation's criminal history record repositories has been the widespread application of computer technology to improve their efficiency and increase the quality of the information they maintain" (U.S. Department of Justice, 1993). Although 23 states have legislation on privacy and security (U.S. Department of Justice, 1992), "the right of privacy issue generally arises from poor police security methods which allow exposure of the contents to unauthorized persons" (Freedman, 1987).

Another form of records that contain personal information is medical records. Patients' diagnoses of diseases, if known by insurers, could "ensure their inability to receive health and life insurance by grouping them into a high risk pool" (Madsen, 1992). Nonetheless, "insurance companies, professional review organizations, and employers who administer their own health insurance programs are some of the third parties generally encountering little or no opposition when requesting access to medical records" (Linowes, 1989).

Although employees have a legitimate fear that their employers might find out about their psychiatric treatment that has been paid for by group insurance (Linowes, 1989), there is legislation against disclosure in every state, but it varies by the types of treatment given. Tennessee holds that the "privilege against disclosure exists only for the psychiatrist, and hospital records are simply the property of the hospital available for disclosure" (Freedman, 1987).

There are over 3,500 colleges and universities in the United States (Culligan, 1994); practically all of them have automated their records systems for currently enrolled students as well as for their alumni. Schools may, at their discretion, release "directory information" about an individual including birthdate, attendance and degrees, honors, and awards received (Culligan, 1994). In the students' interest, several universities, including the University of Memphis, state full compliance with the Family Educational Rights and Privacy Act of 1974 (Privacy Rights, 1993). Laws differ by state; California gives parents full access to their children's records while Connecticut limits their access (Freedman, 1987). Those outside the school systems in Tennessee are authorized access to pupil records for purposes of research (Freedman, 1987).

Another form of personal records often yielding to attempts to protect an individual's privacy is financially related records. These include credit records, bank records, and other financial records. By not being able to locate the exact piece of information for which they are searching, businesses' "quality of work could be impaired and their practices placed at a competitive disadvantage" (Melton, 1990).

Credit bureaus solicit and accumulate various types of information about individuals. They know the person's "age, social security number, balances on credit cards and mortgages, judgments or liens, and payment patterns" (Simon, 1992). "Credit card companies sell lists of their customers' spending habits" to other companies (Detweiler, 1993). Dishonest employees of companies to which you release your credit card number can breach your privacy. A *Time* magazine customer service center employee in Tampa, Florida, sold 3,000 credit card subscription transactions for one dollar each (Menkus, 1992).

Bank records are also a source of personal information. "It is generally unlawful for the bank or the state to disclose publicly a list of depositors or debtors of the bank" (Freedman, 1987). However, some banks do provide loan-payment information to credit bureaus and share customer names with affiliated brokers, insurance agents, or others who will sell financial services (Simon, 1992).

Several other sources of financial records exist. The Tax Reform Act of 1976 "reversed the federal government's thinking that individual tax returns were public information" (Freedman, 1987). Some states may, however, release the "net income tax or gift tax reported by another individual or corporation" (Freedman, 1987). In addition to means of direct access to one's financial records, information can be derived from various other sources. "Companies make heavy use of U.S. Census Bureau data. Even though specific data are confidential, users can extrapolate information about you. For example, they can come close to figuring your earnings by using a Census Bureau neighborhood average" (Simon, 1992).

By using personal information about an individual, insurance companies identify potential customers for their insurance agents. They also use this information for determining policy premiums (Simon, 1992). "Insurance company representatives need and get a great deal of medical, financial, and social information about you—much more than you furnish them. The applicant entering into an insurance transaction usually has no idea how extensive or intrusive the information-gathering process will be" (Linowes, 1989). Telemarketing and direct mail advertisers constantly invade an individual's privacy with a bombardment of junk mail and telephone solicitations. "Without your knowledge you are placed on many lists, whether you like it or not. These lists are used for marketing solicitations as well as many other purposes, often affecting how others interact with you" (Linowes, 1989).

In her article on privacy and direct marketing, Mary J. Culnan (1993) says, "Organizations seeking information on consumers tap into the information network in two ways. First, they use their own data to profile their existing customers. They subsequently use this information to target their existing customers or to rent mailing lists reflecting certain characteristics. Second, the organizations may have an information compiler or broker overlay their existing files with additional personal information matched against a third-party marketing database." This allows the organizations to better serve their existing customers. There are many small firms that "compile and rent specialized mailing lists such as newsletter subscribers or real estate investors, while bigger companies act as middlemen to resale information to marketers that was collected by bigger compilers" (Simon, 1992). These services are provided or facilitated by information brokers. These information brokers offer services such as abstracting and analyzing information, customizing information services, compiling directories, and updating specific subject information (Everett and Crowe, 1988). Further, they "cull information from public records, keying it into private databases where it can be organized, packaged, and eventually sold" (Sussman, 1993).

Additionally, governmental agencies participate in these direct mail activities. There are 23 companies that pay for the U.S. Postal Service's $48,000 annual list of U.S. addresses; this list is updated twice each month. "Marketers buy this information to update their lists and to target people who have moved recently, because those people are likely to spend more on household goods and lawn care" (Simon, 1992).

With all the public records, compiled information, and misuse of restricted information, the individual does have some preventive control over protecting his own privacy. There are several things that may be done to protect one's privacy. As stated earlier, the most important key to obtaining one's personal information is his social security number. This number accesses a wealth of information about the individual and should be carefully guarded (Detweiler, 1993; Marshall, 1989; Simon, 1992).

Guarding one's credit card account numbers not only makes good financial sense, it prohibits unauthorized access to confidential purchasing information. Another tactic to protect one's privacy is to have one's name removed from direct mail and direct telemarketing lists. This practice will significantly reduce the amount of mail received. By not answering surveys or product registration cards, the individual is limiting the amount of information available about his particular preferences. However, a manufacturer will have difficulty finding the person in such circumstances as product recalls or enhancements (Simon, 1992).

To the end of protecting an individual's privacy, several federal laws dealing with the issue have been passed:

- •1968 Omnibus Crime Control and Safe Streets Act — Prohibits interception of wire or oral communications without a court order.
- •1970 Fair Credit Reporting Act — Prohibits credit agencies from disclosing information to anyone but customers, and requires them to allow individuals to see their own files and make corrections.

•1974 Family Education Rights and Privacy Act — Requires federal agencies to allow individuals to see and have an opportunity to amend any records kept on them.

•1978 Right to Financial Privacy Act — Imposes limits on the disclosure by banks of customers' financial records.

•1980 Privacy Protection Act — Prohibits police from searching press offices without a search warrant if no one in the office is suspected of committing a crime.

•1986 Electronic Communications Act — Broadens the protection of the 1968 Omnibus Crime Control and Safe Streets Act to include virtually any type of electronic communication, including computer data transmissions, electronic mailboxes, cellular phones and fiber-optic transmissions. The act does not protect the radio portion of a cordless telephone call.

•1988 Computer Matching and Privacy Protection Act — Sets standards for federal computer-matching programs, with the exception of matches performed for "statistical, law enforcement, tax and certain other purposes."

•1988 Video Privacy Protection Act — Prohibits video rental stores from disclosing which films a customer has rented or bought.

"Privacy should be carefully protected and extended to everyone" (Telecommunications Policy Roundtable, 1994). How can organizations help to ensure individual privacy? Comprised of representatives from several nonprofit and public interest organizations, the Telecommunications Policy Roundtable (1994) says, "The collection of personal data should be limited strictly to the minimum information necessary to provide specific services, and sharing data collected from individuals should be permitted only with their explicit, uncoerced consent." The Roundtable also contends that individuals "should have the right to inspect and correct files containing personal data about them, and that innovative billing practices should be developed to increase individual privacy and minimize misuse of the statements."

Additionally, businesses must improve their privacy practices. They should inform the consumer of how they use information and make it easier for customers to keep personal data private.

Finally, each individual is responsible for the information that he disseminates about himself. If a person wants a certain fact kept private, he must do everything in his power to guard that information. Businesses and governmental organizations must do their best to ensure individual privacy, and the ultimate responsibility lies with those organizations to be self-regulating in matters of personal privacy or risk being legislatively controlled.

REFERENCES

Anis, N. (1993, Fall). "How Beating Traffic Paved a Road to the Future." *Artisoft Chronicle*, p. 2.

Culligan, J. J. (1994). *You, Too, Can Find Anybody: A Reference Manual* (rev. ed.). Miami, FL: Hallmark Press.

Culnan, M. J. (1993). "How Did They Get My Name?: An Exploratory Investigation of Consumer Attitudes Toward Secondary Information Use." *MIS Quarterly*, 17 (3), pp. 341–361.

Detweiler, G. (1993). *The Ultimate Credit Handbook*. New York: Penguin Books.

"Diamond Bar Creates Public Network to Become a Lantastic 'City online.'" (1993, Fall). *Artisoft Chronicle*, pp. 1-2.

Everett, J. H. and Crowe, E. P. (1988). *Information for Sale: How to Start and Operate Your Own Data Research Service*. Blue Ridge Summit, PA: TAB Books.

Freedman, W. (1987). *The Right of Privacy in the Computer Age*. New York: Quorum Books.

Lee, L. (1992). *The Day the Phones Stopped* (rev. ed.). New York: Donald I Fine.

Linowes, D. F. (1989). *Privacy in America: Is Your Private Life in the Public Eye?* Urbana, IL: University of Illinois Press.

Madsen, W. (1992, November). "U.S. Moots Medical Data Privacy Bills." *Computer Fraud & Security Bulletin*, p. 4.

Marshall, P. G. (1989). "Your Right to Privacy." *Editorial Research Reports*, 1, (3), pp. 30–42.

Mason, R. O. (1991). "Four Ethical Issues in the Information Age," in H. J. Watson, A. B. Carroll and R. I. Mann (Eds.), *Information Systems for Management: A Book of Readings* (4th ed.). Homewood, IL: Richard D. Irwin.

McKeown, P. G. (1993). *Living with Computers* (4th ed.). Fort Worth, TX: Dryden Press.

Melton, D. C. (1990). "Information at Your Fingertips." *Journal of Accountancy*, 170 (6), pp. 42–48.

Menkus, B. (1992, November). "Computer Analyst Sells Credit Data." *Computer Fraud & Security Bulletin*, p. 2.

National Center for Health Statistics (1987). *Where to Write for Vital Records: Births, Deaths, Marriages, and Divorces* (DHHS Publication No. 87-1142). Washington, DC: U.S. Government Printing Office.

Privacy in the Workplace: When Employer-Employee Rights Collide. (1987). New York: Modern Business Reports.

"Privacy Rights of Parents and Students." (1993, April). *Bulletin of Memphis State University: Undergraduate 1993-94* catalog, p. 34.

Simon, R. (1992, March). "Stop Them from Selling Your Financial Secrets." *Money*, pp. 98–106.

Smith, H. J. (1993). "Privacy Policies and Practices: Inside the Organizational Maze." *Communications of the ACM*, 36 (12), pp. 105–122.

Sussman, V. (1993, December 6). "Policing the Digital World: Electronic Advances May Strain Some Basic Constitutional Principles." *U.S. News & World Report*, pp. 68–70.

Telecommunications Policy Roundtable. (1994). "Renewing the Commitment to a Public Interest Telecommunications Policy." *Communications of the ACM*, 37 (1), pp. 106–108.

U.S. Department of Justice (1988). *Public Access to Criminal History Record Information* (Contract No. NCJ-111458). Washington, DC: Bureau of Justice Statistics.

U.S. Department of Justice (1992). *Criminal History Record Information: Compendium of State Privacy and Security Legislation* (Contract No. NCJ-137058). Washington, DC: Bureau of Justice Statistics.

U.S. Department of Justice (1993). *Use and Management of Criminal History Record Information: A Comprehensive Report* (Contract No. NCJ-143501). Washington, DC: Bureau of Justice Statistics.

ABOUT THE
CONTRIBUTORS

DOUGLAS ADENEY

Douglas Adeney is a lecturer in philosophy at the University of Melbourne, Australia. He has an M.A. from Monash University, Australia, and a Ph.D. from St. Andrews University. He has published articles on ethics and political philosophy, which are his main areas of interest.

EDWARD BEWAYO

Edward Bewayo is an associate professor of management at Montclair State University in New Jersey where he teaches courses in management, business ethics, small business and entrepreneurship, and human resources management. He holds a Ph.D. from the State University of New York at Albany. His research interests are currently in small business ethical issues and international entrepreneurship. He has published extensively in these areas. He is the director of the Small Business Institute at Montclair State University.

KAY L. BURNETT

Kay Burnett is a software usability specialist with experience in design and implementation of business information systems, management of software development projects, and technical training development and delivery. She has a master's degree in information technology and human effectiveness from DePaul University in Chicago.

BRIAN P. CLIFFORD

Brian Clifford is an instructor in computer information systems and business at Freed-Hardeman University in Henderson, Tennessee. He holds a B.S. in computer information systems and a B.B.A. in management both from Freed-Hardeman University, and an M.S. in business from the University of

Memphis. He is the editor of the Mid-West Tennessee Genealogical Society's quarterly publication *Family Findings* and has published the *History of the New Friendship Community*, Chester, Tennessee, 1995.

B.C. DAY

B.C. (Chic) Day is a professor at the University of Tennessee at Chattanooga in the computer science and electrical engineering department. He graduated from American University, Washington, D.C., and the United States Naval Academy, Annapolis, Maryland. He is a veteran of twenty years' service in the United States Marine Corps. His areas of professional interest include systems development, systems analysis and design, fourth generation languages, prototyping, decision support systems, MIS, human design factors, microcomputer software, programming languages, and computer ethics. He is a member of the Association of Computing Machinery, Upsilon Pi Epsilon and the International Association for Computer Information Systems.

PAT C. DAY

Pat Day has served as an adjunct professor of education at the University of Tennessee at Chattanooga. She has also been a supervisor of student teachers for the university. She graduated from the University of Miami and the University of Tennessee at Chattanooga. She taught in public schools in Florida, North Carolina, Virginia, and California. She has business experience in the fields of real estate, journalism, and sales.

RICHARD G. EPSTEIN

Richard Epstein is a professor of computer science at West Chester University of Pennsylvania. He holds a Ph.D. in computer science and information sciences from Temple University. His "Killer Robot" project has been expanded to include materials that can be used to introduce social implications of computing as well as computer ethics into the classroom. His *Case of the Killer Robot* is due to be published by John Wiley. He served on the ACM/IEEE Joint Task Force, and he is a co-author of *Fundamentals of Computing: Volume II* published by McGraw-Hill.

INGER V. ERIKSSON

Inger Eriksson is an associate professor of computer science at the Swedish School of Economics and Business Administration in Helsinki, Finland. She holds a B.Sc., an M.Sc., a Lic. of Ph., and a Ph.D. in computer science from Abo Akademi University in Finland. She was a Fulbright scholar at the

University of Arizona in 1994-95 and a visiting associate research professor at the University of Colorado at Colorado Springs in 1991-92. She also spent a semester as a visiting scholar at the University of Lund in Sweden in 1988 and a short period of time at the University of California, Los Angeles, in 1993-94. She was the program committee chair for the IFIP WG8.2 International Conference on Women, Work and Computerization in 1991 and is the organizing chair for ICIS '98 to be held in Helsinki. She is a member of the national doctoral program in information systems in Finland and a member of the expert committee of the Science and Technology Commission of the Academy of Finland.

PATRICIA H. FARRAR

Patricia Farrar is an instructor in the department of computer information systems at Middle Tennessee State University. She has a master's degree in statistics and decision theory.

JOHN LÁSZLO FODOR

John Fodor is senior research associate at the Research Center on Computing and Society, president of Educational Media Resources, Inc. (a not-for-profit corporation specializing in educational programming), and a video producer/director. His academic degrees include a Ph.D. and an M.A. from Washington University, and a B.A. from SUNY Albany—all in philosophy. His awards—as a video producer/director—include a Calop Award, an Emmy Award, and two Cheta Awards. He has produced or directed over a dozen video documentaries on computing and human values including the following: *Teaching Computer Ethics, Equity and Access to Computing Resources,* and *Privacy in the Computer Age.* He is co-editor (with Bynum and Maner) of *Teaching Computing and Human Values, Equity and Access to Computing Resources, Computing and Privacy, Computing Security, Ownership of Software and Intellectual Property,* and *Human Value Issues in Academic Computing.* He is currently project director and co-principal investigator for a National Science Foundation grant developing interactive, multimedia CD-ROMs on computer ethics.

DONALD GOTTERBARN

Donald Gotterbarn is a professor of computer science at East Tennessee State University. Prior to moving to East Tennessee State, he taught at the University of Southern California and Dickinson College. He holds a Ph.D. from the University of Rochester. His research has appeared in more than a dozen professional journals, and he has written several encyclopedia articles.

He has done funded research on performance prediction for a distributed Ada closure, on object-oriented testing, and on software engineering education. He is currently directing the SIGCAS task force on licensing and certification of computer professionals and is co-chair of the IEEE/ACM Software Engineering Ethics and Professional Practices committee. He is a member of the ACM and belongs to SIGCOMM, SIGCAS, SIGCSE, SIGSOFT, Computer Professionals for Social Responsibility, and the IEEE Computer Society. He is also a regular reviewer for *Computing Reviews*.

PAUL C. GRABOW

Paul Grabow is an associate professor of computer science at Baylor University where he teaches software engineering, formal software specification and design, parallel systems, data structures, and about the cultural impact of the computer. He received a B.A. in physics and mathematics from Luther College in Decorah, Iowa, and an M.S. and a Ph.D. in computer science from Northwestern university. His research interests include the specification and design of real-time systems and the cultural effects of technology on society. He is a member of the IEEE Computer Society, the ACM, and Sigma Xi.

ALAN HOLT

Alan Holt graduated from Wolverhampton University with a B.Sc. (Hons) in computer science. He joined AT&T Network Systems in 1989 and currently works in its information systems department as a senior engineer. He is a chartered engineer and a corporate member of the Institution of Electrical Engineers and the British Computer Society. He is currently working towards a Ph.D. with the Open University.

JOSEPH M. KIZZA

Joseph Kizza is currently an assistant professor of computer science at the University of Tennessee at Chattanooga. He holds a B.S. in mathematics from Makerere University, an M.S. in computer science from California State University, Sacramento, an M.A. in mathematics from the University of Toledo, and a Ph.D. in computer science from the University of Nebraska at Lincoln. His research interests are in social computing, artificial intelligence and computer architecture. His recent work in social computing has focused on computer ethics, and he has organized three conferences on computer ethics. He has published several works examining social computing and artificial intelligence, and he has taught courses in software engineering, artificial intelligence, computer architecture and operating systems. He is a member of IFIP, ACM, SIGCAS, and the UNESCO IT Expert Group.

JOHN MAGNEY

John Magney is an assistant professor in the department of technical resources and management at Southern Illinois University at Carbondale. He holds a B.S., an M.A., and a Ph.D. all from the University of Michigan, Ann Arbor. His current interests are in quality control, teamwork and cooperative learning, and the effects of computing on the workplace.

ANDREW B. MORRIS

Andrew Morris is a lecturer in the department of information systems at the University of Cape Town, South Africa. Information ethics is his primary area of research, and he is working towards his master's degree. His work in this area has been presented at a number of conferences including the IFIP World Congress in Madrid 1992 and Hamburg 1994, and the ACM's SIGCPR Conference, St. Louis, 1993. He has been a member of the IFIP Ethics Task Group since it began in 1992 and is now South Africa's TC representative. He is involved with the Computer Society of South Africa and has been chairman of the local chapter and national vice president and editor of its newsletter *IT News*. He is also a computer correspondent for a local newspaper and has contributed to a variety of other newspapers and magazines.

CAROL J. ORWANT

Carol Orwant is an adjunct professor in the information science department at Montgomery College in Maryland, where she teaches a variety of computer science courses, many with ethics components.

CHARLES WILLIAM PALMITER

C. William Palmiter is a pastor at Bethel Baptist Church in Greenview, Tennessee. He holds a bachelor of business administration degree from the University of Cincinnati, and a master of divinity degree and a doctor of ministry degree from Southern Baptist Theological Seminary. He has also received an M.B.A. from Middle Tennessee State University. He has written extensively on Christian ethics. Besides his work in the ministry, he has also served as an instructor in seminary extension, as a member of the executive board of the Tennessee Baptist Convention, and in various civic and community capacities.

DAVID PRESTON

David Preston is a reader in information management at the East London Business School, University of East London. He worked for twelve years as a project manager and consultant, largely within the oil industry. His research interests include ethical policy making, the history and the use of ethical codes, philosophically based approaches to information systems development and philosophical issues raised by information technology (IT).

RICHARD RUBIN

Richard Rubin is an associate professor at the School of Library and Information Science at Kent State University. His research and publications focus on issues in human resource management. He is the author of two books entitled *Human Resource Management in Libraries: Theory and Practice*, and *Hiring Library Employees*. He has also written on ethical issues in human resource management and is co-author of the forthcoming article on ethics in the *Encyclopedia of Library and Information Science.*

THOMAS J. SCOTT

Thomas Scott has experience running an academic computer center and has chaired a computer science department. He has also taught computer science every term since 1972 at Western Illinois University. He received his Ph.D. from the University of Georgia, and his teaching interests include operating systems, computer networks, facilities management, computer marketing and ethics, and systems programming. He has been published widely in the areas of team dynamics, computer arithmetic, benchmarking computer systems, network issues, establishing and maintaining computer priorities, learning theory, and computer ethics.

PATRICK SULLIVAN

Patrick Sullivan is the executive director of the Computer Ethics Institute in Washington, D.C. He is also a faculty associate at Johns Hopkins University where he teaches bioethics. He holds a Ph.D. in philosophy from the University of Kentucky. He is chair of the IEEE/ACM task force on software engineering ethics working group on privacy, and the IEEE Computer Society committee on public policy subcommittee on computing and persons with disabilities. He is an associate editor of the Social Philosophy Research Institute book series, and of the journal *Philosophy in Context.*

KEITH TAYLOR

Keith Taylor is a doctoral student, working under David Preston, at the East London Business School, University of East London. He has degrees from Exeter and Cambridge universities. His research is centered around philosophical approaches to and issues raised by information technology (IT).

RICHARD B. VOSS

Richard Voss is an assistant professor of finance at Western Illinois University, Macomb. He has a B.S. in business from the University of Nebraska at Lincoln and a J.D. from the Nebraska College of Law. He taught at Fort Hays State College and at the University of Nebraska College of Business before moving to Western Illinois University.

NANCY J. WAHL

Nancy Wahl teaches at Middle Tennessee State University in the computer science department. She received her Ph.D. in computer science from Vanderbilt University in 1989. Her research areas include distributed debugging, software testing, intellectual property rights with respect to software, and liability issues relating to computing. In addition to her research and teaching responsibilities, she is in charge of developing the MTSU Web site. She is a member of the Association for Computing Machinery (ACM) and the IEEE Computer Society. She is also involved in local, regional, and national ACM activities. She is the faculty advisor for the MTSU student chapter of the ACM and is on the Extended Steering Committee for ACM Computing Week 1996 and 1997. She is also on the steering committees for the ACM Computing and the Quality of Life conferences 1996 and 1997.

JOHN WECKERT

John Weckert is a senior lecturer in information technology at Charles Stuart University, Australia. He has a Ph.D. in philosophy from the University of Melbourne, Australia. His research interests and publications are primarily in computer and information ethics and in knowledge based systems (in particular their applications in information management).

JACQUELINE E.C. WYATT

Jacqueline Wyatt is a professor of computer information systems in the college of business, Middle Tennessee State University. A former industrial practitioner, she continues to consult for business and industry. She has also held positions in academic administration. She holds degrees in accounting, education, behavioral management and anthropology. She has published extensively and is a member of several editorial boards of academic journals. Her current research interests include privacy issues (especially concerning individuals), the sociological issues of technological change, artificial intelligence, and computer integrated manufacturing.

INDEX